D0081278

LIBERAL DEMOCRACY

NOMOS
XXV

NOMOS

Lieber-Atherton, Publishers

New York University Press

NOMOS XXV

Yearbook of the American Society for Political and Legal Philosophy

LIBERAL DEMOCRACY

Edited by

J. Roland Pennock, *Swarthmore College*

and

John W. Chapman, *University of Pittsburgh*

New York and London · New York University Press · 1983

Liberal Democracy: Nomos XXV
edited by J. Roland Pennock and John W. Chapman
Copyright © 1983 by New York University

Library of Congress Cataloging in Publication Data
Main entry under title:

Liberal democracy.

(Nomos ; 25)
"A quarter-century of NOMOS (Index)": p.
Includes bibliographical references and index.
1. Democracy—Addresses, essays, lectures.
2. Liberalism—Addresses, essays, lectures.
3. Judicial review—Addresses, essays, lectures.
I. Pennock, J. Roland (James Roland), 1906–
II. Chapman, John William, 1923–   . III. Series.
JC423.L517   1982   321.8   82-14430
ISBN 0-8147-6584-X

CONTENTS

CONTRIBUTORS

CHARLES R. BEITZ
Political Science, Swarthmore College
DAVID BRAYBROOKE
Philosophy and Political Science, Dalhousie University
ROBERT A. DAHL
Political Science, Yale University
STEPHEN L. DARWALL
Philosophy, University of North Carolina at Chapel Hill
AMY GUTMANN
Politics, Princeton University
BARRY HOLDEN
Politics, University of Reading, England
GEORGE KATEB
Political Science, Amherst College
ROBERT E. LANE
Political Science, Yale University
ROBERT B. McKAY
Law, Institute of Judicial Administration
WILLIAM C. MITCHELL
Political Science, University of Oregon
ROBERT F. NAGEL
Law, University of Colorado
J. ROLAND PENNOCK
Political Science, Swarthmore College
PETER RAILTON
Philosophy, University of Michigan
FREDERICK SCHAUER
Law, College of William & Mary
DAVID G. SMITH
Political Science, Swarthmore College

FREDERICK G. WHELAN
   Political Science, University of Pittsburgh
KENNETH I. WINSTON
   Philosophy, Wheaton College, Massachusetts

FOREWORD

The appearance of this volume of NOMOS calls for a word of explanation and appreciation. The twenty-fifth meeting of the Society coincided with the publication of Roland Pennock's magisterial study, *Democratic Political Theory*. To celebrate this happy confluence I exercised my presidential authority to designate Liberal Democracy as the topic for the meeting and for the consequent volume. Professor Pennock may disapprove of this as an act of democratic centralism, but to have given him a *liberum veto* would have been far more inadmissible.

This volume, then, is a tribute to Roland Pennock for his outstanding contributions to the vitality both of NOMOS and of democratic theory in the larger world of thought.

Paul A. Freund

PREFACE

This volume of NOMOS rounds out a full quarter-century's worth of the series. To observe the occasion we offer in addition to the usual index a somewhat bare index to all of the volumes to date. It was not feasible to make anything like a complete and comprehensive twenty-five year index, but we do present the names of all two hundred and seventy-six of our authors, the titles of their essays, and the major concepts, topics, and theorists that are considered.

On this occasion it seems appropriate to reflect upon the founding of the Society and its purposes. It was organized in 1955 on the inspiration and initiative of Carl J. Friedrich of Harvard University. It continues to serve as a living recognition of his great contributions to both political and legal philosophy. In keeping with his wishes our early meetings were rather cozy affairs. Since then we have grown, and our international membership stands at around five hundred.

Carl Friedrich's views as to what he wanted to accomplish were quite precise. In his "Preface" to the first volume of NOMOS, *Authority*, he spoke of those ". . . who share an interest in the range of problems traditionally treated within the broad framework of political and legal philosophy." He went on to say that, "It is our belief that these problems are of vital importance and that they require interdisciplinary exploration, treatment and discussion." The title of our annual publication, according to Friedrich, was decided on for the following reasons. "We are calling the series NOMOS, which is the broadest Greek term for law, because in this term there are also traditionally comprised the notions of a basic political order and of customs and a way of life. It describes reasonably well, and perhaps better than any term of modern English, what must be the focus of a society such as ours, uniting the several social sciences, law,

and philosophy." Over the years we have sought to hold fast to
these Aristotelian themes and ambitions.

At this time it may also be fitting briefly to survey the changes
in our intellectual landscape that have occurred since the Society was established. In those days many were inclined to think,
perhaps in an Hegelian mood, that political philosophy was dead
and that the end of ideology was at hand. Unsurprisingly, neither of these forecasts turned out to be accurate. After all, we
are "ideological" animals, as John Plamenatz once remarked,
and we cannot be other than preoccupied with how we ought
to live, with the ambiguities that are inherent in human society,
with justice, and with the strains between freedom and equality.
If we are entering an age of scarcity these preoccupations will
intensify.

Perhaps the most significant alteration in our political and
philosophical landscape is the way in which equality has become detached from and opposed to freedom. It was not always so. For the liberal conception of equality had freedom built
right into it as the equal right to freedom, to equality of opportunity. Today we find much more interest in substantive forms
of equality, especially equality of political influence and condition or well-being. Procedural confront substantive conceptions
of justice. And justice itself has been rethought, notably by John
Rawls with a view to lasting integration of our supreme commitments to both liberty and equality.

This interest in equalization, in what ought to be done about
human inequality, underlies various currents of thought, including the resurgence of Marxism and the call for more participatory forms of democracy. Sometimes it seems that craving
for community threatens to overwhelm respect for individuality. Concern for equality renders problematic, and possibly illegitimate, the concentration of authority and power that we
find in the modern corporation. This concern has transmuted
natural into human rights. But life would not be political, nor
would moral equilibrium be so difficult to establish, if we were
not pluralistic beings living in a pluralistic moral universe. So
even as regard for equality has deepened, doubts arise as to the
justice and vitality of the modern welfare state. Whether the
next twenty-five years will witness continuation of current trends
of thought, or their modification or reversal, is an open ques-

tion. In any event, we may all be grateful to Carl Friedrich for having organized a forum in which to think and write about the contrary impulses and sentiments that inform our law and politics.

This is an opportune moment also to tender thanks to our officers, our program committee chairmen, and above all to two men who have made our Society go, namely, John Ladd and Martin Golding, our only and successive secretary-treasurers. That our annual meetings have gone forward smoothly and that we are financially sound is tribute to their efforts and continuing loyalty.

Liberal democracy has for long awaited our direct attention. It was the topic of the annual meetings of the Society held in conjunction with those of the American Philosophical Association (Eastern Branch) in Boston, December 1980. All but one of the paper readers and commentators at those meetings have contributed to the volume. The others, some of whom were present at the meetings and participated in the discussions, responded to invitations from the editors. We owe special thanks to Carl Cohen of The University of Michigan who chaired our program committee. Eleanor Greitzer, our editorial assistant, is nothing less than a *sine qua non* of our series.

And finally on behalf of the Society we wish again to express our appreciation for the philosophical acumen and foresight of our founder, Carl J. Friedrich. He saw what needed to be done and how to do it. Systematic thinking about fundamental problems requires organization, and sustained thinking could be elicited through an annual publication, no better name for which, in a civilization dedicated to freedom under law, could be found than NOMOS.

J.W.C.
J.R.P.

INTRODUCTION

J. ROLAND PENNOCK

Notoriously, democratic theory is not just a single, unified *corpus*. Various theories purport to justify democracy or to describe and explain how it works, or both. As for "liberal democracy," while it may be cogently argued that the addition of the modifier only makes explicit what is already implicit in the concept of democracy, by no means all theorists agree with this interpretation. One philosopher has recently contended that liberal democracy entails both liberal self-determination and democratic choice and that it is unlikely that these two imperatives can be so delineated that they never in principle conflict. Hence it is impossible to construct a coherent liberal theory of democracy.[1] Whether that proposition is sound depends partly upon how one defines coherence. If it means "consistent," one dictionary definition, I believe some theories of democracy can pass the test. If however it means "tight," "closely knit"—another accepted usage—the charge is more readily sustainable. In any case, this issue will be given some attention here and will receive further consideration in the Epilogue.

John Locke, Jean(-Jacques) Rousseau, John Stuart Mill, and John Dewey have more in common than their first names: but their theories are by no means so closely related as, say, those of Adam Smith, David Ricardo, and Alfred Marshall. The differences in democratic theories derive not only from the divergence between rights-based and utilitarian theories but also from the fact that some theories are directed primarily toward justi-

1

fication, others toward the operation of institutions, and still others ("deductive, positive" theories, as I shall call them) toward explaining the workings of democracy by the methods of economic theory, especially those of welfare economics. While to some extent these varying types of theory deal with different problems and thus do not conflict with each other, this is not completely true, especially in the case of the last-mentioned type of theory.

Whether or not democratic theory can be coherent, it, and especially liberal democratic theory (if the two differ), exhibit tensions that first appear in their philosophical foundations and psychological assumptions.[2] The most basic of these tensions has to do with the nature of the individual and his role in the polity. It is often said that democratic theory, whatever else it may be, is individualistic. The contrast intended is with a philosophy that is often called "holism." Just what holism is and whether it is compatible with democracy will not be discussed here. What is clear however is that the individualism with which it may be contrasted covers a broad spectrum. The individual at one extreme may be seen as atomistic, as self-centered, as autonomous, and as having a fixed nature. At the other extreme, he is held to be born plastic and practically blank, receiving his developed nature from his interactions with other individuals in society and with the group as a whole, a nature too that is not only dependent upon society but that, in its fully developed form, far from being self-centered, is primarily interested in the welfare of the whole, with which he identifies, being aware of no self-interest that conflicts with this welfare. While I have expressed this as one end of the spectrum of individualism, if "holism" is anything other than this, I find it hard to define. Certainly it would not be *liberal* democracy.

Anything short of holism, then, can be thought of as a brand of individualism. The democratic theory most sharply opposed to holism would be an individualism so radical that men (or at least families) were thought of as completely self-sufficient and self-regarding, asocial, living in a condition of virtual anarchy. Anything between these extremes would be a form of liberal democratic theory.[3] The existence of these differing theories does not prove that any one of them is incoherent or even that it contains internal tensions (although many of them do). It may indicate simply and only that different theorists have differing views of man's nature. In some measure they clearly do, especially with regard to the extent to which that nature is given, fixed, and the extent to which it is subject to development or other change. But for the most part political philosophers recognize that persons—most persons, at least—cannot be described as either completely selfish or completely dedicated to the welfare of their fellow-citizens, or entirely governed by their sense of justice or a complex of generally accepted rights and duties. They see them as in some measure partaking of each of these features, with resulting internal tensions that reflect themselves in any political theory that does justice to their nature.

Individualistic political theorists hold that each individual is worthy of respect, of dignity; democratic political theorists hold that they are *equally* entitled to respectful and dignified treatment. It is frequently said too that the individual is autonomous, meaning that he is capable of acting rationally and deliberately, of being self-governing rather than completely subject to external controls. (The word "completely" must be stressed if the latter idea is to be realistic.) All that is required to satisfy this condition is (1) that it is individuals, not communities or other "wholes," that constitute the *ultimate* value, whose flourishing is to be fostered, and (2) that the individual must be able, as far as is possible and compatible with justice, to share equally in deciding what is essential for that flourishing. The "as-far-as-possible" qualification is essential because, insofar as liberty (however defined) is among the necessary conditions for flourishing, it may require limitations on what questions should be decided collectively and even on what decisions should be made. It may be thought that introduction of the term "justice" opens a Pandora's box; yet it is essential, for example, that no majority, however large, should be permitted to condemn a man to death because his hair is red or his skin black.

Between the concepts of autonomy and ideology lies another democratic tension. Some hold that the degree of autonomy sketched above is an impossible dream, contending that all political ideas are imposed by a reigning ideology. This issue is the subject of Chapter 12, wherein Barry Holden probes the controversy, and shows the strength of the anti-autonomy arguments and the way in which, if successful, they would cut the heart out of democratic theory. Against this position, he contends that true ideas are possible and that individuals can rationally adopt them, making them their own, not imposed upon them. In this and other ways he refutes the most common arguments against the possibility of an intellectually autonomous electorate. At the same time he shows that the whole subject is exceedingly complex, bedeviled by problems that he brings to light but which he cannot resolve in the allotted space.

Democratic theory in its justificatory aspect is generally based either on a consequentialist ethic or on rights. When these justificatory theories are not held by the same writer they are not a source of tension within a particular democratic theory; but that leading theorist of liberal democracy, John Stuart Mill, is often charged with trying to square the philosophical circle by holding to both of these theories, creating strain if not a downright contradiction within his thought.

The most frequently remarked tension in democracy theory is between twin ideals of liberty and equality. Although the terms *can* be defined so that no discord exists, recent democratic theorists do not commonly take this line; tension between them is normally to be found. In fact, analysis of the concepts is likely to reveal internal tugs as well. Thus political philosophers are seldom content with a definition of liberty that refers only to the absence of legal restrictions. But, if one tries to include in the definition whatever may make it difficult for individuals to do as they please or even what is in their interest, the term tends to get out of control and even to interfere with liberty in the stricter sense. Definitions that try to avoid this difficulty inevitably reflect this internal tension.

Likewise with equality. Equality of what? Should persons be treated identically, or in a way that gives equal consideration to their circumstances? Should the goal be equality of opportunity or equality of condition? Equality of resources or equality of welfare? Equality of satisfaction or equality of development?[4]

Turning to theories of democratic institutions (the heading under which most of the contributions to this volume fall), they may deal with how particular institutions do actually operate (explanatory theory), or with how under stated conditions they would probably operate, given certain assumptions about human behavior or human rationality (hypothetical theories), or with how they ought to operate in order to implement an assumed or previously vindicated set of philosophical foundations. All three of these types of theory may be "positive," avoiding justifications or other value judgments.

Perhaps the first question, logically, for a theorist of democratic institutions to consider is the selection of the unit that is to be self-governing. This is the problem of boundaries, yet it is almost universally ignored. Democratic theorists almost invariably take the territorial unit as given, discussing neither how it ought to be estblished in the first place nor under what conditions, if any, democratic principles would justify part of a democracy in seceding from the whole. The latter omission is especially surprising in view of the emphasis placed upon consent in most democratic theory, and also in the light of current movements for autonomy if not outright secession by Welshmen, Scots, Quebecois, and numerous other national and ethnic groups. In the Prologue to this volume, Frederick Whelan devotes himself to a careful discussion of the boundary problem. He does not pretend to have found a satisfactory answer, but he does provide some valuable ground-clearing by disposing of a number of potential contenders for a solution.

Once the political unit has been determined, what institutions should be established? First is a direct or an indirect democracy more desirable?[5] Once the city-state was replaced by far larger polities, this question became largely academic. However, the Progressive movement in the United States, late in the nineteenth century and in the early part of this century, brought with it new interest in, and demand for, direct democracy in the limited form of the Initiative, Referendum, and Recall. The Initiative and Referendum were made available for ordinary legislation in some twenty states, while a dozen also adopted the Recall, as did over a thousand municipalities. No one who has ever been confronted in the polling booth by a battery of several long and complicated propositions will be surprised to learn that response to this opportunity to practice direct democracy is typically quite low.

In recent years we have seen the rise of a new interest in direct democracy—one that is differently motivated and that takes a different form from that of its predecessor. I refer to the movement for "participatory democracy." The emphasis of the Progressive movement was primarily on giving "the people" more effective control of their government. Although this aim is by no means lacking in contemporary demands for greater popular participation at all levels, extending beyond government to economic organizations as well, the stress is now heavily upon getting more citizens actively involved in policy-making—partly for the purpose of obtaining effective representation of interests that are thought to be overlooked, often by the very people whose interests are involved, and partly for securing that personal development of the participants that was for Mill such an important feature of the value of representative government. Perhaps because this topic has been discussed so widely of late, and was the subject of NOMOS XVI, *Participation in Politics,* none of our authors has chosen to deal with it.

Once it has been settled that the government of a country should take the route of indirect democracy, numerous questions arise: How unified should the central government be? What should be the nature of the representative body? How should representatives be selected? How centralized should the government be? In what way, if any, should its domain be restricted? With the partial exception of the first, each of these questions receives attention here. The first question, which amounts to asking whether the powers of government should be fused (as in the cabinet or parliamentary form) or separated (as in the presidential form), is not dealt with by any of our authors, with the important exception that the chapters on judicial review (of which more anon) assume a system of separated powers and evaluate one aspect of it as it operates in the United States. (Certain elements of the separation of powers are treated in Part IV of NOMOS XX, *Constitutionalism.*)

Turning to the matter of representation, one approach considers what agencies should or do serve that purpose. Although we properly associate it with the legislature, the bureaucracy and, where the separation of powers prevails, the chief executive and to some extent the judiciary, also serve that purpose in important even if only supplementary ways. Assuming that the legislature will be the main avenue for institutionalizing the representative function, or at least the one whose structure should be determined with that end chiefly in view, the question of whether it should consist of one, two, or even more chambers, and, if of more than one, of what each should represent, raises interesting theoretical issues. However, none of them is discussed by our authors.

Most treatments of the subject of representation deal with what that term means or ought to mean and how it can be best effectuated. That is to say they deal with the representative role of the legislature and of the individual members of that body. Should they reflect public opinion in all its variety (to say nothing of its prejudice, self-interest, confusion, ignorance, and misinformation), or should they, in Madison's famous phrase, "refine" it? May electoral and representative systems be constructed in such a way as to favor the one or the other objective? For discussions of these topics, the reader must look elsewhere, e.g., to *Representation,* Volume X of this series.

In Part I, two of our authors deal with the question of what it takes to make a representative body representative, and *equally* representative, of its constitutents. Stephen L. Darwall argues that the principle of Equal Accountability requires a high degree of property redistribution because substantial inequalities of wealth tend to negate political equality. Charles R. Beitz is concerned to find out just what democratic "equality" means, as applied to representative government. More particularly, he examines the "principle of procedural equality," especially as to whether it is a fundamental right. He concludes that at least the usual or conventional arguments for this position are unsound.

Another feature of liberal democracy to which attention should be called grows out of the fact that representative bodies are also lawmaking bodies—the makers, or the validators or invalidators, of major public policies. As such they must be deliberative bodies if they are to serve as agencies for transmuting inchoate or at best highly inspecific (and at worst nonexistent) public opinion into public policy. Furthermore, as agencies of government they must be capable of making decisions, not so fractionated as to be incapable of action, but rather able to govern (or play their crucial role in the governing process) in a reasonably coherent and effective way. I make these obvious points because the literature on representation largely neglects them leaving these matters to others.

Closely related to representation are the topics of electoral and party systems and voting theory. So also is the theory of pressure groups as alternative modes of representation. These topics are also not considered in this book, except for certain limited aspects of voting theory to be discussed in the Epilogue.

The question of how centralized a democratic regime should be is one the answer to which, within broad limits, will vary from country to country. One aspect of it, however, raises an important general question: how does democratic theory relate to federalism? A democratic state does not need to be federal, nor does a federal state need to be democratic, although most of them are. The important question for us that is discussed in these pages is whether federalism is in some measure incompatible with democratic principles. In particular, does the fact that, under the federal form of government, neither the central government nor the governments of the individual "states" has complete control of its agenda contravene democratic principles? Not only does the jurisdiction possessed by the "states" limit the central government, and vice versa, but it also means that the states, at least in some sense, can limit each other. These problems are considered in Part II. Robert Dahl finds that although in a federal system "no single body of citizens can exercise final control over the agenda" this fact does not in itself make it less democratic than a unitary system. Acceptance of the majority principle as fair does not alter this conclusion, assuming that that principle operates within a proper unit. This assumption, about the proper unit, is the one dealt with in Whelan's chapter. Whelan and Dahl are in agreement that no clear and definitive principles seem to govern the decision as to what constitutes a proper unit for democratic decision making.

David Braybrooke, commenting on Dahl under the heading "Can Democracy Be Combined with Federalism or with Liberalism?," points out the relation between federalism and liberalism and at the same time shows that in combining each with democracy a problem arises—the same problem in each case. While he argues that Dahl dismisses too easily and indeed mistakenly his first problem, that of control of agendas, he agrees with Dahl's conclusion that federalism cannot be judged less democratic than a unitary system. Liberalism, in withdrawing certain issues from the domain of government, is like federalism in that it conflicts with Arrow's requirement of Unrestricted Domain. He argues, however, that Arrow and Amartya Sen themselves, perhaps unwittingly, had modified this restriction, in effect accepting the conclusions of Whelan and Dahl that no definitive principles appear to govern the determination of the proper unit for democratic decision-making. These matters receive further attention in the Epilogue, where I argue that federalism has a positive side that is often overlooked, and that Sen's "impossibility of a Paretian liberal," while true, uses a procedural definition of democracy that needs to be corrected by the ultimate values upon which the case for the procedural concept rests.

The next question posed above, that of democracy's proper domain, has already been broached. The most obvious and extensive restriction of domain is an aspect of constitutionalism (as, indeed, is federalism). The very purpose of individual rights and other constitutional restraints is to restrict the scope, the powers, of government. Moreover, the institution of judicial review not only reinforces these restraints but also gives to persons not usually accountable to the electorate extensive positive as well as negative powers. Several of our authors have chosen to deal with this aspect of our subject. Robert McKay leads off, in Part III, with a defense of the United States Supreme Court not only as compatible in principle with liberal democracy but also as having, on balance, carried out its task in a satisfactory fashion. George Kateb, commenting on McKay, agrees that judicial review has served the liberal purpose of protecting minority rights. The charge that it is undemocratic because judges are not elected and have life tenure misses the point that the disinterested position in which this places them actually contributes to their ability to shield minorities.

Peter Railton, on the other hand, argues that the record does not support the "bulwark" theory. Moreover, he contends, this fact adds force to the general critique of elite theories of democracy. Robert Nagel is also skeptical of judicial review's contributions to liberalism. Finding that we have less to fear and more to gain from leaving constitutional interpretation to the political branches of government than is widely believed, he pleads for a revivification of judicial self-restraint.

Concluding the general consideration of judicial review, David

G. Smith discusses various approaches, process-oriented or value-oriented, that the Court may take to constitutional issues. He finds no single formula that is likely to give lasting satisfaction, but concludes that the Court will do well to hold fast to Herbert Wexler's admonition to act in such a way that the losing party will feel that justice has not been violated.

Two more specialized papers (in Part IV) deal with certain theoretical issues relating to freedom of speech. Schauer contends that the argument for freedom of expression deriving from democracy gives it major reinforcement and also lends a distinct coloration to another one of its intellectual supports, the argument from truth. Amy Gutmann, using a recent case involving Princeton University as an example, explores the special problem of academic freedom and argues that it can be defended from either a "corporate pluralist" set of assumptions or from those of liberal democracy. The former tend to be absolute and, in certain circumstances, to sacrifice "citizenship" rights to "membership" rights. Because she wishes to preserve both, she favors reliance on the assumptions of liberal democracy.

Part V brings together four chapters loosely related to each other under the broad heading "Rationality, Responsibility, and Individuality." In various ways they are related to earlier chapters. Barry Holden's contribution is the one exception to my general statement that the volume lacks any consideration of justificatory theory, for Holden supports the belief that truth is not completely relative. Kenneth Winston deals with a more specific but not unrelated problem that has to do with rationality. His concern is with the quality of legislation and especially of its avoidance of favoritism to special interests. Traditionally liberals have relied upon devices (of which the Equal Protection Clause is an outstanding example) to guarantee the generality of rules, legislative and adminstrative, on the theory that that will insure what might be called their social rationality, their avoidance of unjust discrimination. He concludes that the supporting liberal theories are incoherent and also that their motivating ideal of personal autonomy has been displaced by a theory of basic goods.

The other two chapters in this part relate more to individualism than to rationality, although these two concepts are closely linked. William Mitchell argues that the welfare state undertakes more than it can handle. The difficulty is not just over-load, "system-capacity," although that is important; it is also that the *kind* of problems that the welfare state calls on voters and legislators to tackle often calls forth self-interested and selfish behavior, men's private will as contrasted with their public wills (the problem treated by Winston). Paradoxically, the market, relying entirely on self-interest, achieves a more efficient and therefore, at least from this point of view, a more socially desir-able result.

Completing this part, Robert Lane, drawing extensively upon relevant social-psychological materials, investigates the effects that a market society has upon that individualism which histor-ically has been so closely connected with liberal democracy. He finds that it encourages cognitive complexity, psychological mo-bility, personal differentiation, and imaginative thinking, all of which an individualistic society needs. And a money economy, which tends to go with a market economy, reduces dependence upon other individuals, and increases self-awareness and self-criticism, and a feeling of responsibility for one's fate. In all these ways, the market fosters "functional" individualism (by which he means that which contributes to the functioning of society as distinct from the development of the individual).

My concluding Epilogue deals with a variety of issues that fall under no single heading, some but not all of which are dis-cussed elsewhere in this volume.

In closing, let me simply repeat the message of the title of the book, the table of contents, and this introduction: these es-says on liberal democracy make no pretense to being compre-hensive. The foundations of democratic political theory, lib-erty, equality, the autonomy or dignity of the individual are considered only incidentally or at most with respect to their coherence or incoherence, not in terms of their ultimate justi-fication. Rather the authors, assuming the validity of the insti-tution as a whole, deal with theoretical problems that arise at the next level. Even here the book is necessarily selective. So be it.

NOTES

1. Andrew Levine, "A Conceptual Problem for Liberal Democracy," *Jour. of Philosophy,* 75 (1978), 302–08.

2. The question of the relation, if not the identity, of "democracy" and "liberal democracy" is discussed in J. Roland Pennock, *Democratic Political Theory* (Princeton, N.J.: Princeton University Press, 1979), chap. I. Chapters II and III of that book explore most of the issues about to be mentioned here.
3. See chapter V of my *Democratic Political Theory*.
4. Discussion of these issues and references to fuller treatments will be found in my *Democratic Political Theory*, chap. II. For two recent discussions of certain aspects of the problem of equality, see Douglas Rae, "Two Contradictory Ideas of (Political) Equality," *Ethics*, 91 (1981), 451–56, and Ronald Dworkin, "What Is Equality?," *Philosophy & Public Affairs*, 10 (1981), 185–246 and 283–345.
5. In this brief, overall discussion of democratic institutions, it would be tedious to keep repeating the distinction between normative and explanatory or hypothetical theories and to deal separately with each. In any case, they tend to be expounded together.

PROLOGUE: DEMOCRATIC THEORY AND THE BOUNDARY PROBLEM

FREDERICK G. WHELAN

I. THE PROBLEM

The concept of democracy, although protean, always makes reference to a determinate community of persons (citizens)—a "'people"—who are collectively self-governing with respect to their internal and external affairs. The process of self-government may be organized in different ways consistently with common usages of the term and our intuitive notions of what democracy means, although individual theorists may defend a best or truest set of democratic institutional arrangements. Still, any democratic theory must face the logically prior and in some ways more fundamental question of the appropriate constitution of the *people* or unit within which democratic governance is to be practiced. I shall argue not only that the drawing of boundaries around these units is a significant problem for democratic theory and practice, but that democratic theory itself offers no clear guidance on the matter. The difficulties posed by controversies regarding boundaries thus present an important practical limit to the scope of democracy as a method of making collective decisions.[1]

Mention of boundary problems suggests territorial disputes involving sovereign states, or entities aspiring to statehood, and it is in this form that the problem arises most conspicuously.

13

More generally, however, the problem is one of defining or bounding not geographical units but the membership of the democratic body, or citizenry; it is in this form that the problem first arises in the more abstract varieties of democratic political theory.

Democracy is sometimes considered, for example, to be an essentially *participatory* mode of collective decision-making, one in which all citizens have an opportunity for involvement in public affairs. While the exact degree, methods, and distribution of participation that are required or desirable in a democracy are debatable, it is clear that some participatory element, at some significant point(s) in the political process, is a necessary and distinguishing feature of a democracy.[2] The participatory formula for democracy, however, presupposes an answer to the prior question: who may participate? Or, how do we determine membership in the group whose members are entitled to participate? And who is to participate in making this decision?

Another common view regards the *majoritarian* principle as the heart of democratic governance: democracy is present where, when a collective decision is to be made, votes are counted (each person, or citizen, having one) and the alternative preferred by the greater number, or at least a plurality of those choosing to vote, is enacted.[3] Any other method, it is said, would place the decision-making power in the hands of some minority, which violates the basic democratic value of equality among the self-governing citizens. Again, this is a formula that may be accepted, although with qualifications. Since only a small proportion of public decisions made in democratic governments can actually be made by majority rule, the practical democrat generally falls back on the free elections of officials as the hallmark of a real-world democracy, assuming that these are generally although indirectly determinative of policies; it is here that the majority principle is applied.[4] All this is no sooner said, however, than we are again faced with the same problem of boundaries: how do we delimit the group within which, for purposes of making a particular decision, votes are to be counted and a majority preference identified? Or, to note a distinction passed over above, how are *citizens*, those with the right to be counted, distinguished from other persons? Majority rule as a procedural principle is not inherently democratic, but must be combined with relatively inclusive qualifications for citizenship. Determination of the criteria or bounds of the citizen body, however, is a matter that is logically prior to the operation of the majority principle, and cannot be solved by it.[5]

A final and more general idea of democracy is that it is government with the *consent* of the governed. This formula is indeterminate with respect to institutional forms, or the procedures by which consent is to be expressed—questions on which consent theorists have historically differed.[6] Again, however, we may always ask: *whose* consent is required? Or, within what group of people must public policies and laws win the requisite approval or acquiescence? To say simply the consent of "the governed" suggests that this is an arbitrary matter, that democratic theory requires only that consent be obtained for public decisions within political boundaries that are themselves the product of historical accidents, and usually of other-than-democratic forces. But this seems contradictory: it may well be the case that the appropriate boundaries, or the extent and composition of the community, is itself something about which the people involved have preferences; so if democracy is government by consent, then this too is a matter on which, in a democracy, consent ought to be determinative.[7]

The problem of determining the proper boundaries of the self-governing unit thus arises in all forms of democratic theory, and it therefore can be discussed without entering into the debates that arise among proponents of various specialized versions of democracy. Whatever form a democracy takes, collectively binding decisions are made, laws and policies are enacted, and these things are done for and in one way or another by a particular group or *people* that is set apart—and *bound* together[8]—for the purposes of self-government from other people or peoples, who are correspondingly excluded. Democratic theories usually focus on the internal decision-making arrangements, taking for granted the prior existence of a well-defined group with respect to which the question of democratic governance arises. But while individuals, and humanity as a whole, are entities that are naturally given, groups of people sharing characteristics that obviously destine them for collective self-government are not—or, at least, theories that assert oth-

erwise are seriously open to question. The establishment of political boundaries, or the formation of a group of people sharing a common political identity, on which a democracy can be
erected, is a matter that may occasionally appear to have been
satisfactorily resolved by history, but it is often a matter of continuing controversy and conflict. It is itself a matter of political
decision, actually or potentially: boundary-drawing, and the determination of political membership, are perhaps the most fundamental political decisions. Democratic theory then cannot
simply take the matter for granted. Democracy is advanced by
its advocates as the sole legitimate method for making political
decisions; democratic norms accordingly suggest that these decisions, like others, ought to be made with the consent and participation of the people involved, or by the will of the majority
of them. Boundaries comprise a problem, however, that is insoluble within the framework of democratic theory, and it may
be that democracy is practicable only when a historically given
solution of this issue (justifiable or not, by some theory other
than democratic theory) is acceptable. The following argument
to this effect is not intended to discredit democratic theory, but
only to establish one of its inherent limitations.

II. THE ALL-AFFECTED PRINCIPLE

Perhaps the most intuitively plausible proposal with respect
to the proper scope of democratic governance is that all those
people who are affected by a particular law, policy, or decision
ought to have a voice in making it. Woodrow Wilson appears
to have implied some such principle when he called for the
"settlement of every question, whether of territory, of sovereignty, of economic arrangement, or of political relationship,
upon the basis of the free acceptance of that settlement by the
people immediately concerned;"[9] recent democratic theorists
have frequently expressed the same idea.[10] The all-affected
principle would thus distinguish those who are qualified to be
citizens with respect to a particular decision from other persons
by reference to the content, or the prospective impact, of the
decision. Applied to the different types of democratic theory,
this formula indicates the appropriate scope of participation,

or of majority rule, or of the consent requirement; in practice this formula has often been advocated by proponents of a more participatory and egalitarian form of democracy than that prevailing in contemporary states, in which, it is said, many of the people who are actually affected by social decisions are rarely consulted, at least in any direct fashion.

I shall argue shortly that the all-affected principle is an untenable proposal; first, however, two aspects of its *prima facie* plausibility may be noted. This proposal appears to be offered in a spirit of defensiveness: it seems to conceive of social decisions as normally imposing burdens or costs on the passive many, and its intent seems to be to provide people with the means of protecting themselves, to the end either of avoiding these costs or of seeing that they are distributed more evenly. Such a defensive attitude—traditionally with respect to government, more recently with respect to concentrated economic power—has historically been an important part of the demand for democracy; the right to participate in government, like other rights, is (at least) an instrument with which individuals can safeguard their important interests against invasion or deprivation. As such this principle is morally plausible; it is perhaps not so intuitively clear that the recipients of benefits should have a voice in the decision to confer the benefits, although this is a decision that affects them. The applicability of the principle, in this perspective, depends on whether a given decision-making entity is regarded as (typically, or on balance) a source of burdens or of benefits; where the answer is mixed, as is presumably the case with the state and other relevant entities, the force of the principle is blurred, although it may be responded that wherever there is a question of costs, or of weighing relative costs and benefits, the potential bearers of the costs should have a voice.

The all-affected principle in democratic theory, furthermore, resembles the usual solution to the problem of scope in formal utilitarian theory, and may even be derivable as a political application of it; it may therefore derive strength from the appeal of this larger moral theory. Utilitarianism holds that the right action (or decision) is that which in the circumstances produces the greatest net increase in happiness or welfare of those affected by it. The utilitarian principle may serve as a prescription for individual choices, and as such its requirements are clear, although they encounter formidable difficulties, both epistemological (knowing of what others' happiness consists) and intellectual (calculating correctly about means). It may also serve as a standard for political decision-making, prescribing that public policy aim at the greatest overall welfare of those over whom rule is exercised. The utilitarian argument for political democracy—that those affected should not only be benefited by governmental decisions, but should also participate in making them—follows from either or both of two additional points. It may be claimed that each individual is the sole, or best, judge of his own interests, which he defends and promotes with his vote in the democratic process. Or, it may be denied that any ruler or group of rulers other than the people (those affected) as a whole can be depended upon to be motivated by the utilitarian principle: democratic decision-making is the procedure most likely to lead to utilitarian results even in the absence of benevolent motives in individuals. Utilitarianism suitably developed thus may yield the all-affected principle for collective decision-making, and appeal may be made to it in support of this variety of democratic theory.

While resort is occasionally had to the all-affected principle for democratic decision-making in small groups, where it is obvious to all concerned with respect to a given issue just who *is* likely to be affected by the outcome, this principle has not been and cannot be implemented in the context of the state, to which democratic theory is normally applied. Public decisions, authoritative and binding as they are, are made (when they are made democratically) not by those affected, but rather by all the eligible voters or citizens (or their representatives) in the previously delimited political unit on whose agenda the question has arisen. Political democracy is in practice associated with states, that is, authoritative institutions that claim jurisdiction over, and, if democratic, are responsive to the collective preferences of the people residing in, geographically bounded territories. And while all of these fellow-citizens may share some common concerns, it is not likely to be the case that all issues arising on the public agenda are matters of common concern, nor are all citizens likely to be affected by every decision. Consideration of the reasons for the usual resort to the territorial principle rather

than the all-affected principle reveals the fundamental unten-
ability of the latter, despite its superficial attractiveness.

An obvious practical difficulty with the all-affected principle
is that it would require a different constituency of voters or
participants for every decision: the status of fellow-citizens would
not be permanent, as is the case in the territorial states with
which we ordinarily associate the concept of citizenship, but
would shift in relation to the issue proposed. This is more than
a mere inconvenience, which a committed democrat might be
willing to tolerate. The deeper problem is that before a democratic decision could be made on a particular issue (by those
affected), a prior decision would have to be made, in each case,
as to *who* is affected and therefore entitled to vote on the substantive issue—a decision, that is, on the proper bounds of the
relevant constituency. And how is this decision, which will be
determinative of the ensuing substantive decision, to be made?
It too should presumably be made democratically—that is, by
those affected—but now we encounter a regression from which
no procedural escape is possible.[11] In many cases of political
decision-making, moreover, the question of who is affected by
a given law or policy depends on *which* law or policy is enacted
from among the available alternatives; in fact, the scope and
nature of the impact of different laws or policies on different
categories of people is often their most controversial feature.
Thus to say that those who will be affected by a given decision
are the ones who should participate in making it is to attempt
to bypass the crucial question, and to propose what is a logical
as well as a procedural impossibility.[12]

III. TERRITORIAL STATES

Given the failure of the all-affected principle, democratic
theory is normally advanced with reference to some established
community of people, all of whom are citizens and thus entitled
to participate in public business and to make, through majority
rule, collective decisions, regardless of their diverse personal
interests or differential stakes in the issues that appear on the
public agenda. Some citizens may indeed choose to defer, on
particular issues, to those who seem to be especially affected,

but they are not required by democratic principles to do so. The same effect may be attained when those who are unaffected by or have only weak preferences with respect to proposed alternatives fail to exercise their right to vote, or conversely when comparatively intense minorities achieve disproportionate influence through their activism in the political process. In these cases political decision-making, as practiced in countries generally regarded as democratic, may sometimes seem to approximate what is called for by the all-affected principle. Despite the broad and undifferentiated category of legal citizenship, with its territorial basis, the effective constituencies for particular decisions consist of self-selected groups of individuals with special interests in the matter at hand; the boundaries of effective citizenship fluctuate. Familiar criticisms of pluralistic politics, however, call into question the assumption that all those who are affected by a policy normally succeed in exercising influence by informal processes. These phenomena thus seem anomalous, and sometimes even illicit, in light of democratic theory, although they may nevertheless be defended pragmatically.

A democratic political system is therefore one in which all the citizens of a particular community enjoy the right to have their preferences taken into account in public decisions, even though they may be differentially affected by the outcome. Worries that this might lead to unfair results may to some extent be alleviated by the reflection that *liberal* democratic theory, at any rate, not only calls for collective self-determination, but also insists that authority be exercised in accordance with other norms as well. One of these is the rule of law, and in particular the requirement that everyone enjoy the equal protection of, or equal treatment under, the laws that are made by the democratic process. If laws and policies literally treated everyone equally, of course, the all-affected principle would be satisfied even when democracy is implemented, in the usual way, within a fixed territorial community: the democratic regime would simply have to confine itself to matters that affect all of its members, and equally so at that. In practice democracies do not adhere to such limited agendas, and the "equal treatment" provision is usually taken to require only equal treatment for persons who are similarly situated, or who share similar, relevant characteristics. Subject to this condition democracies do enact policies that impose special burdens, or distribute special benefits, to distinct categories of persons, and in normal practice it is the entire citizenry who are entitled to vote on such policies, and to determine the appropriate categories of persons to whom special treatment is given. The determination of relevant differences, which justify departures from absolute generality in law, is in fact one of the fundamental types of political decisions that a community must make, one that reflects its basic collective values and goals as a community. It is thus a decision that must be made (according to democratic theory) democratically, with equal opportunity to participate for all members of the community, even if the effect of such a decision is to identify and prescribe policies for special groups. Thus for example it is the whole citizenry who decide that eighteen-year-old men (and not everyone, nor other descriptions of persons) shall register for military service, and not the affected group—partly because states are organized territorially, and partly for the logical reason, mentioned above, that we cannot know who the especially affected *are* in advance of the larger community's decision. The requirement of the rule of law, with which such decisions as this are generally held to be compatible, does not therefore go very far in reconciling the all-affected principle with the usual structure of democracy.

Democracy therefore is practiced within communities all of whose members may vote and otherwise participate equally. According to what principle, then, or by what decision-making procedure, are the boundaries of the community determined, given that the all-affected principle is not workable for this purpose? The question of boundaries is essentially the question of defining eligibility for membership in the community: democracy refers to self-government by a people, and so *a people* or political "self" must be bounded or set apart from other peoples.[13] In the case of states, however, the boundary problem refers in practice to the geographical borders of the territory over which authority is to be exercised; although in democratic theory territory is a consideration secondary to that of the composition of the people, in modern states it comes for the most part to the same thing, since the principal conditions of citizenship are birth or a period of residence within a certain territory.

How then are the boundaries determined within which democracy is practiced?

In democratic theory democracy is usually offered as the exclusively legitimate method of making binding decisions for a collectivity, yet brief reflection suffices to show that the boundary problem is one matter of collective decision that cannot be decided democratically. Just as in trying to implement the all-affected principle we would need to make a prior decision regarding who is affected, so in attempting to solve the problem of territorial boundaries we would need to make a prior decision regarding who are entitled to participate in arriving at a solution—and this prior question is frequently just as controversial as the substantive question, and procedurally insoluble. A boundary has two sides, and the inclusion of some means the exclusion of others, all of whom are, by this fact, affected by its existence. Thus a boundary cannot be democratically established solely by the collective will of those who are to be included within it, even if we could identify them, although this group is to be self-governing in other respects. When the membership of two adjacent groups is well-established, they can perhaps negotiate their common geographical boundary; but when boundaries in the larger sense of the composition of the self-governing units are in dispute, no democratic procedure seems applicable. Democracy can be practiced for making collective decisions once the collectivity has been defined, but democratic methods themselves are inadequate to establish the bounds of the collectivity, whose existence democratic theory simply presupposes.

This is more than a minor shortcoming of democratic theory, and the logically prior boundary question is often controversial for good reason. Not only are boundaries often an issue about which disputes arise, and with regard to which individuals have preferences; the resolution of this matter is also frequently determinative of the substantive questions that follow, since the alternative possible decisions respecting boundaries or membership may (predictably) generate majorities on different sides of the substantive questions. This case is similar to what may be observed at party conventions and similar proceedings, where the fiercest contests are over rules, procedures, agendas, and the like, since decisions made at this stage can be seen to influence if not predetermine the ostensibly democratic decisions of the plenary sessions. The boundary problem seems more intractable than the problem of alternative procedures or agendas, however, since at least in the latter case the group whose business is to be conducted is definitively constituted. When there is disagreement over the composition of the relevant decision-making body, however—a sub-group demands decision-making autonomy for itself, for example, or people outside the group as currently constituted claim that they are entitled to be included—an impasse occurs, and an outcome that some will denounce as undemocratic will be the likely result.

The boundary problem and its insolubility by democratic means may be vividly illustrated by the case of Ireland, where the most troublesome political issue has long been precisely the proper boundaries of autonomous communities. Other important political questions, both in the north and south of the country, would no doubt be decided differently than they have been as a consequence of a different drawing of political boundaries, which are controversial at least in part because their definition can be seen by all to be determinative of other issues. In the eyes of an old-fashioned Unionist the appropriate sovereign unit (for historical, strategic, and economic reasons) was the United Kingdom of Great Britain and Ireland, the entity that existed from 1800 until 1922. A plebiscite taken among the population of this entity during that period would no doubt have revealed a substantial majority in favor of the established boundaries, a fact reflected in the refusal of the U.K. Parliament to acquiesce in demands for Irish independence. In the eyes of an Irish nationalist, however, the proper unit is the island of Ireland, which seems—both geographically, and for a different set of historical reasons—to be an entity distinct from Great Britain. A vote among the inhabitants of Ireland would probably confirm this opinion. Instead, in order to appease a local majority of Irish Unionists, the boundary settlement of 1921–22 embodied a third possibility: Ireland was divided into what became the present Republic of Ireland and a new entity called Northern Ireland, which remained associated, by a vote of its people, with Great Britain in a new state called the United Kingdom of Great Britain and Northern Ireland. A vote taken among the inhabitants of Northern Ireland would confirm this *status quo,* as would, presumably, a vote among the inhabitants of the present United Kingdom; yet the impasse remains, since the present boundaries appear arbitrary and illegitimate (a kind of international gerrymandering) to Irish nationalists. It may be conceded that all parties to this dispute are *bona fide* democrats, inasmuch as all of them are prepared to rest their case with a popular vote; what they adamantly differ about is the appropriate boundaries within which the vote should be taken. Democratic theory offers no guidelines on this question, and so the essence of the Irish problem is that no solution could generally be accepted as legitimate, given the prevailing contemporary acceptance of democracy as the exclusively legitimate method for resolving political questions. It is for this reason that all parties to the dispute, democrats though they may be, are found appealing additionally to non-democratic principles (historical tradition, nationality, economic rationality, and so on), none of which carries decisive weight, to support the case for their preferred boundaries.

IV. CONSENT

Is there any way, in specialized types of democratic theory or through congenial principles, to resolve such conflicts? In this and the following sections I consider the boundary problem as it appears in consent theory and the theory of nationalism, both of which have historically been associated with modern democratic theory; I also consider some geographical approaches to boundaries, and some theories that make reference to system autonomy as a desirable feature of political regimes, including democratic ones. None of these, I shall argue, offers a generally satisfactory solution to the problem.

Modern democratic theory is an outgrowth of a longer tradition of political thought that focuses on consent as the requisite foundation of government. Consent theory characteristically takes political and legal obligation as the central issue of political theory, and it asserts that (at least in the public realm) only an individual's consent, as expressed for example in an agreement or promise—that is, a free act of his will—can create a valid obligation for him. It follows that governmental authority is legitimate, and subjects are obligated to obey it, only if they have consented to its existence in some fashion. The requirement of consent, which was at first applied to the original establishment and form of the state, was gradually extended until, in the democratic version of consent theory, it is conceived as the mainspring of government. Consent means deliberate choice by the people among alternatives on an ongoing and regular basis; every law and policy is supposed to reflect the will of the majority expressed through the democratic process, while the participation of all the citizens reflects their general consent to the procedural norms of democracy and the constitution of the state in which these are embodied.

Does democratic consent theory offer any guidance on the problem of political boundaries? The original establishment of political authority among previously unattached individuals was the problem typically posed by the classical consent (or contract) theorists, and so one might have expected them to confront the question of how determinate communities come to be set off from one another in the boundary-less state of nature. This question tends to be avoided, however, although they generally appear to hold that any group of consenting individuals can become a people, their unity deriving entirely from their agreement and the laws that are made in consequence of it.[14] Instead these theorists (Hobbes, Locke, Rousseau, Kant), like most modern democratic theorists, begin by presupposing the existence of a community, in the sense of a collection of individuals residing in a delimited territory, and they concentrate on the questions of how these persons could agree among themselves to establish authority, and what form it would take. The proper method of determining appropriate boundaries is left undiscussed.

Consent theory does, however, suggest a principle that seems consonant with the underlying values of democratic theory: the appropriate group within which democracy is to be practiced, and over the members of which collective decisions are to be binding, should be a group that each individual member has joined, or to whose authority he has consented. This principle conjures up the picture of a voluntary association, reminding us that democracy may be adopted as the mode of governance of such associations, of many and varied purposes. Modern political democracy has even been said to have its roots in the congregational self-government of certain Protestant churches, membership in which was entirely optional and, indeed, supposed to be a matter of self-conscious choice.[15] For voluntary associations, consent theory does appear to indicate a plausible and feasible method of determining the bounds of the democratic community. Boundaries in such cases are open and fluid, at least in the sense that dissatisfied members are always free to leave, and also in the sense that, normally, new members may be admitted, if they are attracted to the group's purposes, and subject to its rules, but only on a voluntary basis.

Significant difficulties arise, however, when the attempt is made to assimilate states to this model. States are territorial and compulsory associations, claiming jurisdiction over all residents from the time of their birth or arrival within their borders; and these features seem to be necessary if states are to fulfill their minimal functions of apprehending criminals and exercising compulsory adjudication over disputes between individuals. Actual consent in the sense of a deliberate decision to adhere to a polity is the infrequent exception, characterizing mainly naturalized citizens. Emigration, moreover, is a costly and unfeasible option for most people, even when states permit it, as Hume pointed out.[16] Citizens may learn to approve of the governmental institutions of their country, and they may, if it is a democratic government, have the opportunity of consenting to, or seeking to change, its laws; but the boundaries within which these processes take place are something they normally find settled—or, if unsettled, not a matter to which the principle of consent is readily applicable.

The consent principle may work, to a limited degree, in establishing the composition of groups enjoying local self-government within a federal state. The formal boundaries of the subnational units are of course usually territorial, like those of the larger state, and the same problems of arbitrariness, non-democratic origins, and even manipulation (gerrymandering) arise at this level. Federalism also presents democratic theory with the additional problem of deciding on the appropriate level within the federal structure for making a particular decision— a prior decision that is frequently controversial because, like the drawing of political boundaries, it may predetermine the "democratic" outcomes on substantive issues.[17] If one can assume geographical mobility within a federal system, however, one may imagine individuals "voting with their feet," migrating and settling where they like, thus becoming citizens (at the local level) of a community they choose for themselves. The possibility of migration does not of course alter the established territorial boundaries, but it may (in principle) determine the more important question of the composition of communities in a way that seems consistent with democratic theory.

The assumption of perfect mobility is unrealistic even for a country like the United States; it is of course even more so internationally, which is what most seriously undermines the portrayal of the establishment of states on a voluntaristic basis in classical contract theories. An individual may be fortunate enough to find that democratic institutions exist within the boundaries of the country in which he was born, or he can work for their realization there, but the boundaries themselves are normally given. The background assumption of Madison's advice (in *Federalist* #10) to choose a large republic over a number of small ones was that the Americans of 1788 had such a choice before them, but this is a rare occurrence in political life. Boundaries are not only usually given, but their origins more often than not do not bear scrutiny in light of democratic and related types of political theory.[18] As Hume says in the essay cited above, consent when present is no doubt a ground of legitimate government, but consent historically grows within states founded by other means (usually force), as a consequence of good government. Consent may even come to be routinized in democratic institutions within the state, but it cannot normally be the basis of the existence or of the boundaries of the state in the first place.

The issue of secession may also be mentioned in connection with consent theory. If it is held to be a principle of democratic theory that membership in a particular self-governing unit ought to be contingent on the consent of each individual, it clearly follows that, barring special circumstances, a right of emigration ought to exist for individuals.[19] More controversially, however, it might also appear that a territorially concentrated group whose members (or a majority of them) are disaffected with the larger community ought to be entitled to

secede, along with their territory, and to constitute themselves
as a new state. Compelling them to remain within the larger
state may be compatible with democracy understood solely as
majoritarianism (since they are a minority of the whole), but it
seems at variance with the principle of consent as the basis for
determining membership or the boundaries of the polity.

The right of secession is nonetheless not recognized by modern democratic states, although it sometimes is successfully asserted by arms and afterwards accepted. The other side of this
question was maintained in familiar words by Abraham Lincoln, who combined the roles of state-builder and democratic
theorist. The Union must be preserved, he says, precisely in
order to assure the success of the American experiment in democracy; secession is incompatible with democracy because it
denies the principle of majority rule, and perhaps also because
of its tendency, if not checked, to anarchy. Still, to accept the
verdict of the majority of the larger union, rather than that of
the majority in a smaller but viable geographical unit, is arbitrary in terms of democratic theory, and no doubt reflects a
view of the desirability of large and strong states based on other
than democratic grounds. Nor does it tell us how large the larger
union ought optimally to be: the United States had, after all,
seceded from the British Empire. It is superior force, not adherence to principles of democracy or consent, that generally
resolves such disputes, as in the United States itself.[20]

V. NATIONALITY

Democratic political movements in the past century and a half
have frequently been associated with nationalism, and much
modern democratic theory has acquiesced in what appears to
be the verdict of history by accepting this additional principle
as offering the best practical solution to the problem of political
boundaries for sovereign states. Nationalism, however, contains
difficulties of its own, and a boundary principle based on nationality does not always fit well with democratic theory.

The nationalist principle holds that states ought to corre-
spond to pre-existing national units, and that the claim of independent statehood and self-government arises from the col-

lective right of a distinct nation to determine its own affairs and destiny. While states are artificial creations of political will, nations (it is said) are given, either by nature, or by history, which has differentiated nations from one another on the basis of distinctive languages, cultures, traditions, and common memories. No single objective criterion of nationality appears to be definitive, and defenders of the principle usually end by saying that a nation is simply a group of people united by their common feeling of being a single body in some respect(s) other than their being under a common government.[21] The nation then is held to comprise the *people* or community presupposed by democratic theory, and when a particular nation moveover occupies (or has a historical claim to) a definite territory as well, the criterion of nationality seems to provide a solution to the boundary problem in both of its forms.

Democratic nationalists hold not only that the nation-state is the appropriate unit of self-government, but further that all members of the nation are by that fact qualified to be citizens, with an equal right to participate in managing their common affairs. This conjunction of nationalism and democracy seems largely fortuitous, attributable to the historical fact that democratic ideology discredited dynastic and in some cases colonial boundaries together with dynastic and colonial rule, leaving a void with respect to the legitimate foundation of modern states that nationalism filled.[22] The nationalist principle is nevertheless fundamentally different from democratic principles, since its central tenet appeals to non-voluntaristic criteria.

John Stuart Mill's qualified acceptance of political claims based on nationality illustrates the effort of liberal democratic theorists to reconcile themselves to the currents of the times. "Where the sentiment of nationality exists in any force," Mill says, "there is a *prima facie* case for uniting all the members of the nationality under the same government. . . . This is merely saying that the question of government ought to be decided by the governed."[23] This effort to construe nationalism as somehow implied by democratic theory, however, is circular: one must have decided in advance that "the governed" should be the nation, in order to conclude that they would (democratically) choose to be an independent nation-state. Retreating from this high ground, Mill also offers several arguments to the effect that nationality (as a distinct principle) may be expected to contribute to the success of democratic government: a common nationality facilitates the communications, confidence, and mutual respect that are necessary or desirable in a democracy, permitting compromise and the pursuit of the public interest; it ensures sympathy between the army and the people, thus precluding a common tactic of despotic governments. Nationality as a "sense of belonging together" and as a foundation for the requisite sense of equality thus may be among the conditions favorable to successful democracy.[24]

These arguments notwithstanding, however, nationality provides only a *prima facie* case for statehood. Mill's more fundamental utilitarian principles lead him to the important qualification that it is desirable for small and backward peoples to be absorbed into more highly civilized states—as for example the Scottish Highlanders and the Welsh have been merged with England, the Bretons and the Basques of Navarre with France. It is better, he says, for the average Welshman or Breton to enjoy membership in a more advanced community—rather than "to sulk on his own rocks, the half-savage relic of past times"— and it is also in the general interest of the progress of civilization as a whole, which often emerges as the decisive consideration in Mill's moral theory.[25] This reasoning suggests a different principle for the boundaries of political communities: they should be drawn so as most efficiently to spread the influence of higher civilizations, by absorbing less advanced groups as minority elements into larger democratic states, where their members may be elevated to the higher level. This is a perfectly coherent principle, although it is no more conceptually related to democracy than is the alternative nationalist principle. It is also no doubt of fairly limited applicability, and in default of it Mill is prepared, like most nineteenth-century liberals, to embrace nationalism.

The union of democratic and nationalist principles remains prominent in world politics today, the United Nations having affirmed both the "right of self-determination" of "peoples" and equal democratic political rights for individuals.[26] Political boundaries should be drawn, on these principles, in accordance with the geographical distribution of distinct peoples or nations, the members of which are entitled—and required—to practice democracy among themselves. The existence of "peoples" is presupposed, as in nationalist theory generally, although the concept is no better defined; thus groups aspiring to self-government continue to seek legitimacy by trying to establish their claim to be genuine peoples.

The nationalist principle is theoretically clear, although its empirical applicability to disputed cases is doubtful. Before considering the difficulties, however, we should note how it qualifies democratic theory. Democracy refers to a method of making collective decisions which, holding as it does that collective preferences or majority will (suitably informed by deliberation) should prevail, appeals to values such as voluntarism, freedom (from an alien will, or from mere tradition), and rationality. When it is combined with nationalism, however, democracy appears to be a subordinate and circumscribed principle, even if decisive in its intra-national sphere. Democratic rule is exercised, but within a context that is not itself freely chosen, nor reflective of the will or the reason of the people concerned. Democratic politics takes place in a framework that is held to be outside the scope of political choice, and identified in accordance with criteria supplied by a theory other than democratic theory. Thus while as a matter of putative practical necessity democratic theorists may subscribe to the claims made on behalf of nationality, it should be recognized that in so doing they acknowledge the limitations of democracy.

Beyond this, however, several major difficulties with the nationalistic principle severely weaken its acceptability as a general solution to the boundary problem of democratic theory. The first of these concerns the large number of actual cases (frequently the subject of controversy) where one or another of the tenets of nationalist theory does not in fact hold true, and where therefore the principle offers no guidance. There may in a given region be no agreed-upon nation or people, but rather some other state of affairs: a politically united but heterogeneous population (the United States), or a population sharing a common language and culture but lacking the common interest or sense of unity requisite for a nation (Ireland and Britain, the U.S. in 1860), or two or more different nations whose people are apparently content to live associated in a larger, multi-national state (United Kingdom, Soviet Union), or a number of ethnic groups, each below the size to which the principle of self-determination is conventionally held to apply (some African countries). These examples reveal the inadequacy of nationality as the exclusive determinant of acceptable boundaries, and they point to the fact that political choice and creativity can be brought to bear on the problem, sometimes in a benign and stable fashion.

Another sort of empirical difficulty arises when a claim of nationhood is advanced but not accepted by other groups whose established boundaries would be affected (Basques, Kurds, Palestinians). Such a claim may be rejected either because of doubts about its procedural validity, that is, whether those who make it really represent those in whose name they purport to speak; or it may be problematic simply because the theory of nationalism lacks precise and universally valid criteria for identifying a genuine nation. In such cases neither nationalist nor democratic theory offers any acceptable method for resolving the question.

A final type of difficulty presents itself when two or more nations, with clearly distinct collective identities, exist, but their members are intermingled in the same territory. Since independent states require mutually exclusive and reasonably continuous territories, the nationalist principle cannot be applied in such cases except through a transfer of populations—something that usually cannot be accomplished except forcibly. Even when it is done, the determination of the boundaries into which the populations are moved cannot be made in accordance with the principles of nationalism (nor of democracy), but only through some other method, such as war, or negotiated compromise. It is well known how this difficulty emerged in the Versailles settlement, when the victorious Allies set out to apply the principle of national self-determination (which they associated with democracy) to the peoples of the defeated empires. The residential intermixture of peoples in central Europe was such that it proved impossible to draw boundaries so that each nation had its own state, and each state contained only one nationality.[27] While democracy was to be practiced within the new states, the founding decisions could not be made democratically, but were imposed from without; resentments arising from these decisions—which involved the denial of some national claims, and the creation of new national minorities—were an important factor in the outbreak and course of the Second World War.[28]

A device that has been used on occasion to settle national boundaries in an apparently democratic fashion is the plebiscite, in which a group of people are permitted to decide for themselves, by majority vote, of what country they wish to become a part, or in some cases whether they wish to form an independent state. The plebiscitary process is necessarily so constrained by extraneous forces and arbitrariness, however, that its consonance with the democratic principle (decision in accordance with the will of the people) is illusory. An outside authority must set the alternatives and delimit the electorate, decisions that will appear unfair to some interested parties, especially as they will predetermine the outcome of the vote (and may even be framed for this purpose).[29] A plebiscite is a plausibly legitimate method for settling the independence or affiliation of an area whose national identity and geographical boundaries are already firmly settled by history and not in dispute (as is arguable, for example, in the case of Quebec); but when it is boundaries themselves that are in question, a plebiscite can provide only the appearance of democracy and is likely in consequence to stimulate cynicism about democratic government generally.

I turn now from difficulties in application to another problem in the theory of nationalism, one that casts doubt on its claim to be anything other than an acquiescence in the verdicts of history, so far as the territorial foundations of states are concerned. Contrary to the claim in nationalist theory that nations exist independently of, and prior to, states, thus predetermining their proper boundaries, a careful reading of history suggests otherwise. Nations are more often than not created by states, by the deliberate policies of rulers of states in the process of their establishment and consolidation, or otherwise by the endeavors of political activists who seek to realize the nation-state ideal. Thus attempts have been made to develop national foundations for aspirant states by reviving or standardizing declining languages (Irish, Ukrainian) and by other cultural efforts; in the "new nations" there are many cases of newly invented national identities being promoted by political leaders and superimposed on the ethnic pluralism that exists within the established boundaries (India, Algeria, Ghana, etc.)[30] Macpherson, who acknowledges that the creation of national loyalties in underdeveloped countries is usually undertaken by one-party authoritarian regimes, nevertheless regards this process as "democratic;"[31] but it is not, in the senses of democracy admitted in this paper. Nor is such nation-making a feature only of the contemporary third world: the national unity of apparently clearly defined states such as Britain and France is actually the product of similar efforts by successful state-builders in the past.[32] Thus the boundaries and common culture of the units that may be destined to become self-governing states is rarely natural or simply given, as nationalists hold, but rather is determined by political will. This will, however, is not and cannot be a democratic will, but that of rulers and activists; it is made effectual more often by their initiatives and by force than by any consultation of the preferences of the people concerned.

VI. GEOGRAPHY AND SALIENCE

Geographers have naturally been interested in political boundaries—their origins, consequences, and relationships to other features of the human geography of an area; several topics from this literature may be briefly considered. Geographers have called attention to the fact that precise, linear boundaries for political units, as a concept and a practice, are in large part distinctive of the modern West, and may be contrasted with the more fluid and indeterminate zones or frontiers that characterized Medieval Europe and some non-Western cultures.[33] Well-defined territorial boundaries are probably to be associated with the emergence of the modern sovereign state of the Western type, with its claim to a monopoly of coercive authority within an area (and possibly also with the concept of private property as exclusive *dominium* in European civil law).[34] This type of state, in any case, and this conception of state boundaries, have become universal norms, and thus it is primarily boundaries in this sense that pose the main practical problem for democratic theory.

The literature of political geography contains several normative suggestions regarding boundaries, though not especially ones that are advanced with concern for their conformity to democratic principles. The idea that the best boundaries are defensible ones is frequently proposed, and it is morally plausible if such boundaries would serve to decrease the likelihood of armed conflict between states. Three difficulties, however, attend this suggestion. The defensibility of borders varies to an extent with changes in military technology and thus does not offer a secure basis for boundaries over time. One country's strong borders, moreover, are frequently its neighbor's weak ones; defensible boundaries, however, would be mutually acceptable, and thus stable, only if they were equally defensible from both sides. There is no agreement, finally, on whether the goal of peace is more effectively advanced by boundaries that act as barriers between peoples, or by those that facilitate intercourse and hence mutual understanding. It thus appears that strategic considerations, while they may often (and perhaps properly) enter into boundary determinations, do not provide clear or generally applicable criteria. Geographers have also explored the relationship between boundaries and patterns of economic activity, a topic that suggests that desirable (in the sense of efficient) boundaries would be those that embrace regions that function as economic units. Economic patterns more often than not develop, however, in response to political boundaries previously established. More importantly, it would seem that facilitation of economic growth could never be a neutral or non-controversial principle for boundaries, since any alternative in this respect would tend to advance some interests at the expense of others. Thus while strategic and economic principles may occasionally offer useful considerations, neither very often provides generally acceptable criteria.[35] Neither, furthermore, is democratic, except insofar as one can assume that military security or economic rationality is everyone's (or the majority's) paramount interest, and impute preferences accordingly.

The most-discussed geographical issue pertains to the claim that "natural boundaries" ought to delimit the territory of states, a claim that has at times had an important impact on political practice. The natural-boundary principle, moreover, can be adduced as an adjunct of democratic theory by being brought under the more general heading of salience. Salient factors may be the basis of democratic choice, first, insofar as they determine the popular preferences that democracy must take into account. Secondly, resort to salient features of the objects among which a choice is to be made, merely because they are salient, can be defended in general as a rational basis for a collective decision in some circumstances. When it is important to everyone that a decision be made, but when it is a matter of comparative indifference to each party *which* alternative is chosen, salience provides a criterion that facilitates both agreement itself and observance of the agreed-upon rule or convention thereafter.[36] Accepting the model of rational choice from which this conclusion emerges, a democrat might accept salience to settle disputes when, as in the case of boundaries, democratic procedures are unworkable. This reasoning may partly explain the attractiveness of the notion of natural boundaries, in the sense of conspicuous features of the physical terrain, as the basis for political boundaries.[37]

The first difficulty with this suggestion is of course that in many instances there simply are no obvious physical indicators for boundaries where, on other grounds, boundaries seem to be needed. A more serious, and usually decisive, objection, however, calls into question the very concept of salience or "naturalness" as an objective quality of geographical features. It is clear, to take the most famous case, that the alleged naturalness of the Rhine-Alps-Pyrenees frontiers for France was a distinctively French (not German or Italian) perception. Prescriptions and actions based on this claim were therefore manifestations of a particular political will, notwithstanding appeals to "nature" and inevitability; while this claim was advanced most vociferously to justify annexations of territory in the wake of the French Revolution, the anti-dynastic ideology of natural frontiers was evidently a product of the nationalistic rather than the democratic element in the Revolution.[38] French expansionism led Fichte to reply that the "truly natural boundaries" of a nation are "internal," spiritual ones, marked externally by a common language—that is, to appeal from physical to what might be termed cultural salience, which is even less likely to offer grounds for consensual agreement.[39] The objective quality of geographically salient features may be questioned more generally. Rivers have cartographic salience and have therefore sometimes been used by boundary-drawers, but in actuality rivers in inhabited regions more often unite than separate the people who live on the two banks. The case of Ireland casts doubt on the naturalness (to all observers) of islands as political units. That mountains form obvious dividers, it has been said, is the distinctive perception of lowlanders.[40]

Salience may be a suitable basis for collective choice when a given thing is equally salient—and salient as a solution to the same problem—to all concerned. Boundaries established on this basis, therefore, if they are to accord with democratic values, must be equally salient, *as* proper boundaries, to the people living on both sides. The salience of physical features as political boundaries, however, is likely to differ among the disputing parties depending on their particular historical associations and political ambitions. Salience, furthermore, figures in theories of rational choice as a means of selecting among comparatively indifferent alternatives, and thus it will not work when, as is often the case with boundaries, the alternatives are the objects of differing and intense preferences. For both of these reasons, then, attempted resort to "natural" boundaries comprises a mistaken and usually futile effort to deny the essentially *political* (and thus artificial) quality of boundaries and the political nature of their determination. In some cases political boundaries may be drawn so as to conform to conspicuous features of the terrain, in which case salience, in addition to custom, no doubt plays a role in sustaining them. But it is unlikely that appeal to salience could resolve a political dispute over proper boundaries.

VII. AUTONOMY

The concept of autonomy may finally be considered for whatever guidance it may offer on the question of appropriate boundaries for a democratic system. Autonomy denotes both self-governance from within and independence from external control, ideas that may be combined with democratic procedures for decision-making in order to capture more completely what is usually meant by a democratic system. Two suggestions may be made regarding the bearing of autonomy on appropriate boundaries—neither of them, however, comprising a solution to the problem.

Democratic theorists have frequently raised the question whether it is desirable, in general, for a democratic community to be large or small. The latter has often appeared to be desirable from the point of view of realizing such democratic values as equality, fraternity, and participation. Dahl and Tufte pose this question more systematically as involving a trade-off between "citizen effectiveness" (a sense of real involvement in decision-making), which is attainable only in comparatively small units, and "system capacity," which requires large ones.[41] System capacity refers to the democratic system's control over a significant agenda, or its ability to act effectively on all the matters that affect the interests of its members, and it is thus related to the concept of autonomy: a unit that is too small, however democratic it may be internally, will inevitably have some of the decisions on matters that affect it made by outsiders—or not made at all—and in either case its impotence renders it something less than a fully self-governing or autonomous democracy. The requirement of autonomy thus implies generally that democracies ought to be larger rather than smaller; more precisely it suggests that boundaries ought to be drawn such that each unit has the capacity to control all the matters that affect it. This principle, however, is unworkable: the "matters" for political decision are not always congruent with stable territorial boundaries; more seriously, "affectedness" is a controversial matter itself, invocation of which raises the difficulties discussed above in connection with the all-affected principle. Dahl and Tufte suggest that democratic theorists should think in terms of a hierarchy of different sizes and levels of government, in which the different goals and values of democracy could be realized in differing degrees at different levels; but this in itself does not offer a solution to the problem of how the various units ought to be bounded.

Deutsch relates the concept of the autonomy of a system to a "communication differential" between it and its environment: "among members or parts of an organization there should be more rapid and effective communication than with outsiders."[42] Deutsch mostly argues descriptively that self-governing organizations *are* marked by such differentials, which can be observed and measured, but the argument can take a prescriptive form: boundaries of political systems should be drawn in accordance with such differentials, thereby enabling the system to derive maximum benefit from a common set of historical memories, an unambiguous symbolic system, and facility of internal communications. This argument can, moreover, be applied with special force to democratic systems, since ease of communication is conducive to the deliberative process and the sense of common purpose that are especially important in democracies.

Deutsch's suggestion accords with one of the common arguments relating nationality to democratic government: national sentiments, where they exist, facilitate communication within the national group, thereby conducing to the operation of democracy. It is also reminiscent of Dewey's idea of a "public" as constituted by common perceptions of the consequences of collective actions, and thus by a conscious common interest in controlling these consequences, which is the function of the state. The proper scope of a state, Dewey suggests, corresponds to the extent of such shared perceptions, which no doubt can be related to concentration of communications.[43]

Something resembling this proposal may occasionally provide grounds for drawing boundaries, but its general applicability may be doubted. One difficulty is that communication differentials, and shared perceptions, like the incidence of national sentiments, are usually a *consequence* of political boundaries previously drawn and maintained for a period of time. National boundaries especially, once drawn, however arbitrarily, become important factors in determining subsequent patterns not only of economic and communications networks, but of people's habits and outlooks as well.[44] Another difficulty is that this criterion may conflict with that of autonomy in the sense of system capacity: it may be that pressing matters in need of political solution may be larger in scope than present concentrations of communications, which are related to the past experience of groups, and may be outdated, and thus that optimal boundaries would be more inclusive than indicated by this criterion. While the idea of a communication differential thus provides insights into how political systems function, and into the meaning of autonomy, it is not likely to offer a clear principle for boundaries in many cases.

VIII. CONCLUSION

I shall conclude by reviewing the ways in which the issue of boundaries may be said to constitute a problem for democratic theory. First of all democratic theory cannot itself provide any solution to disputes that may—and historically do—arise concerning boundaries. This is generally the case with versions of democratic theory, including those that emphasize participation, majority rule, consent, autonomy, and the all-affected principle, and it is likewise often the case with the principle of nationality that (though distinct) is often allied with democratic theory. It may not be surprising that democracy, which is a method for group decision-making or self-governance, cannot be brought to bear on the logically prior matter of the constitution of the group itself, the existence of which it presupposes. Nevertheless, strong claims are frequently made for democracy, both by its philosophical advocates and by ideologues and activists of the modern world; democracy is commonly put forward as the sole foundation of legitimate government, and as the sole legitimate method for making binding public decisions of all sorts. Thus that democratic methods cannot be brought to bear on the determination of political boundaries, even though this is usually an important political decision, about which people may have strong preferences, has the effect of rendering controversies over boundaries among the most intractable and bitter types of political conflict. In default of democratic theory, boundaries may occasionally be resolved in accordance with the principle of nationality, in which there is also widespread concurrence, or on the basis of physical features of the landscape. When these criteria also fail, like democracy, to offer clear guidance, it appears that our only choices are to abide by the arbitrary verdicts of history or war, or to appeal on an *ad hoc* basis to other principles, none of which commands general respect.

In addition to the fact that democratic procedures cannot accommodate preferences regarding boundaries as such, there is the secondary problem that the establishment of boundaries (undemocratic as this must be) generally predetermines the outcomes of substantive political issues. This is a matter that is conspicuous and therefore a source of overt controversy only when boundaries are in actual dispute, and a choice must somehow be made among various proposed alternatives; on these occasions the parties concerned can usually see that different resolutions of the boundaries will inevitably lead to different subsequent decisions and policies, and this can greatly enhance the bitterness of the conflict attending the boundary question. Boundaries *generally* determine substantive political outcomes, however, or at least significantly restrict the range of alternatives that will be considered and that have a realistic chance of being adopted—although this is not ordinarily recognized when boundaries are well-established and not themselves in dispute.[45] A literal application of the all-affected principle calls attention in a vivid way to the arbitrariness of virtually all established political boundaries. Doubts may therefore arise concerning the validity of democratic procedures when it is considered that, however impeccable democratic decision-making may be within a given community, the outcomes are in a sense determined by the previous and inescapably undemocratic decisions that defined the community in the first place.

Before democratic procedures can begin to operate, boundaries must be established in one fashion or another. Continuing dissatisfaction with the boundaries as given can, finally, threaten the viability of the established democracy. It is often said that a successful democracy in practice depends on a consensus among its citizens on fundamental democratic values (equality, respect for persons, the right to dissent, and so forth) and on the validity of democratic procedures themselves. Beyond this a healthy democracy must also be characterized by a fundamental consensus on the boundaries of the system, an absence of which among the citizens will be accompanied by a sense of unfairness and alienation if not active efforts to overthrow the system, together with a repudiation of its "democracy" as a fraud. Similarly, a belief among outsiders that the boundaries are illegitimate may pose an external threat to the viability of the system. Thus it must be a matter of concern to all democrats—both the citizens of an existing democratic system and well-wishers of

democracy in general—that boundaries of democratic communities be generally acknowledged as fair and appropriate. In
arguing, as I have, that democracy itself has no resources for
bringing about such a state of affairs, I intend no disparage-
ment of democratic principles in their proper sphere. The
boundary problem does, however, reveal one of the limits of
the applicability of democracy, and acknowledgment of this may
have the beneficial effect of moderating the sometimes excessive claims that are made in its name.[46]

NOTES

1. This is one of the few questions of democratic theory that is not
   systematically discussed in J. Roland Pennock, *Democratic Political
   Theory* (Princeton: Princeton University Press, 1979).
2. See for example Carole Pateman, *Participation and Democratic Theory* (Cambridge: Cambridge University Press, 1970). Michael
   Margolis, *Viable Democracy* (Harmondsworth: Penguin, 1979), seeks
   ways of enhancing opportunities to participate. Equality of participation, or of access to decision-making, may be held to be required.
3. Robert A. Dahl, *A Preface to Democratic Theory* (Chicago: University
   of Chicago Press, 1956), chap. 2.
4. *Ibid.*, chap. 3.
5. Jack Lively, *Democracy* (New York: St. Martin's, 1975), pp. 11–13.
6. Consent may be construed as a weak democratic principle. Consent of the people to what the government proposes is different
   from the government's doing what the people want. A.D. Lindsay,
   The Essentials of Democracy, 2nd ed., (London: Oxford University
   Press, 1935), pp. 29–30. See generally P.H. Partridge, *Consent and
   Consensus* (New York: Praeger, 1971).
7. As the preceding discussion shows, I take "collective preference"
   (in Braybrooke's terms) to comprise the essential meaning of democracy. If democracy is taken to mean a system that upholds
   personal rights, it may be that the boundary problem is less significant. It does not seem to me that welfare is conceptually related to democracy at all. See David Braybrooke, *Three Tests for
   Democracy: Personal Rights, Human Welfare, and Collective Preference*
   (New York: Random House, 1968). On welfare and the meaning
   of democracy, cf. Ernest Barker, *Reflections on Government* (London: Oxford University Press, 1942), p. 315.
8. "The boundary indicates certain well-established limits (the bounds)

of the given political unit, and all that which is within the boundary is bound together, that is, is fastened by an internal bond." Ladis K.D. Kristof, "The Nature of Frontiers and Boundaries," in Harm J. de Blij, *Systematic Political Geography,* 2nd ed. (New York: John Wiley and Sons, 1973), p. 137.

9. This was Point II of Wilson's "Four Additional Points," July 4, 1918, quoted in Samuel Flagg Bemis, *A Diplomatic History of the United States* (New York: Holt, 1936), p. 635.

10. Carl Cohen, *Democracy* (Athens, Ga.: University of Georgia Press, 1970), p. 8: "In a perfect democracy all who are thus affected [by a decision] play some part." Robert A. Dahl, *After the Revolution? Authority in a Good Society* (New Haven: Yale University Press, 1970), p. 64: "Everyone who is affected by the decisions of a government should have the right to participate in that government." Peter Bachrach, *The Theory of Democratic Elitism: A Critique* (Boston: Little, Brown, 1967), p. 74: ". . . the democratic principle that those who make decisions should be accountable to the people who are affected by them . . ." A.D. Lindsay, *The Modern Democratic State* (New York: Oxford University Press, 1962), p. 231, calls the all-affected principle a revolutionary form of democratic theory.

11. Cohen, *Democracy,* p. 27, says with respect to this problem that determination should be made "upon the merits of particular cases;" but this begs the question: who decides what the merits are? Cf. also p. 16: "It is no reasonable requirement to make of any democracy that it enlarge its community to include all of those who may prove to be concerned in the sequel of any of its acts." Of course, after the fact it would be too late in any case; but on Cohen's all-affected principle it is not clear why this would not have been a reasonable requirement before the decision was made.

12. When a decision-making unit is constituted for very limited purposes, as in a water conservancy district, it may be technically feasible, and appropriate, to assign the power of decision to those (and only those) who are affected. This assumes, however, that there are no external effects of such decisions, and that those excluded from the unit have no claim whatever to be included—a situation that is no doubt rare.

13. Democracy is a *politeia,* in Aristotle's sense, defined primarily by the composition of its citizen body and by the conception of justice that determines the structure of authority within it. Territory is a secondary consideration in democratic theory, though not of course in the practice of modern states.

14. See Bernard Crick, *In Defense of Politics,* 2nd ed. (Chicago: University of Chicago Press, 1972), p. 80, for a defense of this view against nationalism.

15. Lindsay, *Essentials of Democracy,* pp. 20–21, 35–36, 48, 52–54. The democracy of such congregations is consensual, due to both their small size and the like-mindedness of the members—the latter a fact due to the voluntaristic basis of membership. For a discussion of similar themes, see Jane J. Mansbridge, "The Limits of Friendship," in J. Roland Pennock and John W. Chapman, eds., *Nomos XVI: Participation in Politics* (New York: Lieber-Atherton, 1975), pp. 246–75.

16. David Hume, "Of the Original Contract," in *Essays Moral, Political, and Literary* (Oxford: Oxford University Press, 1963), p. 462.

17. Sidgwick considers the thought that, humanity being a natural collectivity, the whole world is the natural unit for democratic government. Since such a government would have to be federal, with numerous subdivisions, however, significant controversies would continue regarding *internal* boundaries, as well as over the distribution of powers among the different levels. Henry Sidgwick, *The Elements of Politics,* 4th ed. (London: Macmillan, 1919), p. 218.

18. Cf. Dahl, *After the Revolution?,* p. 62: "the philosophers take up where history leaves off." Dahl also acknowledges the boundary problem in *Preface to Democratic Theory,* pp. 52–54.

19. See Frederick G. Whelan, "Citizenship and the Right to Leave," *American Political Science Review* 75 (1981), pp. 636–53.

20. On secession see Sidgwick, *Elements of Politics,* pp. 226–27, 648–49; and Robert R. Bowie and Carl J. Friedrich, eds., *Studies in Federalism* (Boston: Little, Brown, 1954), pp. 765–66. The amicable achievement of independence by a former colony may be seen as a kind of successful secession, but in such cases the colony was usually (in principle) regarded as a separate entity, destined for eventual self-government. New boundaries are not drawn; the bounded units rather by mutual consent acquire a new relationship.

21. Sidgwick, *Elements of Politics,* p. 224. National sentiments are, however, sometimes generated through a common identification with a past state, real or legendary (the German *Reich,* Zimbabwe); see Raymond D. Gastil, *Freedom in the World: Political Rights and Civil Liberties 1978* (New York: Freedom House, 1978), p. 183.

22. Cf. Christopher J. Berry, "Nations and Norms," *Review of Politics* 43 (1981), p. 85, who suggests a stronger connection.

23. John Stuart Mill, *Considerations on Representative Government,* with *Utilitarianism* and *On Liberty* (London: J.M. Dent and Sons, 1910), pp. 360–61.

24. Lindsay, *Essentials of Democracy,* p. 45; and Charles Frankel, *The*

Democratic Prospect (New York: Harper and Row, 1962), pp. 31–32.

25. Mill, *Representative Government,* pp. 363–64. Mill restricts the applicability of the nationalist principle in a manner parallel to that in which he limits the principle of liberty in *On Liberty:* it is not for barbarians, or, it is subordinate to considerations of progress and civilization.

26. Democratic political rights are declared in Art. 21 of the Universal Declaration of Human Rights; the right of peoples to self-determination is added in the International Covenants on Civil and Political and on Economic, Social, and Cultural Rights. For the documents, see Maurice Cranston, *What Are Human Rights?* (New York: Taplinger, 1973), pp. 91, 95, 108. Self-determination, however, may be understood by some members of the U.N. as connoting only anti-European colonialism, and not necessarily democracy within the new countries. Gastil, *Freedom: 1978,* pp. 193–94.

27. See generally Alfred Cobban, *The Nation State and National Self-Determination* (New York: Crowell, 1969).

28. The disputes of the 1930s are enumerated in Richard Hartshorne, "A Survey of the Boundary Problems of Europe," in Charles Carlyle Colby, ed., *Geographical Aspects of International Relations* (Freeport, N.Y.: Books for Libraries Press, reprint of 1938 ed., 1969), pp. 162–213.

29. Cf. Dankwart A. Rustow, *A World of Nations* (Washington, D.C.: Brookings Institution, 1967), p. 59.

30. Eugene Kamenka, "Political Nationalism—the Evolution of the Idea," in E. Kamenka, ed., *Nationalism* (New York: St. Martin's, 1976), pp. 13–14. See also Rupert Emerson, "Nationalism and Political Development," *Journal of Politics* 22 (1960), pp. 10–11.

31. C.B. Macpherson, *The Real World of Democracy* (Oxford: Clarendon Press, 1966), pp. 27–29.

32. Charles Tilly, ed., *The Formation of National States in Western Europe* (Princeton: Princeton University Press, 1975), pp. 43–44, 78–79, and generally. Nationality is not especially important among the factors that determined the success of the 25 states that emerged by 1900 from the 500 or so candidates of 1500. War was the most important factor in determining boundaries.

33. See Robert L. Solomon, "Boundary Concepts and Practices in Southeast Asia," *World Politics* 23 (1970) 1–23. See, more generally, Stephen B. Jones, "Boundary Concepts in the Setting of Place and Time," in de Blij, *Systematic Political Geography,* pp. 162–75.

34. Kristof, "Nature of Frontiers and Boundaries," pp. 136–39.

35. See de Blij, *Systematic Political Geography*, p. 132–35; Julian V. Minghi, "Boundary Studies in Political Geography," in Roger E. Kasperson and Julian V. Minghi, eds., *The Structure of Political Geography* (Chicago: Aldine, 1969), pp. 140–60. On military technology and defense, see John H. Herz, "Rise and Demise of the Territorial State," in de Blij, *Political Geography*, pp. 454–65.

36. For a lucid treatment of salience in relation to contract theory, see David Gauthier, "David Hume: Contractarian," *Philosophical Review* 88 (1979) 3–38. Cf. also Thomas C. Schelling, *The Strategy of Conflict* (London: Oxford University Press, 1960), pp. 67–71.

37. The concept of natural boundaries sometimes connotes militarily defensible features as well; in some nationalist theories the "naturalness" of certain geographical limits is related to the alleged destiny of a particular nation.

38. Norman J.G. Pounds, "France and 'Les Limites Naturelles' from the Seventeenth to the Twentieth Centuries," *Annals of the Association of American Geographers* 44 (1954) 51–62. Cf. also the psychological appeal of the symmetrical hexagon by which French children are taught to visualize their country; Laurence Wylie, "Social Change at the Grass Roots," in Stanley Hoffmann et al., *In Search of France* (New York: Harper and Row, 1963), pp. 205, 227.

39. Johann Gottlieb Fichte, *Addresses to the German Nation,* ed. George Armstrong Kelly (New York: Harper and Row, 1968), p. 190. See also Elie Kedourie, *Nationalism* (London: Hutchinson University Library, 1960), pp. 122–26.

40. Solomon, "Boundary Concepts," p. 10.

41. Robert A. Dahl and Edward R. Tufte, *Size and Democracy* (Stanford: Stanford University Press, 1973); a similar point is made in Dahl, *After the Revolution?*, pp. 98–103. Considerations of efficiency with respect to economic development may lead to the same conclusion; see Joseph S. Nye, "Nationalism, Statesmen, and the Size of African States," in Martin Kilson, ed., *New States in the Modern World* (Cambridge, Mass.: Harvard University Press, 1975), pp. 158–68.

42. Karl W. Deutsch, *The Nerves of Government* (New York: The Free Press, 1966), p. 205. This work is not especially about democracy.

43. John Dewey, *The Public and Its Problems* (Chicago: Swallow Press, 1954), chap. 2, esp. p. 43; see also pp. 26–28.

44. Eric Fischer, "On Boundaries," *World Politics* 1 (1949) 196–222.

45. Only consider the extreme case: questions of social justice or the distribution of resources would be resolved differently than they are if the *world* were a single democratic unit. Cf. the argument of Charles R. Beitz, *Political Theory and International Relations*

(Princeton: Princeton University Press, 1979), part 3, that national boundaries ought not to limit the scope of social justice.

46. Cf. F.A. Hayek, *The Constitution of Liberty* (Chicago: University of Chicago Press, 1960), pp. 105–06.

PART I

REPRESENTATION

1

EQUAL REPRESENTATION

STEPHEN L. DARWALL

In 1830, nonfreeholding white male citizens of the city of Richmond addressed this plea to a convention considering amendments to their state constitution:

> But the same qualifications that entitle him to assume the management of his private affairs, and to claim all other privileges of citizenship, equally entitle him, in the judgment of your memorialists, to be entrusted with this, the dearest of all his privileges, the most important of all his concerns.[1]

The "this" in question, the "dearest of all his privileges" and "most important of all his concerns," was the franchise—the right to vote in public elections.[2] In arguing that what entitles a person to self-governance equally entitles him to a role in political governance, these men sounded a theme that is by now thoroughly familiar. Carl Cohen, to take but one recent example, echoes it when he writes:

> Every man has a life to lead; it is a life, unique, irreplaceable, having dignity but no price. In living such a life all men are equal, and that is why they have, every single one, equal stake in the decisions of the community. . . .[3]

Because they have this equal stake, all persons who can be presumed to have the capacity for rational choice requisite for self-direction must be thought to have the same claim to participate in political decision.

This argument takes at least an important part of the justification for democracy to lie in its intrinsic value as a political decision-making process taken quite independently of its consequences. It supposes the ideal of democracy to be the projection into the political realm of the ideal of autonomy. Just as, this argument holds, we do not take the main justification for treating individuals with respect for sovereignty over their own lives to rest on their greater wisdom with respect to themselves, neither should we take the justification for collective self-governance to be primarily dependent on its effects.[4] In each case, what grounds the ideal is a conception of the person as capable of rationally self-directed living, and entitled thereby to respect, whether in decisions that concern primarily himself or in taking part in decisions of properly collective concern.

In this essay I shall assume that this argument is, in broad outline, correct. Doubtless, important qualifications must be made. To begin with, neither the self-regarding decisions of individuals, nor those of democratic collectivities more generally, should be respected in all instances.[5] Individuals may choose alternatives that both diverge widely from what they would themselves have chosen given more careful consideration and threaten severe harm to themselves (not least importantly to their very capacity for self-direction). In some such cases even a concern for autonomy itself counsels restricting individual choice.[6]

Because political societies are constituted by individual persons their decisions are doubly risky. Not only, as with individuals, may decisions be ill-considered or threaten the group or its capacity to govern itself. They may also threaten the individuals who constitute it. Liberal political philosophies that have embraced autonomy of the person as grounding democracy have often been concerned, therefore, to place it within a constitutional framework of protected rights of two sorts. First, rights such as freedom of association, thought, speech, and the press help to ensure that the people's choices express their considered judgments. Second, rights such as freedom of the person, freedom from arbitrary arrest and seizure, and rights to due process and privacy, protect individual persons from some potentially obnoxious group decisions by removing these freedoms, more or less, from within its scope.[7] I shall take it, therefore, that the sort of democracy that concern for autonomy of the person best supports is a liberal one, placed in the context of certain familiar rights and freedoms.

Now just which rights and freedoms a defensible democracy must recognize is, of course, an important and vexed question of political philosophy. All of those I have listed to this point would, I think, be relatively uncontroversial among those who would call themselves liberal democrats. But others are not. In particular, it is unclear what rights with respect to private property fit best with a liberal democracy grounded in autonomy of the person. Some writers, most notably Robert Nozick, have argued that any political society that does not accord individuals virtually unrestricted rights of private ownership is incompatible with moral side constraints arising from the fact that individuals are capable of directing and giving meaning to their lives.[8] Others, including John Rawls, Amy Gutmann, and Robert Dahl, have argued that liberal democracy requires significant restrictions on private ownership.[9]

This, then, is the issue that will concern us: What is the proper attitude to take toward private ownership if one is a liberal democrat because of a concern for autonomy of the person? We shall approach this question through the mediating notion of *representation*. This will enable us to divide our single question into two which are perhaps more manageable. First, what sort of representation in the political process is supported by a concern for autonomy of the person? And second, what restrictions on private ownership are necessary if individuals are to be represented in that way? Let us take these question in turn.

I

In her famous study of representation, Hanna Pitkin considers, among others, what she calls the "accountability view," which states that a person is politically represented only if his or her representative is in some way responsible or answerable to him or her.[10] Pitkin rejects this as a theory of representation since it is purely "formal" and says nothing at all about what a representative is supposed to do.

But even if accountability to the represented is not fully adequate as a theory of representation it may still be a necessary condition for genuine representation. In particular, it may be a necessary condition of the sort of representation mandated by autonomy of the person. In fact, if the right to vote (for representatives) is grounded in individual autonomy then so must the corollary right to accountable representation.

This is true whether one takes representatives as delegates of the represented or as empowered to make their own independent judgments. And with respect to the latter, whether about the interests of the represented, or of some larger group, or in terms of some conception of justice or other political ideal. Whatever principles or criteria representatives appropriately apply in political choice, if they are answerable for their choices to the represented, then they must *justify* their choices to them.

We may take it, then, that if autonomy of the person supports the claim of any citizen capable of self-direction to vote for his or her political representatives, it supports a claim to *accountable representation,* for these amount to the same thing. Indeed, we may draw a stronger conclusion. Since what supports the claim of each is, as Rawls puts it, being within a "range" of capacity for rational self-direction,[11] and since everyone within the range is no more nor less within it than anyone else, everyone has an equal claim to accountable representation.

To be sure, rational self-direction is an ideal that can be more or less closely approximated. And it is doubtless true that people differ in their capacities with respect to this ideal, though social factors are also crucial. But as the nonfreeholders of Richmond saw, what is at issue is not excellence, or the capacity for it, that *merits* the franchise. Rather, what matters is whether one has a competence that entitles or "qualifies" one, as they put it, for the franchise. And this is a different matter. Of course, the mere conceptual distinction between a level of competence or qualification and a level of excellence does not itself show much. Qualifications may be set higher or lower, and some political thinkers have held that the most judicious should have the most weighty, or perhaps, the only, influence over political decisions. But what the nonfreeholders of Richmond saw is that an independent criterion determines where the level of competence for political decision making must be placed if it is to be consistent with the autonomy of the person. Or, to be more precise, they saw that whatever level of competence one holds to entitle a person "to assume the management of his private affairs, . . . equally entitle[s] him" to take part in political decisions. To base liberal democracy on the autonomy of the person is to believe that the same level must serve for both.

Each person who has a claim to respect in the direction of his or her own life, then, also has a claim to partake in and share in determining political decisions equal to that of any other person. When decisions are made by representatives, then not only should representatives be accountable to every person, they should be equally accountable. Or, to be more precise, the represented should have an equal *opportunity* to hold representatives to account. When I shall speak of representatives being equally accountable to all rather than all having an equal opportunity to participate effectively in the choice of representatives, it should be understood that it is the latter that is supported by the equal claim of all to participate in political decisions. We shall say, then, that a liberal democracy grounded on autonomy of the person will include a *Principle of Equally Accountable Representation.*[12] This, then, is the answer to our first question.

II

When is representation equally accountable to all? One necessary condition seems to be that when the represented elect representatives, each should have an equal vote. But is this sufficient? Plainly, it is not if some, but not others, can nominate candidates, run for office, participate in political debate, and take part in political organizations. Even if all have the same right to vote, there is a clear sense in which if some have these freedoms and others do not, elected representatives will be more answerable to some than to others.

The most uncontroversial cases, of course, are those where some are *permitted* a larger range of political activity than are others. Liberal democrats generally speak with one voice in condemning political arrangements that formally limit access to the larger range of political activities that gives voting its meaning. And so we recognize an equal claim to run for public office, to engage in political debate, and so on, as grounded as much in the autonomy of the person as is the right to vote.

But what if individuals differ not in respect of the formal freedom to participate in these activities, but in social and economic resources that both create opportunities for participation and also enhance the likelihood that they will be politically successful? How do such differences fit with the claim that each person has to equally accountable representation?

Clearly they do not fit with it well at all. If people differ in their ability to influence which candidates will run, or be taken seriously, which issues will be thought important, which candidates, of those who run, will be able to put forward their case in persuasive ways, and so on, then this does affect the accountability of representatives to them.

The reason the ability to vote for representatives makes them at all accountable to a person in the first place is that it gives him or her some influence over who is to represent. But it is surely not the only thing that does, nor even necessarily the most important. In fact, a person might reasonably give up his vote if it meant he would have a greater influence of some less formal sort. If, the autonomy of the person gives each a claim to equally accountable representation, it must also give each a strong prima facie claim to the circumstances that make such representation possible.

Differences in individual wealth create differences in ability to influence the political process. Successful electoral campaigns require resources, and those with greater wealth are, other things equal, in a better position therefore to influence which campaigns will be successful. This is perhaps the most obvious instance of how social and economic inequalities can create political inequalities, but probably one of the less important. Probably more important are the many ways in which those with greater wealth can better influence the terms of political debate, the issues that are thought to be important and which are spoken to by candidates. For example, those with greater wealth are more likely to own or advertise in the various media through which most public political debate takes place. Through their consequent influence over editorial policy, information gathering, and reporting, those with greater wealth can better influence which issues are taken seriously.

Again, research on complex policy issues of a sort that can command respect may often require significant cost. Those with greater wealth are better able to sponsor research, and, of course, advocacy, that supports their political views and are thereby better able to influence political debate. This, then, is another "political market" in which wealth can purchase political influence.

Electoral campaigns are only a small part of poltical activity. Individuals (and groups to which they belong) can employ wealth in a great variety of ways to further their political agendas. Some of these ways are familiar and obvious: for example, lobbying legislators or bringing a case with political import to court. But there are many others that are perhaps less obvious: for example, it is a not insignificant advantage to be in a position to offer "suitable" employment for those with political ambitions, or for those present office-holders who will want such employment in the future. Differences in wealth can make a political difference in many ways other than their influence on electoral campaigns.

These are but a few examples. I have not mentioned any related to the phenomenon of class, understood either in Marxist or in social stratification terms. This is not because I deny their significance; quite the contrary, many studies have now documented their importance in our own society.[13] Rather, my argument does not require it. I am not concerned to argue that the wealthy *as a group* exert a greater political influence than do other groups. My claim is simply that greater wealth enables a person to exert greater political influence.

Personal wealth is not the only sort that can wield political power. Corporate entities also act in the political realm. If an individual is in a position of influence in a corporation, if his political views coincide in some measure with the corporate interest, and if the corporation has resources to spend in political markets, then this can enhance the individual's influence.

This is true in principle of any corporate body: of churches, unions, and universities as well as firms. But the effects are especially noteworthy in connection with the extremely large and powerful corporations that mark our recent history. Most obviously, such firms and their decision-makers have enormous resources at their command. And in many cases, spending a good deal of these resources in political markets will make good business sense. Moreover, some recent commentators have remarked on what one has called the "privileged position" that corporations have in the political arena.[14] When the economic health of a political society depends on the health of its corporations and on the good will of corporate decision makers and investors, then the latter will exercise a coordinate influence over political representatives.

The placement of individuals in a corporate structure, through which they earn their livelihood, can be relevant to their political influence in another important way. If the structure of relations is hierarchial, then significant questions of *independence* are raised. In this connection it is illuminating to recall earlier debates about who should have the right to vote. Kant, to whom we owe the very idea that capacity for rational choice gives a person a dignity beyond any price, argued that although all persons are equal citizens in some sense, not all are fit to vote. Among those he excepted from having a right to the franchise were women, minors, and "anyone, who must depend for his support (subsistence and protection), not on his own industry, but on arrangements by others."[15] These he considered "passive" citizens with no right to vote. Because they are not fit to vote, representatives need not be accountable to them. Indeed, the point seems to be that even if they could vote, representatives would not be accountable to them in the same way that they are to more independent "active" citizens. They would not, because they would never be made accountable to the person's own independent political judgment.

It is worth remembering that even some of the Levellers were apparently prepared to make similar exceptions in their seventeenth-century demands for the franchise, and therefore accountable representation, in England. One spokesman, Maxmillian Petty, declared:

> I conceive the reason why we would exclude apprentices,
> or servants, or those that take alms, is because they depend
> upon the will of other men and should be afraid to dis-
> please [them].[16]

If, however, it is the case that hierarchical work relations tend
to undermine independent political judgment and its expression, then, *pace* Kant and the Levellers, what seems to follow is
not that those who are employed by and "subject to the orders"
of others, should be denied the vote. On the contrary, if what
grounds a person's title both to direct his own life and to a
share in the direction of society's common life is the competence to make practical judgments, and not whether he is actually placed so as to exercise that competence, then the most
reasonable conclusion would seem to be that he has a claim to
the social circumstances required to enable its exercise, so that
political representation will be equally accountable to him.

It appears difficult, then, to contain democracy within a circumscribed political realm. Political representation cannot be
equally accountable to all if some are less able to develop and
express their own political judgments because they must be
"subject to the orders" of others in order to earn their livelihood.[17] This constitutes a strong prima facie argument for some
form of what is often called industrial democracy, if that is necessary for workers to be free to form and express political judgments. This kind of argument for industrial democracy is of a
different sort than others that are perhaps more familiar. It is
an instrumental argument for it as a necessary condition of
genuine political democracy, rather than on the strength of its
own merits.[18] The claim is that equally accountable political
representation is impossible without it.

Let us sum up the argument of this section. If individuals
have a claim to equally accountable representation that is
grounded in the autonomy of the person, then they also have
a strong prima facie claim to its social and economic prerequi-
sites. Inequalities in personal wealth, in influence over corporate wealth, and in positions of command in employing hierarchies all create inequalities in the degree to which political
representation is accountable to different individuals. There is,

therefore, a strong prima facie claim, based on autonomy of the person, to substantial equality in wealth and in control over corporate assets and over more specific issues relating to work within firms.[19]

III

What are some of the ramifications of basing a case for substantial equality of wealth and control over production on the Principle of Equally Accountable Representation? The first thing we should notice is that the argument is plainly only a prima facie one. Of course, other reasons, indeed some based on a concern for autonomy of the person, may support arrangements that tend to conflict with this principle. For example, consider the pattern of reasoning that takes the parties in Rawls's original position from the benchmark of equality to a Difference Principle that permits inequalities in primary goods other than the basic liberties if that gives the worst-off group a higher absolute level.[20] We can imagine that people equally well situated with respect to wealth and social control, and who are not behind a veil of ignorance, might similarly vote (perhaps even unanimously) to allow some inequalities in these matters if doing so is necessary to increase the wealth of each. That is, people might rationally trade off some of their economic equality, and, I have argued, some of their consequent equality in the accountability of their representation, for increases in absolute wealth. Other values, for example community and self-esteem, might also tell in the other direction.[21]

Second, it is worth noting that the argument for equality of wealth and control over production from the Principle of Equally Accountable Representation is not subject to the familiar objection that egalitarianism (especially with respect to wealth) is born of envy or, at best, of sympathy with those who are envious.[22] Egalitarians, according to this objection, are guilty of thinking of relative deprivation or poverty as though it were itself a kind of absolute deprivation; as though being worse off than others amounted to being badly off. How, the objector asks, can a person's position be worsened just because others are better off than he? It is one thing to want to be better off, to want an absolute improvement in one's condition, but it is quite another to be want to be as well off as others, to be at the *same* level as they. The latter desire is nothing other than envy. And if someone who is better situated wants those who are worse off to be as well situated as he, it can only be because of sympathy with their envy.

Regardless of whatever force this argument has considered in its own terms,[23] it has no force at all if equality of wealth is based on the Principle of Equally Accountable Representation. For even if an increase in one person's wealth does not thereby affect the wealth of others, this is not the case when we consider how wealth affects political influence. By its very nature, if one person gains in political influence, then others must lose. To be concerned about how wealth affects political influence is to be concerned about how relative wealth affects *relative* political influence—no other kind exists.

Third, we should appreciate how the present argument differs from Norman Daniels's argument against Rawls that if it is rational for parties in an original position to opt for Rawls's first principle of equal basic liberties, it is also rational for them to opt for a principle of *equal worth* of the basic liberties (which, Daniels argues, is probably inconsistent with the Difference Principle).[24] By the "worth" of a basic liberty, Rawls and Daniels mean the contribution that the liberty makes to the person's ability to pursue his conception of the good. Thus the same basic liberty (say, freedom of the press) may have greater worth to one person than to another if the one is in a better position to take advantage of it.

If we distinguish what we might call the "political worth" of a basic liberty (the contribution it makes to a person's political influence) within the more general category, then at least a prima facie principle of equal political worth of the basic liberties finds support. That is, basic liberties should work, in the larger social and economic context, to give individuals roughly equal influence over political outcomes—the Principle of Equally Accountable Representation. But that does not itself amount to a conclusive argument for equality of the general worth (to individuals) of the basic liberties. For, unlike the political worth of a liberty, an increase for one person in the more general worth of a liberty (say, to an individual's pursuit of his personal conception of the good by his having greater resources to avail himself of freedom of speech) does not necessarily imply a decrease to another person. Moreover, as I have emphasized, the equal political worth of basic liberties might itself be something that parties in the original position would rationally trade off to some extent against increases for all in other primary goods such as absolute wealth.

Fourth, we may notice how the present argument can be used to defend Rawls's Difference Principle against some objections from less egalitarian critics. A number of writers have agreed with Rawls that parties to an original position would want to protect themselves against certain worst case possibilities under utilitarianism or laissez faire, but urge that this can be done by what R.M. Hare has called an "insurance strategy" of choosing a principle that first establishes a minimum level of wealth and then requires either utility maximizing or laissez faire once everyone has been assured the minimum.[25] There is, of course, no satisfactory way to specify an absolute monetary minimum behind a veil of ignorance, but the late Arthur Okun has proposed that it can be set in relative terms, at, say, one-half of either the mean or median income level.[26] One problem, however, with setting a minimum in either absolute or relative monetary terms is, as Okun himself recognized that there will be no way to know whether the particular bundle of goods necessary for a minimally decent life (Okun's benchmark) can be purchased with that amount. Consequently, he proposes that a monetary minimum must be buttressed by guarantees to various sorts of in-kind aid. These proposals against Rawls are well summarized by Roland Pennock:

> But again why cannot one simply postulate principles of justice that guarantee both basic liberties and basic necessities? Surely one can "buy" parts of Rawls's package without taking the whole thing![27]

The question that these criticisms pose to Rawls is really this: If from an original position one can choose a principle that assures one of living at a tolerable absolute level (together with a system of equal basic liberties), why prefer some other principle whose main effect may well be not to raise the lower level much above a guaranteed minimum, but rather to ensure that higher levels not get too far above lower ones? This is to a large extent the question: Why be concerned about relative levels of primary goods rather than absolute levels? [28]

The argument of the preceding section must surely provide at least some answer. One clear reason to be concerned about relative levels, as well as absolute levels, of primary goods, especially of wealth and control over production, is that these affect political influence and the accountability of political representation. This will not only be of general concern in the original position, it will specifically concern the person who wants to be assured that everyone will be provided basic necessities; no detailed specification of what is needed for a tolerably decent life can be given in a principle of justice that could be chosen from behind a veil of ignorance. Even if everyone in an actual society agrees about the general kinds of things that are basic necessities, these can only be given more detailed specification, and guarantees to them institutionalized, within a political process. The possibility that those who are better off will both have an interest in the enactment of a relatively narrow specification of basic necessities and a greater ability to influence legislations must be especially worrisome to the hypothetical choosers in an original position. [29] This, then, is a clear reason for favoring the Difference Principle to a mixed principle that fixes a minimum and then is largely unconcerned about relative inequality above that point. In fact, it is a prima facie reason for favoring a principle that is even more egalitarian than the Difference Principle.

But can it not be objected that this reply, and indeed the general argument from the Principle of Equally Accountable Representation to substantially equalizing wealth and control over production, has force only if no effective way of insulating the political process from the effects of differential wealth and control is available? A prophylactic approach to achieving equally accountable representation would, by such measures as public funding of campaigns, limits on private contributions to candidates, and so on, seek to ensure that economic influence cannot be translated into political influence.

The fatal flaw with this approach is its premise that the political process can be isolated from the rest of our social and economic life without risk to essential freedoms. But this cannot be done. Some of the most important sorts of political influence are, I have argued, the most subtle and informal. Any society that, for example, sought to prohibit individuals from using their private resources to engage in acts of communication or association with potentially political import or effect would seriously threaten freedoms that are themselves essential for liberal democracy. The prophylactic approach is faced, therefore, with a dilemma: either it will be ineffective in achieving equally accountable representation or, if it is effective, it will threaten essential freedoms such as speech and association.

I have argued that a strong prima facie case for equalizing wealth and control over production can be made from the Principle of Equally Accountable Representation, which is in turn grounded in the autonomy of the person. According to this argument, good reasons, rooted in a concern for genuine democracy, support restricting private ownership and maintaining substantial equality of wealth and control. In closing, I wish to consider very briefly what must surely be the most challenging objection my argument faces: namely, that it treats wealth and control as something that can permissibly be redistributed rather than something to which individuals already have absolute rights of ownership.

This objection is faced with a dilemma. On the one hand, if it is taken so seriously as to rule out any redistribution, then it will turn out that there is not even an equal formal right to political participation. Running a proper election may take resources that some but not others are able to provide. An indigent person may only be able to exercise his or her right to vote, then, if a redistribution of relative wealth is in effect.[30]

On the other hand, if redistribution is allowed to insure formal political participation, then why not redistribute even more to achieve equally accountable representation? The idea that individual property rights are side constraints provides no principled way to avoid this further move since its line has already been crossed. It appears that a libertarian can resist the case for redistributing in the direction of equally accountable representation only by rejecting any right to political participation at all.

NOTES

1. "Memorial of the Non-Freeholders of the City of Richmond (1830)," in *Political Thought in America,* ed. Andrew M. Scott (New York: Rinehart & Company, Inc., 1959), p. 20.
2. It is worth pondering that "franchise" originally referred to certain freedoms (from servitude, from arbitrary arrest, etc.) and only later came to be understood as referring to the right to vote in public elections. See *The Oxford Universal Dictionary* (Oxford: Oxford University Press, 1955), p. 746.
3. "The Justification of Democracy," *Monist* 55 (1971), 16–17.
4. It is, of course, possible to hold with John Stuart Mill that the justification for recognizing both a claim to individual autonomy and to individual participation in collective governance is the utility of doing so, where that utility includes the inherent pleasure or intrinsic value of self-directed choice. That is, that we value these for their utility, though not simply for the value of their effects.
5. By "respect" here I mean "taken into consideration as restricting one's freedom of action," not "esteemed or appraised positively for respect-worthiness." On the difference between these see my "Two Kinds of Respect," *Ethics* 88 (1977–78), 36–49.
6. In this connection see Gerald Dworkin, "Paternalism," in *Morality and the Law,* ed. R.A. Wasserstrom (Belmont, Calif.: Wadsworth Publishing Co., 1971), pp. 107–126.
7. I do not mean to suggest that these categories are mutually exclusive; some rights have both rationales.
8. In *Anarchy, State, and Utopia* (New York: Basic Books, Inc., 1974), see esp. pp. 26f.
9. John Rawls, *A Theory of Justice* (Cambridge: Harvard University Press, 1971), esp. pp. 221f; Amy Gutmann, *Liberal Equality* (Cambridge: Cambridge University Press, 1980), esp. p. 173; Robert Dahl, "On Removing Certain Impediments to Democracy in the United States, *Dissent* (Summer 1978), 310–324.
10. Hanna Pitkin, *The Concept of Representation* (Berkeley: The University of California Press, 1972), pp. 55–59.
11. Rawls, op. cit., pp. 504–512.
12. Rawls discusses what he calls "the principle of [equal] participation" (pp. 212f.) which requires an equal freedom for all to participate in the political process. I have formulated the principle in the text to focus on representation.
13. I have in mind here primarily the so-called "power structure" re-

search deriving from the work of C. Wright Mills (*The Power Elite* [New York: Oxford University Press, 1956]) and G. William Domhoff (*Who Rules America* [Englewood Cliffs, N.J.: Prentice-Hall, 1967]); *The Higher Circles* (New York: Random House, 1970); and *The Powers That Be* (New York: Random House, 1979). An interesting set of recent studies in this tradition is contained in *Power Structure Research,* ed. G. William Domhoff (Beverly Hills: Sage Publications, 1980). Of particular interest are Michael Useem's "Which Business Leaders Help Govern?" (pp. 199–226), and Harold Salzman and G. William Domhoff's "The Corporate Community and Government: Do They Interlock?" (pp. 227–254). The latter is a reply to Thomas Dye's influential study, which attempts to refute a significant corporate/government connection (*Who's Running America* [Englewood Cliffs, N.J.: Prentice-Hall, 1979]), that uses Dye's own data. Much of this research relates not simply to a connection between personal wealth and political influence, but to the connection between the latter and corporate position. I discuss this below.

14. Charles E. Lindblom, *Politics and Markets* (New York: Basic Books, Inc., 1977), pp. 170–188.

15. Immanuel Kant, *The Metaphysical Elements of Justice,* trans. John Ladd (Indianapolis: The Bobbs-Merrill Company, Inc., 1965), p. 79 (*Akademie* p. 314). See also Kant, *On the Old Saw: That May be Right But It Won't Work in Practice,* trans. E.B. Ashton (Philadelphia: University of Pennsylvania Press, 1974), p. 63 for a similar passage.

16. In A.S.P. Woodhouse, *Puritanism and Liberty* (London: J.M. Dent, 1938), p. 83 (quoted in C.B. MacPherson, *The Political Theory of Possessive Individualism* [Oxford: Oxford University Press, 1977], p. 123).

17. It seems clear that the mere fact of working for a wage or a salary does not undermine political independence. What is important are more vague notions like freedom from intimidation and reprisals, having a range of acceptable employment options, freedom to exercise at least some range of independent choice, and so on.

18. See Amy Gutmann, *Liberal Equality,* pp. 203–208; Edward Sankowski, "Freedom, Work, and the Scope of Democracy," *Ethics* 91 (January 1981), 228–242; and Martin Carnoy and Derek Shearer, *Economic Democracy* (White Plains: M.E. Sharpe, Inc., 1980).

19. But why should we stop here? If one person is a more articulate advocate of his political position than another, won't that also have an effect on the accountability of representatives? Why not restrict the opportunities of the more articulate to participate in political

debate if that is necessary to ensure that political representatives are not more accountable to them than to the relatively inarticulate?

This objection must be taken seriously. While I cannot deal with it adequately here, I am inclined to think that a satisfactory response would have to argue that the contemplated restrictions are more central and serious restrictions of the person than are restrictions on wealth or status. They also make the contours of the very freedom to participate in the political process unacceptably open to dispute and, consequently, unstable.

I am indebted to Laurence Thomas for reminding me of this objection.

20. Rawls argues that were one to take up the perspective of a person who was behind a "veil of ignorance" with respect to any information about himself and his society in particular, and pick principles of justice which would be best from the standpoint of his being able rationally to pursue his conception of the good (whatever it might be), it would be rational to choose a principle which permits inequalities in such goods as wealth only if they work to make the worst-off group as well off as possible. See *A Theory of Justice*, pp. 151f.

21. See Rawls's discussion of the limitation on the "principle of participation" (pp. 228f). He argues that any change in the equal *liberty* to participate must be balanced by a gain in the basic liberties (perhaps other, more important, ones) of those whose liberty is to be restricted. For example, in their freedom of person and conscience.

22. For this objection see, for example, Keith Joseph and Jonathan Sumption, *Equality* (London: J. Murray, 1979), pp. 15f.

23. It is not at all clear, by the way, what the force of this argument is supposed to be. After all, if there are circumstances which tend to create envy in those circumstances, then, given the connection between envy and low self-esteem this seems a good reason to try to alter the circumstances. After all, people can only control their feelings to some degree. Nozick, for example, argues that one of the reasons for not allowing people to violate just any right of another, as long as they are willing to compensate the victim, is the substantial *fear* of some rights violations. See *Anarchy, State, and Utopia*, pp. 65f.

24. Norman Daniels, "Equal Liberty and Unequal Worth of Liberty," in *Reading Rawls,* ed. Norman Daniels (New York: Basic Books, Inc., 1974), pp. 253–281.

25. R.M. Hare, "Rawls's Theory of Justice," in *Reading Rawls,* pp. 81–107.

26. Arthur M. Okun, *Equality and Efficiency: The Big Tradeoff* (Washington, D.C.: The Brookings Institution, 1975), pp. 95f.

27. J. Roland Pennock, *Democratic Political Theory* (Princeton: Princeton University Press, 1979), p. 52. Pennock calls this principle "basicmin," to contrast it with Rawls's maximin.

28. Though not entirely since the difference principle assures the worst off that they will do at least as well (absolutely) as any feasible fixed minimal proposal.

29. Recall that all I mean here is that a wealthy person has a better likelihood of being able to do so, not that the wealthy as a group necessarily do (though that may also be true).

30. Note in this connection that Nozick's "dominant protective association" becomes the minimal state only when it extends its protection of rights to independents. To compensate them for the risk that it might violate their rights, he argues that it must provide them coverage at a reduced rate, or, if they cannot afford it, without charge. (See *Anarchy, State, and Utopia,* pp. 108f.) And this, Nozick admits, will require a redistribution of relative wealth (p. 27).

    Note also that this still leaves the political structure of the minimal state quite undetermined. Though we know its function, to protect rights, we do not know, for example, what its forms of participation are. But if the risk of rights violations justifies compensation to independents, why does it not also justify a claim to participation in political decisions? Libertarian rights are, after all, pretty vague. Decisions will have to be made about their contours and about their application in specific cases. While a libertarian recognizes no fundamental right of political participation, perhaps it could be argued to as compensation for the risks that the minimal state poses to the rights of citizens.

2

PROCEDURAL EQUALITY IN DEMOCRATIC THEORY: A PRELIMINARY EXAMINATION

CHARLES R. BEITZ

According to a widely held contemporary view, the legislative mechanism of representative democracy should conform to the *principle of procedural equality:* each citizen is to have a fundamental right to an equal opportunity to influence the outcomes of the legislative process.[1] The interpretation of this principle evokes considerable disagreement. In this paper, however, I shall set this question aside.[2] Instead, I would like to explore the prior question of whether the principle can be given a plausible justification.

Offhand, this might appear to be a pointless, or at least an unnecessary, exercise, since for several reasons it may seem obvious that democrats must be procedural egalitarians. Some will regard the principle as true by definition; that is, they will suppose that a political system simply is not a democracy if its legislative procedures are not egalitarian. However, this is probably false, and in any case it is not very illuminating. It is probably false because there is a natural conception of representative democracy from which nothing definite follows about the distribution of relative influence within democratic procedures. In this conception, the central feature of representative democracy is an electoral mechanism that enables citizens to influence the choice of legislation by participating periodically in the choice of legislators.[3] It would be consistent with this conception, for example, for all citizens to be entitled to vote, but for some to have more votes than others. In any case, it would not be very illuminating to rule out such possibilities by definitional fiat. It is better to regard the distribution and extent of opportunities to participate as posing normative problems in their own right about how the structural details of representative democracy should be arranged.

Another reason it might seem plausible that democrats should be egalitarians is this. Nearly everyone agrees that political democracy, of all the familiar forms of government, most completely embodies an egalitarian ideal, and that its egalitarianism explains (or helps explain) why it is the best form of government. But it is far from clear what is involved in such an ideal, and thus it is uncertain in what sense democratic institutions should answer to it or why their egalitarian features should recommend them to us. The principle of procedural equality resolves this indeterminacy by identifying a precise interpretation of political equality that imposes definite requirements on institutional forms. Obviously, however, the precision and clarity of a principle are not in themselves reasons to accept it. (Indeed, in some contexts we might even regard these properties as invitations to error.) They will recommend a principle only if there are already strong independent considerations in its favor.

In this essay, I shall question whether such reasons can be advanced. My thesis is that it is more difficult than it may seem to give a philosophically compelling defense of the persistent modern conviction that citizens of representative democracies have fundamental rights that their institutions be procedurally egalitarian. I shall not actually argue that the principle of procedural equality is false; indeed, something like it may well be true, at least for the range of cases in which we are most likely to be interested. Rather, I wish to suggest that the most philosophically basic connection between democracy and equality is to be sought elsewhere than in the formal elements of democratic procedures, and that the appropriate distributive characteristics of these procedures should be worked out from this more fundamental point of view.

I

The principle of procedural equality specifies that every citizen is to have a fundamental right to an equal opportunity to influence the outcomes of the legislative process. While a complete analysis of the principle's meaning is not necessary for present purposes, it may be helpful, to fix ideas, to offer a few preliminary observations.

The principle refers to a *fundamental* right to procedural equality: procedural inequalities are impermissible even when they are likely to produce more desirable results than those that would occur under procedural equality. This is an important part of the view I wish to criticize. It assigns a special status to the principle that makes it inappropriate to treat procedural equality merely as one among many considerations that must be balanced or compromised in the design of representative institutions. Thus, for example, the principle of procedural equality rules out from the start the system of plural voting advocated by J.S. Mill;[4] even if (as seems unlikely) Mill were correct in his empirical hypothesis that plural voting would produce legislation satisfying the utility principle, as he understood it, the system would still be unacceptably inegalitarian. Similarly, the principle forbids inequalities in the apportionment of population among legislative districts, even when this is an unavoidable consequence of the effort to realize an ostensibly desirable purpose such as conformity of district lines to pre-existing political boundaries.[5] From the point of view I want to examine, procedural equality is morally basic.

The principle of procedural equality should be distinguished from the principle that each person's interests should receive equal weight in the legislative process. The latter—call it the principle of equal consideration—is result-oriented in the sense that its subject is the relationship between the set of individual interests in a society and the distribution of interest satisfaction resulting from the outcomes produced by the society's legislative institutions. Given an interpretation of the principle of equal consideration (e.g., a social welfare function), the system of representation is to be set up in whatever way promises to yield outcomes maximally satisfying it.[6] The concern for processes is indirect, deriving from the more basic concern for acceptable outcomes. By contrast, the principle of procedural equality is directly process-oriented. Its concern is not (as with equal consideration) the distributive characteristics of political outcomes themselves; rather, it is the distribution of control over the mechanism that produces these outcomes.

The importance of this distinction does not derive only from the fact that procedural equality and equal consideration are not equivalent principles. They may not even be consistent. The view that egalitarian procedures tend to produce results that are in some sense egalitarian is a substantive position requiring an argument. (In the next section, I suggest some reasons to doubt that this position is correct.)

Finally, it should be noted that the principle of procedural equality is indifferent about some questions apparently involving the relative legislative power of individuals and groups. The most important of these arise primarily within representation systems employing separate election districts. A traditional objection to these systems is that they give rise to inequalities in representation resulting from the existence of superfluous majorities and unrepresented minorities within districts.[7] Moreover, since districting systems allow the composition of the legislature to be affected by the distribution of voters across districts, they can produce distortions at the legislative level. Such distortions are familiar in cases of gerrymandering, in which the deliberate manipulation of district boundaries enables a party to gain legislative representation disproportionate to its share of the popular vote; of course similar distortions can come about accidentally.

Although the existence of such distortions is often seen as evidence of procedural inequality, this is not necessarily so. Indeed, one sense of procedural equality (one common in the literature on voting power) is perfectly consistent with distortions in representation of these kinds. Let us say that a representation system satisfies procedural equality if it accords to every voter an equal a priori probability of influencing any particular legislative choice.[8] This criterion will be satisfied whenever the following two conditions are true: (1) each voter has an equal a priori probability of casting the decisive vote (that is, roughly, of making the difference between victory and defeat) in electing the legislator or legislators representing his district; (2) each legislator has an equal a priori probability of casting the decisive vote on any matter coming before the legislature.[9] Clearly, it is fully consistent with these conditions that there be superfluous majorities and unrepresented minorities within districts. Furthermore, neither condition imposes any restriction on how district boundaries should be drawn beyond the requirement of equal population (or, perhaps, equal numbers of qualified voters).[10] Finally, neither condition imposes any restriction on the structure of the representation system beyond the requirements that every district return the same number of representatives to the legislature, and that each representative have an equally weighted vote.[11] These conditions can be satisfied in an extremely wide variety of districting systems, resulting in many different patterns of representation at the legislative level.[12]

This contention is not paradoxical. The principle of procedural equality refers to the distribution of *opportunities* for political influence (that is, of *potential* influence) rather than of *actual* influence. The potential influence that a procedural arrangement confers on any individual can be calculated without knowing how that person or any other person will use the opportunities defined by the arrangement. The extent of one's potential influence depends only on the structure of the procedures themselves. This is not generally true of actual influence, however. A person's actual influence, understood as the probability that he will, in fact, be successful in getting the legislation he wants (or, as the value, to him, of his procedural opportunities) also depends on how he exercises his opportunities and on how others exercise theirs. For example, in a committee in which each member casts one vote and the majority rules, my potential influence equals that of every other member; but if my interests are opposed to everyone else's, my actual influence is zero (assuming that everyone votes his or her interests).

If the subject of procedural equality is taken to be the distribution of potential rather than actual influence, then members of a group that returns fewer than its proportionate share of legislators cannot complain of procedural inequality provided that their votes had an equal a priori probability of being decisive in each district. Their complaint, rather, may be that their

votes had less value than the votes of others: under the circumstances (given the district boundaries and the distribution of
voter interests across boundaries), their interests are likely to
be less well served by the legislature than those of others. Of
course, arrangements that give rise in this way to arbitrary variations in the value of a vote may be open to moral criticism for
a number of reasons. For example, it might be claimed that
such arrangements violate a principle of equal actual influence
(although it is not clear that political procedures in any mod-
erately complex society could ever satisfy this principle.) More
plausibly, perhaps, they may violate a principle of proportional
representation for groups.[13] Whether any such principle can be
given a persuasive justification is a question that I shall not pursue here, except to observe that the considerations involved are
distinct from those associated with procedural equality.

                                    II

    The foregoing observations leave open a number of difficult
problems about the interpretation of the principle of procedural equality, but I do not believe that anything in the criticisms to be advanced below turns on them. Thus, we may ask
whether good reasons support the principle as a constraint on
the structure of representative institutions.
    A likely reply is that procedural equality is required by the
deeper principle that institutions should treat persons as equals,
or, in Dworkin's phrase, as equally deserving of concern and
respect.[14] The difficulty, of course, lies in formulating the
deeper principle with sufficient precision to yield definite implications about the distribution of opportunities for political
influence. I shall comment on two different, although possibly
consistent, formulations.
    What is intended might be that procedural equality expresses
public recognition of (or embodies institutionally the principle
of) equal respect for the autonomy of persons. Political institutions, it might be said, should avoid interfering with, and when
possible should contribute to, their citizens' respect for themselves and for one another as persons equally capable of mak-

ing deliberate choices about their own situations, and of carrying out these choices in action.[15]

The idea of respect for autonomy is frequently appealed to in more general justifications of democracy. In that context it has several aspects, each of which connects with democratic institutions in a different way. Most obviously, that opportunities to influence political decisions are available to everyone ensures that those so motivated will be enabled to defend their interests and to promote their ideals. They will be able to exercise some degree of control over aspects of their lives affected by political decisions, and need not passively accept those decisions as *faits accomplis* that are beyond challenge. Further, since democratic politics requires public discussion and debate, it supports a political culture with incentives for investigation and criticism of government, and for the public presentation of opposing political views. Such a culture both encourages and enables the exercise of the faculties of judgment and choice. Finally, democratic politics creates an environment in which persons confront each other not only to manipulate but to persuade, and so must take seriously each other's nature as a rational being. In this sense, public recognition of rights of participation is a form of "communal acknowledgement of individual worth," providing grounds for the belief that one is regarded by others as a person whose opinions and choices have intrinsic importance.[16]

Although claims like these play an important role in the general justification of democracy, they do not appear to lend support to the principle of procedural equality as well. First, procedural equality does not seem necessary to ensure that citizens will regard themselves as sharing in control rather than as objects of manipulation by an alien power. As Mill observed, this consideration requires that everyone have *some* opportunity to participate in political decision-making; it is not obvious that these opportunities should therefore be equal, particularly if other considerations making for inequality are widely accepted.[17] Similarly, the distinctive political culture of democracy seems to be consistent with some amount of political inequality. The essential condition here seems to be that political competition be extensive enough to generate a continuing interest in having available independent sources of information and criticism regarding a government's activities, and to create recurring situations in which engagement in argument and persuasion will be necessary to compete effectively for power. In both cases, institutions must be sufficiently open to allow conflicting positions to be represented, but it is not obviously necessary that every citizen have an equal opportunity to influence outcomes.

Some forms of inequality are clearly objectionable for other reasons related to respect for autonomy. Consider, for example, the white primary or the use of unequal election districts to dilute the influence of blacks. Such inequalities not only work to the detriment of the disadvantaged group but will also be experienced by them as demeaning. The visible dilution of influence will appear as an insult. This may be true even when there is good reason to believe (which is lacking in the examples cited) that those who are disadvantaged by the inequality will benefit in the long run: the inequality itself comes to symbolize the paternalistic superiority of those advantaged by it. But not every procedural inequality has this effect; few, for example, feel insulted or degraded by the patent inequality of representation in the U.S. Senate. This suggests that inequalities in the voting system that work to the detriment of identifiable groups will be regarded as insulting in the presence of other social practices that single out those same groups for invidiously discriminatory treatment, but not necessarily otherwise. Other types of procedural inequality (for example, limitations on access to the ballot) seem even less immediately degrading, again at least insofar as the inequalities do not reflect discriminatory practices elsewhere in society. Here there is an asymmetry in the basis of procedural equality: considerations associated with respect for autonomy furnish stronger objections to inequalities that reinforce existing patterns of unacceptable social discrimination than to inequalities that are, in this respect, benign.

But it may be objected that this formulation of the argument from equal consideration is too subjective; what is important is not only that persons have equal self-respect, but that their equal self-respect be rational in view of how their interests are treated by their institutions. This objection introduces a second formulation of the argument, for now it is claimed that political institutions treat persons as equals only when the decisions reached give equal weight to each person's interests. Some such criterion is the basis of the arguments for democracy offered by Bentham and James Mill, and by various contemporary "economic" theorists of democracy (insofar as they are concerned with normative issues.) Now it is not clear offhand how this criterion should be interpreted. There are minimal and maximal interpretations. The first—which underpins utilitarian theories of democracy—is that decisions (or, more exactly, a sufficiently long string of decisions) should maximize the overall or average increase in satisfaction; the second, that decisions should (in the long run) yield equal increments in satisfaction for each person. These interpretations are obviously very different. Other interpretations of the equal weight formula might also be suggested, as well as alternative standards of distributive equity based on an objective ranking of sources of satisfaction (such as Rawls's two principles together with the theory of primary goods), and mixed views in which a satisfaction-maximizing principle is constrained by an objective "welfare floor."[18]

While equal-weight formulae initially appear to be especially appropriate in democracies (because each evaluates decisions according to a standard in which, in an obvious sense, each person counts for one) I do not believe that this appearance survives scrutiny. Whatever superficial plausibility attaches to equal-weight formulae is likely to dissolve once it is recognized that these formulae govern the distribution of *increments* in satisfaction resulting from political decisions rather than aggregate levels of satisfaction. If the antecedent distribution is unacceptable, ensuring that increments are equal will only perpetuate an unacceptable distribution.[19]

Nevertheless, let us assume for the sake of argument that some form of the incremental equal-weight formulae provides the most adequate substantive standard for assessing the outcomes of political decision procedures. With suitable modifications our conclusions will apply to other outcome-oriented standards as well. The question is whether egalitarian procedures are sufficient to guarantee that the outcomes will be acceptable from this point of view.

The answer is that they are not. Whether egalitarian procedures will produce egalitarian outcomes depends on whether various further conditions are met in the society in which the procedures operate. As Barry has argued, outcomes that are egalitarian in the maximal sense are likely to result from egalitarian procedures (specifically one person, one vote majoritarian legislative procedures with binary choices, but the result can be generalized) only when two conditions are met: "(1) on each issue, each of those who are in the majority stands on the average to gain as much satisfaction from the law as each of those in the minority stands to lose from it; and (2) on each issue there is an independent probability for each person of being in the majority that is equal to the proportion of the total number in the majority on that issue."[20] A third condition is also needed: all (first order) preferences are equally represented in the decision process. (Suppose that we divide the members of a society into groups on the basis of similarities of preference among the options available in an election. All preferences would be equally represented if the voting rates of all groups were equal.)[21]

Barry's first condition is a weakened version of the idea that each preference must represent an equal opportunity for producing satisfaction (one fulfilled preference adds as much as another to the total amount of satisfaction in society.) Without this condition, fulfillment of the majority's preferences might not produce a greater gain in satisfaction than fulfillment of the minority's preferences. The first condition, therefore, might be said to hold that there are no *intense* minorities. The second condition reflects the pluralist idea that the diversity of interests in society and the presence of many cross-cutting cleavages guarantee that electoral majorities will be constantly shifting, giving each person in the long run an equal chance of being in the majority more than half of the time. Otherwise there is no assurance that in the long run satisfaction will be distributed equally throughout society. This condition might be said to hold that there are no *permanent* minorities. The third condition is more straightforward: it ensures that the electoral system will accurately register the distribution of preferences. To maintain the parallelism, although with some exaggeration, we might say that this condition holds that there are no *silent* minorities.

Egalitarian procedures guarantee egalitarian results in the maximal sense only if society satisfies all three conditions. But surely few (if any) modern democracies satisfy all three conditions. Therefore, in few (if any) modern democracies could the principle of procedural equality be justified by appeal to the principle of equal consideration. The case for procedural equality is not much strengthened by switching to the minimal interpretation of the equal weight criterion. While we could drop the second condition, the first and third would still be necessary, and these in themselves are too demanding for almost any large contemporary democratic society. Matters only get worse if some other equity standard (such as Rawls's difference principle) is substituted for either version of the incremental equal-weight criterion. Since such standards distinguish between legitimate claims and expressed preferences, the required social conditions would be more rather than less demanding than those we have considered.

In practice, any effort to tailor democratic procedures to specific distributional results will be subject to formidable uncertainties about the political behavior of citizens, as well as to variations in the many other socioeconomic conditions that affect political outcomes. These factors are fluid and it is unlikely that much can be said in general about the relation between alternative configurations of procedures and the distributive characteristics of the resulting decisions. In itself this uncertainty might argue for procedural equality a "focal point solution"[22] to the problem of procedural design. But this is only to say that equality serves as a first approximation of the optimal distribution of opportunities for participation, and that the burden of proof lies with those who advocate procedural inequalities for outcome-oriented reasons.

Even if we accept the equal-weight criterion as a standard for assessing political decisions, therefore, it does not necessarily follow that the distribution of opportunities for political influence should conform to the principle of procedural equality. It is true that procedural equality has historically served as a goal of political reform, but if these reflections are correct this is more likely to be justified by the tendency of egalitarian procedures to improve the distribution of benefits and burdens relative to that produced under the old regime. This is a second respect in which the argument based on the principle of equal consideration is asymmetrical, since procedural inequalities might be permissible if reasonably calculated to produce

further improvements in the quality of political outcomes, as-
sessed from the point of view of whatever interpretation of the
principle is adopted.

III

The defects in the two views just considered may be traced
to the fact that each holds procedural equality to be instrumental to the satisfaction of the more basic principle of treating
persons as equals. In each case empirical premises are needed
to connect the more basic principle with procedural equality,
and in each case these empirical premises do not appear to be
true. Indeed, in each case it is even possible to imagine circumstances in which procedural *in*equalities might be necessary to
treat persons as equals (as Mill's advocacy of plural voting illustrates.)

It might be thought, however, that procedural equality has
intrinsic rather than instrumental value. Perhaps its importance
derives from considerations of fairness that override the types
of result-oriented considerations discussed above. Such a view
seems to represent a widely held intuition. Can reasons be given
to back it up?

One plausible account is suggested by an analogy taken with
minor changes from Barry.[23] Imagine a railway car which has
not been designated either "smoking" or "no smoking" and assume that each of the passengers either wants to smoke or objects to others smoking in the car. Assume also that no other
seats are available aboard the train. Finally, suppose that the
consequences of failure to agree on a rule about smoking would
be such that no one would prefer it to either "smoking" or "no
smoking." Now one might think that decisive reasons dictate
one decision or the other; but it seems likely that any such reasons would be disputed by those on the other side. Where there
are "no presumptions as to merits," Barry suggests that the only
decision procedure that has a chance of acceptance all around
is one based on procedural equality: each person casts one vote
and the majority rules.[24]

This might be true in the following sort of case. It may be
that none of the passengers believes that decisive reasons dic-

tate one or the other decision; each regards his or her preference simply as an arbitrary taste, none believes that much damage would be done by either possible outcome of the decision
process, and so on. There are "no presumptions as to merits"
in the sense that no individual passenger entertains any view
about which decision would be best on the merits. In this case
each might reason that deciding by majority vote is the best
decision procedure, because it will satisfy the greater number
of preferences, and no preference has more to be said for it
than any other. Now of course this case has few interesting political analogs, and it is clearly not the sort of case that Barry
intends. However, if the description of the case is brought closer
to the circumstances Barry imagines (and is thereby made more
realistic), his conclusion becomes more problematic. According
to the amended description, each passenger does have a reasoned belief about which decision would be best, but these beliefs conflict. Each has presumptions as to merits, but *shared*
presumptions as to merits are insufficient to generate agreement. Here it is harder to accept majority voting on the grounds
that it satisfies the greater number of preferences. Why should
those who turn out to be in the minority think it a good thing
to satisfy preferences that are unreasonable from their point of
view? [25]

Where not only preferences but also the reasons underlying
them conflict, a more elaborate explanation of the fairness of
procedural equality will be required. One might say that agreement on egalitarian decision procedures represents a compromise that is reasonable when some decision procedure is needed
and agreement on the merits of conflicting claims is unlikely to
be reached.

Peter Singer advances such an account of procedural equality
as a criticism of Mill's plural voting proposal: "Assuming that
we did believe Mill's system of voting to be perfectly fair," we
should still have to recognize "that it would be impossible to get
everyone to agree on who was to have the extra votes." Thus,
"it would be wise to put aside beliefs about what would be perfectly fair, and settle for the sort of compromise represented
by 'one man, one vote'. . . . As a fair compromise, [this prin-
ciple] is greatly preferable to a 'fight to the finish' over each
controversial issue." [26]

Without questioning the wisdom of procedural equality as a strategic accommodation to the threat of chaos, I do not believe that its "fairness," if based on such a compromise, can carry much moral weight. Certainly this "fairness" is insufficient to justify the claim that equal rights to influence political outcomes are fundamental in the sense of being immune in principle from adjustment to obtain desirable patterns of outcomes. For the criterion of "fairness as a compromise" is simply that it is accepted all around: the features in virtue of which a procedural arrangement is fair are set by what those who will be bound to its results will accept, given that everyone prefers *some* decision procedure to none at all. No independent standard of fairness can be invoked to persuade or criticize someone who refused to accept procedural equality, and nothing in principle prohibits dispensing special favors or procedural advantages to such a hold-out if that were the only way to get him or her to go along. More importantly, nothing prohibits procedural inequalities that yield desirable results if the compliance of a sufficient number of those affected could somehow be guaranteed.

But perhaps it will be objected that this criticism caricatures the idea of fairness as a compromise by assimilating it too closely to the equilibrium point in a bargaining situation. Not just any compromise counts as fair, it might be said; at a minimum, we want to exclude compromises arrived at under such threats as that of noncompliance in the case of the hold-out imagined above. Here, the idea of a hypothetical agreement suggests itself. Suppose, to return to our railway car, that the passengers were asked what procedure for group decision-making they *would* agree to if they were required to agree without knowing that one matter for decision would be the question of smoking versus no smoking. Surely *then* they would accept procedural equality.

This may be true, but it does not salvage the account of fairness as a compromise. The force of arguments concerning what people would have agreed to, when in fact they have not agreed to anything, depends on the reasons any particular agreement would have been reached.[27] It is these reasons that explain the significance that should be attached to the claim that certain people would have agreed to some principle. Hence, we need to consider why procedural equality would be accepted by the passengers in our railway car. There are two interesting possibilities: either the agreement would be the result of a compromise (some procedure is required and this is the only one that everyone would accept), or it would be the result of a convergence of individual judgments about what procedure is antecedently most likely to produce acceptable decisions. If the former, then our earlier problem returns at a new level: the terms of the compromise, and hence its fairness, will merely reflect the balance of bargaining power among the passengers. This may have strategic, but it does not have moral, importance. (Simply to stipulate that bargaining power is equal will not help, since this merely smuggles in the conclusion that requires justification. Moreover, it is not clear that procedural equality would be agreed to even if bargaining power *were* equal; some other principle might be Pareto superior to it.) If the latter, then it needs to be argued that the requisite convergence would indeed emerge, and this will turn out to depend on empirical assumptions like those considered earlier; for example, that cleavages among the passengers are not so deep that one group would have reason to expect permanently to be in the minority. In any event on the latter view the fairness of procedural equality would not consist in its compromise character but in its conduciveness to acceptable results, a position that, for reasons already discussed, is not likely to make good the claim that procedural equality is fundamental.

Perhaps there are other ways of defending procedural equality as a fundamental requirement of fairness; if so, there are reasons to doubt that they would be successful. Assertions that some procedural arrangements are fair invite the question of why *those* arrangements should have a special claim on our support. If one wishes to maintain that fairness is morally fundamental, this question must be answered by showing that the favored procedures have a characteristic whose value is both overriding and independent of considerations about results. But then the further question arises of why the indicated characteristic has overriding value. Simply to respond that procedural fairness has *intrinsic* value is unsatisfying when the choice among alternative procedures makes a difference in the expected results and independent standards for evaluating these results are available. This is particularly true when the requirements of procedural fairness are in dispute. The value of fairness should be susceptible to some more compelling explanation than is provided by the unanalyzed claim that its value is intrinsic. But any other response—including the effort to bring to bear a principle of respect for persons—seems to collapse into an argument from desirable results.[28]

IV

A last argument for procedural equality, which I shall call the argument from liberal stability, can be seen as the residue of Singer's conception of fairness as a compromise once the misleading moral connotations of "fairness" are stripped away. If one were in the position to design political institutions, other things equal, one would want to find ways to encourage compliance with the laws and to promote social order with the least coercive interference in individual lives. One possibility—that pursued by Rousseau in *The Social Contract*—is to constrain the decision-making system so that its outcomes will be (and will be regarded as) in the interests of most of the people most of the time. But this is unrealistic in complex and diverse societies. Another possibility is to build into the system procedural devices that will elicit popular support even when particular decisions disappoint some interests.

A familiar part of the justification of representative government relies on something like the argument from liberal stability. As Barry puts it,

The most important point about a system of elections for representatives is that it provides an intelligible and determinate answer to the question why these particular people, rather than others perhaps equally well or better qualified, should run the country . . . [O]nce the idea of the natural equality of all men has got about, claims to rule cannot be based on natural superiority. Winning an election is a basis for rule that does not conflict with equality. Indeed, it might be said to flow from it. For if quality is equal (or, as Hobbes more exactly put it, quality must be taken to be equal as a condition of peace) the only differentiating factor left is quantity. . . . Justification for rule in terms of the specific achievements of the government lacks this essential feature of determinateness. Others can always claim that their performance would be superior, and who is to say it would not be?[29]

As I understand him, Barry does not hold that there *are* no objective moral principles for assessing the performance (or expected performance) of representatives. Rather, the idea is that people are likely to disagree about what these principles require and how they should be applied. Moreover, few are likely to allow that some person or group, by virtue of intelligence, birth, or position, is better qualified than anyone else to arbitrate among contending principles. These observations are to be regarded as generalizations from political sociology. Their function in Barry's argument is to define an empirical condition that must be satisfied by any form of government reasonably likely to be voluntarily supported by the bulk of its population.

If this interpretation of the argument is correct, then it is not simply the "determinateness" of representative systems that recommends them. Many systems for choosing public officials are determinate in the ordinary sense of giving an unambiguous answer to the question of who should rule. Indeed, some non-electoral systems are both determinate and consistent with "natural equality" (selection by lot, for example). What recommends representative government, on this view, must be that it is more likely than any other form of government, in the context of prevailing political attitudes, to elicit continuing popular support.

It is clear that this view rests on several nontrivial empirical premises, but let us grant for the sake of argument at least this much: in modern, industrial societies and in normal circumstances, representative institutions with a universal franchise are more likely than any other kind of political institutions to elicit the willing support of their people. The question I would like to explore is whether considerations of liberal stability should incline us to the more exacting position that representative institutions should be procedurally egalitarian.

This depends on the political attitudes of the members of a given society, particularly the extent to which their acceptance of democratic procedures is based on the perception that those procedures are equally open to all. Some such perception probably plays a role in explaining the stability of most modern democracies; if not, at least it is likely that the type and extent of procedural inequalities that any given population will accept are limited. However, the area of indeterminacy seems to be large; while "the idea of the natural equality of all men"[30] has been about for several centuries, procedural equality is a more recent innovation. In the U.S., striking inequalities continue to be tolerated in the less obvious segments of the electoral system (e.g., access to the ballot, campaign financing) with no discernable adverse effect on public acceptance of political decisions. Indeed, it is sometimes said that considerations of liberal stability militate against procedural equality in some of its aspects. For example, some writers argue that the kinds of procedural inequalities that favor two-party as against multi-party (or no-party) systems make for higher levels of acceptance of political decisions by creating incentives for compromise in the pre-election stage of political competition.[31] Therefore, it appears that at least some procedural inequalities are compatible with, and may even be required for, public acceptance of the outcomes produced by democratic procedures. Other, perhaps more striking, inequalities might become compatible with liberal stability if norms and expectations shift; for example, if it came to be thought that some group had been systematically deprived of its appropriate share of social benefits and that some procedural inequality was a suitable remedy. Thus, while considerations of stability place limits on the distributional characteristics of procedural arrangements in democratic systems, these limits are historically variable and do not obviously favor thoroughgoing procedural equality.

V

The arguments I have criticized appear to represent the most common reasons for accepting the principle of procedural equality. Since there may be other, more persuasive arguments, it would be claiming too much to say that the principle has been shown to be incorrect. Nevertheless, I hope to have raised doubts about the view that procedural equality is a fundamental right, and thus, about the understanding of the democratic ideal that interprets its egalitarian element wholly in procedural terms. Similarly, I hope to have made it plausible that the justification (not to say the rationale) of many of the movements that have historically pressed for egalitarian procedural reforms is to be sought in the redress of substantive inequities in law and society rather than in the realization of some intrinsically important, fundamental procedural right.

It would require another paper to develop an alternative view about the connection between democracy and equality and to explain what such a view implies for controversies about procedural design. Here, I can only indicate briefly and schematically how one might proceed. The alternative view would locate the egalitarian element at a more abstract level: for example, an ideally equal democracy might be said to be one which treats its citizens as moral equals, or perhaps (in the formula cited earlier) as persons equally deserving of concern and respect.[32] Again, this is not very illuminating. To unpack such a formula, one needs a democratic theory in the wider sense, one which addresses substantive problems of liberty and distributive justice. Problems of procedural design—the issues of democratic theory in its narrower sense—would be worked out with reference to these broader concerns. A theory specifying rules to govern procedural design that was instrumental in this way would inevitably be more complex than that associated with procedural equality; it could not proceed from one basic principle, but would, instead, express a compromise among multiple basic concerns (such as respect for autonomy, distributive justice, and stability) as seen from the point of view of citizens conceived as moral equals.[33] Its application would necessarily involve more extensive reference to empirical considerations. As I have suggested, an instrumental view might recommend different institutional requirements for different contexts, and circumstances can be imagined in which it might not only allow but require inegalitarian procedural arrangements. But procedural inequalities that were justified from this broader point of view would not be *unacceptably* inegalitarian; rather, they would be necessary to ensure that persons would be treated as the moral equals that they are.

NOTES

For their critical reactions to previous drafts, I am grateful to David Hoekema, J. Roland Pennock, Thomas Scanlon, Mark Wicclair, and the members of the Yale Legal Theory Workshop, among whom Owen Fiss was especially helpful. The early stages of my work on democratic theory were supported by a Rockefeller Foundation Humanities Fellowship.

1. In formulations differing mainly in details, the principle is endorsed in many recent works of democratic theory. See, e.g., Carole Pateman, *Participation and Democratic Theory* (Cambridge: Cambridge University Press, 1970), p. 43; John Rawls, *A Theory of Justice* (Cambridge: Harvard University Press, 1971), p. 221; Jack Lively, *Democracy* (Oxford: Basil Blackwell, 1975), pp. 8, 16; Amy Gutmann, *Liberal Equality* (Cambridge: Cambridge University Press, 1980), pp. 180–81.

   The principle plays an important role, as well, in American constitutional law. It is evoked, for example, by Chief Justice Warren's declaration in *Reynolds v. Sims*, 377 U.S. 533 (1963), that "the fundamental principle of representative government," "the clear and strong command of our Constitution's Equal Protection Clause," "the heart of Lincoln's vision of 'government of the people, by the people, [and] for the people,' " is "substantially equal legislative representation for all citizens. . . ." *Ibid*, at 560, 568. With respect to the size of election districts, the *Reynolds* Court held further that deviations from absolute equality would be acceptable if "based on legitimate considerations incident to the effectuation of a rational state policy." *Ibid.*, at 579. Contrast the more restrictive language of *Wesberry v. Sims*, 376 U.S. 1 (1964): "As nearly as is practicable, one man's vote in a congressional election is to be worth as much as another's." *Ibid.*, at 7–8. A generous reading of all of the election cases, taken together, might allow a more nuanced position than that described here to be attributed to the Court. See, e.g., Laurence H. Tribe, *American Constitutional Law* (Mineola, N.Y.: Foundation Press, 1978), pp. 737–61.

2. There is a particularly illuminating analysis of the possibilities in Jonathan W. Still, "Political Equality and Election Systems," *Ethics* 91, no. 3 (April 1981), pp. 375–94.

3. Such a view derives from Joseph Schumpeter. *Capitalism, Socialism, and Democracy,* 3d ed. (New York: Harper and Bros., 1950), p. 269.

4. Mill suggested that persons of greater intelligence (measured by level of education) be given extra votes, since their political judgment was likely to be superior. J.S. Mill, *Considerations on Representative Government* [1861] (Indianapolis: Liberal Arts Press, 1958), ch. 8, pp. 136–37.

5. This position is maintained, for example, in Justice Brennan's majority opinion in *Kirkpatrick v. Preisler,* 394 U.S. 526 (1969).

6. See Ronald Rogowski, "Representation in Political Theory and in Law," *Ethics* 91, no. 3 (April 1981), p. 397, and the references cited there.

7. Thus, Mill remarked that "In a really equal democracy. . . . [a] majority of the electors would always have a majority of representatives, but a minority of the electors would always have a minority of the representatives. Man for man they would be as fully represented as the majority." *Considerations on Representative Government,* ch. 7, p. 103.

8. The phrase "a priori probability" may be misleading. The probabilities intended are not literally a priori: they are defined against an information base including all relevant features of the actually existing voting arrangements, with the exception that each voter is assigned an equal chance of choosing any of the alternatives available to him. These probabilities are a priori in the special sense that they express the chance that each voter would have of being decisive on an issue if he were equally likely to take any available position on that issue.

9. This is a crude formulation of the standard view in the literature on voting power. It derives from L.S. Shapley and Martin Shubik, "A Method for Evaluating the Distribution of Power in a Committee System," *American Political Science Review* 48, no. 3 (September 1954), pp. 787–92. See also John H. Banzhaf III, "Weighted Voting Doesn't Work: A Mathematical Analysis," *Rutgers Law Review* 19 (Winter 1965), pp. 317–43; and Alvin I. Goldman, "On the Measurement of Social Power," *Journal of Philosophy* 71, no. 8 (May 2, 1974), pp. 231–52.

10. As Dixon puts it, "all districting is gerrymandering" in the sense that the pattern of legislative representation by group or party will always be affected by the system of districting, even when the system is perfectly egalitarian, and whether the effect is intended or accidental. Robert G. Dixon, *Democratic Representation* (New York: Oxford University Press, 1968), p. 462.

11. For the last point, see Banzhaf, "Weighted Voting Doesn't Work,"

and the same author's "Multi-Member Electoral Districts—Do They Violate the 'One Man, One Vote' Rule?," *Yale Law Journal* 75, no. 8 (July 1966), pp. 1309–38.

12. See Edward R. Tufte, "The Relationship between Seats and Votes in Two-Party Systems," *American Political Science Review* 67, no. 2 (June 1973), pp. 540–54.

13. As Dixon suggests. *Democratic Representation,* p. 463. An argument of this general form is also given in Justice White's majority opinion in *White v. Regester,* 412 U.S. 755 (1973), at 765–69 (multimember districts held unacceptable when they deny adequate legislative representation to groups which were subjects of past discrimination).

14. Ronald M. Dworkin, *Taking Rights Seriously* (Cambridge: Harvard University Press, 1977), pp. 180–83.

15. "Whether it be in the field of individual or social activity, men are not recognizable as men unless, in any given situation, they are using their minds to give direction to their behavior." Alexander Meiklejohn, *Political Freedom* (New York: Harper and Brothers, 1960), p. 13.

16. Lively, *Democracy,* pp. 134–35.

17. Mill, *Considerations on Representative Government,* ch. 8, p. 137.

18. Such a principle is suggested by R.M. Hare, "Rawls's Theory of Justice—II," *Philosophical Quarterly* 23, no. 93 (July 1978), pp. 241–51.

19. A more serious problem—which we need not pursue here—is the reliance of the equal-weight formulae on interests as indices of individual positions rather than on some more objective standard. For a discussion, see Thomas M. Scanlon, "Preference and Urgency," *Journal of Philosophy* 72, no. 19 (November 6, 1975), pp. 655–99.

20. Brian Barry, "Is Democracy Special?," *Philosophy, Politics, and Society,* Fifth Series, ed. Peter Laslett and James Fishkin (New Haven: Yale University Press, 1979), pp. 176–77. It is neglect of these presuppositions that explains G.E.M. Anscombe's peculiar findings in "On the Frustration of the Majority by Fulfillment of the Majority's Will," *Analysis* 36, no. 4 (June 1976), pp. 161–68.

21. This condition is particularly important in view of evidence that participation rates vary with social class in most western democracies. See Sidney Verba, Norman Nie, and Jae-On Kim, *Participation and Political Equality* (Cambridge: Cambridge University Press, 1978), esp. ch. 4.

22. The phrase is Thomas Schelling's. *The Strategy of Conflict* (Cambridge: Harvard University Press, 1960), pp. 57ff.

23. Brian Barry, *Political Argument* (London: Routledge and Kegan Paul, 1965), p. 312.

24. *Ibid.*

25. This thought is the source of Wollheim's "paradox" of democracy. Richard Wollheim, "A Paradox in the Theory of Democracy," *Philosophy, Politics, and Society,* Second Series, ed. Peter Laslett and W.G. Runciman (Oxford: Basil Blackwell, 1962), pp. 71–87.

26. Peter Singer, *Democracy and Disobedience* (New York: Oxford University Press, 1973), p. 35; the order of the phrases has been changed.

27. As Dworkin points out in his review of Rawls's *A Theory of Justice.* See *Taking Rights Seriously,* pp. 150–83.

28. For a helpful further discussion of this last point, see William N. Nelson, *On Justifying Democracy* (London: Routledge and Kegan Paul, 1980), pp. 17–33.

29. Barry, "Is Democracy Special?," p. 193.

30. *Ibid.*

31. For example, Maurice Duverger, *Political Parties,* trans. B. and R. North (London: Methuen, 1954), pp. 216–28, 403–12; Gabriel A. Almond, "Introduction," in G.A. Almond and James S. Coleman, *The Politics of the Developing Areas* (Princeton: Princeton University Press, 1960), esp. pp. 33–45. For a discussion, see Leon Epstein, *Political Parties in Western Democracies* (New York: Praeger, 1967), pp. 73–76.

32. In *On Justifying Democracy,* William N. Nelson defines a similar view. He argues that the most compelling justification of democracy is that it is more likely than any other system for making political decisions to yield just legislation. *Ibid.,* pp. 100–21. While I believe that Nelson is correct in regarding the justification of democracy in instrumental terms, his view is too narrow in concentrating only on the quality of the legislation that democratic systems produce. It is also important that democracies have, historically, been most hospitable to a variety of personal liberties, and that their political cultures have supported the development of habits of critical inquiry and independent judgment about public affairs.

33. An example of a theory of this kind is that developed in Rawls's *A Theory of Justice.* However, Rawls's own discussion of political justice is too abstract, and at some points too ambiguous, to yield clear guidance for many problems of procedural design. *Ibid.,* pp. 221–34.

PART II

FEDERALISM

3

FEDERALISM AND THE DEMOCRATIC PROCESS

ROBERT A. DAHL

Whenever the number of citizens is large—it need be no longer than the adult population of a small country—then citizens will find it inconvenient, even oppressive, to govern themselves in a single unit. To manage public affairs they will need other units, including local governments. Local governments will make binding decisions, enforced if need be by heavy punishments. In principle, a local government might be highly democratic—thanks to the advantages of its size, possibly far more than the national government. Yet it would necessarily fall short of democratic criteria in one respect: its citizens would not exercise final control over their own agenda, which would be restricted by a higher level of government or by the constitution of the country.

Let us now suppose that the national government is constitutionally prevented from infringing on the agenda of the local government. Each level of government is privileged, so to speak, in relation to the other. Yet because each has a protected agenda, neither has a completely open agenda. This is, in essence, a federal system if by federalism we intend to mean a system in which some matters are exclusively *within* the competence of certain local units—cantons, states, provinces—and are constitutionally *beyond* the scope of the authority of the national government, and where certain other matters are constitutionally outside the scope of the authority of the smaller units.

Federal systems have a somewhat ambiguous standing in democratic ideas, partly for purely historical reasons but also because they compel one to raise the following questions:

1. If one requirement of a fully democratic process is that the demos exercises final control over the agenda,[1] and if in federal systems no *single* body of citizens can exercise final control, is it then the case that in federal systems the processes by which people govern themselves cannot even in principle ever be fully democratic?

2. If some conflict over government policies is inevitable and if the only fair and practical principle of decision-making is majority rule (operating within limits set by the obligation to respect the fundamental rights of all citizens, including the minority), then do not federal systems unfairly restrict the majority principle? For in federal systems a national majority cannot prevail over a minority that happens to constitute a majority in one of the local units that is constitutionally privileged.

3. When a people needs more than one unit in order to govern itself well, can we reasonably conclude that one kind of unit, such as the city-state or the nation state, ought to be "sovereign," i.e., ought to be the unit in which the demos should exercise final control over the others?

These are the questions I shall explore in this essay. They involve more than mere issues of terminology or concerns about how one may properly apply the term democracy. They compel us to ask whether a people is able to govern itself fully in a federal system or whether federalism is, as some writers contend, fundamentally defective according to democratic criteria.

To deal succinctly with these questions it is useful to exclude a number of other issues. For example, it is obvious that in practice great and quite possibly irremovable obstacles are likely to prevent any body of citizens from exercising complete and final control over the agenda of public affairs. When the number of citizens is large, these obstacles are doubtless even greater because the need for representation induces a drift of control away from the demos toward the representatives. However, the problems posed by federalism are not a result of representation or of other sources of inequalities. Consequently I am going to assume that all other obstacles, including those created by representation, have been overcome. I shall speak of the demos controlling the agenda as if their representatives were mere agents. The assumption is empirically ridiculous, but making it will help to avoid confounding one problem with another.

I. FEDERALISM AND DEMOCRATIC IDEAS

Before the national state became the focus of democratic ideas, prevailing doctrine insisted that the most appropriate unit of republican or democratic government was the small city-state. Frequently that doctrine also stressed the harm to the public good that must result when autonomous associations exist within the city-state. Thus Rousseau, the last great exponent of views like these, contended that a republic would be best served by a small state without associations.

Yet in Rousseau's day the city-state was already becoming merely a historical vestige incorporated, often by force, into a national state. The historical focus of democratic ideas was now becoming the national state or the country. It happened, however, that the countries in which democratic ideas most deeply influenced institutions and practices were, constitutionally speaking, of two kinds: unitary and federal. In unitary systems our first two questions do not arise, for, constitutionally speaking, all local units are merely creations of the national parliament, fully subject, in principle at least, to its control. The national government delegates authority to local governments; it does not alienate its authority. Thus in principle the national demos has access to an open agenda. And a minority that happens to be a majority in a local unit has no constitutionally privileged position: the national majority may, if it chooses, overrule the decisions of that local unit.[2]

Yet democratic ideas and practices also flourished in federal systems, earlier, in fact, than in unitary systems. Indeed in both Switzerland and the United States, where federalism antedated many of the institutions later regarded as necessary to democracy, the federal system was generally thought to be specially favorable to democracy. So Tocqueville argued in his famous analysis of democracy in the United States. In the twentieth century, however, with the growth of the welfare state and the

expansion of national controls over economic life it was sometimes said that federalism had become obsolete.[3] Yet this view
proved to be premature, among other reasons because of the
emergence of federal insitutions on a transnational scale in the
European Community.

Transnational federalism is the mirror image of federalism
within a country. When a nation with a unitary constitution,
such as France or Britain, enters into a transnational federal
system, such as the European Community, then its national demos no longer has access to a completely open agenda. Yet the
agenda of the transnational unit is also strictly limited. Consequently, even if the larger "community" were to operate according to the majority principle, on many questions a majority
of citizens in the "community" could not overrule a minority,
provided only that the minority of the "community" were a majority in one of the local units: i.e., a country.[4] If we assume
that over the next century transnational federalism will grow
stronger, then the problem of federalism in democratic theory
and practice is far from transitory or obsolete. It simply reap-
pears in a new and perhaps more refractory form. If the application of democratic ideas to the national state first generated the questions of this essay, the attempt to apply them to
transnational governments ensures that the questions will persist.

II. THE AGENDA PROBLEM

The first question—the agenda problem—is more easily answered than the second. For the agenda problem is only partly
real.

To help us determine what is real and what is illusory, I am
going to invent a "democracy" with a closed agenda. Let me
call our closed democracy Sylvania. The government of Sylvania controls only one subject, the schooling of children. To
be sure, schooling is no trivial matter. But if Sylvanians want to
act on other things and have no opportunity to place them on
the Sylvanian agenda, or on the agenda of any other government they control, then we would think the Sylvanians rather
oppressed in spite of their vigorous but closed democracy. Sup-

pose, for example, that Sylvania, though perfectly autonomous and self-governing on questions of schooling, is controlled by a foreign nation, Fredonia, that excludes the hapless Sylvanians from citizenship. No matter if Fredonia itself is the very perfection of the democratic process: Sylvanians are colonials and their thin little "democracy" is a pretty piece of window-dressing staged by their rulers. The Sylvanians may admire the democracy of their Fredonian rulers, but they can never emulate it.

But if Sylvanians are *not* excluded from citizenship in Fredonia, then they are at once citizens of Sylvania and the more inclusive unit, now called Greater Fredonia. If, as Sylvanians, they govern themselves democratically on school matters, and, as Fredonians, they govern themselves democratically on all other questions, if the agenda of Fredonia is completely open and Sylvanians may place matters of interest to them on the Fredonian agenda, then our problem of closed democracy vanishes. I do not say that there are not other problems, but the processes by which the Sylvanian-Fredonians govern themselves satisfy all the requirements of the democratic process, including final control over the agenda of public affairs. Taking the two governments together, the Sylvanians confront a completely open agenda. If we assume that the other criteria are met, then we must conclude that the Sylvanians enjoy a fully democratic process.

But in this description have we turned Greater Fredonia into a unitary rather than a federal system? Has the Fredonian demos merely *delegated* control over school questions to Sylvania and other local units? If so, then our solution appears to be spurious, for it tells us that our problem does not arise in unitary systems but in federal ones, which is precisely where we started. But does our solution also imply something more interesting: that our problem cannot be solved *except* by turning federal systems into unitary ones?

Let us now suppose that under the constitutional arrangements reached when Sylvania joined Greater Fredonia, Sylvania's control over schools is permanent and inalienable. The system is definitely federal. In one perspective, Greater Fredonians have alienated control over schools to Sylvania and other local units. Just as the agenda of Sylvania is closed on everything except schools, so the agenda of Greater Fredonia is permanently closed on matters involving schools. What are we to make of this situation? Though clearly federal, the solution seems to be no different from that provided by a unitary system with local governments. To be sure, the agenda of Greater Fredonia is closed with respect to schools, but on everything else it is completely open. Let me call it quasi-open. As in a unitary system, if we take the two governments together, Sylvanians confront a completely open agenda, for whatever they cannot put on the Sylvanian agenda can be placed on the agenda of Greater Fredonia. If every Fredonian has his own local equivalent of Sylvania, then the federal system does not prevent Fredonians from exercising final control over the agenda of public affairs.

In sum: Provided that in one of their units all citizens have access to a quasi-open agenda, federalism is not inherently less capable of meeting the criteria of the democratic process than a unitary system.

III. FEDERALISM AND THE MAJORITY PRINCIPLE

If federalism can pass the first test question, what about the second? Although democratic criteria might yield other decision rules than the majority principle, no others appear, as general principles, to be equally fair and yet workable in practice. But an even narrower principle would create the problem raised by the second question: a system that gave to a specially privileged minority the power to overrule the majority on questions of policy could hardly be regarded as democratic. Yet in federal systems a national majority cannot prevail over a minority that happens to be concentrated in a constitutionally privileged local unit where its members are a majority. This is an anomaly of federalism that unitary systems avoid.

The anomaly would be much less significant if it could be shown that federalism is necessary in order to protect the primary political rights that must be guaranteed to all citizens (whether in a minority or a majority) in order for the democratic process to exist.[5] But another anomaly would simultaneously be created. For if the primary political rights of citizens required federalism, then it must be the case that unitary systems deny these rights to their citizens. Yet so far as I know even the most convinced federalist would not be prepared to argue, for example, that the political system of Norway, being unitary, is inherently less democratic than the political system of Switzerland. If federalism is necessary to democracy, then unitary constitutional systems are necessarily undemocratic. To show that unitary constitutional systems are necessarily undemocratic, one would also have to show that a small, autonomous city-state with no need for decentralization to even smaller units would *necessarily* be undemocratic. The argument grows absurd.

Is the converse true, that because of their peculiar treatment of the majority principle, federal systems are *necessarily* undemocratic? Some critics have so contended. But if this is so, then a transnational federal system like the European Community is necessarily undemocratic. Are we to conclude that however desirable it might be on other grounds, when a people who govern themselves under a unitary constitution enter into a larger federal order they must necessarily suffer some loss of democracy?

Since the issues are elusive, let me go back for a moment to Greater Fredonia and then go on to an even more abstract system. A moment ago we assumed that the agenda of Sylvania is constitutionally closed on everything except schools, while the agenda of Greater Fredonia is closed only on schools but on nothing else. Suppose that a majority of Fredonians come to the conclusion that their schools are in such a deplorable state that more uniform educational standards must be imposed on the country. If Greater Fredonia were unitary, we should not think it tyrannical or even undemocratic if national policies were imposed in order to bring local school systems up to scratch. But because Greater Fredonia is federal, the majority of the country is barred from acting to improve the schools. Yet the Sylvanians might be a small minority of all Fredonians, and even in Sylvania the majority might be only barely greater than the minority.

One can imagine any number of instances in which justice would seem to support the claims of Sylvania for autonomy on some particular matter. But in this particular instance would it not be both unjust and undemocratic if the minority were permitted to have its way about standards for the schools? If the majority principle is ever justified, is it not justified in this instance? If it cannot be justified in this instance, I do not see how it could ever be justified.

Let me now introduce an abstract system. S is a smaller subsystem in B, the bigger and more inclusive system. Nothing could be simpler.

(I warn the reader not to think that we necessarily have reproduced Sylvania and Greater Fredonia all over again.) Assuming that both B and S are governed democratically within the limits of their agenda, and that the primary political rights of all citizens are respected, should the majority of B always be entitled to prevail against the local majority in S—on, say, schools? Or to put it the other way round, should the local majority in S be constitutionally entitled to prevail on some matters—say schools—against the larger majority in B?

In using the term "entitled" I mean to exclude mere convenience, efficiency, or utility.[6] It might be convenient or efficient for people in B to allow the people in S to govern themselves on certain matters such as schools. This is simply to say that B is a unitary system, and B finds it useful to delegate authority to S. Obviously that is not the problem here. To say that the majority in S is sometimes *entitled* to prevail over the majority in B is to say, in effect, that the people in S have a *right* to govern themselves on certain matters, and that B ought not infringe on this right. At the same time, however, by assumption all citizens in B, including those in S, are fully protected in exercising their primary political rights, that is, the rights necessary if a people is to govern itself. But if the entitlement is not merely convenience or efficiency, and if it is not a primary political right, what sort of "right" is it? Do people have a fundamental moral "right" to a "local" government, like the "right" to free speech—a moral right so basic that it should be constitutionally guaranteed?

Despite my warning, I imagine that all along the reader has thought of S as a local unit like Sylvania and B as a national unit like Fredonia, and as a result may be rather sympathetic to Fredonia's claim. But suppose that S is a country like Britain or France, and B is a transnational system like the European Community. Where now do one's sympathies lie? In this case is not one more sympathetic to the claims of the people in S to exercise control over the education of their children than with the claims of B to govern over the people of S on these matters? Are we to say that B merely *delegates* authority over education to S? But in what sense does B possess this authority to begin with? Certainly not legally or constitutionally. Morally? Ought any larger unit *always* to have authority over any smaller unit? Even the most severe critic of federalism will begin to dig in and resist somewhere.

A solution to the apparent conflict between federalism and the majority principle is elusive because it depends on an answer to the third question—which, unfortunately, admits of no satisfactory answer on purely theoretical or philosophical grounds.

IV. THE PROBLEM OF THE DEMOCRATIC UNIT

The Greeks of course believed that only a city could be a good state and as late as the eighteenth century Rousseau and Montesquieu agreed that the best state for a self-governing people could not be larger than a city. Since their day, democratic orthodoxy has claimed the national state or country as the proper unit—even if the country in question is no more than a fragile aggregate of regions or tribes. But like its predecessors, the national state is a moment in history. In Europe its claims are already dissolving into a larger entity. In the year 2100 will the nation-state still seem to be the natural site and limit of the democratic process?

The fact is that one cannot decide from *within* democratic theory what constitutes a proper unit for the democratic process. Like the majority principle, the democratic process *presupposes* a unit. *The criteria of the democratic process presupposes the rightfulness of the unit itself.* If the unit itself is not a proper or

rightful unit, then it cannot be made rightful simply by democratic procedures. If the United States were to compel Costa
Rica to become the fifty-first state, would not Costa Ricans
rightly feel—and we too—that a grave injustice had been done?
That they had been deprived of their right to govern themselves? In a national referendum a majority of Norwegians chose
not to enter the European Common Market. Was this not in
part from a feeling that in entering the Common Market they
would wrongly yield up to others some of their own authority
over themselves?

To ask what kind of unit is proper or best, whether abstractly
or in the concrete case, spills out a whole bagful of questions,
few of which have a crisp answer. The ancient question presents itself: what kind of unit is most capable of providing the
essentials of a good life? This question immediately suggests a
further one: in whose judgment, that of the citizens concerned
or our own? Are we to play the role of the omniscient judge,
or shall we simply let the citizens have their way? I am going to
take the easy way out and assume for the purposes of this discussion that the two converge.

We then come to the problem of "system capacity."[7] Imagine
that the Sylvanians are perfectly free to decide what is to go on
their own agenda and what, if anything, on the agenda of
Greater Fredonia. The extent of Sylvania's association with
Greater Fredonia is wholly under Sylvania's control. Politically
speaking, then, Sylvanians are as independent or autonomous
within Greater Fredonia as they choose to be. It is reasonable
to think that Sylvanians would find it advantageous to ask
Greater Fredonia to perform certain functions that Sylvania is
less capable of undertaking by itself. Defense might be an example. Some functions might be flatly beyond Sylvania's capacities—material, economic, technological. For example, Sylvania
probably could not prevent upstream and upwind pollution
from damaging the environment and health of Sylvanians. Thus
Sylvanians might consider three options.

1. They might want to keep full control over their own
agenda, even though Sylvania will not function very effectively
on matters of defense or controlling pollution.

2. They might want to delegate control over these matters to
Fredonia, and retain control over all other questions.

3. To gain other advantages from the greater system capacity of Fredonia they might want to enter into a full union with Fredonians, believing that a majority of Fredonians would be predisposed to delegate certain local functions to the Sylvanians even though final control over the agenda of public matters would rest with the citizens of Fredonia as a whole.

By choosing (1), in effect the Sylvanians would give up the advantages of Fredonia's greater system capacity in order to retain exclusive control over their own agenda. By choosing (2) they would gain some of the advantages of Fredonia's greater system capacity in return for some loss of control over their own agenda, but Sylvania would still have a "quasi-open" agenda. By choosing 3 they would gain all of the possible advantages of Fredonia's greater system capacity; in return they would completely yield up final control over any part of their own agenda, though in all likelihood a majority of Fredonians would delegate to Sylvanians some authority to govern themselves within a closed agenda.

Two questions arise: Is one option in some reasonable sense *more democratic?* And is one option in some reasonable sense *more desirable?* On the information before us, on what ground could we conclude that one is more democratic than another? I see only two possibilities. One is sheer numbers. As Rousseau suggested long ago, it is necessarily the case that the greater the number of citizens, the smaller the weight of each citizen in determining the outcome.[8] If the greater the weight of each citizen, the more democratic a system is, then other things being equal a larger system is bound to be less democratic than a smaller system. However, this statement is subject to an obvious difficulty: if it were true, and a smaller system must always be more democratic than a larger, then the most democratic system must consist of one person, which is absurd. On the other hand, if a system is more democratic to the extent that it permits citizens to govern themselves on matters that are important to them, then in many circumstances a larger system would be more democratic than a smaller one, since its capacity to cope with certain matters—defense and pollution, for example—would be greater. Yet it is obvious that just as the criterion of numbers alone leads to absurdity, taken by itself the criterion of system capacity compels us to say that an absurdly large system is the most democratic—quite possibly one consisting of the entire human population of the globe. If in order to avoid these absurdities we take the two criteria together and search for an optimum balance between system size and capacity, we can no longer proceed theoretically. We shall need to make complex and debatable empirical and utilitarian judgments. In addition, since empirical conditions will vary, there is every reason to suppose that even if an optimum can be found it will not be the same in different circumstances and historical periods. Finally, we can not assume that a single aggregate of persons would be best served by only one system. Garbage removal, water supply, schools, pollution, defense—each may in principle produce a different optimum. The result might well be a complex system with several or more layers of democratic government, each operating with a somewhat different agenda.

If we are prepared to assume that one solution might be more democratic than another but less desirable on balance, and conversely might be more desirable though less democratic, can we decide, with the information at hand, which would be the best or most desirable? If we believe that democracy is good, and if we cannot say whether one solution is more democratic than another, we shall be hard put to decide that one solution is better than another, for a crucial ingredient in a reasonable judgment about desirability will be missing.

Furthermore, if we introduce additional criteria for judging a desirable solution, their application will also require empirical knowledge—or guesses—not found in abstract descriptions of the alternatives.

Thus it does not seem possible to arrive at a defensible conclusion about the proper unit of democracy by strictly theoretical reasoning: we are in the domain not of theoretical reason but of practical judgment. Yet even practical judgment cannot, it seems, yield a general answer that holds for all times and places; the answer depends too much on particularities.

To say that an answer cannot be derived theoretically is not to say that judgments need be arbitrary. If this were so, then almost all political judgments would be arbitrary. Certain assumptions on which the validity of the democratic process itself depends can be brought into play. In particular, a reasonable judgment would require one to appraise alternative solutions in the light of two prior principles: that the interests of each person are entitled to equal consideration, and that in the absence of a compelling showing to the contrary an adult is assumed to understand his or her own interests better than another. These principles are too general to lead to conclusive answers, particularly in the face of great empirical complexity. But they may help us to find reasonable answers.

I have tried to show, first, that although in federal systems no single body of citizens can exercise final control over the agenda, federalism is not for this reason less capable than a unitary system of meeting the criteria of the democratic process, provided only that at some level of government every citizen has access to what I have called a quasi-open agenda.

Second, if one assumes the fairness of the majority principle, then it is an anomaly of federal systems that a national majority cannot always prevail over a minority on questions of policy, if that minority happens to constitute a majority in a local unit with a constitutionally protected agenda. Yet on that ground alone federalism cannot be judged less democratic than a unitary system, except on the premise that the proper unit in which majorities should prevail is the nation or the country.

Third, such a premise is arbitrary and highly contestable. By purely theoretical reasoning from democratic principles it appears to be impossible to establish that the city-state, the country, a transnational system, or any other unit is inherently more democratic or otherwise more desirable than others.

NOTES

I wish to express my appreciation to members of the Yale Faculty Seminar on American Democratic Institutions for help in clarifying some aspects of this essay. The argument is part of, and to some extend depends on, a more extended interpretation, some of which has appeared elsewhere and is cited below.
1. I am assuming here that a fully democratic process would satisfy the following criteria: (1) equality of voting; (2) opportunities for effective participation; (3) opportunities for enlightened understanding; (4) final control over the agenda by citizens; (5) inclusiveness. These criteria are explained and justified in "Procedural De-

mocracy," in Peter Laslett and James Fishkin, eds., *Philosophy, Politics, and Society,* Fifth Series (New Haven: Yale University Press, 1979).

2. To avoid misunderstanding, it may need to be said that in practice all "democratic" countries are politically pluralistic and not monistic, no matter whether their constitutions are federal or unitary. That is, in both kinds of systems relatively autonomous associations, organizations, and other sub-systems exist in great variety. Federalism may magnify political pluralism but other causes ensure that even unitary systems, if they are "democratic," will also be pluralistic. Cf. my *Dilemmas of Pluralist Democracy: Autonomy v. Control* (New Haven: Yale University Press, 1982).

3. Harold Laski, "The Obsolescence of Federalism," *New Republic* 98: 367–69 (1939).

4. In the European Community, the power of a majority of citizens of the Community to overrule "local" (i.e., country) decisions is even more limited because of the relative ease with which one of the constituent nation-states can withdraw—and the bargaining power such a threat gives to the "local" governments.

5. By "primary political rights," that is, the rights necessary to the democratic process, I mean the rights of all adult citizens to vote in free and fair elections, to organize political associations, to express themselves freely, to seek access to alternative sources of information, etc. See my "The Moscow Discourse: Fundamental Rights in a Democratic Order," *Government and Opposition* (Winter, 1980).

6. For an argument that federalism has consequences for the distribution of costs and benefits of alternative policies, and thus for (rational) voters' choices, and so, presumably, for policies, see Susan Rose-Ackerman, "Does Federalism Matter? Political Choice in a Federal Republic," *Journal of Political Economy,* 1981, vol. 89, no. 1, 152–165. Rose-Ackerman contests the contrary argument by William H. Riker, "Federalism" in *Handbook of Political Science,* Vol. 5, *Governmental Institutions and Processes,* ed. by Fred I. Greenstein and Nelson W. Polsby (Reading, Mass.: Addison-Wesley, 1975).

7. Cf. the discussion on system capacity in Robert A. Dahl and Edward R. Tufte, *Size and Democracy* (Stanford: Stanford Univ. Press, 1973).

8. I am aware that this is not Rousseau's language and that his treatment, which is in places obscure, might admit of other interpretations, though the general thrust of his argument seems to me perfectly clear. I am also aware that the proposition could be much more rigorously stated and proved than I have tried to do in the text. For example, one might present the famous Shapley-Shubik power-index. But the language here is, I believe, sufficient to sustain the argument.

4

CAN DEMOCRACY BE COMBINED WITH FEDERALISM OR WITH LIBERALISM?

DAVID BRAYBROOKE

The question whether democracy is compatible with federalism and the question whether democracy is compatible with liberalism are so closely connected that each can be regarded as a special case of the other. Both have to do with specifying certain matters that are to be reserved from democratic action by the whole body of citizens. Inquiry into each may be expected to throw some light on the other. I shall be specially concerned with inquiring how what is at stake for democracy in combining with liberalism throws light on what is at stake for it in combining with federalism.

There is more at stake in combining with federalism, I think, than Dahl allows in his treatment of his first question, about whether it is democratic to have some matters taken off the agenda of a larger jurisdiction and reserved for the agenda of a smaller one. Does this question really "vanish"? Are "all the requirements of the democratic process, including final control of the agenda" satisfied if citizens in the smaller jurisdiction can put anything on the agenda of the larger jurisdiction that they cannot put on the agenda of the smaller one? I think not.

In the first place, some issues that Dahl takes up only later can properly be brought up here. By accepting a division of agendas, the citizens of the smaller jurisdiction are giving up a chance to count for as much in deciding the matters on the agenda of the larger jurisdiction as they count for in deciding matters on their own agenda. In this sense, the answer to Dahl's question, "When a people who govern themselves under a unitary constitution enter into a larger federal order [must they] necessarily suffer some loss of democracy?" is straightforwardly yes. If "democracy" is taken to mean, given a body of citizens, and given alternatives on each issue within their reach, differing in ways that they care about, it is more democratic for them to have more control over matters that affect them rather than less, then it is less democratic for them to have their control diluted in the larger jurisdiction.

But "democracy" may also be taken to mean, given a body of citizens, it is more democratic for them to get what they (or what most of them) want more rather than what they want less. Whether the division of agendas is more or less democratic in this sense is less certain. Because of what Dahl calls its greater "system capacity," the larger jurisdiction may be able to pursue successfully various policies on a given matter that are beyond the capacity of the smaller jurisdiction; people in the smaller jurisdiction may prefer some of those policies to anything that on its own the smaller jurisdiction can do about the matter in question. Putting something on the agenda of the larger jurisdiction may advance democracy if these things are true.

On the other hand, the policies that the smaller jurisdiction would prefer to have the larger jurisdiction pursue may not in fact be policies that the larger jurisdiction is likely to adopt. People in the smaller jurisdiction may prefer the best of the less satisfactory policies within their reach. If so, putting something on the agenda of the larger jurisdiction will not advance democracy for the smaller jurisdiction. As Dahl maintains at the end of his paper, the citizens of the smaller jurisdiction cannot tell whether it will be worthwhile to divide agendas— losing some control but getting more of what they want—until they have carefully studied empirically the conditions facing them and balanced one thing against the other.

The citizens of the smaller jurisdiction may wonder on other grounds whether divided agendas offer such a good bargain. For, in the second place, how much confidence can they place in Dahl's assurance that they can put everything that they want on one agenda or the other? Will not the other citizens of the larger jurisdiction constitute at least one other smaller jurisdiction? Perhaps not; possibly even on matters parallel to those that are reserved to the smaller jurisdiction the other citizens of the larger jurisdiction accept the participation of the citizens of the smaller jurisdiction. The smaller jurisdiction, for example, chooses its own pension policies; the larger jurisdiction chooses pension policies for everybody not in the smaller jurisdiction. Such an arrangement, queer though it sounds, is not only possible, it is sometimes found in fact. (Quebec has its own public pension plan and also participates in making decisions about the public pension plan for the rest of Canada.)

However, the usual situation is one in which there are other smaller jurisdictions. If there are, the citizens of any given smaller jurisdiction may contemplate with dismay not being able to put on any agenda open to action in which they have a part matters reserved to other smaller jurisdictions. This is so whether or not those matters are parallel to matters reserved to their own jurisdiction. A citizen of Nova Scotia, for example, which depends on the public pension plan for the rest of Canada, might have reason to think that the decisions made by Quebec in carrying on its own public pension plan affected him adversely by jeopardizing the financial security of the more general plan. A citizen of Ontario or New Brunswick, where schooling in French is available for Francophone families moving into the province (though not everywhere in either province), might well wish for the power to change the Quebec law under which Anglophone newcomers are not permitted to have their children schooled in English.

Thus, if we suppose Fredonia to be divided into several smaller jurisdictions, so that "every Fredonian has his own local equivalent of Sylvania," it is not true that every Fredonian will exercise control as a Sylvanian over any agenda items that he does not exercise control over as a Fredonian. So it is not on the ground alleged a good bargain for Sylvanians. But neither is it necessarily a good bargain for Fredonians. Dahl has so divided his discussion as to concentrate under his first question, about control over the agenda, on the bargain from the point of view of the smaller jurisdiction. He looks on federalism in the other direction, from the point of view of the larger jurisdiction, only when he turns to his second question (about whether it is acceptable for a majority in the larger one not to prevail). However, I think this question is best looked upon as an aspect of the first. If we ask, is it compatible with fully realizing democracy for a smaller jurisdiction to divide agendas with a larger one, we should demand to know both whether it is compatible with fully realizing democracy for the smaller jurisdiction and whether it is compatible with fully realizing democracy for the larger jurisdiction. Even if it were compatible for the smaller jurisdiction, in the sense that people there could on one agenda or the other count for something in deciding any matter of concern to them, it might not be compatible for the larger jurisdiction. Fredonians outside Sylvania in the larger jurisdiction, whether or not they belong to Sylvanias of their own, and however democratic their situations are in other respects, confront in the agenda reserved to any given smaller jurisdiction matters that they cannot put on any agenda under their control.

An issue arises here that is logically more general than majority rule or the difference between federal and unitary systems. If part of the agenda is devolved upon two or more smaller jurisdictions, can the larger jurisdiction meet certain elementary formal conditions, which democrats would be loath to forego, on the relations between the preferences of its citizens and its social choices? Amartya Sen's "Liberal Paradox" suggests not.[1] Sen formulates a Condition of Minimal Liberalism: There are at least two people (k and j) and two distinct pairs of alternatives (x, y) and (z, w) such that one person can decide, irrespective of the wishes of the other (or of anybody else), which of one pair shall be adopted, and the other person can similarly decide respecting the other pair. The condition may be applied to federalism by letting k stand for all the people in one smaller jurisdiction and j for all the people in the other. Sen proves that the condition cannot be met for the larger jurisdiction without sacrificing at least one of three things. One is the Pareto Principle, in the form that simply says, if everyone in the jurisdiction prefers one alternative to another, it is preferred socially. Another is the condition of Unrestricted Domain, according to which any combination whatever of all persons' preference orderings for all alternatives may offer itself as the input into social choice. The third is that the process of social choice, given such an input, shall amount to at least a Social Decision Function, that is to say, a system of aggregation from which will reliably emerge a choice set free, for example, of the drawback manifested by cyclical majorities in the Paradox of Voting.

A democrat could hardly waive the Pareto Principle; having a Social Decision Function, concerned as a democrat must be, among other things, with relating social choices to personal preferences, is not much easier to give up. Without one, one may have determinate social choice founded on personal orderings only by grace of the order of voting and of a procedure that precludes every alternative being put to a vote against every other.[2] A democrat cannot lightly set aside Unrestricted Domain either. Is every combination of personal orderings in which k's preference between x and y conflicts with j's just to be disregarded? It does not seem democratic to refuse in advance to consider certain preferences that k may have; she may in fact attach a good deal of significance to this one. Must the democrat then stay with these conditions and give up liberalism—and federalism simultaneously?

Actually, if he divides agendas in the right way, he can keep both faiths, and meet the other conditions as well, at the cost of explicitly relativizing the condition of Unrestricted Domain to sets of alternatives and sets of persons. Sen (followed on this point by Levine)[3] divides choices, but lets the pairs of alternatives overlap with pairs open to choice by the larger jurisdiction. Thus j alone chooses between x and y and k alone chooses between z and w, but together (along with anyone else in the larger jurisdiction) they choose between x and z and between z and w. But if both x and y (having one's children given schooling in French, say, as against having them given schooling in English) are set apart on j's agenda and both z and w set apart on k's, Sen's proof is blocked.

Unrestricted Domain is fulfilled if we take it to mean that all possible orderings by j and anyone else in her smaller jurisdiction for x and y (and any other alternative figuring uniquely on its agenda) are to be taken into account. This relativized interpretation of the condition has been available in social choice theory all along. In effect, by not asking which persons the orderings were to be taken from, social choice theorists like Arrow and Sen have relativized the condition to sets of persons in accordance with Dahl's dictum, "The criteria of the democratic process presuppose the rightfulness of the unit itself."[4] In other words, the set of persons presupposed in social choice theory is a variable determined by external considerations, among which may be found the division of jurisdictions. Relativizing Unrestricted Domain to sets of alternatives does not accord quite so neatly with the practice of social choice theorists. The alternatives that Arrow assumes he is dealing with are grand amalgamations of ordinary political alternatives; they are all-encompassing social states.[5] He is inclined to assume also that every distinct social state figures as an alternative.[6] However, he does not persist with the second assumption; neither assumption does any work in his formal reasoning or in Sen's.[7]

A liberal democratic federalist would wish to have agendas divided on some reasonable principle; logical correctness—freedom from paradox—would not in itself suffice him. In practice, federations originate in various ways, both by larger jurisdictions dividing into smaller ones below and by smaller ones erecting larger ones above, as Dahl notes; and also by doing one thing first, and then doing the other, as has happened both in the United States, with the addition of further states to the original union of thirteen, and in Canada, with the addition of further provinces to the original four.[8] Canada presents the further complication that the legislation creating Confederation was enacted by an authority theretofore substantially as well as formally superior—the Queen in the Parliament of the United Kingdom—to the jurisdictions agreeing to federate.

Whether a federation originates in one of these ways, pure or mixed, rather than another, may make little difference in the end. It is tempting for Eastern Canadians to argue that since Alberta was a creation of the government set up by the Eastern provinces, its claim to riches from oil is contingent and revocable. However, evidently on being made a province, Alberta in fact gained all the rights and privileges generally possessed by the original provinces. On the other hand, the terms of federation sometimes differ between the smaller jurisdictions: Newfoundland claims to have entered Confederation on special terms; Quebec can claim to have done so, too. Are the terms of origin to be written off as accidents of circumstance? Even if they are, in the sense of corresponding to no reasonable general principle for dividing agendas, they may be legally decisive. In some cases, moreover, the terms do reflect general principles.

For example, paragraph 133 of the British North America Act guarantees people in Quebec the right to use French or English when they take part in the business of the legislature or of the courts in that province. This provision reflects the contingent historical fact that people in Quebec were very much attached to the use of French, to the point of taking up arms to make sure of it. (They still are.) Is this an accident of circumstance? I think the trouble that might have been expected from not accepting this division of agendas in favor of Quebec can be taken as a measure of the value French-speaking Quebeckers placed on having the choice of speaking French. From the existence of the provision, we can infer, on the other side, that the value to English-speaking people in the other jurisdiction of denying Quebeckers this choice was not, even if it was substantial, great enough to outweigh the net advantages in other respects of agreeing to federate with Quebec. The provision is thus the outcome of mutually advantageous free exchange.

"The minority that happens to constitute a majority"[9] in Quebec is, of course, a very special sort of minority (or majority). It is not transitory; it is not even (like the majority in Alberta for keeping a lion's share of riches from oil in the province) composed, on a geographical basis, of any miscellaneous lot of Canadians who happen to be there. It is a minority with its own language and distinctive culture continuously established on that terrain since the early seventeenth century. The English-speaking provinces might be regarded, in dividing agendas, not only as having found it not worth their while to deny Quebec the reservation for its agenda of certain matters vital to its culture. They might also be regarded as having agreed to divide agendas so that every province would have with Quebec parallel powers to protect the culture indigenous to it. Hence to each province is reserved legislation on education.[10]

Looked at in this way, the rationale of Canadian Confederation brings us to another principle for bargaining, a principle that may be used in supplementation to the principle of free

exchange to encourage some exchanges without regard to differences in bargaining power. This supplementary principle is
that in bargaining over agendas each smaller jurisdiction should
accord to the others matters parallel to those that it believes it
must keep off the agenda of the larger jurisdiction to protect
itself from significant losses.

Bargaining under this principle will go some distance in giving effect in federalism to the liberal principle that people
should be free to choose for themselves in matters where there
is no threat of harm to others that the others can reasonably
regard as substantial. That principle, though along with all the
other strands of liberalism it is still alive, in spite of continual
premature rumors to the contrary, has been persistently vexed
in theory by difficulties about defining what harm is to be
counted as both substantial and pertinent.[11] If we adopt a bargaining approach, we can hope to manage these difficulties; we
shall be managing them, furthermore, in illuminating concurrence with another strand of liberalism. A federation, like any
government, may be called upon to accord with a social contract; it generally differs from a unitary government, and so a
democratic federation differs from a unitary democracy, in
being called upon twice over.[12]

NOTES

1. Amartya K. Sen, *Collective Choice and Social Welfare* (San Francisco:
   Holden-Day, 1970), Chap. 6* (pp. 87–88).
2. Cf. Charles R. Plott, "Axiomatic Social Choice Theory: An Overview and Interpretation," *American Journal of Political Science,* 20
   (August 1976), 514.
3. Andrew Levine, "A Conceptual Problem for Liberal Democracy,"
   Journal of Philosophy, 75 (June 1978), 302–308.
4. Robert A. Dahl, "Federalism and the Democratic Process," in this
   volume.
5. Kenneth J. Arrow, *Social Choice and Individual Values,* 2nd ed. (New
   York: Wiley, 1963), pp. 17, 109.
6. Ibid., pp. 17, 24.
7. "Without loss of generality we may suppose that the entire universe is the set of three alternatives mentioned in the statement of
   Condition 1." Arrow, op. cit., p. 51. Cf. the statement p. 59 of his
   central theorem, which begins "If there are at least three alterna-

tives . . ." Sen says, op. cit., p. 42, "We assume throughout this book that there are at least two persons in the society and at least three alternative social states." In both works, the formal arguments go through for alternatives specified no further than by the symbols x, y, and z, though the significance of the results depends on what the alternatives are interpreted to be.
8. Prince Edward Island did not come in right away.
9. Dahl, this volume.
10. British North America Act, par. 93.
11. A comment by Roland Pennock has led me to see that the analogy between liberalism and federalism may not carry through in the itemization of harms. As liberals, we may regard anybody as free to pick up and leave any jurisdiction that does not suit him; as federalists, we may not be ready to concede smaller jurisdictions the freedom to detach themselves by secession. The analogy assumed in this paper, therefore, is best conceived as an analogy in which individual persons like smaller jurisdictions stay put geographically.
12. While I was revising this paper, I had the benefit of reading an unpublished paper by Brian Barry, "Lady Chatterley's Lover and Doctor Fischer's Bomb Party: Liberalism, Pareto Optimality and the Problem of Objectionable Preferences," which he kindly sent me after the A.S.P.L.P. meetings in Boston. In his criticism of Sen, which is much more comprehensive than mine, he comes out in much the same place as I do on the questions that we treat in common; in particular, my point that Sen's paradox vanishes if the agendas are as thoroughly divided as liberalism traditionally calls for is consistent with Barry's views. In an article, "Liberty, Unanimity and Rights" (*Economica*, 43 [August 1976], 217–245), cited by Barry, Sen surveys the literature generated by his paradox. At several places, he seems inclined to favor a thoroughgoing division of agendas as a way out; but his conceptual apparatus—in particular his classification of possible ways out as weakening the Pareto Principle, or weakening the Condition of Liberalism, or weakening Unrestricted Domain—stands in the way of his squarely accepting the idea. On a proposal by M.J. Farrell, which comes closest to the idea among the solutions that Sen discusses—it would have the set of alternatives partitioned into "socially equivalent subsets"—Sen comments, in accord with my own remarks here, that it "involves a significant departure from the usual format of social choice theory." I would follow Barry in his contention that social choice theorists working in the usual format have been led astray by unresolved ambiguities in the term "social choice." In Sen's paradox the term equivocates between the idea

that society has renounced any objection to how people choose within the scope of their rights and the idea that it is still somehow pertinent to think of society as endorsing what they choose within that scope. However, I have left the notion of social choice uncriticized in the present paper, thinking that my argument against Sen may be accepted even by people who think (as I myself am half of a mind to think) that with more cautious handling the notion could be rescued from criticisms even as telling as Barry's.

PART III

JUDICIAL REVIEW

5

JUDICIAL REVIEW IN
A LIBERAL DEMOCRACY

ROBERT B. McKAY

Sir Kenneth Clark, in the Foreword of his book *Civilization* concedes that he cannot define "civilization," but he is sure that he prefers it to barbarism.

I feel somewhat the same about "judicial review" and "liberal democracy," the terms whose relationship I seek to explore in these comments. At least I am sure that I prefer judicial review and liberal democracy to the reverse—whatever that may be.

Despite obvious definitional difficulties, it is important to define at least in a general way the terms at issue. Let me begin with liberal democracy, which for me presents fewer difficulties. I suggest the following definition for liberal democracy: Majority rule through representative government, as limited by a public commitment to individual freedom and government under the rule of law.

It is more difficult, and for a lawyer more embarrassing, not to be able to identify precisely the components of judicial review. The problem is that there are a number of rival theories about the proper exercise of judicial review. I am reminded of the judge who said, after hearing the plaintiff's argument, "He's right." Upon hearing defense counsel the judge observed, "She's right." When reminded by the bailiff that both lawyers could not be right, the judge rose to the occasion stating firmly, "You're right, too."

The present topic has much the same quality. The several disparate views—and the variations thereon—present a problem not unlike that the judge confronted. That is the fascination of judicial review. Despite many divergent views, none is demonstrably wrong. It is probably also true that none is demonstrably right.

I propose to defend current manifestations of judicial review, particularly the role of the Supreme Court of the United States, against the critics. My views are likely to appear more dogmatic than in fact they are; it may be necessary to state a categorical position in order to defend the relatively wide range of discretion in judicial review that I do in fact favor. I shall offer a defense of activist (or whatever name may be preferred) judicial review. I shall defend the "Warren Court" *and* the "Burger Court," espousing the proposition that they are distinguishable in detail, but not in broad concept of the judicial role.

Part One of this paper, "The Conventional Wisdom," is intended to be relatively noncontroversial. Part Two will develop the proposition that the Supreme Court understands what judicial review is all about and is reasonably successful in its performance of that function—even in the absence of carefully articulated theory. Indeed, perhaps judicial review is more art than philosophy so that efforts to pin it down in neat terms are destined to fail. In the second part I ask the question: "What's so bad about judicial review?"

I. THE CONVENTIONAL WISDOM

No topic more excites contemporary scholars in law, philosophy and political science than the effort to determine the proper scope and function of judicial review. If not quite timeless, judicial review emerged on the American scene almost two centuries ago and has been inconclusively debated ever since. The various alternative resolutions of the issue produce significantly different results. Yet no answer is demonstrably right or provably wrong. The only thing agreed upon is the statement of issues, which might go something like this:

1. A written constitution provides at least some occasions when judicial review is necessary to set aside legislative and ex-

ecutive decisions. The very premise of a higher law requires some higher authority—often called a "supreme" court—to make those determinations.

2. Judges, however, are not free to do whatever they want. The principle of self-restraint necessitates guidelines for the exercise of discretion; that is where the trouble begins, since there is no agreed-upon definition of the controlling principles.

3. In order to limit the possible abuse of discretion, it is postulated that judges should dispose of matters presented to them for decision in a manner as value-free as possible.

Professor Mark Tushnet identifies the principles and the problem in this trenchant observation:

> Judicial review is needed to avoid the tyranny of the majority, and constraints on judges are needed to avoid the tyranny of the judiciary. The difficulty is that liberalism provides no means of accomplishing that result.[1]

That statement catches the dilemma of judicial review. The teachings of liberal democracy point ambiguously in several directions. We are told that decisional authority rests with the people and their chosen representatives (some elected, some appointed by those elected), and majoritarian democracy requires respect for their views. We are also reminded that those spokespersons of the majoritarian impulse may not transgress the more or less ill-defined limits imposed by constitutional text. Those restrictions are of three kinds: (1) The restraint of federalism provides for the national government and the state governments to operate in partially separate, partially concurrent spheres of authority, definable only by some authority superior in this regard to both. (2) The restraint of the separation of powers stipulates that the three branches of the national government shall operate in sometimes distinct, sometimes blurred areas of competence, definable only by an authority charged with neutral and dispassionate resolution of disputes. (3) The final restraint is intended to protect minority rights from the occasional tyranny of the democratic majority, definable by an authority committed to principles of limited governmental authority rather than to democratic majoritarianism.

The assignment is formidable and fascinating. The remarkable thing is that it has worked passably well for almost 200 years, despite doubts expressed at the beginning and the objections of commentators ever since. The system has survived both simplistic and sophisticated assertions about how to satisfy Chief Justice Marshall's dictum that the obligation is to "say what the law is."[2] Excitement remains in the quest for the elusive right answer to justify the travail of the search. Excitement is not enough. Workable principles are necessary in the search for solution of real-life problems. The questions are no less troublesome than inquiry into the nature of the judicial process with an overlay of the special difficulties of a constitutional court charged with answering ultimate questions about distribution of power. In the effort to work through the maze of conflicting views, it may be useful to begin with several propositions believed to be noncontroversial.

1. A written constitution poses problems of interpretation that differ from ordinary legislation. When legislative or executive action is challenged on the ground that it contravenes a constitutional provision, some authority—preferably a court—is required to assess the claim and perhaps to invalidate the law or rule or executive action. The matter is not as easy as Justice Owen Roberts once asserted,[3] but it is indispensably necessary. Judge Learned Hand said it well: "A constitution is primarily an instrument to distribute political power; and so far as it is, it is hard to escape the necessity of some tribunal with authority to declare when the prescribed distribution has been disturbed."[4] The distribution of powers at issue is the division of authority between nation and state, the separation of powers among the coordinate branches of the national government, and the protection of minority interests against majority decisions.

2. Even apart from constitutional issues, courts are called upon to decide the compatibility of one statute with another, as well as the congruence of regulations, rules and executive actions with expressions of legislative will. Performance of this function is scarcely less difficult and sensitive than deciding on constitutional questions—with one important exception. When the legislative body disagrees with a nonconstitutional ruling, it can be set aside (although the practicalities sometimes make statutory interpretations almost irreversible). Not so with rulings

of constitutionality, which can be overturned only by judicial reconsideration or by constitutional amendment, neither of which is easily achievable. Nevertheless, questions of judicial philosophy and personal judgment intrude in nonconstitutional decision-making as in those carrying the heavier burden of near-finality.

3. Even when neither constitution nor legislative act is directly at issue, courts are regularly required to decide matters that involve sensitive judgments about the kind of society in which we live. This is the stuff of the common law, the "interstitial" lawmaking of which Justice Holmes spoke. There was, for example, a time in England when courts were strong and Parliament was still developing its potential. The common law judges molded and shaped the law to meet the perceived needs (primarily property) of the times.[5] Similarly, strong courts in the United States have modified the law of torts, contracts, property, consumer rights and environmental needs to meet the varied demands of successive generations. The effort is to decide in ways that comport with the needs of society without departing too far from the legislative text or the common law heritage.

4. Each of the above propositions is limited to some not easily definable extent by the restraining hand of stare decisis. No judge asserts freedom from precedent, but no judge worthy of the calling finds precedent an absolute shackle in instances where the desire to be free of such restraint is sufficiently compelling. The skillful judge can distinguish; the bold judge can risk overruling the out-of-date or erroneous rule. Oddly, the current debate about judicial review takes little notice of this issue, which in earlier days captured at least equal attention.[6]

It is instructive that the public has been largely quiescent in its acceptance of an activist role for the judiciary in the construction of statutes and regulations and in the development of the common law, even though courts may, in the seemingly innocent guise of interpretation, reshape the legislative will more significantly than in the usual case of outright invalidation. Indeed, the American public seems to approve in general of the way in which the courts function, including the most controversial aspect of the judicial operation, constitutional review. Public opinion surveys reveal that popular respect for all institutions has declined, but courts have suffered less than others, federal courts less than other courts, and the Supreme Court least of all.[7]

The theory and practice of judicial review have always had a powerful attraction for judges, political leaders, academics and ordinary people. The reasons are perhaps twofold: (1) The answer to the basic questions about the extent of power are important in the world of practical affairs; and (2) although many answers are offered, each with solemn assurance of correctness, there is no way of ascertaining the assuredly true answer. There may even be some disagreement about the basic question(s). Perhaps the most straightforward is that of Professor Thomas Grey, who puts the issues thus:

> In reviewing laws for constitutionality, should our judges confine themselves to determining whether those laws conflict with norms derived from the written Constitution? Or may they also enforce principles of liberty and justice when the normative content of those principles is not to be found within the four corners of our founding document?[8]

These questions move beyond what was once the threshold question: Do courts have *any* authority to overturn legislative decisions? Thomas Jefferson, Spencer Roane and others would have denied any invalidation function to the federal courts,[9] but even the most restrictive contemporary concept of judicial review acknowledges that some scope must be allowed for such review. Judge Learned Hand, probably the most eloquent of the "self-restraintists," put it this way:

> [It] was altogether in keeping with established practice for the Supreme Court to assume an authority to keep the states, Congress and the President within their prescribed powers. Otherwise, the government could not proceed as planned, and indeed would almost certainly have foundered, as in fact it almost did over that very issue.[10]

Continuing, he noted that the power of judicial review is "not a logical deduction from the structure of the Constitution but only a practical condition upon its successful operation. . . . [Therefore,] it need not be exercised whenever a court sees, or thinks that it sees, an invasion of the Constitution."[11]

Many other commentators have taken a less restrictive view of judicial review, as will be apparent from the following brief reminder of the principal issues that have surfaced in the effort to define its limits.

The Historical View. Although the Constitution nowhere explicitly confers the power of judicial review upon the federal courts, Alexander Hamilton had little difficulty in finding an intention to do so, particularly as stated in *Federalist Paper* Number 78. His powerful argument is still the basic statement of the case for judicial review:

> There is no position which depends on clearer principles than that every act of a delegated authority, contrary to the tenor of the commission under which it is exercised, is void. No legislative act, therefore, contrary to the Constitution, can be valid. To deny this would be to affirm that the deputy is greater than his principal; that the servant is above his master; that the representatives of the people are superior to the people themselves; that men acting by virtue of powers may do not only what their powers do not authorize, but what they forbid.

> If it be said that the legislative body are themselves the constitutional judges of their own powers and that the construction they put upon them is conclusive upon the other departments it may be answered that this cannot be the natural presumption where it is not to be collected from any particular provisions in the Constitution.[12]

In *Marbury v. Madison* [13] Chief Justice Marshall found the same arguments persuasive, along with evidence of a number of state courts that had already accepted the principle of judicial review. Once the principle was established, however, the power of invalidation was long used sparingly.

Then came the troublesome *Lochner* era, so-called because of the most celebrated exercise of judicial review to upset a state statute on substantive due process grounds,[14] in a decision commonly believed to have been motivated by judicial disapproval of the economic policies that motivated the statute. Judicial invalidation of significant New Deal legislation, between 1933 and 1937, on similar grounds, and widely believed to have been similarly motivated, produced the constitutional crisis of 1937 in the form of President Roosevelt's "Court-packing" plan. The President's proposal was defeated by an interesting coaliton of Court-defenders, including both supporters and critics of the economic and social views embodied in the challenged legislation. It was an impressive affirmation of the power of an idea, the necessity to defend the integrity and independence of the Supreme Court of the United States.

The principle of judicial review may have been made secure, but substantial disagreement remained as to the rationale for judicial review, and more particularly as to the circumstances for its exercise.

The "Preferred Position" Controversy. In 1937, shortly after the failure of the Court-packing plan, the Court was confronted with the need to rationalize its intention to "incorporate" some parts of the Bill of Rights into the due process clause of the Fourteenth Amendment without recourse to the recently repudiated use of substantive due process to upset disfavored statutes. The result, in *Palko v. Connecticut*,[15] was to adopt the new principle of "ordered liberty" as a vehicle for preserving the most vital portions of the Bill of Rights as limitations against the states. In Justice Cardozo's words:

> [Some] immunities that are valid as against the federal government by force of the specific pledges of particular amendments have been found to be implicit in the concept of ordered liberty, and thus, through the Fourteenth Amendment, become valid as against the states.[16]

To solve one problem was, however, to create another. What indeed were the criteria for "ordered liberty?" How could that concept be confined where substantive due process could not? The Court's initial answer to that perplexing question came one year later in *United States v. Carolene Products Co.*,[17] specifically in the now famous footnote 4 to Justice Stone's opinion.

There may be narrower scope for operation of the presumption of constitutionality when legislation appears on its face to be within a specific prohibition of the Constitution, such as those of the first ten amendments, which are deemed equally specific when held to be embraced within the Fourteenth.

It is unnecessary to consider now whether legislation which restricts those political processes which can ordinarily be expected to bring about repeal of undesirable legislation, is to be subjected to more exacting judicial scrutiny under the general prohibitions of the Fourteenth Amendment than are most often types of legislation.

Nor need we enquire whether similar considerations enter into the view of statutes directed at particular religious, or national, or racial minorities: whether prejudice against discrete and insular minorities may be a special condition, which tends seriously to curtail the operation of those political processes ordinarily to be relied upon to protect minorities, and which may call for a correspondingly more searching judicial inquiry.[18]

In those cryptic paragraphs the footnote enunciated three rather distinct propositions that have been profoundly significant in the development of constitutional law, and the footnote has generated an enormous body of academic comment.

The first paragraph (added, we are told, at the suggestion of Chief Justice Hughes) asserts what is now called the "interpretivist" position, that "judges deciding constitutional issues should confine themselves to enforcing norms that are stated clearly or [are] clearly implicit in the written Constitution. . . ."[19] As Professor Ely points out, this notion can neither be called activist nor self-restraining, and thus the need for a new term. Justice Black is generally regarded as the pre-eminent interpretivist, since he was a primary exponent of adherence to constitutional text (as he read the Constitution); but the common perception was that he was activist in his views on civil liberties, civil rights and the power of government to act.

The second paragraph suggests the possible appropriateness of closer scrutiny to legislation that restricts access to the democratic political process and thus arguably thwarts expression of the will of the people. This is now sometimes described as process-based constitutional theory.[20]

The third paragraph states the rationale for according special protection to "discrete and insular" minorities that might be the targets of discrimination resulting in curtailment of the normal operation of the political process.

This footnote, especially the second and third paragraphs, has been particularly rich in its progeny of more or less direct lineage. The "preferred position" doctrine for First Amendment freedoms[21] and the various standards of special scrutiny[22] are the most notable examples.

The *Carolene Products* footnote and its offspring have had a notable revival of academic interest, especially in connection with academic expressions of alarm over the supposed over-reading of the footnote to encourage a return to substantive due process in reviewing the constitutionality of legislation. These concerns will be discussed in the final portions of this paper.

The Undemocratic Character of Judicial Review. A principal argument in favor of limitations on the power of judicial review has always been that it is fundamentally inconsistent with the majoritarian premises on which the nation is founded. And certainly it is true that legislative bodies, state and local, are chosen in more or less democratic fashion, and the President is also chosen on a reasonably representative basis, while the members of the federal judiciary (and an increasing proportion of the state judges) are given what amounts to life tenure *plus* the power to upset the acts of the democratically chosen representatives of the other parts of government. Professor Eugene V. Rostow provided appropriate answers when the issue was at its most active in 1952. He boldly argued in support of "The Democratic Character of Judicial Review,"[23] asserting, as did Hamilton in *Federalist Paper* Number 78, that constitutional interpretation by the courts does not "by any means suppose a superiority of the judicial to the legislative power. It only supposes that the power of the people is superior to both. . . ."[24] Continuing on his own, Professor Rostow reminded of the wide discretion irrevocably delegated to appointed officials, and that "democracies need not elect all the officers who exercise crucial authority in the name of the voters."[25]

While that thoughtful paper did not, and cannot, wholly still the charge that the exercise of judicial review is somehow inconsistent with democratic values, at least the point was made that judicial review need not mean judicial supremacy and that revisory authority is sometimes essential to preserve the values enshrined in the Constitution.

The Neutral Principles Debate. As the debate about the democratic or nondemocratic nature of judicial review cooled off in the mid-fifties, new attacks emerged in terms that seemed at first most appealing. Professor Herbert Wechsler, an eminent constitutional lawyer, enlarged on Judge Hand's argument that judicial review is suspect but occasionally (if rarely) necessary. Wechsler offered an attractive rationale, which came to be known as "neutral principles" of adjudication. His argument was this:

> I put it to you that the main constituent of the judicial process is precisely that it must be genuinely principled, resting with respect to every step that is involved in reaching judgment on analysis and reasons quite transcending the immediate result that is achieved.[26]

The piece created a considerable stir because of its argument that *Brown v. Board of Education* [27] and other recent civil rights decisions lacked neutral principles and were therefore wrong. Many applauded the notion of neutral principles, but few agreed with its application in the particular instances; the Wechsler thesis seems oddly anachronistic upon rereading it today.

The late Professor Alexander Bickel provided a different, more elegant support for the notion of restraint, suggesting the areas into which he believed the Court should not intrude, including reapportionment and affirmative action.[28] But the Supreme Court rejected that advice in *Baker v. Carr* [29] and the subsequent reapportionment decisions and in the *Bakke* [30] case and its related successors. After the initial clamor of distress about opening up the reapportionment process, few today deny the justiciability of the issue and the appropriateness of the application of the equal protection clause to the resolution of the issue. In fact, the apportionment cases are generally regarded as one of the major triumphs of the Court. It may be hoped that the affirmative action principle will be similarly accepted as its constitutional base becomes more firmly anchored in the public consciousness. These things take time.

Contemporary Versions of Judicial Review. The more recent critics may be divided into two principal classes, which I call the rejectionists and the perfectionists. The rejectionists are those who would limit judicial review most sharply, as suggested by the titles they select to express their views.[31] Although those writers are well received by a considerable audience, most members of the academic community reflect a more moderate attitude toward the work of the judiciary. Among this larger group the views are extraordinarily diverse. The only justification for collective identification as perfectionists is that each in his or her own way supports a reasonably activist role for the judiciary in some kinds of cases, but rejects the work of the Supreme Court in other respects for failure to meet the critical standards imposed by the commentator. An important manifestation of the "new criticism" is that each author advances a personal jurisprudence of judicial review and, in the process, explains what is wrong with the jurisprudence of fellow critics.[32]

The disparate theories range widely over constitutional law and moral philosophy. Thus, Professor Dworkin argues candidly for "a fusion of constitutional law and moral philosophy," recommending as a text Professor Rawls's "abstract and complex book about justice which no constitutional lawyer will be able to ignore."[33] Taking a more restrained view of the process, Professor Ely avoids such value-laden terms as activist and strict-constructionist by speaking of "interpretivism" and "noninterpretivism" to categorize two principal concepts of judicial review. The distinction is not easily drawn in specific cases, but the broad directions are understandable. Interpretivists are those who stay relatively closer to the specifics of the constitutional text than the noninterpretivists. But even that difference is somewhat elusive.

Professor Jesse Choper offers a different view, arguing for a functional division as to areas appropriate for judicial review and those in which restraint is called for. He would have the Court exercise the power of judicial review

> in order to protect individual rights, which are not ade-
> quately represented in the political processes. When judi-
> cial review is unnecessary for the effective preservation of
> our constitutional scheme, however, the Court should de-
> cline to exercise its authority. By so abstaining, the Justices
> both reduce the discord between judicial review and ma-
> joritarian democracy and enhance their ability to render
> enforceable constitutional decisions when their participa-
> tion is critically needed.[34]

Despite the logical appeal of the suggestion, doubt remains whether this dichotomy between discretion asserted and discretion withheld is any more principled than other theories of judicial review, all of which Choper rejects.

And so it goes. It is perhaps not surprising that scholars do not agree and that there seem to be almost as many theories as there are commentators. Meanwhile, the Court proceeds on its more or less placid way, largely unaffected by the outpouring of comment and criticism. No single jurisprudence of judicial review has emerged to dominate the academy, and the Su-preme Court continues to be more pragmatic than philosophical about the process, taking the matters that come before it a case at a time.

The continuity of the judicial process is perhaps best illustrated by comparing the course of decisions in the so-called "Warren" and "Burger" Courts. For a time it was widely believed that the Supreme Court, as partially reconstituted by Presidents Nixon and Ford, would turn its back on civil rights and individual liberties, would become more strict (whatever that means) in its construction of the Constitution and statutes and would in general exercise more restraint. In 1976, the Society of American Law Teachers asserted that this was happening: "The Supreme Court is making it harder and harder to get a federal court to vindicate federal constitutional and other rights."[35] Most observers now conclude, however, that the judicial philosophy of the Burger Court is not very different from that of the Warren Court. Some in fact are angered that their raised expectations of restraint have been frustrated. Professor Lusky, for example, laments as follows: "Since 1954 and especially since 1962, and *most* especially since 1969 [the year Warren Burger became Chief Justice], the Court has engaged in constitutional innovation on a large and expanding scale. . . ."[36]

Other commentators are less likely to condemn (or praise) the Court of the 1970s on the ground of notably greater activism than in the 1960s. Yet Professor Lusky is right at least to this extent. While Earl Warren was Chief Justice many complained that the Court had gone too far in the vindication of individual rights and liberties, but in only one instance was the Court accused of a return to the generally discredited notion of substantive due process not grounded in constitutional text. In that case, *Griswold v. Connecticut*,[37] the Court did not concede that it had overstepped the magic line, but Justice Black so argued in dissent, as did many disapproving commentators. In the 1970s the principle of personal autonomy and privacy was extended in the abortion cases[38] to reach even more controversial results; the criticisms became even more intense.[39]

In other cases, too, whether the decisions raise substantive due process objections or not, the Burger Court clearly advanced the libertarian line. Most strikingly, the gender cases, the capital punishment cases and the affirmative action decisions all significantly advance the frontiers of constitutional law in a liberal direction. They are the more remarkable because in each such instance (including the abortion case) the same result was beyond any realistic expectation of legislative accomplishment.

The absence of any consensus among the most perceptive Court-watchers as to a coherent theory of judicial review, particularly since the criticism comes from the right and left, from above and below, raises anew the question whether perhaps the Court is doing a better job than it is given credit for. The balance of this paper is devoted to that question. It is easy to criticize the work of an institution as vulnerable to subjective evaluation as the Court. It is more difficult to defend the Court and its practice of judicial review, especially since the Court itself offers neither an explicit statement of overall philosophy nor a line of decisions that is manifestly self-revelatory. When nine strong-minded individuals must compromise personal views to reach a common judgment, it is unlikely that an institutional philosophy will emerge. I sometimes like to speculate as to how vulnerable would be the work product of a Court composed of nine constitutional scholars selected by a succession of chief executives.

II. WHAT'S SO BAD ABOUT JUDICIAL REVIEW?

The Supreme Court of the United States does not lack detractors, whether related to the result in individual cases or in regard to consistency with earlier decisions on similar matters. What the Court appears to lack are defenders of the process of judicial review over time. Particular lines of decision have their enthusiasts, but those approving views often turn critical when the line of development does not go the whole distance favored by individual commentators. And even those who express enthusiasm for particular results seem reluctant to commend the process by which those results are achieved. It is as though right answers have been achieved by good luck, not by right principles or methods.

None of this should be particularly surprising. Commendation is never as strongly motivated as criticism. Courts in general, and the Supreme Court in particular, are uniquely vulnerable to charges of inconsistency and absence of coherent theory. In the case of the Supreme Court, which is the principal target of a substantial body of Court-watchers, the Court itself provides the first line of attack in the dissents and concurrences of Justices who proclaim to the world the failures of the majority. Since all members of the Court are sometimes in the majority and sometimes in dissent, no single member of the Court can be said to have discovered the Holy Grail of unflinching truth. Moreover, no member of the Court, now or in the past, can be accused of having developed and adhered to a resolutely consistent philosophy of judicial review. General approaches to judicial review are discoverable in the opinions of almost all Justices; but specific articulation and consistent application of a philosophy of judicial review are qualities not yet attributed by the Court-watchers to any Justice. Heads in the clouds, feet of clay.

This, too, is understandable. The matters that come to the Supreme Court ordinarily involve close questions; otherwise, the issues would not be there. Gone are the days when the Court resolved a considerable number of private disputes, sometimes brought to the Court by force of jurisdictional requirement and sometimes by choice. Nearly all matters now involve issues of public concern and come to the Court by exercise of its own discretion. To its credit the Court generally accepts the hard cases. For every instance of postponing decision on a troublesome matter for which the public may not yet be ready, such as the refusal to determine the rights of homosexuals, the Court has taken and decided dozens of cases that it must have known in advance would be severely criticized, no matter how decided.

What Is the Role of Constitutional Courts? As noted in Part I of this paper, the evidence is strong that judicial review was intended by the drafters of the Constitution. It is far less clear that the founders had any conception of the uses to which judicial review might be put. That is not to suggest at all that there has been usurpation or abuse of function. Just as the founders did not anticipate the role of political parties in the electoral process or the use of administrative agencies in the adjudication process, they could not have anticipated the expanded role of judicial review. Nor should we conclude that they would have been dissatisfied with the development of judicial review as we know it today. What we do know, at least from the testimony of Hamilton and Marshall, is that the balance-wheel function of judicial review was intended. The Court has been from the beginning, is now, and presumably ever will be the guardian of the division of authority between nation and states, the preserver of the separation of powers and the protector of minorities against the sometime tyranny of the majority.

That there are times and tides in the jurisprudence of the Supreme Court should neither surprise nor dismay. The looseness of key constitutional phrases in the original text, in the Bill of Rights and in the Civil War Amendments is both a protection against early demise of the instrument and an invitation to flexible interpretation. This may be illustrated by what we know of original intent and subsequent developments in the area of economic liberty.

We need not doubt that an important purpose of the 1787 Constitution was to protect property rights, including the prohibition against state laws impairing the obligation of contracts, the interstate privileges and immunities clause, even the negative implications of the commerce clause. These are all measures that

> "nationalized" the protection of certain private rights and the entrepreneurial liberties: principally, the conjunction between John Locke's *Second Treatise of Civil Government* (published in 1690) and Adam Smith's *The Wealth of Nations* (published in 1776).[40]

In recent decades of primary preoccupation with the Bill of Rights and the Fourteenth Amendment, we tend to forget the original importance of economic liberty. Those values have not been altogether abandoned; in recent decades they have had a certain revival, albeit in forms not contemplated by the founders. Professor Van Alstyne notes at least four areas of protection of property as liberty.[41] (1) In *Hudgens Corp. v. NLRB*[42] the Court upheld the right of the owners of a large shopping center to exclude those who sought to exercise free speech on matters not related to the business enterprise. (2) The provision against laws impairing the obligation of contracts has been revived after a long eclipse.[43] (3) Freedom of speech rights have been enlarged for those who can afford to advertise.[44] (4) The invalidation of Florida's right-of-reply statute when sought to be applied against newspapers may have been in part attributable to the private ownership of the paper, carrying with it the free exercise right of expression unrestricted by any obligation to permit reply.[45]

The Enduring Strength of Judicial Review. Every present member of the Supreme Court of the United States accepts the principle of judicial review;[46] it is unlikely that any future President of either major political party will nominate or the Senate confirm an individual who rejects it. Judicial review is an integral part of the American social and political fabric. But what good is it? If judicial review can neither be defined nor confined within predictable bounds, as I suggested, how are we to live with such a wild card? My answer is in several parts.

1. The Supreme Court is a significant force in the shaping of values in American society. It is a mistake to think of the High Court as we think of other courts, whose primary function may still be dispute resolution. As Professor Owen Fiss notes, "Adjudication is the social process by which judges give meaning to our public values."[47] And what are those values? He explains:

> The values that we find in our Constitution—liberty, equality, due process, freedom of speech, no establishment of religion, property, no impairments of the obligation of contract, security of the person, no cruel and unusual punishment—are ambigious. They are capable of a great number of different meanings. They often conflict. There is a need—a constitutional need—to give them specific meaning, to give them operational content, and, where there is a conflict, to set priorities.[48]

Courts may not do that job perfectly, but neither do the other branches. "History is as filled with legislative and executive mistakes as it is filled with judicial ones."[49]

The Supreme Court has gradually moved into an expanded role in this value-setting function. In response to the demand of the litigious American people, the Court has increasingly been asked to pass judgment on the great social controversies of the day and to decide not only the constitutional issues, but as well to devise and monitor the remedial phase of litigation involving desegregation of schools, the conditions of confinement in prisons and mental institutions, reapportionment, siting of nuclear plants, and many others.[50] The courts may not be perfect instruments for the management of social change in these extended-impact cases, but it is hard to say that courts should not take jurisdiction of matters properly brought to them by counsel who perceive the advantages of judicial resolution of disputes in preference to reliance on the legislative and executive branches. What are those advantages that bring unsolicited, and sometimes unwelcome, business to the courts?

The advantages are several. Judges are more independent

and more value-free than members of the political branches. Moreover, courts *do* answer questions addressed to them, and relatively more quickly than is usual in the legislative process. Surprisingly, the courts provide a better forum for the airing of diverse views than do legislative bodies; they are even better at fact-finding than legislatures. The authors of one recent study found that

> the courts are able to accommodate diverse and vigorous interest representation; that judicial procedures facilitate information gathering and focus presentation of opposing expert viewpoints in an "analytical" fact-finding format that is distinct from the "political bargaining" patterns of legislative deliberations, and, that in implementing remedies, courts have been able to employ effectively the full panoply of resources available to the litigants themselves in fashioning and implementing policy reforms.[51]

2. The Supreme Court performs a vital public education function. It has been asserted that law is the American religion. If so, surely the Constitution is the Bible. In the absence of divine revelation exegesis is provided by the Supreme Court of the United States. In that capacity the Court engages in a continuing dialogue with the American public in relation to the public issues of the day. The legislative and executive branches are not very good at performing this educational function. The Court supplies the material to assist in the shaping of values in public life. Whatever the ultimate outcome of current debates on gender discrimination, abortion, capital punishment and affirmative action, the Court's opinions provide the basic data and information about the various points of view that are relevant to the vital national discussion.

Significantly, the work of the Court is useful for, and is being used for, law-related education in primary and secondary schools as well as in post-secondary schools and in adult education.

3. The Supreme Court is a useful foil to the legislative and executive branches of government. Legislatures commonly approach politically sensitive issues like a dog circling a porcupine—carefully. It is convenient for legislatures to use the Court for two purposes: (1) to resolve politically difficult questions

that they paper over with legislative ambiguities; and (2) to avoid the necessity of taking too seriously borderline questions of constitutionality. It is not unknown for legislators to blame the Court for denying the popular will, no matter how clear the invalidity of the act in question. Courts and legislators alike understand the game. Where judges have life tenure and are truly independent, they can safely absorb a certain amount of such punishment. Indeed, the Supreme Court represents a kind of moral force in our society, above the battle, not quite accessible, and yet sufficiently human for the rest of us to understand and respect their entirely natural foibles. It is in this connection that *The Brethren* may in the long run have enhanced the regard in which the Court is held. No scandal was unearthed, and the Justices were revealed, as we all should have known, to be much like the rest of us, sometimes petty, sometimes irritable, nearly always strong-willed and self-confident.

4. Finally, the Court continues to perform its bedrock function of protecting the weak and the powerless against the tyranny of the majority (and sometimes as well protecting an apathetic majority against the tyranny of an intense and well-organized minority).

CONCLUSION

The Supreme Court of the United States, like other courts, is not perfect. It is not possible, perhaps not even desirable, to define a coherent and altogether defensible theory of judicial review. The Court is not disturbed that consistency is not entirely possible. In the practice of judicial review the Supreme Court has admirably served the cause of justice for nearly two centuries. My advice is not to worry too much about the matter. So long as we are free to tell the Court, the world—and each other—about its failings, things should turn out pretty well.

NOTES

1. Tushnet, "Darkness on the Edge of Town: The Contributions of John Hart Ely to Constitutional Theory," 89 *Yale L.J.* 1037, 1061 (1980).

2. Marbury v. Madison, 5 U.S. (1 Cranch) 137, 177 (1803).

3. "When an act of Congress is appropriately challenged in the courts as not conforming to the constitutional mandate, the judicial branch of the government has only one duty, to lay the article of the Constitution which is involved beside the statute which is challenged and to decide whether the latter squares with the former." United States v. Butler, 297 U.S. 1, 62 (1936).

4. Hand, "The Contribution of an Independent Judiciary to Civilization," in Dilliard (ed.), *The Spirit of Liberty,* 3rd ed., 121–22 (Chicago: University of Chicago Press, 1977).

5. Horowitz, *The Courts and Social Policy,* 1–3 (Washington, D.C.: Brookings Institution, 1977).

6. See Cardozo, *The Nature of the Judicial Process* (New Haven: Yale University Press, 1921) and *The Growth of the Law* (New Haven: Yale University Press, 1924). For a more recent discussion, see Bayles, "On Legal Reform: Legal Stability and Legislative Questions," 65 *Kentucky L.J.* 631 (1977).

7. National Center for State Courts, *The Public Image of Courts, in State Courts: A Blueprint for the Future* (Williamsburg, Va: NCSC, 1978).

8. Grey, "Do We Have an Unwritten Constitution?," 27 *Stan. L. Rev.* 703 (1975).

9. Baker, *John Marshall: A Life in Law,* 373–77, 627–29 (N.Y.: Macmillan, 1974).

10. Hand, *The Bill of Rights* 15 (Cambridge: Harvard University Press, 1958).

11. Ibid.

12. *The Federalist Papers,* No. 78 at 467 (New York: Mentor, 1961).

13. 5 U.S. (1 Cranch) 137 (1803). See Van Alstyne, "A Critical Guide to *Marbury v. Madison,*" 1969 *Duke L.J.* 1.

14. Lochner v. New York, 198 U.S. 45 (1905).

15. 302 U.S. 319 (1937).

16. Id. at 324–25.

17. 304 U.S. 144 (1938).

18. Id. at 152, n. 4 (citations omitted). For a full explanation of the genesis and development of the footnote, see Lusky, *By What Right?,* 108–12 (Charlottesville, Va.: Michie, 1975).

19. Ely, *Democracy and Distrust,* 1 (Cambridge: Harvard University Press, 1980). See also Grey, 27 *Stan. L. Rev.* 703 (1975).

20. See Tribe, "The Puzzling Persistence of Process-Based Constitutional Theories," 89 *Yale L.J.* 1063 (1980).

21. See, e.g., McKay, "The Preference for Freedom," 34 *N.Y.U.L. Rev.* 1182 (1959).

22. See Tribe, *American Constitutional Law,* 1000–1060 (Mineola, N.Y.: Foundation Press, 1978).

23. 66 *Harv. L. Rev.* 193 (1952).
24. *The Federalist Papers, supra* note 12, at 467–68.
25. Rostow, *supra* note 23, at 197.
26. Wechsler, "Toward Neutral Principles of Constitutional Law," 73 *Harv. L. Rev.* 1 (1959).
27. 347 U.S. 483 (1954).
28. See Bickel, *The Least Dangerous Branch* (Indianapolis, In.: Bobbs-Merrill, 1962) and *The Supreme Court and the Idea of Progress* (N.Y.: Harper and Row, 1970). And he disagreed with Wechsler about *Brown,* which he thought correctly decided. See Bickel, "The Original Understanding of the Segregation Decisions," 69 *Harv. L. Rev.* 1 (1955). See also Black, "The Lawfulness of the Segregation Decisions," 69 *Yale L.J.* 421 (1960).
29. 369 U.S. 186 (1962). For the principal substantive decision, see *Reynolds v. Sims,* 377 U.S. 533 (1964).
30. *Regents of the University of California v. Bakke.* 438 U.S. 265 (1978). See also *United Steelworkers of America v. Weber,* 443 U.S. 193 (1979) and *Fullilove v. Klutznick,* 448 U.S. 448 (1980).
31. See, e.g., Berger, *Government by Judiciary* (Cambridge: Harvard University Press, 1977); Glazer, "Towards an Imperial Judiciary?," 41 *The Public Interest 104* (1975); Kurland, "Government by Judiciary," 2 *U. of Ark. at Little Rock L. Rev.* 307 (1979); Lusky, *By What Right?, supra,* note 18.
32. See, e.g., Choper, *Judicial Review and the National Political Process* (Chicago: University of Chicago Press, 1980); Dworkin, *Taking Rights Seriously* (Cambridge: Harvard University Press, 1977); Ely, *Democracy and Distrust* (1980); Fiss, "The Supreme Court 1978 Term: Foreword: The Forms of Justice," 93 *Harv. L. Rev.* 1 (1979); Grey, "Do We Have an Unwritten Constitution?," 27 *Stan. L. Rev.* 703 (1975); Rawls, *A Theory of Justice* (Cambridge: Harvard University Press, 1972); Richards, *The Moral Criticism of Law* (Belmont, Ca.: Dickenson Pub. Co., 1977); Tribe, "The Puzzling Persistence of Process-Based Constitutional Theories," 89 *Yale L.J.* 1063 (1980); Tushnet, "Darkness on the Edge of Town: The Contributions of John Hart Ely to Constitutional Theory," id. at 1037; Unger, *Knowledge and Politics* (N.Y.: The Free Press, 1975).
33. Dworkin, *Taking Rights Seriously,* 149.
34. Choper, *supra* note 32, at 2.
35. Society of American Law Teachers, *Supreme Court Denial of Citizen Access to Federal Courts to Challenge Unconstitutional or Other Unlawful Actions: The Record of the Burger Court,* ii (New York: Society of American Law Teachers, Monograph, 1976).
36. Lusky, *supra* note 31, at 9. See also "Symposium, The Burger Court: Reflections on the First Decade," 43 *Law and Contemp. Prob.*

(Summer 1980). In a representative comment Professor Henry Monaghan concludes that: "One can quarrel about the details, but taken in the main, the Burger Court has left intact the federal edifice bequeathed by its predecessors." Id. at 50.

37. 381 U.S. 479 (1965).
38. Beginning with *Roe v. Wade,* 410 U.S. 113 (1973).
39. See, e.g., Ely, "The Wages of Crying Wolf: A Comment on *Roe v. Wade,*" 82 *Yale L.J.* 920 (1975).
40. Van Alstyne, "The Recrudescence of Property Rights as the Foremost Principle of Civil Liberties: The First Decade of the Burger Supreme Court," 43 *Law and Contemp. Prob.* 66, 71 (1980).
41. Id. at 70–82.
42. 424 U.S. 507 (1976). In an interesting sequel to *Hudgens,* the Court was confronted with a similar fact situation, except that the case came from the California Supreme Court, which had upheld an exercise of free speech on the premises of the shopping center under the provisions of the California Constitution. The Supreme Court of the United States unanimously affirmed the California decision, but five opinions were required to explain the various avenues to that result. *Pruneyard Shopping Center v. Robins,* 100 S. Ct. 2035 (1980). Justice Brennan had earlier urged state courts to protect individual liberties under state constitutions more generously than the Supreme Court interpretation of similar provisions in the United States Constitution. Brennan, "State Constitutions and the Protection of Individual Rights," 90 *Harv. L. Rev.* 389 (1977).
43. *United States Trust Co. v. New Jersey,* 431 U.S. 1 (1977); *Allied Structural Steel Co. v. Spannaus,* 438 U.S. 234 (1978).
44. See, e.g., *First National Bank v. Bellotti,* 435 U.S. 765 (1978); *Buckley v. Valeo,* 424 U.S. 1 (1976); *Bates v. State Bar,* 433 U.S. 350 (1977).
45. *Miami Herald Publishing Co. v. Tornillo,* 418 U.S. 241 (1974). Compare *Red Lion Broadcasting Co. v. FCC,* 395 U.S. 367 (1969).
46. If Justice Rehnquist is considered the Justice most reluctant to upset legislative judgment, it is apparent that he is willing on occasion to go further in invalidation of federal statutes than some of his "liberal" colleagues. See, e.g., *National League of Cities v. Usery,* 426 U.S. 833 (1976). It is not useful to identify Justices as "liberal" or "conservative." The fact is that every member of the Court is more willing to uphold civil rights and liberties than the public as a whole. The Court as a whole is to the "left" of its constituency.
47. Fiss, "The Supreme Court 1978 Term: Foreword: The Forms of Justice," 93 *Harv. L. Rev.* 1, 2 (1979).
48. Id. at 1.
49. Id. at 15.

50. Chayes, "The Role of the Judge in Public Law Litigation," 89 *Harv. L. Rev.* 1281 (1976).
51. See Rebell and Block, Educational Policy Making and the Courts, 215 (Chicago: University of Chicago Press, 1982).

6

REMARKS ON ROBERT B. McKAY, "JUDICIAL REVIEW IN A LIBERAL DEMOCRACY"

GEORGE KATEB

I appreciate—in fact, I admire—the worldly way in which Professor McKay responds to the supposed perplexities concerning the institution of judicial review. Attentive to those who seriously question whether judicial review is defensible as a prominent feature of democratic government, he counsels us to remain unalarmed. For a variety of good reasons, he says, judicial review is not merely reluctantly defensible but positively praiseworthy. And just as "The absence of any consensus among the most perceptive Court-watchers as to a coherent theory of judicial review . . . raises anew the question whether perhaps the Court is doing a better job than it is given credit for . . ." so "It is not possible, perhaps not even desirable, to define a coherent and altogether defensible theory of judicial review." His next to last line is, "My advice is not to worry too much about the matter."

What makes this worldliness possible is, of course, a certain quantity of experience that he has pondered deeply. I imagine McKay saying to himself that critics of judicial review have their points, make their case, should be listened to—but, really, they come and go; judicial review stays. The good it does far exceeds its harm: Warren Burger no less than Earl Warren deserves credit for his strength and wisdom. The test—I take

McKay to be saying—is ultimately pragmatic. Judicial review works in spite of all theories that are spun out in its behalf or against it. The tendency of its theoretically unencompassable functioning is to protect and inspire basic values.

Yet I think that for people (like myself) more jittery or less experienced than McKay the seeming inability to defend judicial review coherently is greatly troubling. It might one day come again under terrible assault. Perhaps, therefore, we should continue the theoretical effort. I am sure a final theory is out of reach—as a final theory is out of reach on any major matter in political and legal philosophy. I also grant that some can never be reconciled to judicial review whatever theory may do to defend it; some, including myself, will always be more grateful for its existence than theory may strictly allow us. At the same time, I do not pretend that I am able to provide a theory to defend judicial review. I hope that I can offer a few suggestions, guided in part by what McKay (and others) say.

I would begin with the functions of judicial review: review of federal and state laws, regulations, and acts. Several functions figure prominently in the literature; some are structural, like adjudicating jurisdictional disputes arising from the federal and separated nature of American government; others are important though informal, like schooling officeholders and the American public in matters of constitutional principles, and thus, of moral philosophical principles. I would like, however, to enter a plea for a particular understanding of the functions of judicial review. When McKay refers to the "bedrock function" of judicial review as "protecting the weak and the powerless against the tyranny of the majority" he approaches the heart of the matter, in my judgment. But I would prefer a somewhat different formulation. The bedrock function of judicial review is to protect individual rights against government[1] and, where relevant, against any concentration of private or quasi-public power. I do not want the stress put on the weak and powerless, because this wording suits harassed or persecuted racial and religious minorities, but does not suit too well harassed or persecuted individuals involved in the exercise of the rights of free mind, or persons caught in the toils of the law. I do not want the stress put on the tyranny of the majority, a phrase with conservative Tocquevillian associations, because harassment or persecution—or any effort to abridge or defeat a right of individuals—is rarely traceable to the will, judgment, or even caprice of the majority; that is, the majority of citizens in the country or a state. Nevertheless, I concede that what I have mostly in mind is the protection of (in some loose sense) unpopular, deviant, distasteful, or even unvirtuous exercises of rights.

My hope, then, would be that courts when engaged in judicial review would conceive their purpose as the Supreme Court did when Earl Warren was Chief Justice: to affirm, even if not in so many words, that the highest purpose of judicial review is to protect constitutionalism, to protect the Constitution as a charter of constitutionalism, as a charter commanding the defense of the rights of individuals against the continuous, even if *characteristically mild,* encroachments by public, quasi-public, and private power. (Obviously unpopular exercises of rights could not long survive unless officials and people alike were steadily disposed to accept constitutional restrictions on their immediate, particular dispositions.) My hope would be that we would all see that the Constitution is an addendum to the Bill of Rights as much as the Bill of Rights is an addendum to the Constitution.[2] Of course, I am not foolishly saying that courts can always find for individuals. Instead, it is a matter of judicial self-understanding when judges engage in judicial review. The wrong self-understanding consists in judges seeing themselves as officials of government, part of the process of governance. The right self-understanding is to see themselves as members of an independent judiciary—that is, independent of governance and vocationally committed to chastening political, and if need be, other kinds of authority in the name of rights of individuals. Judges are to have a special, a tender regard for individuals, even when law and principle compel them to find against them. As time goes on, this revised self-understanding will be more urgent for the reason that emergencies, necessities, and opportunities will crowd in on political authority (to confine myself to that kind) that will increase the temptation to encroach. And even without these encouragements to temptation the technological capacities to encroach will grow ever greater and more refined, and will, by themselves, be a temptation.

If the principal function of judicial review is thus concep-

tualized, certain criticisms suggest themselves. (Other criticisms
will also figure when other conceptualizations of judicial review
are made.) I will, by the way, disregard a criticism powerfully
operative, but almost always tacitly: the view that judicial review
is wrong because it obstructs the will of the government, of the
state, majestically conceived, altogether apart from the question
of majority rule. Piety towards government—indeed the very
notion of the State—are antithetical to the meaning of American democracy, which was built in defiance of such piety and
such a notion. Let us be aware of this secret motive in the
thought of some critics of judicial review, and turn, sketchily,
to some pertinent criticisms (guided again by McKay).

It is often said that judicial review in the name of protecting
rights of individuals violates the principle of majority rule. The
late Alexander Bickel, inspired by Justice Frankfurter, based
his analysis of judicial review on this supposed "counter-major-
itarian" quality. The content of this criticism is various and not
always specified with a great deal of precision. Let us isolate
some strands. One argument holds that judicial review obstructs the will of the majority of citizens and substitutes for
that will the will of a minority of citizens. Judicial review thus
violates the high principle of equality according to which each
is to count for one and no one is to count for more than one.
Another argument holds that judicial review means that unelected judges obstruct the will of the majority of elected legislators and elected executives, and hence, even if indirectly, obstructs the will of the majority of citizens. Thus, judicial review
not only may produce a substantive inegalitarian result but is
in itself structurally inegalitarian in allowing the will of the unelected to prevail over the will of the elected. Judicial review is
convicted of being doubly undemocratic. A third argument
holds that judicial review often means that minority or individual interests prevail over the interests of the majority.

I believe that the main response to these allied but separable
criticisms must proceed by way of affirming the idea that the
majority (whether directly or through their elected officials)—
if we may posit its existence for the sake of discussion—have
no right to abridge or defeat rights of individuals. What judicial review may take away from the majority, the majority could
never claim.[3] The legitimate will of the majority is the consti-

tutional will, the constitutionally restricted will of the majority. Judicial review is not a morally dubious or perplexing obstruction. Its mere existence does not engender a conflict of values. I would add a tangential consideration. I believe that the principle of equality expressed in such practices as universal suffrage and eligibility for office, and majority rule, is traceable to the same root as the principle of constitutionalism expressed in such guarantees as are found in the first, fourth through eighth, ninth and tenth, and fourteenth amendments, to the Constitution (as well as in places in the original articles). Perhaps, the concept of respect for persons can be used to name that root, problematic as the concept is. The consistent politics of equality—that is, consistent democracy—is constitutional democracy.

In replying to critics, something can be made of the imperfectly democratic nature of the American political system. It is thought that, since representative democracy is, in many ways, not really representative and hence not really democratic (or only representative and hence not really democratic), the essentially undemocratic institution of judicial review should not be made to bear an especially heavy apologetic burden. My preference, however would be to use that as a secondary argument only, partly because of its reliance on changing circumstances and furiously contestable interpretations of those circumstances.

One aspect of the criticisms especially must not be handled too quickly. That is that judges are not elected. Why should the unelected be entrusted with the work of protecting rights of individuals? Such work is an exercise of authority, and all authority should exist only as the result of contested elections in which the people are given a choice and then choose. The one genuinely democratic moment in supposedly democratic politics—to leave aside the infrequent and localized uses of the power of referendum—is electoral choice. Why profoundly abridge it by reserving to the unelected a significant authority—perhaps, the highest authority? I do not think it will do to say that judges represent the real will of the people as found in the Constitution as contrasted to particular laws, regulations, and acts made by or in behalf of temporary majorities; or to say that over time the people have given their practical consent to the institution of judicial review. I believe that a more theo-

retical argument is needed, and is found in the idea that an
electoral procedure for filling judicial offices is not compatible
with the work of that office when that work is understood as
protecting rights of individuals. The work must be done by
judges, but ideally not by elected judges.

The work should be done by judges because what is needed
is a corrective to the energies that animate laws, regulations,
and acts. These energies are political, of course; that means
they are often the energies of interests. The tendency of ener-
getic interests is not to be too patient with niceties, but the life
of rights of individuals resides in niceties. Only disinterestedness can protect niceties. We expect disinterestedness from
judges: they will not be judges in their own case, as political
interests are, and are for morally allowable and existentially desirable reasons. Within constitutional limits, self-interest is a political virtue. We have disinterested judges to defend the limits
against encroachment. In general, politics is initiative and is
driven by the question, What shall we do? A disinterested reactive agency must exist to ask, What has been done? Has anyone paid an unacceptable cost by having a right abridged or
defeated? Further, if we need judges, because we need disinterestedness, we should not want them elected, because we want
them unbeholden to anyone, to be free of identifiable supporters, to have only one preposession—namely, that in favor of
protecting rights of individuals.[4] I think, therefore, that the
strongest majoritarian complaint against judicial review—that
judges are not elected—can be rebutted.

Election is contrary to the nature of the office of judge, when
that office is defined as protecting rights of individuals. To be
sure, the process of selecting judges is hardly devoid of political
considerations. The hope is that the office transforms the person, once selected.

The life of the law is not logic or experience, but interpretation,[5] the interpretation of the logic of constitutional experience. Judges engage in continuous acts of interpretation. I
would emphasize this banality because I do not want to be
thought so innocent as not to know that the work of protecting
rights will normally—not merely incidentally—engender disagreement as to what protecting a particular right entails on a
given occasion; or whether, in fact, a claimed right is at stake

or is a right at all. I must acknowledge that a misguided or tendentious effort may be made by judges to clothe their dislike of policies in the assertion that a right is being abridged or defeated. The line between policy—political initiative undertaken at the behest of interests—and the protection of rights— a disinterested and reactive act of judgment in behalf of constitutionalism—is not always sharp. On the other hand, especially in a period in which government is continuously active, continuously generative of policies, individuals may be encouraged to claim a right, when actually they are claiming a privilege or demanding assistance. These conditions of ill-definition—in which the line that separates political dispute over policy and judicial determination of the meaning of constitutionally guaranteed rights becomes ever less easy to draw, yet more necessary to draw—jeopardize the account of judicial review I have been sketching. I would locate in such ill-definition the true problematic of judicial review; because of ill-definition the constant possibility of judicial encroachment on the political domain will persist. The encroachment would be troubling whether it presumptuously validated government action or improperly obstructed it. Not *every* policy issue is translatable into a matter of rights. A boundlessly fluid notion of rights is not compatible with the idea of judicial review as protection of rights.

NOTES

1. Risky as it is to invoke Hamilton's authority on the subject of rights, we might say that the essence of the matter is found in his *Federalist,* no. 78.
2. In *Federalist,* no. 84, Hamilton says, ". . . the Constitution is itself, in every rational sense, and to every useful purpose, *A Bill of Rights.*" The *Federalist Papers,* ed. Clinton Rossiter (New York: Mentor, 1961), p. 515. That Hamilton wrote these words in order to discredit the idea of a bill of rights does not diminish the relevance of his formulation. The original seven articles and the first ten amendments are cut from the same cloth. They both affirm the ultimate priority (to speak paradoxically) of individual rights in general, and confine one particular right, the high political right of equality, expressed as majority rule, to its proper sphere.
3. Speaking of the regulation of expressed opinion, Mill says, ". . . I

deny the right of the people to exercise such coercion, either by themselves or by their government. The power itself is illegitimate. The best government has no more title to it than the worst." *On Liberty* in *The Philosophy of John Stuart Mill,* ed. Marshall Cohen (New York: Modern Library, 1961), chap. 2, p. 204. His point on the liberty of thought and opinion is generally applicable to all basic rights.

4. See Hamilton, *Federalist,* no. 78, p. 471. The idea of judge requires either life-long tenure or a limited but not renewable term.

5. See Hamilton, *Federalist,* no. 80, p. 476.

7

JUDICIAL REVIEW, ELITES, AND LIBERAL DEMOCRACY[1]

PETER RAILTON

1. THE PROBLEM OF JUSTIFICATION

The power of judicial review claimed by the Supreme Court since *Marbury v. Madison*—the power to rule authoritatively on the constitutionality of Congressional legislation[2]—has been a source of continuing controversy among democratic theorists. How can a democrat justify vesting in a small, appointed group the authority to overturn the acts of elected representatives or to rule decisively on basic questions about the founding principles of the republic? Although it is possible for citizens to work their way around the Court by various routes—amending the Constitution, impeaching justices, changing the size of the Court, or simply ignoring its rulings—these routes may be difficult and are not frequently traveled. Certainly, an intransigent Court can set a great many obstacles in the way of majority rule, and if the majority is not large, lasting, and committed, these obstacles may be insuperable. What might a democrat's justification of judicial review look like?

We face here a familiar question that nonetheless involves a number of ambiguities not always adequately noticed. Is the democrat to justify judicial review in terms of the Constitution? Its *direct* conformity to peculiarly democratic values? Its tendency to support democratic institutions, albeit through un-

democratic means? Its *moral rightness* or *justice*, whether or not
it is particularly democratic or contributory to democracy? Let
us sort out at least some of these issues before proceeding.

It is an intriguing question of legal and political history
whether or not the framers of the Constitution intended the
Supreme Court to exercise the power of judicial review as in
fact it has done. This question has no one answer: the framers
had various ideas about the Court. Moreover, great difficulties
face any attempt to interpret what particular framers—or state
legislators during ratification—had in mind. I do not think a
democrat would be well advised to look here for justification of
judicial review. The Constitution, after all, is no social contract.
It did not receive unanimous assent originally, and it has not
been assented to by subsequent generations (the notion of tacit
consent being both dubious in itself and of doubtful applicability in this case). Further, it is within our right to amend the
Constitution or call a new Constitutional Convention. So even
the democrat who accepts social contract theory must be prepared to look for justification beyond the existing Constitution
and its history. (A democrat holding a *hypothetical* contract view
would at the least have to ask whether, in the right sort of circumstances, consent *would* be given to the existing Constitution
as amended and interpreted.) Thus the Constitution cannot
plausibly be considered an expression of "the will of the people," or the *ultimate* basis for justification within our polity. While
it is part of the *perceived* justification for many institutions that
they can somehow be linked to the Constitution, deification of
the framers or reification of their words will not make a justification sound if it is not already so.

Looking beyond the Constitution, we may search for a *democratic* justification of judicial review or an outright *moral* justification. I propose to concentrate on the problem of fitting judicial review into a liberal-democratic scheme of things.

This is not the place to launch an inquiry into criteria of liberal democracy. But we need a starting point, and I propose
the following. It seems to me more useful to think in terms of
degrees of liberal democracy than to attempt to lay down necessary and sufficient conditions for it. Let us say that a society
achieves a higher *liberal-democratic profile* to the extent that it
meets these criteria: *popular sovereignty* (in the broad sense that

government policy should be subject to regular and effective public review), *political liberty* (comprising at least freedom of conscience, speech, press, assembly, and association), *political equality* (in the broad sense that individuals do not face unequal legal or social obstacles to exercising influence over public decisions, and that the effects of economic and social inequalities on the *worth* of a citizen's rights to participation—to vote, to run for office, to initiate referenda, etc.—are reduced as far as possible), *political competition* (such that there are no legal or social obstacles to the appearance of opposing groups that may compete for power through attraction of public support so long as they abide by certain rules—e.g., that competitors will not sanction institutionalized violence, that power will be given up and an orderly transition will occur if an incumbent group loses popular support to a competitor, and so on), *political participation* (such that an active role in deciding public matters is part of a typical citizen's life—Mill would add, part of his personal development as well—and no large blocs of the public have reason to feel themselves *de facto* disenfranchised, i.e. excluded from effective participation), and the *free and equal availability of information* (excluding, of course, certain sorts of personal or strategic information). Some of these criteria are controversial, but it seems to me minimally controversial to claim that they are liberal-democratic *values,* partially constituting an *ideal* of liberal democracy that may be more or less fully realized by actual liberal democracies.[3] These values may enter into tradeoffs against one another or against other values, including social efficiency and personal freedom. I do not assume it to be possible to maximize satisfaction of all the criteria at once, and know of no uniquely right way of combining the criteria into a single measure for ranking societies along a liberal-democratic continuum. At any rate, assessments of how fully a society satisfies the various criteria will inevitably be rough.[4] Moreover, several of the criteria can only sensibly be applied dynamically, over time, and thus at a given time may be somewhat indeterminate how well they are satisfied. These criteria attend to *process* as well as *outcome.* Outcome-based criteria cannot be decisive since even an ideal liberal democracy may fail to meet the wishes of its people, while a dictatorship may succeed.

Judicial review of acts of the national representative assembly does not seem at first to be a likely candidate for boosting a society's liberal-democratic profile. It appears to conflict directly with popular sovereignty, political equality, and political competition. Further, the Court could use this power to hinder political liberty rather than promote it. Finally, if the Court is allowed final say on constitutional matters, participation (and self-development through participation) on the part of both the general public and their representatives may be impaired: people may be discouraged from becoming active, even on behalf of liberal-democratic values, if their efforts can be frustrated by a tiny group of judges. Ordinary citizens and members of government alike may fail to develop an adequate understanding of constitutional issues if these become the special preserve of others. Procedurally and substantively, then, judicial review would seem to pose a serious problem of justification for the liberal democrat.

2. A STANDARD RESOLUTION: THE COURT AS BULWARK

For various reasons, democracy cannot be mere majority rule. After all, it is a precondition for a majority's being democratic that the rights of all to an equal vote, to certain political liberties, etc. be respected. If a democracy is to be to a considerable degree a *liberal* democracy, respect for these rights and liberties must come up to a rather high standard. And even when a majority has been formed under conditions of political liberty, equality, and competition, it may yet go on to act undemocratically or illiberally by denying liberal-democratic rights or freedoms to some or all. A *check* of some sort would seem needed if liberal democracy is to be prevented from putting an end to itself through a "tyranny of the majority."

A constitutional court—already empowered to review state laws in light of the federal constitution and to serve as an appeal court in federal cases—might be adapted to fill this need. If appointed for life with unlowerable salaries, the justices could have substantial independence from passing public enthusiasms. If empowered to subject acts of Congress to constitutional scrutiny, they could stand as protectors of basic rights and liberties against majoritarian forces. Moreover, an independent court could also serve as a check against legislative violations of constitutional prerogatives, including the balance of power among branches and levels of government. Since the Constitution does not interpret or enforce itself, and since citizens may lack expertise or be vulnerable to illiberal sentiments while members of Congress may be eager to enlarge their powers by encroaching on the rights or bailiwicks of others, it seems to some a plausible remedy to assign the power of constitutional review to an elite judicial group "above the fray" of politics. Robert McKay represents this Federalist "bulwark" position when he writes:

> The Court has been from the beginning, is now, and presumably ever will be the guardian of the division of authority between nation and states, the preserver of the separation of powers, and the protector of minorities against the sometime tyranny of the majority.[5]

It is of relatively little interest that a constitutional court *might* play a bulwark role, since it is equally easy to say that a national majority *might* check its own illiberal or undemocratic tendencies. Proponents of the bulwark defense must see the Court as substantially more likely than the people themselves or their representatives to play this role.[6] McKay, for example, describes judges as "more independent and more value-free than members of political branches," and (perhaps somewhat contradictorily) says that "the Supreme Court represents a kind of moral force in our society, above the battle, not quite accessible," concluding that "In the practice of judicial review the Supreme Court has admirably served the cause of justice for nearly two centuries."[7]

The bulwark argument does not defend judicial review by showing the Court to be itself a democratic institution. On the contrary, the Court is viewed as a decidedly elitist institution, a moral aristocracy, which earns its place and powers by defending liberal-democratic values that would otherwise be at risk from unchecked popular rule. To abolish judicial review might enhance a country's liberal-democratic profile temporarily, but in the end, the argument runs, basic rights and freedoms would suffer a loss that would more than offset this gain.

3. REFORMULATING THE BULWARK DEFENSE

Democratic theorists of a realistic bent may find the notion of a Supreme Court "above politics" too implausible to serve as a basis for the defense of judicial review. They would point to the political character of judicial appointment,[8] to a rate of turnover on the Court that would, on average, permit a two-term president to appoint four justices, nearly a majority,[9] and to the historical record, which suggests that the Court has been reoriented after a number of major shifts in electoral politics, including shifts on issues regarding basic civil and economic rights.[10] Perhaps the gravest majoritarian threats to liberal-democratic values would come from determined, even fanatical popular movements, yet many have argued that the Court is not far enough above politics to resist such trends more than briefly.[11]

It is worth emphasizing that the argument against the transcendental character of the Court need not be confined to an argument that the Court will tend to follow major electoral shifts. Equally important are the influences of ideologies common to competing elites and other effects arising from the class and cultural background and current status of the justices. Such constitutional provisions as life tenure and unlowerable salaries and such self-imposed requirements as the use of "neutral principles"[12] or "strict interpretation" hardly serve to annul these powerful influences. If a justice's robe is a very imperfect shield against political forces from without, it certainly does not exorcise the personal and ideological forces within. It goes without saying that such influences politicize the Court, and raise questions about whether the Court would in fact be a "moral aristocracy" equally protective of the rights of all.

However, democratic theorists may offer a defense of judicial review that does not rely on excessive claims for the Court's moral and political transcendence. Some democratic theorists have discarded the notion that the people *as such* rule in existing Western European and North American republics, replacing it with the idea that (1) elites actually rule: majority rule is the myth, "minorities rule" the reality.[13] They nonetheless hold that in these republics (2) elite rule is "democratized" and "liberalized" as follows: (a) the elites must compete for popular support; (b) entry into elites is relatively open, meritocratic or electoral rather than hereditary; (c) political freedoms exist to a significant degree—e.g., freedom of speech, the press, association, etc.—and competitors generally "play by the rules"; (d) the elites are heterogeneous and fragmented—no unified elite controls politics, business, religion, and culture; and (e) the electorate itself is heterogeneous, exhibiting a plurality of interests and many cross-cutting loyalties, so that no one group can altogether dominate over long periods. Also typical of such approaches to democratic theory are the following theses about those countries labeled liberal democracies: (3) the average citizen is apathetic—his political involvement consists at most in voting—and his information about the world is scanty; (4) members of the various elites are generally more committed to liberal-democratic values than the average citizen, better informed, and less vulnerable to the appeals of demagogues, extremist religions, illiberal parties, etc.; and (5) the relatively low rate of political participation by ordinary citizens helps the system achieve stability and efficiency and preserve liberal-democratic values. These versions of democratic theory owe a great deal to earlier students of elites and oligarchy, including Mosca and Michels, and to Schumpeter's market analysis of democratic politics. While there is no single elitist theory of democracy, various writers advance theses that partly constitute the view—e.g., analyses of voting behavior by Plamenatz, Berelson, and others,[14] Lipset's theory of "working-class authoritarianism,"[15] Dahl's pluralist or "polyarchical" approach to democracy,[16] and Sartori's "democratic theory of elites."[17] To avoid entanglement in interpretive issues, let us identify (1)–(5) as the central theses of what will be called an *ideal-typical elite theory of democracy.*[18]

Against the background assumption that democracy is majority rule, the Court's power of review appears anomalous and in need of special justification. If instead one adopts an elite theory, the Court finds a place among the various non-majoritarian institutions of a working democracy. The fact that it is not *wholly* isolated from political pressures merely makes it fit more naturally in an elite-democratic framework. Moreover, it can be argued that the Court, among elites, is especially able and likely to promote liberal democracy. It is especially *able* to do so because it has relatively great autonomy and recognized constitutional authority. It is especially *likely* to do so for four reasons. First, it is entitled to assert its power of review only on constitutional grounds, and the Constitution, as amended, is a liberal-democratic document. Second, the Court's actions are subject to careful scrutiny by the press, the legal profession, and the legislative and executive branches of government. It can only stand to lose prestige if its actions are seen as grossly at variance with its constitutional mandate or canons of legal reasoning. Third, since the Court lacks means of enforcement or control over a large budget, it must be particularly careful not to lose its symbolic authority by violating expectations. Similarly, it has a strong incentive to be relatively neutral in mediating contests among the branches or levels of government. Fourth, we may expect that those chosen to be justices are particularly likely to possess that allegiance to liberal-democratic values found among Western elites.

Realism may compel us to abandon any view that treats the Court as above politics, but the "bulwark" defense of judicial review may survive in a slightly revised form. After all, we need not imagine that constitutional interpretation is a matter of transcendental communion with fixed principles in order to believe that the Court will use their independence and authority to oppose illiberal or undemocratic tendencies.[19] Even as a *secular* priesthood justices are able to lend the aura and inertia of fundamental law to their interpretation of constitutional rights, thereby giving these rights an importance in the political process that they might not otherwise possess.[20]

4. A HISTORY FOR SKEPTICS

It is plainly an empirical question whether the Court actually has played a bulwark role, and as a philosopher I am at a disadvantage on empirical turf. I do not mean to suggest that I think empirical issues are irrelevant to philosophy—I believe just the opposite—only that I have no special expertise in these matters. Fortunately, others have done the historical work for us.

Writing in 1940, Robert Jackson, later Justice Jackson, surveyed the history of judicial review, somewhat broadly construed: *Marbury v. Madison,* in which Chief Justice Marshall was able to secure the constitutionally controversial power of judicial review by, in effect, making Jefferson an offer he could not refuse; *Dred Scott,* which ruined hopes for a constitutional resolution of the problem of slavery; the series of decisions on black civil rights, beginning in 1873 and including *The Civil Rights Cases* and *Plessy v. Ferguson,* wherein the Court, which had not played an active role in the *extension* of black civil rights during Reconstruction, came back to life in time to give judicial approval to the *reversal* of Reconstruction; the extended period of "substantive due process" during which the Court showed great willingness to use the Fourteenth Amendment to prevent states from developing legislation to protect consumers, unions, unorganized workers, farmers, women, and children against corporate abuses, but little interest in using the Amendment for its original purpose of protecting black civil rights against state encroachment; the "discovery" of an alleged Constitutional "freedom of contract" and its use to strike down progressive federal legislation; the curious vacillation between denying federal authority when it was directed against trusts, while asserting it when states attempted reforms; the prolonged struggle against federal child labor laws and the income tax, which in the latter case ultimately led to a constitutional amendment; and the concerted effort to roll back New Deal legislation, which precipitated Roosevelt's "court-packing" scheme. He calls the role of the Court in reviewing acts of Congress since the 1870s "one of the most amazing chapters in the history of popular government."[21] Moreover, Jackson argues, it is largely forces *outside* the Court—amendments to the Constitution, the creation of new legal forms, popular pressure on the Court—not judicial self-correction, that have been responsible for undoing those court-created or -protected harms that have been remedied.

Now Jackson has an axe to grind, being an advocate of the

New Deal, but so has virtually every legal historian who has passed judgment on the record of judicial review. It is therefore perhaps all the more striking that his conclusions seem widely shared. For example, a more recent study by John P. Frank concludes:

> The actual, overt exercise of judicial review of acts of Congress has been of almost negligible good to civil liberties, and has probably harmed those liberties more than it has helped them.[22]

Because serving the bulwark function would be a matter of resisting illiberal or undemocratic actions, assessments ordinarily focus on cases in which the Court has *struck down* a law or practice—if the Court *upholds* a liberal or democratic act on the part of another unit of government then its role is not that of a bulwark but of a legitimator. Now the role of legitimator can be of considerable importance, and moreover the Court by its mere presence and authority may be able to influence legislation and practices. However, Frank argues that even when its indirect effects have been reckoned in, judicial review of acts of Congress "has not been of any great significance to the civil liberties of the American people."[23] One must also consider cases in which the Court *failed* to act as a check upon legislators who have trod on basic rights. Frank identifies six major repressions in American history—the Alien and Sedition Acts (1795–1801), the Anti-Masonry period (circa 1830), the Nativist period (climax circa 1850), the Espionage and Bolshevik scare (1917–1927), and the McCarthy era (1946–1956)—and finds:

> The bald fact is that, except for the very narrow points involved in the *Garland* and *Lovett* cases, Congress has never yet passed a statute in a fit of repression which the Supreme Court has invalidated. On the contrary, except for the very special and unusual reaction after the Civil War . . . , the Court has stamped the repressionist acts "Approved."[24]

We should add that when in this century Congress has made repressive use of its power of *inquiry*, the Court has refused to intervene. Moreover, in *The Insular Cases* the Court failed to extend the protection of the Constitution to those under Congressional authority in annexed territories.

It is not difficult to multiply negative verdicts on judicial review. In his 1967 discussion, Leonard Levy concludes that a bulwark thesis cannot "command the preponderance of historical evidence" and thus "[o]ver the course of our history, in other words, judicial review has worked out badly. . . ."[25] Henry Steele Commager, writing in 1943, argues that the majoritarian Congress has been a much better friend of civil liberties and the downtrodden than the Court, and is unable to find a single case in which the Court defended basic rights against congressional attack.[26] Thirteen years later, Robert Dahl, too, is unable to discover such a case.[27]

When we turn to the question of the Court as a protector of the separation of powers, we again find historical assessments contrary to the bulwark thesis. Oliver Field concludes a survey by observing what few would challenge, that the national government has gradually come to occupy a dominant position in the federal balance of power, and that the Court "has both led and been led in this development."[28] Jackson notes that while the Court often used the issue of states' rights opportunistically to block congressional reforms, it seldom has accepted a state's petition for protection of its constitutional rights "upon its own demand."[29]

A full appraisal of the Court's performance in promoting liberal-democratic values would go beyond judicial review of national legislation and include a thorough survey of judicial review of state laws, the interpretation of statute, and so on. While I know of no systematic study of this kind, I gather from the work of a number of commentators that (at least in the last four decades) the Court has made a more credible show of defending liberal democracy in areas outside the sphere of congressional review: its recent work in desegregation, reapportionment, and criminal procedure is highly praised. At the same time, however, its earlier work in these areas, and its overall record on freedom of speech and several other civil liberties, are more or less strongly criticized.[30] But it would be out of place to venture here any overall judgment of the Court's behavior: the issue before us is judicial review as descended from *Marbury v. Madison,* and it seems possible to form a rough, and largely skeptical, judgment on that.

Yet, it may be asked, does this survey do justice to a Court that has in recent years made such fundamental contributions to basic rights? Perhaps the Court has overcome its questionable past and truly become a bulwark? There certainly is no denying that the post-New Deal Court has taken a number of courageous positions on behalf of civil rights. But it must be noted that these positions did not come as a countervailing force against an illiberal national majority; rather, they were consonant with the policies of the dominant New Deal political coalition. This coalition had certain basic liberal commitments on economic and social matters, was under pressure from its own constituency and for foreign policy reasons to promote black civil rights, and stood to benefit politically from "one man/one vote" redistricting and the effective enfranchisement of blacks. Prior to the *Brown v. Board of Education* decision, and partly in response to A. Philip Randolph's March on Washington Movement, President Roosevelt had created the Fair Employment Practices Committee, which put "no discrimination" clauses in most wartime contracts; President Truman had ordered the desegregation of the armed forces; and the NAACP had fought a long campaign against lynching and had organized a series of legal challenges to unequal schooling.[31] While the Warren Court led the way in attacking *de jure* school segregation, its effectiveness was limited by a number of factors, including its failure to call for immediate integration. Its policy on housing, public accommodations, and *de facto* desegregation was more cautious still. The great leap forward in civil rights, and even in school desegregation, did not occur until Congress, under growing pressure, passed the Civil Rights Act of 1964.[32] Most recently, it has been in *upholding* and *enforcing* congressional civil rights legislation, not in checking majority curtailment of minority rights, that the federal courts have been most prominent. Whether the Court will continue to play a leading role in civil rights now that the legislative and executive tides have turned and the civil rights movement has grown quiet, is far from clear. My aim is by no means to belittle the recent contributions of the Court to civil rights, but only to place them in perspective as (1) an exception in the Court's history, (2) part of a large and complex political realignment, and (3) playing a significant initiating, implementing, and legitimating function *within* that new political order rather than following a bulwark script.[33]

5. ORIGINS OF AN ILLUSION

If such good reasons exist for skepticism about the claim that the Supreme Court is a bulwark for liberal-democratic rights and freedoms, why has this view been so persistent? Like many illusions, I will argue, this one is explained in part by the effects of *expectation* and *perspective*.

Expectation. Discussions of constitutional issues too often take the words of the framers as the truth of the matter. If Hamilton and Madison called the Supreme Court a "bulwark,"[34] then, by God, that is what the Court must *be*. If at some point in history it fails to play this role, this is an aberration, not a clue to the real nature of the Court.

A kind of legal essentialism is at work here, leading people to look to the letter of the law and to historical intentions as definitive of the character of actual institutions. Legal essentialism commits what might be called the "anti-naturalistic fallacy" of inferring "is" from "ought," an unlikely mistake to make on the face of it, but one that seems to have been rather tempting in the case of the *legal* "ought." Perhaps this fallacy has special currency in constitutional discussions in this country because even relatively cynical citizens like to think of the Constitution as the "real foundation" of society. Moreover, those most given to thinking about the Court, academics and lawyers, may have special difficulty in resisting the urge to treat words over-seriously. One result has been the prevalence of positive expectations about judicial review that have been remarkably resistant to facts.

There may also be deeper reasons for this resistance than an overdose of school-board-approved U.S. history or a scholarly fetishization of the word. Presumably one such reason is the quite general tendency to see the symbolically central institutions of one's society as legitimate. Most of us regard our society as basically legitimate despite its flaws, and this we readily think of as stemming from the soundness of its "real [read:

symbolic] foundations." In American moral discourse, no notion is more basic than that of *rights,* and it therefore is natural to look to rights as the key to an explanation of the Court's legitimacy. If this justification is linked in the sacred texts of the republic to the Court's power of judicial review, we have the makings of a very powerful dogma. Small wonder each generation debates the matter anew.

Perspective. If pre-existing expectations distort perception, the problem is intensified, psychologists tell us, when a conspicuous and recent example appears to bear out our preconceptions. When stereotyper meets stereotype, the truth appears to be luminously revealed.

The Supreme Court has received an enormous amount of attention in our lifetimes, much of it focused upon the controversial stands of the Warren Court on behalf of the rights of blacks, religious (or anti-religious) minorities, and suspected criminals. The "proximity effect" of this attention, and its coherence with expectation, gives us an unusual perspective on the Court's history.

The popular and scholarly historiography of the Court reveals such a shift in perspective: up until the mid-1950s, one finds a succession of critiques of "judicial supremacy" or "black-robe aristocracy" as an illiberal and oligarchical force in society; after that time, a quite different set of authors launches attacks on the "nine old men" and their "judicial tyranny" on behalf of liberal and progressive values.[35]

Of course, the Warren era is now behind us, but the existence of residual distorting "proximity effect" is shown in the continuing tendency to conflate judicial activism *as such* with judicial activism on behalf of liberal-democratic values. For instance, McKay, in his advocacy of a bulwark defense, draws comfort from the sheer *activism* of the Burger Court.[36] The survey of historical surveys in section 4 makes it clear that the pre-New Deal Court often took activist stances on behalf of positions antithetical to the enhancement of America's liberal-democratic profile.[37] However much the Warren Court may *explain* a positive association in people's minds between the Court and liberal-democratic values, it goes no further to *justify* this association than the ratio of the Warren Court's tenure to the whole duration of the Court. This ratio is low enough (about one to ten) to undermine the contention that the Court has a *reliable* propensity to be active on behalf of liberal democracy.

"So what," it might be asked, "if the Court's contributions to basic liberties come only occasionally and then mainly in the context of social and political movements already favorable to such rights—isn't it better than nothing to have these contributions?" It is a good deal better than nothing, but in assessing judicial review we must look at the debit side as well as the credits. Scholars who have done so largely agree that the contribution of judicial review to basic rights—or to liberal-democratic values generally—has been on balance either slight or negative. Finally, we must also enter into the ledger the costs of judicial review to popular sovereignty and political equality. As far as I can see, it does not seem plausible that the contribution of judicial review to basic rights has been sufficient to offset its undemocratic character.

6. AVOIDING PAROCHIALISM

Making such a judgment involves asserting, at a minimum, a counter-factual to the effect that *without* judicial review, liberal democracy would not have fared worse in this country. I gain some confidence in this counter-factual not only from the record of judicial review, but also from the state of liberal democracy in North American and Western European republics that do not have judicial review in the American form. Perhaps certain liberal-democratic values are more fully realized in the United States than in various Western European democracies (e.g., freedom of the press and information), but other liberal-democratic values seem less fully realized here (e.g., political equality, participation, and competition). It is by no means clear that the United States has the highest overall liberal-democratic profile.[38]

There is an intolerable degree of parochialism in explanations of the survival and growth of liberal democracy in the United States that place great credit in the Constitution, the Supreme Court, the two-party system, or "the genius of American politics," while ignoring that other nations have made similar progress though lacking these features. Of course, the path of democratization and liberalization has been quite bumpy in a number of European countries, but in our own history that path has traversed some extremely rough stretches. The Supreme Court and the Constitution did not spare us a civil war as bloody as any history had yet seen. Indeed, in the crisis over slavery judicial review was a *destabilizing* force.

7. JUDICIAL REVIEW AND ELITE THEORIES OF DEMOCRACY

The actual practice of the Court has general relevance to democratic theory because it may be viewed as an example of behavior in a system of competitive elite rule. While elite theorists do not all agree on the proper analysis of judicial review, it is part of the ideal-typical theory (see section 3) that elites, rather than what is held to be an apathetic and often illiberal mass, are the most reliable friends of liberal democracy. The lackluster performance of the Court over the history of judicial review can hardly be said to *refute* elite theories—such theories speak only of broad tendencies, and the Court is but a single and in many ways singular case. But surely the history of judicial review must be a *disappointment* to elite theorists, particularly since the Court's special position among elites would seem to make it peculiarly well suited to be a bulwark. If any elite is in a position to act as a countervailing force on behalf of liberal democracy, it is the Supreme Court.[39]

Commager, among others, argues that the units of federal government *more* vulnerable to popular pressure than the Court, especially Congress, have better overall liberal-democratic records. Thus popular pressure may be an important liberalizing and democratizing force, and isolating an elite from such pressures, even when that elite is pledged to defend basic rights and freedoms, may *lessen* its likelihood of living up to that pledge.

This should be unsurprising. Popular sovereignty, political equality, freedom of information, etc., where they exist to any significant degree, do not make the lives of elites easier. It is reasonable to assume that governmental and non-govermental elites subject only to oligopolistic competition before an apathetic and poorly informed audience will endeavor to preserve the asymmetry of their power and information relative to the rest of society and to translate it into comparable asymmetries in their own favor in social outcomes. From this modest supposition we may draw the conclusion that we should not expect the ordinary workings of elite politics to generate potent forces for the full realization of liberal-democratic values.[40]

Indeed the conspicuous pattern in American history is that by far the greatest amount of pressure for the full realization of liberty and democracy has come from "below" and "outside" elite-dominated politics-as-usual, including judicial review. The most significant source of such pressure has been popular movements—for abolition, workers' rights, women's suffrage, black civil rights, and so on. As an explanation of liberalization and democratization, pressure from non-elites has the advantage of non-parochialism: similar patterns are to be found in the history of Western Europe. To be sure, some popular mobilizations have been highly illiberal and undemocratic in aim or effect, while others have managed to combine liberal-democratic and illiberal, undemocratic aims and effects in complex ways. "The people" refers not to a homogeneous mass with unified interests, but to individuals differing in class, ethnicity, regional identification, and gender, and these differences have led to wide variation in what has gone under the blanket label "popular movement." Any meaningful generalization about popular movements simple enough to state here would be false. But if we restrict our attention to North America and Western Europe during the last two centuries, a crude hypothesis may be advanced that is perhaps near enough the truth to serve our purpose: while not all popular movements have pushed for greater liberal democracy, the largest source of pressure for such reform has been mobilization by non-elites, and this pressure has been more or less vigorously opposed by existing elites.[41]

Of course, it has been a central tenet of elite theories of democracy that elites are subject to political pressure and competition in the normal course of events. But the point being urged here is that major advances in liberal democracy have tended to involve routes that lead outside the framework of politics-as-the-alternation-of-elites and involve non-elite initiatives.[42] The peculiar contribution of Euro-American elites to the development of liberal democracy has not been in protecting it against proto-authoritarian masses, but rather in showing restraint in a number of instances in the use of the power of the state or the military to repress popular movements (in contrast, say, to Latin America).

Again, none of this should be surprising, and perhaps only the proclivity of certain enthusiastic elite theorists for standing the dynamic of liberalization and democratization on its head makes all this worth pointing out.[43] But there is also a more immediate reason for reminding ourselves of these broad patterns in the past: the bulwark defense of judicial review owes some of its persistence in the face of contrary evidence to tacit or explicit acceptance of central elements of elite theory. It is not difficult to understand why the notion that elites are more trustworthy partisans of liberal democracy than the "mass" has had such a grip on the intellectual imagination: it is common to take a dim view of the "mass," and the twentieth century affords us examples of illiberal and undemocratic political movements with impressive popular support that seem splendid confirmation of our worst fears. But we must not mistake these sad facts for something that they are not, namely, evidence that it is elites after all who are the truly dependable force for liberal democracy.[44] However comforting this latter view may be to those of us who lead the life of the mind, history simply does not bear it out, even in one of its most plausible and venerated forms, the "bulwark" defense of judicial review.

The history of judicial review has bearing not only on the tenability of elite theories of democracy, it also provides additional evidence that, contrary to the hopes of certain eighteenth-century political architects, fundamental social conflicts of interest cannot be transcended in the political sphere through careful design of government or consensus on certain basic principles. It is a gross simplification of the political sphere to see it as a mere reflection of social forces, but it is an equally gross exaggeration to think that politics can make a society whole when interests and powers do not.

Judicial review is not about to go away merely because it has disappointed hopeful expectations. Even those most aware of the Court's failings are reluctant to tamper with entrenched

constitutional practice. This may at times be more of a concession to symbols than good practical politics would dictate, but
if the electoral college can survive as long as *it* has, judicial review seems assured of a long life.

Suppose that one accepts the elite theorists' description of
the Court as one of the many elite institutions that dominate
the political process, but suppose in addition that one doubts
their contention that elites are in practice the political sector
most firmly committed to liberal democracy.[45] What might one
expect or hope for from judicial review? Experience suggests
that one would only be let down if one were to expect the Court
to serve as a bulwark during periods of illiberalism or repression. Indeed, it would seem that in the main one is entitled to
have only the hopes for judicial review that one has for the
dominance of liberal-democratic political trends, if that. But
even in a liberal-democratic political climate there may be special functions the Court might serve through judicial review.
For example, if certain basic rights are supported by a majority
of the people but opposed by well-organized and strategically
placed minorities, legislators may be afraid of the political costs
of affirming these rights. The Court could then promote liberal
democracy by upholding acts that protect these rights, thereby
giving them greater legitimacy in the public eye, or by striking
down acts that abridge them passed by a fearful Congress. A
presidential veto could also serve the latter function, but presidents, like legislators, may be less willing than the Court to absorb certain short-run political costs, and a presidential veto may
lack some of the moral and legal authority of Court action. A
look at history suggests that the Court is unlikely to perform
this function reliably or often, and so those concerned to protect the basic rights in question would be well advised to organize themselves politically rather than leave matters in the hands
of the Court. To succeed in the end they will need an active
social base, not just a good legal case. But it is not overly opti-
mistic to think that the Court might on occasion perform this
function. Perhaps something like the situation imagined here
existed at the time of the school desegregation rulings (although in that instance it was not *national* legislation under review).[46] Such a role for judicial review does not presuppose that
the Court is above majoritarian politics or dominant ideologies,

or more committed to basic rights than the general populace. Far from posing a threat to popular sovereignty or political equality, such Court action would directly promote them.[47]

NOTES

1. This essay is based upon a comment on Robert B. McKay's paper "Judicial Review in a Liberal Democracy," in the version presented at the Twenty-Fifth Annual Meeting of the American Society for Legal and Political Philosophy in Boston, December 1980.

   In writing this essay I have received help and encouragement from more people than I can thank here, but I should mention John Agresto, William Bennett, Vince Blasi, Thomas Holt, Arthur Luby, Donald Regan, Rebecca Scott, and the editors of this volume, to all of whom I am especially grateful.

2. Broadly construed, judicial review also includes the review of *state* legislative actions and state and federal *executive* actions on constitutional grounds. I follow most commentators in concentrating (although not exclusively) on judicial review narrowly construed, since the thorniest problems for democratic theory appear to arise when the acts of a national legislature are subject to judicial review.

3. I do not mean to suggest that the liberal-democratic ideal has always involved all of these elements; on the contrary, contemporary notions of liberal democracy are the product of considerable historical evolution.

4. We can say at least this much: if one society is lower than another in *all* categories, then it is less liberal-democratic. However, more sophisticated measures would be needed for serious comparative use of the criteria.

   After writing this essay, I learned that Robert A. Dahl has used a similar notion of a social "profile" in assessing the extent to which a society meets the social and historical conditions favorable to the development of democracy. Since that is a different question from the one we are addressing here, it is not possible to compare Dahl's list directly with the list I offer above. See his *Polyarchy: Participation and Opposition* (New Haven: Yale University Press, 1971), esp. ch. 10.

5. McKay, "Judicial Review in a Liberal Democracy."

6. It would not suffice to sustain the argument to say that a constitutional court would be called upon to serve as a check *only* when a majority is acting illiberally or undemocratically, for the Court

is able to strike down legislation even when the majority is acting in a liberal and democratic way.

7. McKay, "Judicial Review in a Liberal Democracy."

8. It is difficult to assess just how much the power of appointment has influenced the political character of the Court. One study reports that some 90 percent of appointees to the federal bench from 1885–1955 came from the same party as the president. See Jack W. Peltason, *Federal Courts in the Political Process* (New York: Random House, 1955), p. 31. Of course, presidents have been known to appoint justices with whom they have disagreed politically.

9. Robert Dahl calculates that from 1789 to 1956 a Supreme Court justice was appointed, on average, once every twenty-two months. See Robert A. Dahl, "Decision-Making in a Democracy: The Supreme Court as a National Policy-Maker," *The Journal of Public Law,* 6 (Fall 1957): 282–295. At this rate, if a party were able to hold onto the presidency for three out of four consecutive terms, it would be able to reproduce its outlook on the Court. It may not be necessary to assume that the Senate, too, is dominated by this party; at least in recent years, the Senate has been reluctant to turn back qualified candidates on political grounds.

10. Dahl, "Decision-Making;" see also the more detailed study by Richard Funston, "The Supreme Court and Critical Elections," *American Political Science Review,* 69 (September 1975): 795–811.

11. See for example H.B. Mayo, *An Introduction to Democratic Theory* (New York: Oxford University Press, 1960), p. 199; also, Paul A. Freund, "Review and Federalism," in Edmond Cahn (ed.), *Supreme Court and Supreme Law* (Bloomington, Ind.: Indiana University Press, 1954), p. 159: "the force of judicial review is apt to be felt in delay, not in final veto."

12. It is, furthermore, questionable in what sense "neutral principles" are related to "value neutrality." So-called "neutral principles" are not morally neutral, but rather moral principles of a certain kind. On one interpretation, for example, a "neutral principle" with regard to freedom of speech should make no mention of whether what the person says is "right" or "wrong" according to whomever is doing the judging. To make a fully general demand that principles be indifferent among world views, conceptions of the good, etc. would beg the question against teleological moral principles. Obviously, to beg so important a normative question is hardly to be morally neutral. "Neutral principles" simply cannot be wholly neutral in a normative sense since they distinguish between permissible and impermissible acts.

13. The latter phrase is Dahl's; see his *Preface to Democratic Theory* (Chicago: The University of Chicago Press, 1956), p. 132.

14. Bernard R. Berelson, Paul F. Lazarsfeld, and William N. McPhee, *Voting* (Chicago: The University of Chicago Press, 1954); John Plamenatz, "Electoral Studies and Democratic Theory, I: A British View," *Political Studies,* 6 (1958): 1–9.

15. Seymour Martin Lipset, *Political Man: The Social Bases of Politics* (Garden City, N.Y.: Doubleday, 1960).

16. Dahl, *Preface.*

17. Giovanni Sartori, *Democratic Theory* (Detroit: Wayne State University Press, 1962).

18. Those who have become partly identified with "elite theories of democracy" have differed considerably in where they place greatest emphasis among the various components of the ideal-typical theory. If names must be attached, I suppose that the ideal-typical theory outlined here is quite a bit closer to Sartori's view of things than, say, Dahl's. Moreover, it must be added that acceptance of the descriptive theses of the ideal-typical theory does not entail endorsement of competitive elite rule. Political scientists associated with elite theories have in general been careful to emphasize the *empirical* character of their claims, although Dahl's remark that the American form of "minorities rule" is not "so obviously a defective system as some of its critics suggest" (*Preface,* p. 150) is not atypical. In what follows, I will criticize some of the empirical theses of the ideal-typical theory but adopt others in the process.

    For an extended discussion of elite theories and some of their problems, see Peter Bachrach, *The Theory of Democratic Elitism* (Boston: Little, Brown, 1967), Introduction by Sheldon Wolin. I am indebted to Bachrach's and Wolin's presentations at several points.

19. This is not to say that all of those associated with elite theories have taken such a view of the Court and judicial review. For example, cf. Dahl, *Preface,* pp. 58–60.

20. It is a troublesome problem that the Court's symbolic function might be impaired if the public had an accurate understanding of the extent to which it is a part of the political system. However, the Court is such a potent symbol that it might well command special respect even from those well aware of its political character; certainly this sort of thing is true of a number of institutions in our society, e.g., the leadership of churches and universities.

21. Robert H. Jackson, *The Struggle for Judicial Supremacy* (New York: Vintage, 1941), p. 37.

22. John P. Frank, "Review and Basic Liberties," in Cahn (ed.), *Supreme Court and Supreme Law,* p. 129.

23. Frank, "Review and Basic Liberties," p. 136.

24. Ibid., p. 114.

25. Leonard W. Levy, "Judicial Review, History, and Democracy," in Leonard W. Levy (ed.), *Judicial Review and the Supreme Court* (New York: Harper and Row, 1967), p. 36. Levy does see merit in the argument that judicial review *could*, if wisely exercised (as in *Brown v. Board of Education*), have the effect of "releasing and encouraging the democratic forces in American life" (p. 37) or at least of winning grudging public acceptance of constitutional limitations on acts against "obnoxious or despised members of society" (p. 41).

26. Henry Steele Commager, *Majority Rule and Minority Rights* (New York: Oxford University Press, 1943), p. 53.

27. Dahl, *Preface*, p. 59. The record of the Court in protecting basic rights of minorities might be defended on the grounds that it successfully protected the rights of propertied minorities against various sorts of popularly-backed legal incursion. After all, protection of property rights against the less well-off majority is certainly one of the functions that a number of the framers hoped the Court would serve. However, despite its historical connection with liberal democracy, it is doubtful that property in this sense can figure as a central liberal-democratic right. It surely increases one's freedom to own property, but property occupies a peculiar place in the triumvirate "life, liberty, and property" since even in a fully liberal-democratic society property rights—unlike the right to life or civil liberties—belong by law to but one class of citizens, owners.

28. Oliver P. Field, "State vs. Nation, and the Supreme Court," *American Political Science Review*, 28 (April 1934): 233–245, p. 244. Paul Freund also concludes that judicial power has not served well as a check on national power, adding that it "performs its most useful task in repressing the parochialism of interest at the local level." ("Review and Federalism," p. 96.)

29. Jackson, *Struggle*, pp. 19–20.

30. See, for example, Frank, "Review and Basic Liberties," pp. 136–139. Notice that in such areas as redistricting and criminal procedure, a constitutional court may come into its own as the most likely governmental device for achieving reform. It still may not be *highly* likely to play such a role—witness the long pre-Warren history of bias in districting and of the lack of certain important protections in criminal procedure—and moreover the Court arguably does not need the power of judicial review to carry out this role. However, its possession of the power of judicial review may contribute to the Court's prestige in ways that are important to its ability to operate successfully in these areas.

31. For a description of the role of the NAACP in initiating the legal struggle against racism, and in carrying it on well before the Supreme Court became a champion of black rights, see Richard Kluger, *Simple Justice: The History of* Brown v. Board of Education *and Black America's Struggle for Equality* (New York: Knopf, 1976).

32. In 1964, ten years after *Brown,* only two Southern states had more than two percent of their black students in integrated schools. One year later federal threats to withhold aid on the basis of Title VI of the 1964 Civil Rights Act had raised to six percent the proportion of black students in the South in integrated schools. By 1967, the figure was 22 percent. Statistics from *The New Columbia Encyclopedia,* ed. by W.H. Harris and J.S. Levey (New York: Columbia University Press, 1975), p. 1347. See also Vince Blasi, "Observation: A Requiem for the Warren Court," *Texas Law Review,* 48 (1970): 608–623, esp. p. 615.

33. Similar qualifications seem *less* appropriate concerning the Warren Court's activism on behalf of the rights of suspected criminals, although most of these do not fall under the heading of judicial review. More relevant, perhaps, is the early Warren Court's poor record of resisting Congressional actions that violated the rights of alleged "subversives." It seems to be characteristic of governmental institutions everywhere that the civil rights of genuine dissidents and alleged "subversives" are liable to special abuse.

34. For Alexander Hamilton, see *The Federalist,* No. 78, ed. by Jacob E. Cooke (Middleton, Conn.: Wesleyan University Press, 1961), p. 526; for James Madison, see *The Debates and Proceedings of the Congress of the United States,* comp. by Joseph Gales (Washington, D.C.: 1834), 1st Congress, 1st Session, I, 439.

35. For a sense of the contrasting variations possible on a theme, compare Drew Pearson and Robert S. Allen, *The Nine Old Men* (Garden City, N.Y.: Doubleday, Doran, 1937) or Fred Rodell, *Nine Men: A Political History of the Supreme Court from 1790 to 1955* (New York: Random House, 1955), on the one hand, to Rosalie M. Gordon, *Nine Men Against America* (Boston: The Americanist Library, 1958), on the other.

36. McKay, "Judicial Review in a Liberal Democracy:" "I shall defend the 'Warren Court' *and* the 'Burger Court,' espousing the proposition that they are distinguishable in detail, but not in broad concept of the judicial role."

37. See also Philip B. Kurland, *Politics, the Constitution, and the Warren Court* (Chicago: The University of Chicago Press, 1970), pp. 17–18.

38. Moreover, it is not obvious how decisive a role judicial review, as

opposed to other factors, would play in an explanation of the high points in the profile of United States.

39. This claim could be challenged on the ground that the power of the Supreme Court is more symbolic than real, so that it would be unable to serve as a last line of defense of liberal democracy even if it sought to do so. A strong government geared up to wage a war or suppress "subversion" may not be much deterred by a court ruling, as Thayer discovered when he challenged Lincoln's suspension of *habeas corpus* during the Civil War. And powerful groups opposed to liberal-democratic policies, such as segregationists in the South, may be able to evade a decree that is not backed up by financial or physical force that the Court cannot by itself command. But the Court has proven that it can *obstruct* popularly supported measures (e.g., during the period of "substantive due process") and can help *legitimate* popular reform movements (e.g., the civil rights movement), thereby making a difference to the course of events.

40. The "modest supposition" made here is hardly contrary to the liberal tradition in political thought. John Stuart Mill took a much stronger position:

> All privileged and powerful classes, as such, have used their power in the interest of their own selfishness, and have indulged their self-importance in despising, not in lovingly caring for, those who were, in their estimation, degraded, by being under the necessity of working for their benefit.

From his *Principles of Political Economy,* ed. by W.J. Ashley (London: Longmans, Green, 1926), p. 754 [IV.vii.1]. As Marx pointed out in a letter to Weydemeyer (5 March 1853), it was bourgeois historians and political theorists, not he, who discovered class antagonisms and traced "the economic anatomy of the classes." Madison, for example, wrote in *Federalist* 10 that "the most common and durable source of faction has been the various and unequal distribution of property. Those who hold, and those who are without property, have ever formed distinct interests in society." Of course, both Mill and Madison still harbored hopes for elites and for transcending class antagonisms in society without the elimination of actual class hierarchies. These positions were in some tension with their own theories and with liberal political theory in general (which rejects organic hierarchies and posits a rational, utility-maximizing individual).

The "apathy" of the American public cannot be viewed here

simply as a social "given." A primary cause of apathy, especially among the less well-off, is a sense that politics-as-usual does not provide an adequate vehicle for the representation of one's interests. For a discussion of inequality of resources, class differences in rates of participation, and the consequent greater influence of the well-off on social decision-making, see Sidney Verba, Norman H. Nie, and Jae-On Kim, *Participation and Political Equality: A Seven-Nation Comparison* (Cambridge: Cambridge University Press, 1978), esp. chs. 1 and 4.

41. Crude as it is, this hypothesis is uncontroversial enough to be granted even by someone as identified with the thesis of "working-class authoritarianism" as Seymour Martin Lipset:

> Despite the profoundly antidemocratic tendencies in lower-class groups, workers' political organizations and movements in more industrialized countries have supported *both* economic and political liberalism. Workers' organizations, trade-unions, and political parties played a major role in extending political democracy in the nineteenth and twentieth centuries . . . . The upper classes [by contrast] resisted the extension of political freedom as part of their defense of economic and social privilege. [*Political Man*, pp. 126–127.]

Is there any reason to think that a deep change has occurred in the past few years to invert these roles?

It might be objected that the leadership role often played by intellectuals or religious leaders in popular movements shows that this sort of political activity is just another part of the competition of elites. But this is wrong on two counts. First, it fails to distinguish *status* elites from *power* elites. Second, while popular movements often leave in their wake new hierarchical structures with power elites (e.g., political parties or labor unions), during their periods of formation these movements are conspicuously not part of the ordinary competition of elites, and are greeted as such by existing elites.

42. It is also worth pointing out that the sorts of competition faced by American elites in normal circumstances are not as effective at representing non-elite interests as some elite theorists have suggested. Both political and economic competition are imperfect and oligopolistic. Further, many of the most powerful elites, most notably corporate leadership, are not subject to direct *political* competition at all, despite the fact that their decisions may be as significant in people's lives as the decisions of elected government. The *economic* competition these elites face is quite different in na-

ture from democratic political competition—those with more money *ipso facto* have more "votes," information is highly protected, the "agenda" is quite restricted, and so on. The private sector "countervailing forces" to corporations—public interest groups, unions, consumer organizations, etc.—are in general much less able to influence public policy than corporations, and public sector countervailing forces—e.g., regulatory agencies—have notoriously been unable or unwilling to challenge corporate power vigorously for long.

43. For example, Sartori has written in his *Democratic Theory* that:

> [Democracy] is so difficult that only expert and accountable elites can save it from the excesses of perfectionism, from the vortex of demagogy, and from the degeneration of *lex majoris partis*. . . . It has been said that leadership is needed only to the extent that the role of the people remains secondary. But I had rather say that it is when pressure from below is greatest that eminent leadership is more necessary than ever. . . . [P. 119.]

44. We also must not be too hasty in the conclusions we draw from, for example, the rise of fascism between the World Wars. In particular, we should note that fascist movements drew much greater support from some non-elite groups than others; they were not expressions of a homogeneous "mass" of the kind often summoned up in fearful discussions of the political character of "mass society."

45. The claim being made here is *not* the claim usually tested when a survey is made of the professed views of people from various social classes. Such surveys are frequently cited by elite theorists to support their contention that elites are more committed to liberal-democratic values than the bulk of society. Unfortunately, however, such surveys do not tell us who in society is likely to *act* on behalf of liberal-democratic values; for this we would need, among other things, an analysis of interests. *Prima facie,* non-elite groups have a greater interest in political equality, popular sovereignty, political competition, etc. They also may have a greater interest in freedom of the press, information, assembly, etc., since if these are officially controlled, it is safe to say that it will not be the non-elites doing the controlling. I have no doubt that members of the Supreme Court throughout its history would have scored in the top percentiles of "professed commitment to liberal-democratic values;" it is more doubtful whether they have promoted these

values as vigorously as other, "lower" social groups that would look less liberal-democratic in surveys.

46. For those who think it a basic right, the freedom to choose abortion might be another example. A majority appear to support this right, but legislators have often been unwilling to go on record supporting it in light of the organization and intensity of its opponents. In Michigan, the state legislature regularly votes to cut off public funding for abortions and the governor regularly vetoes such bills, to the relief of a majority of the populace. It is not difficult to imagine a national parallel in which the Supreme Court plays the vetoing role.

47. For the Court to play such a role would of course require that it be willing to reinterpret Constitutional rights in light of changing beliefs and values, but this would not constitute a departure from existing practice.

I would not claim that the role suggested here for judicial review is the only one with any substantial likelihood of occurring that would constitute a special contribution to liberal democracy. See note 30 for another suggestion.

8

INTERPRETATION AND IMPORTANCE IN CONSTITUTIONAL LAW: A RE-ASSESSMENT OF JUDICIAL RESTRAINT

ROBERT F. NAGEL

INTRODUCTION

Since *Marbury v. Madison* the moral and legal authority of judicial review has been justified in part on the ground that constitutional principles were "designed to be permanent . . . unchangeable by ordinary means."[1] Variations of this theme continue to play an important part in constitutional theory. Alexander Bickel wrote that enforcement of constitutional principles by the courts "may meet a need for continuity and harmony in our values."[2] Henry M. Hart, Jr. sought a justification for judicial review in the need for "articulating and developing impersonal and durable principles."[3] Moreover, the persistent tendency to base constitutional interpretation, at least in part, on the intent of the framers also assumes the feasibility of permanent meaning for constitutional provisions. Although much of the legitimacy of constitutional law continues to depend on the possibility of durable meaning, a general proposal that important constitutional provisions can have relatively plain, stable meaning would be met with widespread skepticism among constitutional scholars. Armed with sophisticated understanding about the inherent inaccuracies of written communication and about the demands created by social change, most legal scholars would regard it as naive to suggest that constitutional principles could have or should have consistent meaning through the centuries.

Durable meaning may be more desirable and feasible than is commonly thought. In the first section of this essay, I suggest that skepticism on this point can be traced to the pervasive influence of the legal profession on how we think about the constitution. The second section describes those parts of the constitution that have had relatively constant meaning and that have been fairly consistently realized. I then explore the relationship between heavy reliance on interpretation and the preconditions for durable meaning. I conclude that to an unexpected extent judicial restraint may be consistent with a stable constitutional order.

I. THE INTERPRETED CONSTITUTION

The legal profession monopolizes the opportunity both to present arguments to courts and to render authoritative interpretations. Lawyers, therefore, affect not only what the constitution, as a practical matter, is but also how it is thought about and understood. Our conception of the constitution has been shaped by their instincts and intellectual habits.

Legal training emphasizes argumentative skills. These skills require acute sensitivity to the potential for intellectual uncertainty. Does a provision have a plain, established meaning that is adverse to your client's interests? Perhaps its meaning can be nudged off that fixed point if the provision is read together with surrounding provisions; or, if those provisions do not help, perhaps in the light of other cases, or with the perspective of the most recent sociological data, or in the context of some notion of moral philosophy. Does the history of the provision appear to support the established meaning? Parse the speeches of those who favored that meaning to show that they did not have in mind precisely your client's circumstance. Find the quotation from the atypical framer. Contrast circumstances at the time of the provision's adoption with current conditions.

Despite the common public perception of lawyers, such argumentation is not necessarily sophistic. Effective legal argument can be penetrating: it finds ambiguities because a careful reading demonstrates that the text is less clear than it first appeared, and it locates uncertainties in historical intent because history is rich and complex. Indeed, intellectual sophistication is the main ally of those who see the constitution as a "living document," flexible enough to be useful in modern conditions.[4] But, convincing or not in a particular instance, the lawyers' craft is argument and his milieu is unsettled meaning.

Like the veteran policeman who cannot find innocence in his crime-filled world, the lawyer almost never sees meaning as simple or clear. It is something to be argued about and, ultimately, may seem to be no more than the momentary outcome of argumentation. In short, legal thinking builds upon and accentuates contemporary tendencies towards relativism and solipsism. Oddly, then, those most entrusted with the meaning of our fundamental document are by training, role, and instinct inclined to think that it is difficult to discover meaning. Hence one of the most obvious but least considered consequences of lawyers' influence on our understanding of the constitution is the implicit identification of interpretation with importance.

Because our conception of the constitution is so shaped by argument about its meaning, interpretation seems indispensible. The most familiar content of the constitution is simply a series of judicial interpretations. The power of judicial review, often described as the very centerpiece of the constitutional system, was, of course, created out of complex arguments about the nature and purposes of constitutional government as well as from more conventional textual analyses.[5] Validation of broad national powers was accomplished by structural and contextual arguments that gave the words "necessary and proper" in Article 1, section 8 the sense of "convenient."[6] The most commonly praised aspect of the constitution—protection of individuals' rights against state and local governments—is the product of an interpretive device by which some of the bill of rights are deemed "incorporated" into the fourteenth amendment.[7] The "constitution" that is popularly discussed today consists of powerful reasons why the requirement of "equal protection of the laws," which was surely aimed at racial discrimination, does not actually prohibit many significant racial inequalities.[8] The same requirement is also represented by analyses about whether exclusion of women from draft registration (a matter the framers never dreamed they were addressing) can actually meet the "tests" of an "important state interest" and a "substantial relationship" between that interest and the means chosen for its accomplishment.[9] And so on. A relatively short document has come to be represented by hundreds of volumes of judicial interpretation that purport to set forth prudential and moral principles relevant to almost any public issue. Legal scholars summarize byzantine doctrines of "constitutional law" in elaborate and heavy treatises.[10] The law journals swell with ideas for variations on the complex explanatory and interpretative structures that have come to be the constitution: "A 'New' Fourteenth Amendment: the Decline of State Action, Fundamental Rights, and Suspect Classification . . ."; "Due Process as a Management Tool in Schools and Prisons"; "The Newsman's Qualified Privilege: an Analytical Approach"; "A 'Birth Right:' Home Births, Midwives, and the Right to Privacy."[11]

Absorption in recondite interpretation tends to legitimize the primacy of the judiciary in constitutional matters because judges are considered expert in the intellectual tasks associated with legal exegesis. This expertise—skill at assessing evidence about historical intent, at textual analysis, at harmonizing various provisions and cases, at clear and reasoned explanation—is thought to be a qualification for accurate and consistent interpretation. Public respect for judicial methods, therefore, tends to reconcile the fact of pervasive interpretation with the ideal of enduring constitutional principles. Ordinarily, judicial interpretations are viewed as marginal shifts in meaning that merely adapt consistent underlying principles to new circumstances. This view dramatically understates the extent of change brought about by interpretation. Its currency suggests that uncertainty and interpretative variation in constitutional meaning have come to be largely taken for granted and is, in this sense, a testament to the influence of the legal profession. The simple fact is that the lawyers have steadily and fundamentally altered the constitution.[12]

Major organizational principles come and go. The rule that legislative bodies may not unduly delegate their authority to appointed agencies was an important, effective principle for a few years.[13] Hornbooks now describe it as a dead doctrine.[14] But judges and scholars hint the rule may reappear in some new form in the future.[15] For many years it was established that the regulation of commerce among the states could not be used to displace the police powers reserved to the states by the tenth amendment.[16] Then this provision, requiring that unenumerated powers be reserved to the states, became a "mere truism" that did not affect the definition of "commerce."[17] For more than 150 years, according to the doctrine of judicial review, the Supreme Court was the ultimate interpreter of the constitution. In 1966, it was discovered that the Congress had broad power to define the fourteenth amendment.[18] More recently, the Court has again denied that Congress shares interpretative authority with the Court.[19] For decades the power of judicial review was limited by the separation of powers, which was thought to prevent the judicial department from operating prisons or designing reapportionment plans.[20] Now, judicial power routinely reaches both of these matters.

Explanatory doctrines appear and then fade away. The constitution prohibited "irrebutable presumptions" for a while, but that rule is now discredited.[21] Classifications against illegitimates had to be justified under a "strict scrutiny" standard; then "mere rationality" would do; then strict scrutiny" again; then yet a third standard was created.[22] Indeed, constitutional rights themselves exist and then do not. The rights to contract and to hold property were used to void a range of state regulations, but both are now out of favor and are not significantly enforced.[23] Wholly new rights, like the right to contraceptives and abortion, appear after almost two hundred years of absence.[24] Some rights, like the right to have illegally seized evidence excluded at trial, are non-existent, then exist, then mysteriously exist but not necessarily as a part of the constitution itself.[25] The meaning of other rights changes fundamentally. For some 136 years the bill of rights applied only as against the national government, but since 1925 some of these rights at various times have begun to apply against state governments.[26] The prohibition against the establishment of religion did not prohibit voluntary prayers in public schools until 1962.[27] Patronage systems began to violate the first amendment in 1976.[28] For most

of our history, reasonably vigorous public debate somehow co-
existed with traditional defamation rules, but in 1964 it was
discovered that the first amendment required significant alterations in these rules in order to foster vigorous public debate.[29]
Although since the fourteenth century the word "jury" probably had meant a deliberative body of twelve members and although that was the "usual" expectation of the framers of the
sixth amendment, in 1970 the word was reshaped to include
groups of only six.[30]

Judicial changes in constitutional meaning have not been
confined to recent years nor to courts influenced by the bracing
jurisprudence of legal realism. In 1829, the constitution permitted states to regulate their internal affairs even if the effect
was to obstruct interstate commerce, so long as the state rule
did not conflict with any congressional statute.[31] By 1851, however, the Court had discovered in the grant of authority *to Congress* to regulate commerce a basis for *courts* to invalidate state
laws inconsistent with judicial views of properly unimpeded
commercial activity.[32] Prior to 1918, the constitution allowed
the national government to prohibit interstate shipment of
goods considered by Congress to have harmful effects; however, in that year a conservative and formalistic court was able
to explain that the constitution prohibited exclusion from interstate commerce of goods produced by child labor.[33]

Specifics cannot capture the scope of the alterations accomplished by interpretation over the years. A document that was
originally grounded on the importance of personal industry and
private property has come to emphasize a kind of personal
freedom that verges on hedonism.[34] A document carefully designed to constrain strong national power and to protect valued
local authority now permits almost limitless national power and
regards local authority with suspicion.[35] A political theory that
originally appraised individual rights with some caution and
emphasized the distribution of power through the principles of
federalism and separation of powers has become a theory that
views organizational principles skeptically and overwhelmingly
emphasizes the protection of individual rights.[36]

Whether particular changes were justifiable or not, it is surely
true that durable, "permanent" meaning has not been afforded
by judicial expertise. But why, after all, should the judiciary

seem a likely institution for preserving stable meaning? The skills and instincts associated with the legal profession are not those of a scholar. Despite sober demeanors and rigorous training, judges do not approximate truth in the manner of the detached scientist or scholar. They identify and exploit ambiguity and uncertainty.[37] Moreover, the process of adjudication is invoked only when a legal principle is, according to someone's lights, not working. Thus judges stand at the spot in the governmental system where constitutional malfunctions are most certain to appear and where the need for revision will seem most apparent. Interpretation itself is a process that is necessary only when established understandings are challenged, when some change in accepted meaning is called for. Put plainly, the special function of the judiciary is to change constitutional meaning.

All this, of course, is widely understood but is usually phrased differently: the constitution "adapts," "grows," " is kept up to date," and "lives." So great is the influence of the legal profession on attitudes toward the constitution that what is surprising is not the role of judicial interpretation in altering "permanent" constitutional principles but the contrasting notion that the constitution might have plain, durable content. But if meaning is not confused with interpretation, many constitutional provisions have had remarkably stable meaning.

II. THE UNINTERPRETED CONSTITUTION

Much of the constitution draws its meaning from practice[38] rather than from interpretation. This occurs most clearly when the judiciary, for one reason or another, refrains from exercising any significant enforcement role with respect to a provision. For example, the Court early determined that the guarantee to each state of a "republican form of government" in Article IV, section 4 was to be enforced by the legislative branch; since then the Court has made little serious effort to interpret the clause.[39] Nevertheless, with the exception of a few isolated episodes—when the nation was new, and when military governments ruled in the South during the period of Reconstruction—the norm throughout our history has been for every state to have a republican form of government. This fact is in vivid contrast to the frequency with which such judicially enforced requirements as free speech or integrated schooling are apparently violated.[40]

The meaning for "republican form of government" that is immanent in this long practice is not the kind of meaning with which lawyers are comfortable or much interested. Although its core can be summarized—some division of the government into separate branches, the existence of substantial accountability to the electorate, the impartial application of the laws—the idea is not fully formalized, articulated, or closed. It is a recognition based on everyday experience. Different people might assign somewhat different intellectual content to the same institutional patterns, and it is not clear how much of the pattern is "mandatory." The continuation of the practice suggests that most people would be surprised and affronted by any dramatic shift away from the established pattern and would either oppose a change or move quickly to re-establish the norm. This is probably because most people approve of the core meaning. But some are not aware of assigning any meaning to the practice at all. Some who generally tolerate the practice might raise objections to specific aspects, such as the limited scope and equality of suffrage. And some might in the abstract disapprove of the whole idea. The practice is allowed to continue partly because of habit, familiarity, and a sense of normalcy.[41] In sum, the sort of meaning that emerges from practice is readily distinguishable from precise legal rules,[42] but this does not make it any the less real.

Much that is important in the constitutional system rests on the operation of provisions that gain their content from long usage rather than from legal construction. Congress "assembles" every year as the constitution requires.[43] Despite the temptation of power, presidents routinely relinquish office when their constitutional terms expire. The provisions for replacement of a president after death or during periods of incapacity have never been abused.[44] The rules controlling impeachment and removal of civil officers have rarely been used and have never led to removal for purely partisan reasons.[45] With the remotely possible exception of the formation of West Virginia, territorial integrity of the states has been respected, as Article

IV, section 3 requires. Soldiers have not been quartered in private homes. A census has been conducted every ten years, as required by Article I, section 1, without the aid of the Supreme Court. All the presidents have been older than 35. Although the difference between a "treaty," which requires ratification by the Senate, and an "executive agreement", which does not, has never been formalized by the Court, the ratification provisions of Article II, section 1 have never fallen into disuse.[46] The import of "advice and consent" was determined by the behavior of George Washington and the subsequent presidents who followed his example.[47] Procedures for amending the Constitution have been followed some 26 times without judicial intervention. No Supreme Court decision gives an authoritative construction of the ninth amendment's reservation of unenumerated rights to the people, but that provision has been spectacularly realized in the pervasive appeal to the language of rights in political debate.[48] The judiciary has never restricted the plenary authority of Congress to create and restrict the jurisdiction of the lower federal courts, yet the power has not been used to frustrate the enforcement of constitutional rights. In nearly two hundred years, only once has the congressional power to make exceptions to Supreme Court jurisdiction been found to have been used so as to interfere with the independent judiciary.[49] Obviously, whatever consensus or inhibition prevents alterations in some practices is often subject to challenge. But the constitution represented by all of these practices has been remarkably durable.

Constitutional principles can also emerge from practice when judicial interpretations do not supply specific meaning but merely ratify the validity of past practices. The constitutional process by which Congress enacts legislation has largely been defined in this way. For example, the Court defined a "revenue bill," which under Article I, section 7 must originate in the House, in conformity with legislative practice.[50] Similarly, the definition of a quorum for purposes of enacting legislation,[51] the number of votes required to override a veto,[52] the formalities of the presidential signature,[53] and the intricacies of the use of the veto power[54] have all been determined by judicial validation of political practice.

Finally, meaning arises from practice when provisions get only part of their substance from judicial interpretation, so that practice can independently supply additional significance. The breadth of congressional power under the commerce clause has varied with the vicissitudes of judicial doctrine. But as Herbert Wechsler noted, the basic principle of enumerated powers— that national regulation is exceptional and must be specially justified while state regulation is the norm—is embedded in the political process.[55] Moreover, it has not generally taken judicial opinions to prevent the adoption of a national religion, nor classical bills of attainder, nor the use of dismemberment and other tortures as punishments. Overwhelming agreement about the meaning of the constitution prevents such actions, and this agreement reflects and is reflected in prolonged behavior.

In short, while much scholarly and popular attention is focused on the complexities and surprises of constitutional interpretation, much of the constitutional order is consistently realized and derived from practice. To the extent such meaning is conventionally recognized, it tends to be considered exceptional and dependent on the special character of certain provisions.

It is sometimes thought, for example, that durable meaning is possible when provisions are highly specific and sustained agreement about them is therefore likely. The requirement that a president be at least 35 years of age or the definition of the four-year term of office can be contrasted with larger concepts like due process of law, which "gather meaning from experience."[56] However, if sustained consensus were a function of specificity, one would not expect to find so many general provisions among those that have exhibited consistency in practice: the guarantee of a republican form of government, the definition of high crimes and misdemeanors, the reservation to the people of unenumerated rights, and so on. Moreover, it is largely a matter of choice whether to perceive a provision as simple and specific or as complex and general. The phrase "due process of law" probably had quite a definite meaning to the framers, who used it to refer to certain familiar judicial procedures.[57] The term now seems expansive because we have become accustomed to using it in many other ways. On the other hand, although we do not argue about the meaning of a four-year presidential term, argument is certainly possible. Similarly "narrow" terms have generated considerable uncertainty—for instance, the definition of a majority for purposes of defining a quorum,[58] or the definition of "ten days" in Article I, section 7 during which the president can veto a bill.[59] Might a four-year term be extended in an emergency? Might electoral fraud, economic chaos, or military danger constitute such an emergency? If such arguments seem farfetched, consider that economic emergency figured in the Court's validation of a state law that violated the established, and historically correct, meaning of the impairment of contracts clause,[60] and that military emergency influenced the Court's approval of the internment of Japanese-Americans during the Second World War.[61] Certainly, there is widespread agreement that the meaning of a four-year term ought not be disputed, but that agreement cannot be satisfactorily explained simply on the basis of the specificity of the word "four."

It is also sometimes proposed that relatively fixed content is possible when terms are organizational, when they refer to "governing institutions" rather than to substance.[62] This suggestion is in part a variation on the argument based on specificity, for organizational terms like "election," "advice and consent," or "assemble" might be thought somehow more specific and therefore more capable of generating sustained agreement. But, again, the extent to which such terms might seem specific is more a function of tacit consensus than intrinsic specificity. Although history might well support an interpretation of "advice and consent" that required formal, personal consultation with the Senate, this would seem unnatural in light of long practice to the contrary.[63] The requirement that Congress "assemble" could be interpreted to require increased access by the public. But congressional practices regarding executive sessions are sufficiently entrenched and acceptable to make the proposal seem improbable.[64] Moreover, some of the provisions that have not been subject to interpretation, such as "high crimes and misdemeanors" and the prohibition against quartering soldiers, are substantive. And many terms that have prompted considerable argumentation and have undergone large changes in meaning are organizational—for example, "jury" and the tenth amendment's reference to "reserved powers."[65] In any event, the line between substantive and organizational is far from clear. The census provides the basis for apportionment and might be thought organizational, but, if improperly conducted, a census might be thought to violate individual substantive rights.[66]

Finally, it might be said that durable meaning is possible when all real content is lacking. For example, many of the uninterpreted provisions merely lodge decision-making authority in some institution other than the federal judiciary. The ninth amendment at least validates the propriety of invoking non-enumerated rights in state and local forums. Everyone can agree with that since the nature of the rights remains undefined. It also might be that the Court has approved many practices regarding the process of legislating because the constitution largely entrusts the definition of those procedures to each House.[67] In the same way, control over constitutional amendments and impeachment is left to the Congress. Apparently stable meaning for these provisions is easy, it might be thought, since the constitution merely requires that the relevant decisions be made by the appropriate institution. However, these practices have remained within—and have helped to define—accepted constitutional limits. The absence of judicial interpretation of these provisions has as much to do with effective consensus about content as with any textual requirement of judicial abstinence. Article I, section 5 vests the power to judge the qualifications of its members in the House of Representatives, but the Supreme Court invalidated the exclusion of Adam Clayton Powell on the ground that the House had established improper criteria for exclusion.[68] In the course of its decision, the Court stated, "In order to determine the scope of any 'textual commitment' under Article I, section 5, we necessarily must determine the meaning of the phrase to 'be the Judge of the Qualifications of its own Members.' "[69] In short, the grounds for exclusion from the House were subject to judicial interpretation because the House had acted on the basis of a meaning of the word "qualification" about which there could be disagreement. Analogously, if the House were to impeach a president on the basis of his race, the Court might well intervene. Impeachment, then, has been exempt from judicial interpretation because the House has acted within accepted limits, not simply because the matter is textually committed to it rather than to the judiciary.

A variation of the notion that the uninterpreted provisions lack content is that practice can reflect a consistent "meaning" only when that meaning is amorphous. As I have noted, the meaning that emerges from practice is often not fixed or precise. But meaning need not be formalized to be real. It remains both true and important that effective agreement has consistently existed to the effect that presidents are not removed from office over policy differences, that state governments are organized around basic democratic principles, that Congress "assembles" every year, and so on. As these examples suggest, however, it is true that uninterpreted meaning is usually basic meaning—unsurprising and unexceptional. But that the meaning which emerges from practice should seem obvious merely underlines the extent to which tacit agreement about such meaning is widely shared and firmly established. If constitutional meaning is to be durable, it must seem to be plain to those who are governed by it. Perhaps, uninterpreted meaning is both obvious and relatively stable not because of the special characteristics of certain provisions, but because of the special capacity of practice to sustain effective consensus.

III. SOME REASONS FOR DURABILITY

Practice has important advantages over interpretation for sustaining the sense of shared agreement that can eventually make a particular meaning seem plain or inevitable. These include informality, generality, and caution.

Informality. The meaning that emerges from practice is implicit, more a matter of behavior and habit than of verbalization. Congress simply "assembles" every year without considering the meaning of the word; presidents are not declared "unable to discharge the powers and duties of [the] office" although no one has stated a rule that the incapacity must be extraordinary; the difference between a treaty and an executive agreement is not formally articulated, but treaties continue to be sent to the Senate for ratification.

As novelists tell us with regard to social relations, much can be tolerated if left unspoken that might destroy if spoken.[70] Articulation sharpens and focuses attention. It raises the stakes, provokes argument. Individuals who could not agree that three distinct branches are necessary for a republican form of government might nevertheless find acceptable the practice of organizing state governments around three branches. A representative might consistently vote only for narrow impeachment resolutions but still hold to the expansive view that high crimes and misdemeanors are whatever the Congress says they are.

Intellectual informality decreases the range of possible consequences and thus increases the chances for agreement. A legislator might believe, for example, that the president has no power as commander-in-chief to seize private property in peacetime without congressional authorization. Yet the same legislator might accede to a particular seizure for immediate practical reasons if his behavior were not viewed as a concession binding in future cases.[71] Similarly, it would be easy to gain agreement not to remove a president from office for a relatively minor incapacity, because such a decision would not be thought to have any implications for a later, potentially more serious incapacity. The limited, indefinite quality of informal meaning increases the likelihood that stable practices can develop.

Legal meaning, on the other hand, is verbal meaning. It is formalized in written opinions, specified in holdings, and systematized in explanatory doctrines. Losers are identified and suffer reduced stature. Thus interpretive meaning is hard but brittle. Every decision provokes new argument as those who stand to lose attempt to reverse or narrow its scope. The Supreme Court's famous abortion decision, for example, fiercely embittered the losers and raised the controversy to new levels of visibility. The reach of the Court's decision has been tested in every way—skillfully drawn homicide statutes, onerous reporting requirements, parental and spousal consent statutes, and funding restrictions. As a consequence, the Court's own formulation of the constitutional interests involved has begun to shift significantly.[72] And for the first time serious congressional attention has begun to focus on whether the fetus might be defined as a person for purposes of protection under the due process clause.[73] Stable meaning does not easily become established at such levels of visibility and controversy.

Explanatory doctrines and other judicial principles that favor consistency (such as *stare decisis*) can also destablize consensus. These doctrines tie the decisive moral victory of the winning side to a potentially large number of other situations and thus elicit disagreement. In 1979, for example, the Court held that members of the public had no right to attend pretrial hearings in criminal cases.[74] In practice, criminal trials had been open to the public throughout American history and as far back as "the days of the Norman Conquest."[75] It was debatable, however, whether this long practice had been a function of the public's right or the accused's. In its decision the Court explicitly settled this issue by holding that the right was that of the accused. This holding, as well as other aspects of the Court's reasoning and language, strongly suggested that not only public pretrial hearings but also the well-established institution of public trials might be subject to waiver by the defendant. The apparent implication that the press might be excluded from criminal trials provoked harsh public reaction.[76] In 1980, the Court "clarified" its earlier decision by holding that trials, as opposed to pretrial hearings, must be open to the public.[77] This second opinion added a new specification: judges could still close trials if they made a finding of "an overriding interest" in closure. This new decision promises copious new opportunities for interpretative controversy. It will be necessary to examine what circumstances might give rise to such overriding interests and what other sorts of governmental proceedings must, by analogy, be kept open to the public. Within the space of a few months, then, judicial interpretation had succeeded in jeopardizing the long established institution of public trials, reversing itself, and throwing open a host of new questions that would require resolution. Somehow from the days of the Norman Conquest until 1979, the practice of holding public trials had been secure. Perhaps this was in part because the theoretical bases and precise ramifications of the practice had remained somewhat obscure and ambiguous; perhaps in part because whatever exceptions had occurred were of low visibility and were not rationalized.

Generality. To the extent that it is verbalized, the meaning that emerges from practice tends to be general, a characteristic that helps to sustain broad agreement. That presidents are not impeached for policy disagreements does not settle the difficult question of how to distinguish such disagreements from the failure faithfully to execute the law. Nor does agreement on the general practice have any necessary implications for the dispute about whether "high crimes and misdemeanors" must be felonies. Similarly, the core of "republican form of government" is very general and does not settle many specific questions. For example, does issuance of advisory opinions by state courts so violate principles of separation of powers that it contravenes basic requirements of republican government? But by permitting variations on the periphery, practice allows continuing agreement on the general form of republican government. Because the meaning inherent in the practice settles so little, many can abide it.

In contrast, interpretation concentrates attention on specific issues. Judicial elaboration takes place in the context of a concrete controversy. The demands of legal advocacy make it probable that cases with extraordinary facts will be chosen as the occasion for decision.[78] The same demands require that arguments be uncompromising. Moral issues are put in a highly specific perspective, and principles are tested to their limit. If it is agreed that slavery is immoral, courts will be asked whether unpaid labor in mental hospitals is treatment or "slavery." If most can agree that legal discrimination on the basis of race is wrong, courts will have to decide whether the same considerations require the prohibition of gender distinctions. The illusion is created that nearly everything is subject to challenge, and the inhibition against disputing even core meanings begins to weaken. For example, the principle of enumerated powers was pushed to its limit in the period before 1937 when the Court tried to distinguish the national power over commerce from such "local" concerns as manufacturing.[79] In reaction it became common for serious observers to argue that federalism was an outdated principle[80] and, indeed, eventually the Court largely eviscerated the tenth amendment. Similarly, "due process" safeguards at trial have become so elaborate as to prompt serious and widespread reconsideration of the value of even basic aspects of the adversary process.[81] The right against compulsory self-incrimination has been taken to prohibit police from engaging in what many would see as merely informal conversations with suspects. These decisions have opened public discussion of the wisdom of the fifth amendment itself.[82] If, as the

Supreme Court now holds,[83] nude dancing is protected by the first amendment, can some people be blamed for beginning to doubt the seriousness and the wisdom of the principle of freedom of speech?

Caution. Much of the social consensus that permits durable, "plain" meaning is not necessarily substantive. Rather, it can be agreement that certain issues ought not to be contested. One basis for such an inhibition is a shared sense that a matter is too important, too unpredictable, or too complicated to be made uncertain. To adopt an expansive meaning for "high crimes and misdemeanors," for example, would expose everyone to grave risks by making the occupancy of high office precarious. Similarly, Congress's refusal, thus far, to defeat the enforcement of certain constitutional rights by manipulating the jurisdiction of lower federal courts is partly explainable because of the seriousness and unpredictability of the consequences of jeopardizing important judicial machinery. Organizational terms may generally tend to be exempted from interpretation because they define the mechanisms by which all disputes are settled; effective consensus about them is achieved, then, because of widespread acknowledgement that such basic terms ought not be unsettled for fear that the capacity for dispute resolution will itself break down. Such inhibitions rest in part on a long-term view that is willing to forgo principles for a pragmatic sense of caution.

Judicial interpretation occurs in an atmosphere that tends to minimize fears about unsettling meaning. Lawsuits are framed and decided within the confining perspective of a single case and in the absolute language of rights. The finding of a legal violation "entitles" the victim to relief; the loser takes on the aspect of an offender whose interests and difficulties become correspondingly less worthy of concern. In providing legal content, the court is simply doing its duty. Any harm or uncertainty created by an interpretation is merely a necessary byproduct of the imperative process of defining and protecting rights. Secondary and long-run consequences are of less importance than the immediate protection of the aggrieved party. Indeed, there is something generally comforting about the piecemeal process of adjudication—future uncertainties can always be settled in due time by new authoritative interpretations. The full import of adopting the "one man/one vote" principle or of extending free speech rights to school children or of introducing procedural due process into the authoritarian world of prison administration or of opening government decision-making to the public's "right to know"—all surely will require limitations and modifications, but these (it is thought) can be worked out in future cases. In legal argument the concept of endless uncertainty is made a cliché, "the slippery slope argument," and is routinely raised and as routinely dismissed.

In short, many of the attributes of judicial interpretation that most suggest stability and consistency—the formality, the emphasis on timeless principles and rights, the narrow attention to one small case at a time—in fact work to make disagreement and instability the norm. Of course, the judiciary is not the only (or even the major) cause of American contentiousness, and heavy reliance on judicial interpretations of the constitution is partly a result, not a cause, of the lack of political and social cohesion. But the solution has intrinsic characteristics that exacerbate the problem. To the extent that durable constitutional meaning is a reflection of social consensus, the process of judicial interpretation is in many ways at war with the ideal of enduring constitutional principles.

IV. JUDICIAL RESTRAINT
AND CONSTITUTIONALISM

To say that practice had advantages for sustaining a working consensus about constitutional meaning is not to suggest that all uninterpreted meaning necessarily will be permanent. The negotiated distribution of power between the executive and legislative branches, for example, has shifted dramatically over the years and with it the effective meaning of the principle of separation of powers. Nor do I wish to deny that when changes in practices begin seriously to defeat a constitutional value, judicial interpretation can sometimes educate, restrain, and stabilize. What of importance, then, follows from the perspective urged in the preceding sections?

It follows, first, that the judiciary ought not be in constant confrontation with society. Since the desegregation decision in

1954 it has become increasingly common to see the federal courts locked in prolonged political combat over such matters as achieving racial balance in the public schools, improving mental hospitals, and reapportioning legislative districts.[84] Decisions that dramatically alter social and political institutions— for example, the recent invalidation of local patronage systems as violations of the first amendment[85]—have become commonplace. Moreover, influential theories about the function of judicial review depict the judiciary as properly a lonely institution continuously engaged in a struggle to keep the political branches true to the constitution. As Ronald Dworkin would have it:

> Different institutions do have different constituencies when, for example, labor or trade or welfare issues are involved, and the nation often divides sectionally on such issues. But this is not generally the case when individual constitutional rights, like the rights of accused criminals, are at issue. It has been typical of these disputes that the interests of those in political control of the various institutions of the government have been both homogenous and hostile.[86]

Such views require the frequent exercise of judicial power to restrain other institutions because those institutions are thought to have no disposition to honor constitutional rights.[87]

The belief that the judiciary should routinely confront and reshape society is, I believe, a function of narrowed perception. If the practices that give meaning to the constitution are acknowledged, the capacity of the nonjudicial institutions to sustain constitutional standards need not be viewed so pessimistically. It was, for example, public opinion and a censure vote in the legislative branch, not judicial intervention, that stopped Senator McCarthy's threat to first amendment freedoms. It was public indignation at Roosevelt's court-packing plan that protected the independence of the judiciary. Even the illustration Dworkin uses, the rights of accused criminals, ignores the fact that in the famous *Miranda* decision the Court ordered only the warnings that were already standard procedure among agents of the executive branch of the national government.[88] Perhaps more importantly, the confrontation model ignores the constitutional costs of a routinely pugnacious judiciary. Much of the conflict, resistance, and instability that is evidenced in modern constitutional litigation is simply a predictable consequence of over-emphasis on interpretation as the exclusive source of constitutional meaning. Stable realization of constitutional principles depends upon preserving the kind of tacit agreement that interpretation itself tends to break down.

Second, it follows from the perspective proposed in this paper that legalistic standards for evaluating judicial opinions are too limited. These standards emphasize the internal quality of the explanations offered. Because it is assumed that constitutional meaning should be provided almost entirely by the intellectual exercise of interpretation, emphasis centers on such cerebral matters as the deftness with which doctrine is used or the quality of the moral discourse. Indeed, since the function of the interpreted constitution is primarily to restrain nonjudicial behavior, which is assumed often to be a consequence of wayward moods and passions, popular disagreement has sometimes become almost a sign of proper, even heroic, use of interpretive authority. Thus, *Brown v. Board of Education* is actually a small embarrassment to Dworkin, who has to describe it as an exceptional use of judicial power in that it sustained and strengthened a latent national consensus on the impropriety of racial segregation.[89]

If public practices are not viewed as being separate from and antithetical to constitutional meaning, the capacity of a decision to confirm and to build popular consensus and understanding can be properly valued. But such a broadening of the standards used to evaluate judicial opinions would require some subordination of legal standards and legal power. It is not, of course, predominantly the craftsmanship of an opinion that wins popular acceptance. Timing and the basic result communicate most effectively the "normative premise . . . in the ruling itself,"[90] and that unadorned meaning either conforms to the public's understanding of the constitutional values or it does not. Moreover, common sense and history suggest that the number of occasions when the Court can expect to impose or help build a new consensus are probably few.[91] And, as suggested by the discussion in section III, even in those few circumstances the reliance on judicial interpretation may eventually undercut the newly formed consensus, just as the last twenty years of twisting school desegregation decisions may be under-cutting the consensus on racial desegregation that the Court helped to build in *Brown*.[92] Thus, a more usual role for the courts would be to restrain departures from a core of settled meaning—settled both by the clear sense and history of the constitution and by apparent public understandings. Such de-cisions, by appealing to an existing sense of constitutional meaning, can be effective and stabilizing. But this view of the judicial function does not require routine exercise of judicial power, since most modern issues are not clearly settled by con-stitutional text and history and since departures from estab-lished understandings and practices would, by definition, tend to be aberrational.

A third implication is that judicial deference is an appro-priate way to sustain the constitutional system. The more com-mon viewpoint is that, since the meaning of the constitution is declared and preserved only by the courts, any restraint in in-terpreting and enforcing the constitution is a dereliction of the duty to uphold the constitution. For example, Bickel's well-known proposal that courts should sometimes use technical le-gal devices to avoid or postpone constitutional decisions was attacked as profoundly anti-constitutional.[93] In fact, Bickel himself accepted the premise of such attacks and defended ju-dicial deference and avoidance on prudential grounds.[94]

But the various mechanisms that allow for judicial defer-ence—humility and caution in the declaration of potentially far-reaching new constitutional principles, respect for the customs and mores of the times, consideration for the judgments of the other branches and levels of government, and sometimes avoidance of decisions on the merits altogether—all have one characteristic in common: they implicitly or explicitly share re-sponsibility for giving meaning to the constitution. To that ex-tent, lawyers and their interpretative habits are rendered less influential in determining constitutional content. Meaning can then be influenced in part by other values and norms, includ-ing those norms that are formed by reference to established practices. Deference and avoidance, then, are not necessarily an abandonment of the responsibility to enforce constitutional values. They are the major way that courts, controlled as they are by legal norms, can acknowledge and give effect to the various sources of those values. Deference and avoidance are necessarily anti-constitutional only to the extent that lawyers' thinking must monopolize constitutional meaning.

To summarize, I am recommending that the idea of judicial restraint be re-examined and re-emphasized. The lawyers' aggressive instinct for interpretation ought not be permitted to displace the generous understanding that the constitution belongs to all of us. It can be, I think, safer with us than is commonly believed—at least if ambitious and moralistic constitutional interpretation does not undermine the capacity for durable constitutional government.

NOTES

1. Marbury v. Madison, 1 Cranch 137, 176–77 (1803).
2. Alexander M. Bickel, *The Supreme Court and the Idea of Progress* (New York: Harper & Row, 1970), p. 87.
3. H.M. Hart, Jr., "Forward: The Time Chart of the Justices," 73 *Harvard Law Review,* 84, 99 (1959).
4. See, e.g., Terrance Sandalow, "Constitutional Interpretation," 79 *Michigan Law Review* 1033 (1981); Paul Brest, "The Misconceived Quest for the Original Understanding," 60 *Boston University Law Review* 204 (1980); Stephen Munzer and James Nickel, "Does the Constitution Mean What It Always Meant?" 77 *Columbia Law Review* 1029 (1977). See also Laurence H. Tribe, *American Constitutional Law* (Mineola: Foundation, 1978), p. 816 and passim; Charles A. Miller, *The Supreme Court and the Uses of History* (Cambridge: Harvard, 1969), pp. 189–201.
5. Marbury v. Madison, 1 Cranch 137 (1803).
6. McCulloch v. Maryland, 4 Wheat. 316 (1819).
7. E.g., Palko v. Connecticut, 302 U.S. 319 (1937).
8. Regents of University of California v. Bakke, 438 U.S. 265 (1978).
9. Rostker v. Goldberg, 101 S.Ct. 2646, 2661, 2663 (White and Brennan, JJ., dissenting) (1981).
10. E.g., Laurence H. Tribe, *American Constitutional Law* (Mineola: Foundation, 1978).
11. These titles were drawn, as examples, from *Current Index to Legal Periodicals* for September and October, 1980 (University of Washington Law Library and *Washington Law Review*).
12. For an extended analysis that reaches much the same conclusion, see Sandalow, "Constitutional Interpretation," 79 *Michigan Law Review* 1033 (1981).

13. Schechter Poultry Corp. v. United States, 295 U.S. 495 (1935); Panama Ref. Co. v. Ryan, 293 U.S. 388 (1935).
14. J. Nowak, R. Rotunda, J. Young, *Constitutional Law* (St. Paul: West, 1978), p. 147.
15. National Cable Television Ass'n. v. United States, 415 U.S. 336 (1974). John Hart Ely, *Democracy and Distrust* (Cambridge: Harvard, 1980), p. 133.
16. E.g., Carter v. Carter Coal Co., 298 U.S. 238 (1936).
17. United States v. Darby, 312 U.S. 100, 124 (1941).
18. Katzenbach v. Morgan, 384 U.S. 641 (1966). See also Jones v. Alfred H. Mayer Co., 392 U.S. 409 (1968).
19. The Court insists, instead, that the Congress shares only remedial power. Oregon v. Mitchell, 400 U.S. 112 (1970); Rome v. United States, 446 U.S. 156 (1980).
20. As to prisons, see, e.g., Siegel v. Ragen, 88 F. Supp. 996 (1949), cert. denied 339 U.S. 990 (1950), rehearing denied, 340 U.S. 847 (1950). As to reapportionment, see Colegrove v. Green, 328 U.S. 549 (1946).
21. Compare Vlandis v. Kline, 412 U.S. 441 (1973) with Weinberger v. Salfi, 422 U.S. 749 (1975).
22. Levy v. Louisiana, 391 U.S. 68 (1968); Labine v. Vincent, 401 U.S. 532 (1971); Weber v. Aetna Cas. & Sur. Co., 406 U.S. 164 (1972); Trimble v. Gordon, 430 U.S. 762 (1977).
23. Compare, e.g., Allgeyer v. Louisiana, 165 U.S. 578 (1897) and Lochner v. New York, 198 U.S. 45 (1905) with Williamson v. Lee Optical Co., 348 U.S. 483 (1955) and New Motor Vehicle Bd. v. Orrin W. Fox, 439 U.S. 96 (1978).
24. Griswold v. Connecticut, 381 U.S. 479 (1965); Roe v. Wade, 410 U.S. 113 (1973).
25. The exclusionary rule was first applied to the states in Mapp v. Ohio, 367 U.S. 643 (1961). In United States v. Calandra, 414 U.S. 338, 348 (1974), the Court described the right as remedial "rather than a personal constitutional right of the party aggrieved."
26. For a history, see J. Nowak, R. Rotunda, J. Young, *Constitutional Law* (St. Paul: West, 1978), pp. 411–416.
27. Engel v. Vitale, 370 U.S. 421 (1962).
28. Elrod v. Burns, 427 U.S. 347 (1976).
29. New York Times Co. v. Sullivan, 376 U.S. 254 (1964).
30. Williams v. Florida, 399 U.S. 78 (1970).
31. Willson v. The Black Bird Creek Marsh Co., 2 Pet. 245 (1829).
32. Cooley v. Bd. of Wardens, 12 How. 299 (1851).
33. Compare Champion v. Ames, 188 U.S. 321 (1903), Hipolite Egg Co. v. United States, 220 U.S. 45 (1911), and Hoke v. United States, 227 U.S. 308 (1913) with Hammer v. Dagenhart, 247 U.S. 251 (1918).

34. On the original importance of property, see Bernard H. Siegan, *Economic Liberties and the Constitution* (Chicago: Univ. of Chicago, 1980), pp. 30–40. On more recent priorities, consider, e.g., Schad v. Mount Ephraim, 101 S.Ct. 2176 (1981) (nude dancing), Planned Parenthood of Missouri v. Danforth, 428 U.S. 52 (1976) (right to abortion for unmarried minor without parental consent), Carey v. Population Services Int'l., 431 U.S. 678 (1977) (right of unmarried minors to decide whether or not to beget or bear a child); Stanley v. Georgia, 394 U.S. 557 (1969) (right to private use of obscene literature). See generally, Richard Posner, "The Uncertain Protection of Privacy by the Supreme Court," 1979 *Supreme Court Review* 173.

35. On the kinds of concerns that lead to the adoption of the tenth amendment, see Cecelia M. Kenyon, *The Anti-Federalists* (Indianapolis: Bobbs Merrill, 1966). On the present scope of national power with respect to the states, see e.g., Perez v. United States, 402 U.S. 146 (1971), United States v. Darby, 312 U.S. 100 (1941); Katzenbach v. McClung, 379 U.S. 294 (1964). The suspicion with which the Court views state authority is especially evident in the expansion of federal judicial power at the expense of powers traditionally or textually reserved to the states. See, e.g., Baker v. Carr, 369 U.S. 186 (1962); Elrod v. Burns, 427 U.S. 347 (1976); Griswold v. Connecticut, 381 U.S. 479 (1965); Roe v. Wade, 410 U.S. 113 (1973); Columbus Bd. of Ed. v. Penick, 443 U.S. 449 (1979).

36. See Robert Nagel, "Federalism as a Fundamental Value: National League of Cities in Perspective," 1981 *Supreme Court Review* 81.

37. On the ambiguity of legal categories and their relation to change, see Edward Levi, *An Introduction to Legal Reasoning* (Chicago: Univ. of Chicago, 1949).

38. In his study of the British constitution, Dicey used the word "convention" rather than "practice." Albert V. Dicey, *Introduction to the Study of the Law of the Constitution* (London: Macmillan, 7th ed., 1908). Horwill, applying Dicey's idea to the American constitution, employed the word "usage." Herbert Horwill, *The Usages of the American Constitution* (Oxford, 1925). I have chosen a different word to emphasize, as the British tradition does not, that behavior can define the written words of a constitution. For a different treatment of a similar theme, see Charles A. Miller, *The Supreme Court and the Use of History* (Cambridge: Harvard, 1969), pp. 128–142, 189–201.

39. Minor v. Happersett, 21 Wall. 162 (1875); Forsyth v. Hammond, 166 U.S. 506 (1897); In re Duncan, 139 U.S. 449 (1891).

40. As a rough measure, consider that in one year (1977) 13,113 civil

rights cases were commenced in the United State District Courts. Between 1971 and 1977, the total was 63,227. *Judicial Conference of the United States, Report of the Proceedings* (Washington: U.S. Printing Office, 1977), p. 189.

41. Cf. Thomas C. Schelling, *The Strategy of Conflict* (New York: Oxford, 1963), p. 73.

42. For a fuller discussion, see Colin Munro, "Laws and Conventions Distinguished," 91 *The Law Quarterly Review* 218 (1975).

43. Article I, section 4; Amendment XX, section 2.

44. Article II, section 1, para. 6; Amendment XX, section 3; Amendment XXV.

45. Article I, section 2, paragraph 5, section 3, paragraph 6; Article II, section 4.

46. Louis Henkin, *Foreign Affairs and the Constitution* (Mineola: Foundation, 1972), pp. 173–76.

47. See Herbert Horwill, *The Usages of the American Constitution* (Oxford, 1925) pp. 104–105.

48. For an analysis of the meaning of the ninth amendment, see Raoul Berger, "The Ninth Amendment," 66 *Cornell Law Review* 1 (1980).

49. United States v. Klein, 13 Wall. 128 (1872).

50. Flint v. Stone, 220 U.S. 107 (1911).

51. United States v. Ballin, 144 U.S. 1 (1892).

52. Missouri Pacific Ry. Co. v. Kansas, 248 U.S. 276 (1919).

53. Gardner v. Collector, 6 Wall. 499 (1868); Lapeyere v. United States, 17 Wall. 191 (1873); La Abra Silver Mining Co. v. United States, 175 U.S. 423 (1899); Edwards v. United States, 286 U.S. 482 (1932).

54. The Pocket Veto Cases, 279 U.S. 655 (1929).

55. Herbert Wechsler, "The Political Safeguards of Federalism: The Role of the States in the Composition and Selection of the National Government," in *Federalism, Mature and Emergent* (MacMahon, ed., 1955) p. 97.

56. National Mutual Insurance Co. v. Tidewater Transfer Co., 337 U.S. 582 (1949) (opinion by Frankfurter).

57. Raoul Berger, *Government by Judiciary* (Cambridge: Harvard, 1977) p. 193–200.

58. See note 51.

59. See note 54

60. Home Building & Loan Assoc. v. Blaisdell, 290 U.S. 398 (1934).

61. Korematsu v. United States, 323 U.S. 214 (1944).

62. Edward Corwin, "Judicial Review in Action," 74 *University of Pennsylvania Law Review* 639, 659–60 (1926).

63. See Herbert Horwill, *The Usages of the American Constitution* (Oxford, 1925) pp. 104–105.

64. Id., pp. 175–182.

65. For a complete description of the varying interpretations of the tenth amendment, see Gerald Gunther, *Constitutional Law Cases and Materials* (Mineola: Foundation, tenth ed., 1980), pp. 195–211. On the meaning of "jury" see Williams v. Florida, 399 U.S. 78 (1970); Apodaca v. Oregon, 406 U.S. 404 (1972); Burch v. Louisiana, 441 U.S. 130 (1979); Ballew v. Georgia, 435 U.S. 223 (1978).

66. Young v. Klutznick, 497 F. Supp. 1318 (E.D. Mich. 1980).

67. See Article 1, section 2, paragraph 5, section 3, paragraph 5, section 5.

68. Powell v. McCormack, 395 U.S. 486 (1969).

69. Id. at 521.

70. This is a pervasive and complex theme, for example, in Henry James, *The Golden Bowl* (Penguin, 1980).

71. Cf. Youngstown Sheet & Tube Co. v. Sawyer, 343 U.S. 579, 593, 610–11 (1952) (Frankfurter, concurring). Justice Frankfurter proposed that "a systematic, unbroken, executive practice, long pursued to the knowledge of the Congress and never before questioned . . ." might be treated as a gloss on "executive power." This position, consistent with the recommendations in this paper, stops well short of placing undue pressure on every particular Congressional decision. But it does suggest how even judicial deference to a practice might undercut the development of stable norms to the extent that the practice is thereby formalized into an explicit legal rule.

72. Compare the Court's treatment of the governmental interest in potential life in Roe v. Wade, 410 U.S. 113 (1973) with Harris v. McRae, 100 S.Ct. 2671 (1980).

73. S. 158 ("The Human Life Bill") was introduced by Senator Helms in 1981.

74. Gannett Co., Inc. v. DePasquale, 443 U.S. 368 (1979).

75. Richmond Newspapers, Inc. v. Virginia, 100 S.Ct. 2814, 2821 (1980).

76. Noted in Justice Blackmun's concurrence in Richmond Newspapers, Inc. v. Virginia, 100 S.Ct. 2814, 2841, n.2.

77. See note 75.

78. For a general discussion of the characteristics of adjudicatory decision making, see Donald L. Horowitz, *The Courts and Social Policy* (Brookings, 1977), pp. 1–67.

79. E.g. Carter v. Carter Coal Co., 298 U.S. 238 (1936).

80. E.g. Corwin, "National–State Cooperation—The Present Possibilities," 46 *Yale Law Journal* 599 (1937) and Louis Koenig, "Federal and State Cooperation Under the Constitution," 36 *Michigan Law Review* 752 (1938).

81. E.g., Marvin E. Frankel, *Partisan Justice* (New York: Hill and Wang, 1980). See also John Langbein, "Land Without Plea Bargaining: How the Germans Do It," 78 *Michigan Law Review* 204 (1979); Mirjan Damaska, "Evidentiary Barriers to Conviction and Two Models of Criminal Procedure: A Comparative Study," 121 *University of Pennsylvania Law Review* 506 (1973).

82. E.g., Robert Kaus, "Abolish the 5th Amendment," *The Washington Monthly*, 12:10 (December, 1980), pp. 12–19.

83. Schad v. Mount Ephraim, 101 S.Ct. 2176 (1981).

84. For a description, see Abram Chayes, "The Role of the Judge in Public Law Litigation," 89 *Harvard Law Review* 1281 (1976).

85. Elrod v. Burns, 427 U.S. 347 (1976); Branti v. Finkel, 445 U.S. 507 (1980).

86. Ronald Dworkin, *Taking Rights Seriously* (Cambridge: Harvard, 1977), p. 143.

87. For similar views, see Owen Fiss, "The Forms of Justice," 93 *Harvard Law Review* 1, 10–13 (1979); Martin M. Shapiro, *Freedom of Speech: The Supreme Court and Judicial Review* (Englewood Cliffs: Prentice-Hall, 1966), p. 30; Alexander M. Bickel, *The Supreme Court and the Idea of Progress* (New York: Harper & Row, 1970), p. 86.

88. Miranda v. Arizona, 384 U.S. 436, 483–486 (1966).

89. See note 86.

90. The phrase is taken from Hans Linde, "Judges, Critics, and the Realist Tradition," 82 *Yale Law Journal* 227, 230 (1972).

91. See Robert A. Dahl, "Decision-Making in a Democracy: The Supreme Court as a National Policy-Maker," *Journal of Public Law*, 6 (Fall, 1957), 279–295.

92. J. Harvie Wilkinson III, *From Brown to Bakke The Supreme Court and School Integration: 1954–1978* (New York and Oxford: Oxford University Press, 1979). See also Philip Kurland, " 'Brown was the beginning' The School Desegregation Cases in the United States Supreme Court: 1954–79," *Washington University Law Quarterly* 309 (1979).

93. Bickel's proposals were made in Alexander M. Bickel, *The Least Dangerous Branch* (Indianapolis: Bobbs Merrill, 1962). They were attacked in Gerald Gunther, "The Subtle Vices of the 'Passive Virtues'—A Comment on Principle and Expediency in Judicial Review," 64 *Columbia Law Review* 1 (1964).

94. Alexander M. Bickel, *The Supreme Court and the Idea of Progress* (New York: Harper & Row, 1970), pp. 99, 173–181; *The Least Dangerous Branch* (Indianapolis: Bobbs Merrill, 1962), pp. 68–72.

9

LIBERALISM AND JUDICIAL REVIEW

DAVID G. SMITH

The presidential election of 1980 may well have been a turning point in American politics, forcing liberals to take stock of their doctrines and policies and to ask "What went wrong?" and "Where do we go from here?" In the light of recent controversy over Supreme Court decisions and the prospect of new appointments to the Court, that reassessment needs to be extended to judicial review as well.

"Taking stock" in this essay includes analysis of the historic connections between liberalism and judicial review and of the jurisprudence of the Supreme Court in recent years. In deciding "where we go from here" leading philosophies of judicial review are examined, though none seem adequate guides in present circumstances. In the expectation that both the personnel and the policies of the Court will change substantially, liberals need now to decide what they can both conscientiously urge upon such a court and also defend as "liberal." Those issues occupy the concluding part of the discussion.

I.

For those nurtured in the tradition of Charles A. Beard and latter-day populists, such as Arthur Schlesinger, Jr., the association of liberalism with judicial review jars the sensibilities.[1] In this tradition, judicial review was conceived as part of the system of checks and balances, intended to protect property and ward off the two evils of despotism or popular upheaval. Judicial review was, therefore, of aid and comfort mainly to the conservatives, distrusted and disliked by liberals. Although this perspective has some support in the facts, it is only partly valid and unfortunately works against a more balanced appreciation of judicial review that is important for considering it in contemporary context. Indeed, one insight to be gained from American constitutional history is the importance of judicial review in articulating liberal doctrine along with defensive conservatism.

In the American origins of judicial review, one objective as important as checking power with power was to secure the rule of law through separation and independence of the judiciary. Appointed by governors under Colonial charters, the judiciary did not enjoy tenure or independence. Even when later removed from control of the executive, judges still did not become independent but shared powers with the legislature, which in turn often reviewed acts of courts and exercised judicial functions. Thus, judicial review of lower by superior courts and review by the courts of administrative procedures and of legislatively assigned functions were practices that gave the judiciary an "independent will" as well as establishing a sharply defined separation and balance of powers. To that extent, judicial review contributed not only to checking power, but also to upholding a rule of law and a salutary formality in the exercise of political power.[2]

In early America, judicial review was seen as having a "democratic" function, surprising though that may seem today. Constitutions emanated from "the people." And when courts challenged legislation, especially acts in derogation of written constitutions or bills of rights, this was considered not so much judicial usurpation, as holding a legislature accountable ultimately to "the people," who were the authors of the constitution. Indeed, *Federalist* No. 78 notes, in particular, that the representatives in Congress are not, in fact, "the people" but only "servants" of the people, with a limited and delegated authority. And Article II of the Constitution does not vest "legislative power" in the Congress, but only the "legislative Powers herein granted. . . ." So, in upholding the Constitution, a reviewing court was acting "democratically," for it preserved the original terms of the compact.[3]

In keeping with liberalism, the rights protected by early judicial review were not conceived or applied in a mean or narrowly circumscribed way. The American colonists conceived themselves as governed by the English common law and hence entitled to the liberties and franchises of British subjects—which they interpreted generously and to their own advantage. It was a time, moreover, of confluence of legal doctrine and of adaptation of institutions to it. Thus, the Americans were inheritors of an English tradition of Higher Law, applying it through local courts to their own circumstances.[4] They were legatees of the Whig Revolution of 1688 as well as participants in an American republican Enlightenment. One part of their tradition we see in the Declaration of Independence: asserting the right to revolution following a "long train of abuses and usurpation."[5] But an equally vital aspect of their political ethos is revealed in the Bill of Rights: specific protections, redolent of fundamental right, but intended to be enforced in the ordinary courts of the land.[6]

Judicial review in its original American expression has much in common both with the method and the aims of liberalism.[7] On the one hand, that review was narrowly "guarantist," designed to protect vested rights of property, along with life and liberty. But it also preserved many of the historic gains of classical liberalism: separation of powers, rule of law, and important civil liberties, including freedom of speech and religious toleration.[8] Also of significance, along with doctrines of vested right and obligation of contract, was the enlightened and liberal quality of American law, especially as it touched on rights of property and personality. Judges invoked the original contract, natural right, and "law of the land" to infuse into constitutional law doctrines similar to later substantive due process or equal protection. To take but one example, observe what Justice Washington does with the historically particularist and inegalitarian concept of "privileges and immunities" in *Corfield v. Coryell*. He described "privileges and immunities" as "fundamental principles," belonging "of right, to the citizens of all free governments," and goes on to say that they may be comprehended under the following general heads:

. . . protection by the government; the enjoyment of life and property, with the right to acquire and possess property of every kind, and to pursue and obtain happiness and safety; subject nevertheless to such restraints as the government may prescribe for the general good of the whole.[9]

Prominence is given to property. Yet it is a protectionism that includes liberty and life, and that affirms universality and the fundamental rights of all.

Despite the salience of legal and civil rights in early American constitutionalism, judicial review was not very important either for the federal or the state governments during the first hundred years of the new republic. With the exception of a few great constitutional decisions on the organization and powers of government, such as *Martin v. Hunter's Lessee* [10] or *McCulloch v. Maryland*,[11] federal exercise of judicial review dealt almost entirely with but two issues: obligation of contract and interference with interstate commerce.[12] In the states, use of judicial review was equally rare, and more commonly directed at improper organization and procedure rather than at substantive violations of right such as unlawful takings, impairment of contract, or repugnancy to fundamental law.[13] A few scattered decisions presaged later invocations of due process,[14] but the most dramatic use of this concept, in *Dred Scott v. Sanford,* is generally considered a judicial and political catastrophe.

Judicial review became more important in the period after the Civil War largely because of two great changes. The first was the accelerated transition from a sparsely settled agrarian nation to a growing industrial and urban one. The second was the transformation of American federalism, especially with the adoption of the Thirteenth, Fourteenth, and Fifteenth Amendments. Urbanism and industrialism created the occasion for intervention in the economy by subsidy and regulation. The Civil War Amendments provided the jurisdiction and concepts applicable for review, especially of state activities of a promotive or regulative character.

It is usual, and probably correct, to think of the Court in this era as "illiberal," and to associate its authority with the overturning of the income tax, with "dual federalism" and restrictive interpretations of the commerce clause, and with a marked lack of neutrality as between labor and capital, trade unions and trusts. Despite Justice Holmes's pungent observation that "The 14th Amendment does not enact Mr. Herbert Spencer's *Social Statics*," many feared that it did.[15]

Notable also in the period from 1870 to the New Deal was the singular ingenuity of state and federal courts in devising protections for business matched by an equally remarkable obtuseness to the plight of minorities or unpopular causes. To protect business from regulation and labor from undue "paternalism," the courts read "liberty of contract" into due process clauses. And they invented strictures such as "public purpose" in taxation, and "public use" in eminent domain, to strike down municipal and state schemes of regulation and subsidy.[16] Meanwhile, judicial review was little used to protect minority rights or black Americans, the latter being the putative beneficiaries of the Civil War Amendments. From 1900 to 1913, a period of great judicial activity, over 600 cases arising under the Fourteenth Amendment reached the Supreme Court. Only 28 dealt with the rights of blacks.[17] Inclusion of free speech, religious freedom, and rights of the accused, that by a liberal reading of "due process" might well have found their place along with liberty of contract and various freedoms of doing business, did not begin until 1923 with *Meyer v. Nebraska*,[18] a case in which the First Amendment rights were largely assimilated to those of economic liberty and property, and made applicable to the states.

Judicial attitudes from the Civil War to the Great Depression serve to remind not only that one man's liberalism is another's paternalism, class legislation, or treasury raid, but that liberalism can be served in more ways than one. An arguably "liberal" contribution of the courts during this period was to curb local mercantilism and help promote a national economy and system of regulation.[19] Another was to attack subsidies for business and guild-like privileges of various professions. Such doctrines as "implied limitations" on legislative power, tests of public interest or welfare in police power regulation, and the requirement of public purpose for taxation were, no doubt, used meanly by the courts. Yet they were also important in preserving rule of law and public probity in a time of stressful transition to a new kind of civil society, during which other societies have foundered.[20]

Uses of judicial review in aid of modern or "revisionist" liberalism began extensively with the Roosevelt Court, with 1937 as an approximate date. For most of the next forty years the Court was "liberal" in the new sense. And the judicial "creativity" of that era is properly likened to the first decades of the American Republic in the sweeping change of doctrine and adaptation of law to new circumstance. That surge of innovation and creativity is only now drawing to a close.

Probably the one case that most nearly anticipated the philosophy of the new judicial liberalism was *United States v. Carolene Products,* decided in 1938.[21] The controversy itself was unimportant. It dealt with Federal regulation under the Commerce Clause of an unpleasant milk substitute called "Milnut." Justice Stone, for the Court, upheld the Act, saying that "regulatory legislation affecting ordinary commercial transactions" was not to be held unconstitutional unless "of such a character as to preclude the assumption that it rests upon some rational basis within the knowledge and experience of the legislature." The opinion added, in a footnote, that this presumption of constitutionality might be narrowed where legislation:

1. appeared on its face to be within a specific prohibition of the Constitution, such as the first ten Amendments themselves or as embraced within the Fourteenth;
2. restricts political processes that can ordinarily be expected to bring about its repeal;
3. operates with prejudice against discrete and insular minorities, such as particular religions or races.

Foreshadowed in Stone's statement, not precisely but in large measure, are four important elements of modern judicial liberalism. First is the near conclusive presumption in favor of economic regulation, reversing the favored position heretofore enjoyed by liberty of contract. Second is the preference given to some rights, especially those in the Bill of Rights. Anticipated also is a growing concern with "discrete minorities" and "invidious" discrimination, the beginnings of a "new" equal protection. There is, finally, a hint that some or all of the Bill of Rights might be "embraced within" or "incorporated" into the Fourteenth Amendment.

Most of us would say, "That's the kind of liberalism we understand." Yet in the interests of fairness to other conceptions, several observations seem in order. For some, the version of liberalism articulated by the Court in its preference for the Bill of Rights and civil rights over economic liberty seems almost as one-sided as the *laissez faire* liberalism of the earlier pre-Depression Court.[22] Furthermore, such a philosophy entailed vast expansion of judicial power. With active incorporation of Bill of Rights guarantees into the Fourteenth Amendment and the development of preferred fundamental rights and substantive equal protection, the Court not only rapidly nationalized these civil rights but made itself into a standing constitutional convention for their continuing interpretation.[23] Not surprisingly, conservatives objected. But even among liberal friends of the Court, divisions formed between those who believed that the Court should seek "neutral principles," and those who found justification in the belief that it was articulating "deeper lasting currents" in American constitutionalism.[24] Even conceding that the Court ought to proclaim such "deeper lasting currents" or express our fundamental constitutional morality, other quondam liberals raised the issue of how much of that people have to take, and whether the Court was seriously trying to articulate these currents or simply acting on some prejudice of its own.[25]

The decade from 1964 to 1974 bounded roughly the maximum extension of the new liberalism—about half under Warren and about half under Burger. It was a decade of rapid creation of new "fundamental rights," of welfare and other "entitlements," and of new "suspect classes." Debate was sustained as to whether a "minimum subsistence" was a constitutional right or whether the poor, the aged, children and homosexuals ought not be considered "suspect classes," entitled to the "new" Equal Protection of the Fourteenth Amendment.[26] It was, indeed, a time of creativity and progress, but also one in which liberal jurisprudence seemed perilously close to ideology, lacking a grounding in the law. In the words of one commentator: "The Constitution may follow the flag, but is it really supposed to keep up with the *New York Review of*

Books? . . . 'We like Rawls, you like Nozick. We win, 6–3. Statute invalidated.' "[27]

Despite fears to the contrary, the judiciary proved neither "imperial" nor incapable of self-limitation.[28] Some have argued that the Court is in retreat, though it would seem better to say that the Burger Court has mostly failed to extend doctrine than to negate it. In any event, the Court appears to be temporizing. For a number of reasons, moreover, liberal jurisprudence may have reached some natural limits, at least for the present.

One such reason is division within liberalism, doubts about what is truly liberal in a number of difficult or ambiguous situations. How do we choose, for example, between individual rights and various kinds of corporate liberties: Amish children and the Amish family;[29] blacks and the freedom of association of private clubs;[30] free speech for individuals and the self-governance of the university?[31] Or how to choose between procedural protections and other protective interests or welfare benefits: the right to a pre-termination hearing versus a larger benefit pool;[32] or formal commitment proceedings for juveniles versus an interest in therapy? Even if one agreed with Dworkin that "rights trump policies,"[33] which trumps are highest? or does a tenative and not especially weighty "entitlement" clearly trump other important interests?[34] Many would conclude that "no trumps" might be a better suit, that a reasonable person has no clear test for saying that one interest is more "right-ful" than another.

A number of putative liberals also think that judges may attempt too much, especially in making decisions without considering the difficulties of implementation. The courts have vindicated the rights of blacks, women, mental health patients, and children at times when neither the legislature nor administrative authorities could or would act. But implementation has proven something of a nightmare.[35] A court can decree busing; but it cannot prevent white flight or desertion of the public schools. Nor can courts provide the housing and the jobs that would stem deterioration of the urban ghetto. In a recent case, the Supreme Court could also have decreed the "de-institutionalization" of mentally retarded inmates and their placement in community residential settings.[36] But the Court could not simultaneously lift the local zoning restrictions or mandate the supporting community-based services. Nor could the Court assure that rights for the mentally retarded would not come at the expense of the mentally ill.[37] In Lon Fuller's terminology, these are "polycentric" tasks: ones in which a single decision will have ramifications for many others. These ramifications often entail such tasks as the allocation of scarce resources, and the coordination of other branches of government or public and private endeavor, tasks that some believe are better suited to the legislature or left to private orderings.[38]

Defense of judicial liberalism has been embarrassed by many hard cases resting upon soft jurisprudence. A number of these could be mentioned, especially in the areas of fundamental rights and equal protection: abortion, sex discrimination, and busing.[39] But take as one illustration *San Antonio Independent School District v. Rodriguez.*[40] Here, the Court dealt with a suit to equalize expenditures among school districts, raising the issues of whether education was a "fundamental right" and whether "wealth discriminations" between school districts violated the Equal Protection clause. Justice Powell seems both prudent and correct in saying "no" to both, halting the Court on the edge of yet another vast quagmire.[41] Yet, as Justice Marshall pointed out in dissent, the Court had long been in the business of recognizing degrees of invidiousness as well as fundamental rights nowhere specifically mentioned in the Constitution. Why stop now? Is a "nexus" any worse than an "emanation" or a "penumbra?" Why is "district inequality" any harder to accept than "recent immigrant" as a suspect class? The point is that the alternatives are momentous in their potential impact, yet the judicial decision is often justified by doctrine intervening between the constitutional text and the case law that is scarcely distinguishable from political theory in the broadest sense.[42] And while as a liberal one may like the outcome and even admire the political theory, it is hard to defend the decision as good law.[43]

Finally, there is concern, again among liberal defenders of judicial review, that the Court not only stands on insecure ground, but may also tend too much to represent the views of a particular constituency: lawyers and the academic community, the urban and suburban intelligentsia, and leaders of minority groups.[44] No doubt, these groups are also the most important defenders of liberalism; yet as has been said before, it is a liberalism that has an intellectual cast to it, and is far removed from the sentiments of commerce and industry and from Middle America as well.[45] Some warn that judicial review is vulnerable and that, therefore, confrontation to the Court's authority is dangerous.[46] Others, including this author, are troubled that the Court has tended—at least until recently—to express too closely the attitudes of an unrepresentative, elitist constituency more concerned with "doing good" than articulating constitutional values we can live by.[47] Recent challenges to judicial review have taken a variety of forms, from attempts to remove jurisdiction over school-prayer suits or deny funds for enforcing integration orders, to legislation or constitutional amendment that would repeal the abortion decisions. These warning signals are clear and indicate that for practical as well as doctrinal reasons, judicial liberalism in its present form has reached a limit.

II.

Enough may have been said to support the proposition that the judicial liberalism of the future will be of a different sort from that presently in vogue. The question remains, "Where do we go from here?" Is there a different liberal stance for the Court, one that liberals could urge upon it and defend with conviction? Because of its importance, statement of an alternative needs to be attempted, however inadequate it may turn out to be. Therefore, after an examination of three of the most familiar current appraisals of judicial review, I shall outline such an alternative.

One school would limit judicial review drastically. The philosophy of judicial construction shared by this group—in varying measure and in different ways—is usually called "strict construction," though "documentarianism" or "interpretivism" are terms also employed.[48] According to this way of thinking, the Court should stick as closely as possible to the language or the "original intention" of the framers of the Constitution, the Bill of Rights, and the Fourteenth Amendment.[49] Article V provides for amending the Constitution, if need be, and that is the only legitimate method for changing it. Justice Black stated this view eloquently in his famous dissent in *Griswold v. Connecticut* concluding on the note: "That method of change was good for our Fathers, and being somewhat old-fashioned I must add it is good enough for me."[50] Raoul Berger has also defended the "original intentions," though more with respect to the Fourteenth Amendment and uses made of "incorporation."[51] This philosophy, in a less rigorous and more popularized form, has found favor with a succession of Republican presidents. A closely allied position, shared by many, including Justice Rehnquist, is that the Fourteenth Amendment ought to be closely confined to the intent of its framers and applied almost exclusively to racial discriminations.

The "strict constructionists" complain of two separate abuses: one procedural or process-oriented, the other substantive. On the first score, they attack the tendency of the Court, especially since 1965,[52] to view "incorporation" as a device for continuing constitutional amendment.[53] As to substance, they are skeptical that the Court can or should articulate "fundamental rights," and complain of its frequent resort to "subjective considerations of 'natural justice' . . ." in reaching decisions.[54]

Today, this outlook would seem to have little to do with liberalism. "Strict construction" is almost a code word for judicial conservatism, and its strongest supporters appear to be reactionaries, mostly concerned with doing away with the progress made by the Warren and Burger courts. For the sake of perspective, therefore, it may be well to remind ourselves that in early America this attitude would have been seen as distinctly liberal and "republican," since it upheld the original contract and restricted government to its terms. To the extent, furthermore, that this approach would restrict the courts (and judicial whimsy) and give to the legislature and the states a substantial role in constitutional interpretation, it could also be taken as liberal, even today. As Hans Linde has pointed out, had the application of the Equal Protection of the Fourteenth Amendment to the federal government not been decided by the Court in *Bolling v. Sharpe,* but rather debated in Congress, the benefits for American democracy might have been considerable.[55] In a similar vein, the issue of sex discrimination might also have profitably awaited the outcome of the campaign for ratification of the Equal Rights Amendment.[56]

The argument would seem to support judicial self-restraint, though, rather than strict construction. Underlying the proposition about greater reliance upon the legislature and the amending procedures of Article V are two implicit theses. One is that these procedures are more popular and, therefore, more "democratic." Conceded: they involve more people and to that extent are more "democratic." But being more democratic does not make them more liberal, if "liberal" is taken to include rationality and protection of individual rights. The second assumption is that political procedures would be more educational, that the citizens would derive salutary lessons from them. But there seems no good reason why the citizenry might not be as well, indeed better, instructed by a Court still active but less usurpationist, that is to say, more self-restrained. Surely, the Court helps to enlighten political debate, even when, at times, it interferes with the political process.

Much of the strict constructionist argument is based on a concern with legitimacy. The judges are to interpret the Constitution and not remake it, especially not by free-wheeling jurisprudence whereby they write into law their own political theories or convictions about fundamental rights and equal protection. They ought, therefore, to stick close to the text and seek to achieve in their opinions as good a fit between text and case law as possible. That's strict construction, and that's legitimate. Agreed. But surely not the only kind of legitimacy. Another is conforming to acceptable rules, standards or values: say, a neutral principle, or a deep and abiding element of the American ethos. *If* courts successfully elucidate these principles *and* they are accepted, it is hard to see why they aren't as legitimate a base for decision as that of the strict constructionist. In fact, they may serve us much better than a text written for people long since dead. The strict constructionist really avoids the difficult issue: why and when is one mode of interpretation to be preferred to the other?

The point of strict construction is, of course, that judges ought to be quiet, especially where, in Robert Bork's language, "Constitutional materials do not clearly specify the value. . . ."[57] Properly, the issues then should be left up to Congress, the

President, or the states. If courts stick to this counsel, they will indeed say little, for most of our constitutional debate from 1787 to the present has turned on concepts that had little foundation in the text or clear case law about them: vested rights, dual federalism, liberty of contract, "privacy," "invidious discrimination," and so forth.[58] From the perspective of liberalism, the issue really is whether such matters are decided more rationally, fairly, and with greater solicitude for individual rights with the courts or without, and not whether elected officials ought to prevail. It does not greatly matter whether specific authority can be found in the document.

Others see the role of the Court not so much as articulating fundamental rights or expanding equal protection, as supplementing or perfecting the democratic process. Laurence Tribe has called this approach "process-based," and that term seems apt enough to serve.[59] In basic philosophy, it would appear to share something of Learned Hand's "failure of the venture at hand" approach to judicial review,[60] even more of the *Carolene Products* doctrine of Justice Stone.[61] With some variation among various proponents,[62] the basic idea is that of perfecting a democratic agency: ensuring that minorities are represented, that all are heard, political processes are not blocked, and representative bodies really mean, upon sober re-consideration, what they said.

Process-based theories begin with a well-founded skepticism about judicial creativity and the role of the Court as constitution-maker. We face the seeming anomaly of judicial supremacy in a democratic society.[63] With a written Constitution, though, and with separation of powers and federalism, the system needs an umpire to interpret the rules of the game and arbitrate between the majority and the minority. But what if that umpire frequently changes the rules of the game, and on premises that seem neither grounded in the law, nor neutral, nor principled? Then isn't there a real question whether legislatures ought not have an equal role in determining the meaning of the document, especially since we have already said that the Constitution ought to evolve to meet felt necessities of the time?[64] Indeed, the legislature might do a better job, since it's more contemporary.

The process-based approach accommodates judicial review to

the democratic process in two ways. First, it emphasizes those substantive guarantees—free speech, representation, and the regularity of legislative and administrative procedure—that enhance rather than thwart democracy. Prominent would be, of course, solicitude for "insular and discrete" minorities, whether they be racial, religious, or political. Also prominent, especially in John Hart Ely's version,[65] would be assuring equality of suffrage and representation. Second, this conception minimizes substantive restraints on legislative or administrative power in preference to methods of review that would ask of officials, especially lawmakers, "Do you really mean it?" Process-based theory would emphasize concepts such as overbreadth or vagueness; less or least restrictive alternative; means scrutiny and articulation of purpose; the delegation doctrine; and unconstitutional motivation.[66]

A good many liberals, especially these days, would probably feel more comfortable with a process-based theory than with a jurisprudence of fundamental rights. Process-based theory is consonant with the underlying philosophy of the Constitution itself. Like the Constitution, it is strong on procedure, not substance. Aside from the First Amendment, even the Bill of Rights contains mostly procedural guarantees. In keeping with the view that a constitution gives power as it restrains it, process-based theory seeks to perfect the democratic process, not, to use Philip Kurland's language, to "hold it in judicial tutelage."[67] Furthermore, this approach would excuse liberals from defending some of the more egregious and unpopular judge-made rights, quasi-rights, or semi-suspect classifications of recent years. This theory is strong on the First Amendment, but on political speech rather than obscenity. It would enable us to protect political radicals and racial and religious minorities, without bringing in the poor or homosexuals, aged or children as suspect classes. And it would support due process in criminal justice and administration without commitment to the whole panoply of shakily grounded "entitlements" the Court puffed up and then deflated.

Is this way of thinking an attractive alternative for liberals? One wonders about the symbolism and rhetoric of such concepts as "insular and discrete minority" or "political processes which can ordinarily be expected to bring about the repeal of

undesirable legislation." Not very exciting. Nor are they better
dressed up in more current terminology of "representation-
reinforcing" or "clearing the channels of political change."[68]
The problem is that the Constitution is a political as well as a
legal document. Granted that such an approach to constitutional jurisprudence might make better democratic theory and
even more philosophical sense, would it be understood or ac-
claimed by the populace? Possibly so, but much might be lost
in making constitutional doctrine a comprehensible and enriching element of political discussion. Unlike freedom of religion
or speech, due process or equal protection, this judicial rhetoric
inspires little passion and, most likely, little popular loyalty
either.

Emphasis on process would appear to provide an even less
satisfactory jurisprudence than the "fundamental values"[69] approach it would replace. For it is both more result-oriented and
more dependent upon the subjective values of a majority of the
justices. If we have trouble deciding what are fundamental rights
and why, is there any reason to suppose it will be easier to decide which group counts as a "discrete and insular minority?"[70]
Process thinking indeed exacerbates the difficulty by confounding a ground for intervention with its justification. Protection
against invidious discrimination is confused with perfecting the
representative process. But how define a minority? Women, the
poor, the aged, fat people, homosexuals, and a variety of ethnic
and religious minorities are or have been discriminated against.
Which are to qualify for protection and why? The point, of
course, is that the groups that receive protection are those we
deem unfairly deprived of fundamental rights, *whether or not*
they are *incidentally* unable to defend themselves politically. In
the end, concentration on process leaves us with a jurisprudence even less able to generate reasoned distinctions. Maybe a
swamp is better than a quagmire, but its advantages are hard
to perceive.

Process-based theory would also, as the name implies, get the
Court into deciding not about rights but about the political process: suffrage and the electoral machinery, legislation, and the
administration of programs. Ely states that unlike the "fundamental-values approach," a "representation-reinforcing approach" assigns judges a role "they are conspicuously well situ-

ated to fill."[71] Let us leave aside for the moment doubts that courts would find it politic to invoke doctrines like "unconstitutional motivation" or "due process of legislation," or that they could breathe life again into the delegation doctrine. One worries how well suited judges are to reinforce representation in the light of *Reynolds v. Sims*,[72] *Buckley v. Valeo*,[73] or *Elrod v. Burns*.[74] For good reasons, many constitutional scholars have long argued that these topics should be considered "non-justiciable."[75] There is a danger that intervention might not strengthen the political process at all. In any event, intervention would probably show the judicial process at its worst: deciding on weak grounds, provoking political uproar, and leading to perverse results.

Another candidate for a liberal philosophy of judicial review is called by Ely the "fundamental-values" approach,[76] to distinguish it from the "process-based." Proponents of this philosophy are defenders of the Court, especially of its putatively more "liberal" decisions dealing with fundamental rights or equal protection. Here, there are two main variants. One that we can term the "Old School" would stick to precedent and neutral principles, but says that when the Court must, perforce, be innovative it should seek to express the "enduring values of society"[77] or the "deeper lasting currents of human thought that give direction to the law."[78] The "Old School" sees judicial review, then, as creative and presumably "liberal," but without guiding theory or comprehensive vision. This is the point on which the "New School" differs: the importance of an underlying moral or political theory. What distinguishes this group is the importance attributed to intervening theory, rather than precedent or constitutional text, in justifying a particular decision such as *Roe v. Wade*,[79] *Shapiro v. Thompson*,[80] or *Regents v. Bakke*.[81] For some, the argument or implication is that moral or political theory should be taken more seriously, especially the political theory of John Rawls. For Ronald Dworkin, the justification of a decision *is* a political theory: the theory that best decides the case, fits with the "constitutional scheme as a whole,"[82] and also justifies the other decisions the judge proposes to make.[83]

Leaving aside for the moment the "Old School," the question is whether the "New School" of "fundamental-value" theorists would be a good bet for contemporary liberals seeking a new philosophy of judicial review. Implicitly, much has already been said to indicate that it would not, but perhaps a few additional observations are in order.

A realistic point is that going for "New School" jurisprudence would simply make matters politically worse for the Supreme Court and for liberal principles of judicial review. Judges armed with a systematic political theory seem too much like Learned Hand's "bevy of Platonic Guardians," and it is notable that those justices who seem to have a theory—say, Warren, Brennan, or Rehnquist—are often distrusted or condemned as "result-oriented" or lacking in judicial temperament. For them to become and, further, *to appear to become* more definite and self-conscious, especially with the aid of scholarly doctrines about fundamental rights and the political theory of the Constitution, would likely exacerbate criticism of the Court. We already have enough complaints about the tendentious quality of decisions and views that the Court speaks for an unrepresentative elite.

But surely, one might say, clarification of our thinking about fundamental values is always in order. As noted above, contemporary liberal jurisprudence is much vexed by issues of individual versus corporate liberty, the truly worthwhile core of free speech as opposed to abuses, what to do about "entitlements," and so forth. Perhaps theoretical analysis would help. But the trouble with much fundamental-value literature is that it *is* constitutional theory—i.e., it relates the case in hand not so much to precedent or text or to constituent and analytically primitive concepts, but to a theory of the Constitution. It is less a disinterested inquiry into the moral or conceptual foundation of rights than the presentation of plausible alternatives for action, containing within that analysis advocacy of the relevant values. What troubles, as with policy analysis generally, is the issue of who is to decide the alternatives, package the relevant variables, and write in the implicit value judgments.[84] In other words, if between the case in hand and the living Constitution a large body of intervening doctrine relating fundamental values to our governmental institutions is needed,[85] then we properly expect the courts and the judges to develop that doctrine for themselves and case-by-case, not take it over wholesale and ready-made from lawyers, economists, or political theorists.

There is still the question of whether and how the Justices should themselves discover or invent fundamental rights, deliberately and presumably with theoretical forethought. Should the Justices make it their business to define and provide a conceptual and theoretical foundation for free speech, "privacy," substantive Equal Protection, or "entitlements?" In some landmark decisions, they have come close to doing this. Examples would be Frankfurter in *U.S. v. Rabinowitz*,[86] Douglas in *Griswold v. Connecticut*,[87] Brennan in *New York Times v. Sullivan*,[88] or Marshall, dissenting, in *Rodriguez*.[89] Here, the Justices went beyond precedent and emergent doctrine. In a sense, they anticipated rights and sought theroetical foundations for them.

The usual argument against this kind of endeavor is that judges aren't always good prophets and when they aren't you are stuck.[90] On this point, the evidence of the last forty yars is mixed. But the Supreme Court can, by this evidence, do a reasonably good job of stating fundamental rights and developing viable paths of constitutional growth; if they blunder, bad precedents may be "distinguished" or mitigated.

The narrow point at issue, now, is whether judges should seek to "anticipate" our rights, define such rights when they are emergent and as yet inchoate. This is essentially a question of judicial creativity, and of how much is desirable. No doubt, a leap ahead is sometimes justified by events.[91] But against a large amount of creativity one could argue that the "open texture" of the Constitution is an advantage. The vague clauses and concepts permit an accommodation and a casuistry that adapt the law to "felt necessities" and the unpredictability of life. Deliberately to anticipate rights is not only to risk embarrassment, but to lose pragmatic flexibility.

Second, on the advisability of anticipating rights, concept or theory in this area may well come late and in a fragmentary way that eludes closure. The notion of "privacy" is a case in point. It developed from a number of sources, over many years.[92] It has proven to be both creative and protean. Yet, in various applications, for instance with respect to the First and the Fourth Amendments, both the concept and the boundaries of privacy have resisted final statement. Justice Douglas's bold leap toward a general statement and conceptual closure in *Griswold v. Connecticut* said too much and too soon. Clarity and precision are likely to be long in coming. Thus the dangers are, on the one hand, premature statement that risks fatuousness; on the other, a theory that comes late, answers problems we no longer face, made the more awkward by its very elegance.

None of these approaches—strict constructionist, process-based, or fundamental-values—seem to be adequate as a philosophy of judicial review. More will be said, later, about the "Old School" of fundamental-values jurisprudence. And the task of outlining a defensible approach to judicial liberalism remains. As a prelude, though, a few observations about the contemporary political scene are needed.

Whether the Supreme Court follows the election returns or not, those concerned with constitutional jurisprudence of the future can hardly ignore the presidential election of 1980. One justice (Stewart) has already been replaced and five more are prospects for retirement in the next few years. Moreover, American domestic politics seem likely not only to shift from left to right, but also to undergo major changes in the scope and method of public action, raising a variety of new constitutional issues. Both the personnel of the Court and its political environment could change more drastically than at any time since 1937.

In the large, most of the constitutional jurisprudence of an era grows out of the major political issues: the Great Depression; war and conscription; domestic repression; civil rights; the environment and consumerism and so forth. The justices do not make constitutional law in general; they make it in dealing with substantive disputes. With this in mind, it may be useful to anticipate the coming issues.

With the caveat that prophesies are often wrong, four areas have been identified that seem likely to generate constitutional litigation:

1. Defendants' rights: arising from attempts to deal with "crime in the streets," organized crime, and delinquency.
2. Speech, association, and religion: including freedom of religion and establishment issues, pornography, commercial speech, academic freedom and free association.
3. "Entitlements" and substantive equal protection: decline of affirmative action, of job-associated remedies and

protections; remedies against, rather than for, the poor.
4. Deregulation and devolution: "deregulation" of business; decline of environmentalism and consumerism; New Federalism and shifting responsibility for categorical services.

Some liberals inspecting this list would be inclined to say "fight it out" on the doctrinal lines already established. Yet the issues likely to arise in the near future will perplex the judge who is "liberal" but also concerned to be impartial, principled, and mindful of the appropriate limits of the judicial process. What, for instance, should such a judge say about preventive detention of the hardened criminal? About the administrative power of schools to quell disturbances, for instance, resulting from extremist political activities? About investigations of the narcotics traffic or racketeering in the trade union movement? About a fiscally constrained state's attempt to collect from deserting fathers? About limiting standing or remedies for product liability suits, environmental impact statements, accident or malpractice litigation? These are disputes about rights or liberties at the margin, within a zone of doubt where reasonable men can well disagree, and where courts arguably should defer to administrators or to the legislature.

Probably much constitutional dispute will be about what matters are appropriate for government intervention, either for paternalistic reasons or to protect some common interest. Thus, intervention will be directed more at crime and morality and less at economic externalities or welfare benefits. Some, like Robert Bork, deny that, absent a constitutional text, there is any principled way for a Supreme Court Justice to choose between one form of intervention and another: to declare "that sexual gratification is any nobler than economic gratification."[93] His arresting comparison of "gratifications" does make a point important in the present context: that the "preferred position" of First Amendment guarantees over economic liberties or community interests will be increasingly questioned; that "entitlements" and the intermediate level of Equal Protection will probably erode; and that, on the procedural side, the readily available review and sweeping class-action suits that supported administrative and judicial intervention to regulate the economy will be restricted. That would seem to be much of the historic significance of the election of 1980: a swing toward conservatism, with a reversion, in part, to an earlier form of American "liberalism."

On the assumption that the future holds much challenging and reshaping of existing rights, what is a viable conception of judicial review, defensible both as liberal and as realistic given this prospect? In large measure, the answer is compounded of theories already examined: a conception of judicial review that is in part "process-based" and in part a "fundamental-values" approach, though of the "Old School" variety.

One kind of perplexity arises in areas that are genuinely in doubt, where, for instance, a justice is trying to decide about a law or regulation that pits an important economic, administrative, or community interest against another personal or group interest that, for whatever reasons, he is inclined to consider a "constitutional right" but isn't sure how important or compelling it is. It is in this zone of doubt that the process-based theory can be of primary use, by raising doubt without dogmatically asserting the substantive interest or right. Here, three methods can be applied in roughly ascending order of stringency. These are (1) intensified means-end scrutiny; (2) articulate weighing and balancing; and (3) insistence upon a less restrictive alternative.

Intensified means-end scrutiny[94] makes the most of a doctrine that has always been good constitutional law: that legislation is valid if reasonably related to a legitimate legislative end. What this approach does is to take the doctrine seriously, avoiding either the extreme of strict scrutiny or hypothetical rationalizations by the courts of legislative purposes or of delegations to administrative bodies. Means-end scrutiny is traditionally an activity that judges can do well. It would be useful for vague statutes, overbroad delegations, for the "intermediate tier" of Equal Protection, and "important" personal interests, such as "entitlements." It has the further merit of not making an arbitrary distinction between liberty and property interests.[95] Also, means-end scrutiny would enable the courts to exercise a suspensive veto over legislation without denying the legitimacy of the legislative end of the sincerity of motives, and without bringing the courts into direct confrontation with the elected branch of government.[96]

Articulate weighing and balancing is especially appropriate for situations in which an important personal or corporate interest, on the one side, confronts a complex or interdependent set of regulatory objectives on the other. Welfare entitlements, environmental regulation, or interstate taxation are examples. Articulate weighing and balancing would entail an analysis to determine the elements that are to have weight, relating them to the regulative task as a whole, and giving a rationally enunciated decision as to how the scales tip.[97] The point of the method is that it requires a systematic examination or re-examination of the various interests at stake. Where notions about rights are in flux or where the rights involved may be affected in complicated or indeterminate ways by regulatory changes, such a method would seem not only useful, but acceptable to fair-minded persons whatever their politics.

Requiring a less restrictive alternative, especially where readily available, would seem particularly appropriate as government activity begins to trench upon more "fundamental" rights, especially freedom of speech or religion and other personal liberties. In these areas, deprivations are often severe and direct. Furthermore, the consequences of intervention are hard to judge. In the economic sphere, such a constraint—especially if read as "least" rather than "less" restrictive—could become an excuse for injudicious meddling in administration.[98] But in the area of First Amendment rights and due process, liberty it is both well established and lends itself to common-sense application. It might, for example, have value in enabling the courts to sort out some vexed problems of commercial speech or pornography, meanwhile preserving essential First Amendment guarantees and allowing the assertion of important community interests.

The prescription derived from "process" theories of judicial review can provide a way to query legislation and to temporize where liberal values are threatened. But it says nothing about fundamental values as such, and we are not likely to do without them for long. Americans expect the Court to deal with these values, however much they may disagree about what they are.

And the times at which judicial philosophies have clashed have typically been periods of creativity, not passivity. So, it behooves liberals to have a position on fundamental values that they can conscientiously and effectively defend.

Basic to liberal philosophy and the Constitution are a number of "core rights" of personhood and citizenship, such as free speech, right to counsel, suffrage, and so forth. These rights have been greatly extended through a liberal philosophy of incorporation and Fourteenth Amendment interpretation. They have also acquired a baggage of emanations, penumbras, and breathing space along with auxiliary doctrines meant to give them "substance and reality" that arguably are not necessary constituents of these rights. This ambitious elaboration of rights and the preferred position doctrine that has supported it are now challenged. From the liberal perspective, this is the gravest issue of all, for these are the rights most in need of protection and assurance of continuing vitality.

In defending such rights liberals should recognize that their fundamental values are grounded in "constitutional materials"[99] of greatly differing quality. Some such values are supported by text, tradition, and case law; others derive from a one-time majority of the Court. But substantial agreement does exist between liberal and conservative alike on what can be regarded as "strong" and as "weak" constitutional materials or argument. In fairness, liberals should be prepared to concede where the constitutional basis is weak, as they can defend with vigor those fundamental values that are well grounded. For example, no compelling logic or line of precedent requires the exclusionary remedy for unconstitutional searches. Yet the accused's right to counsel rests upon tradition, symbolism, precedent, and reasoned principle of the strongest sort. If such rights are to be challenged, it should be by constitutional arguments of equivalent weight: by a strong line of precedent, a true induction, or a powerful theory of the relevant constitutional materials.

Much the same argument applies with respect to new fundamental rights. From all that has been said, expansive creativity in erecting new fundamental rights is neither prudent nor philosophically defensible. To be recognized, they will need the support of strong constitutional materials. Yet the acceptance of such rights can be firmly and fairly advocated by liberals when they genuinely "press for recognition" in the case law, when they provide a fair resolution for antitheses of legal logic, or when they buttress a tough-minded doctrinal synthesis.

Finally, fairness or even-handed treatment of opposing interests is appropriate to ask of a new Court. The liberal might like to say "be neutral and be principled," but it hardly lies in the mouths of most liberals to say it. Furthermore, the next Court will almost surely re-examine much basic constitutional law, making decisions that contain much implicit policy. It would seem only fair and realistic to appreciate that both neutrality and principle will be more desiderata to be sought than strict criteria of legitimacy. Herbert Wechsler's[100] famous prescription had implicitly, though, a third part particularly apposite for the future: that the Court seek to render decisions that— by the fairness and the adequacy with which opposing authority and cases are treated—are capable of persuading the opposing party, even though that party has lost.[101] That advice would seem important for liberal and conservative alike, so long as they would preserve the American practice of judicial review.

NOTES

1. Charles A. Beard, *The Supreme Court and the Constitution* (New York: Macmillan, 1912), p. 94; Arthur M. Schlesinger, Jr., *The Age of Jackson* (Boston: Little Brown, 1945), pp. 322–323.
2. George Dargo, *Roots of the Republic—A New Perspective on Early American Constitutionalism* (New York: Praeger, 1974) pp. 44ff.
3. Note, too, the use of a Council of Revision in New York and of Councils of Censors in Pennsylvania and Vermont—used to ensure faithfulness to the peoples' will as expressed in constitutions. See, especially, Gordon S. Wood, *The Creation of the American Republic—1776–1787* (Chapel Hill: University of North Carolina Press, 1969); Charles Grove Haines, *The American Doctrine of Judicial Supremacy* (New York: Russell and Russell, 1959) pp. 73ff.
4. Edward S. Corwin, "The 'Higher Law' Background of American Constitutional Law," in *Selected Essays on Constitutional Law* (Chicago: Foundation Press, 1938), Vol. I, pp. 18ff.; Gordon S. Wood, *op. cit.*, pp. 291–292.
5. Carl L. Becker, *The Declaration of Independence—A Study in the History of Political Ideas* (New York: Knopf, 1922).

6. Cf. Gordon S. Wood, *op. cit.*, pp. 291–292, 454 *et. seq.;* George Dargo, *op. cit.*, Ch. 7.

7. "Liberalism," as used in this essay, includes two aims: (1) curbing arbitrary authority; and (2) giving scope to the free expression of personality. Liberalism is both rather than either. The first objective of non-interference, standing alone, would leave the individual at the mercy of nature and group and economic power. The second objective of enfranchisement, especially as state intervention for the sake of "enablement" is involved, could lead to statism, technocracy or elitism, and unbounded discretion. Liberalism seeks a rational and conscientious reconciliation of these two goals and their attendant methods.

8. Thus, consider the Bills of Rights in the state constitutions of 1780, prior to the Constitution. Cf. Donald S. Lutz, *Popular Consent and Popular Control—Whig Political Theory in the Early State Constitutions* (Baton Rouge, La., Louisiana State University Press, 1980), pp. 124ff.

9. 4 Wash. C.C. 371 (1825).

10. 1 Wheat. 304 (1816).

11. 4 Wheat. 316 (1819).

12. Charles Groves Haines, *op. cit.*, pp. 401ff.

13. Ibid.; also, Roscoe Pound, *The Spirit of the Common Law* (Boston, Marshall Jones, 1921).

14. E.g. *Wynehamer v. People,* 13 N.Y. 378 (1856); *Bank of Columbia v. Okely,* 4 Wheat. 235 (1819); *Murray's Lessee v. Hoboken Land and Improvement Co.,* 18 Howard 272 (1856). *Dred Scott v. Sanford,* 19 Howard 393 (1857).

15. *Lochner v. New York,* 198 U.S. 45 (1905).

16. Charles Grove Haines, *The Revival of Natural Law Concepts* (Cambridge, Mass., Harvard University Press, 1930); Clyde E. Jacobs, *Law Writers and the Courts* (Berkeley: University of California Press, 1954).

17. Charles Grove Haines, *The American Doctrine of Judicial Supremacy, op. cit.,* p. 422.

18. 262 U.S. 390 (1923); Cf. also, *Pierce v. The Society of Sisters of the Holy Name of Jesus and Mary,* 268 U.S. 510 (1925). McReynolds wrote both opinions, Holmes dissenting in *Meyer. Meyer* dealt with a Nebraska statute that made it unlawful to teach German in a parochial school. *Pierce* involved an Oregon initiative measure that required children to attend public schools from the ages of eight to fifteen years, and thus would effectively have destroyed parochial schools. Interestingly, McReynolds wrote both majority opinions without once referring to the First Amendment, resting his decision primarily upon the liberty to engage in ordinary law-

ful business. Holmes dissented in *Meyer,* finding the restriction reasonably related to a legitimate legislative purpose.

19. Tony A. Freyer, "The Federal Courts, Localism, and the National Economy, 1865–1900," 53 *Business History Review* 343 (1979); Charles W. McCurdy, "American Law and the Marketing Structure of the Large Corporation, 1875–1890," 38 *Journal of Economic History* 631 (1978).

20. Cf. James Bryce, *The American Commonwealth* (New York: Macmillan, 1924); A.V. Dicey, *Lectures on the Relation between Law and Public Opinion in England During the Nineteenth Century* (London: Macmillan, 1914).

21. 304 U.S. 144 (1938).

22. Even authorities such as Tribe and Miller note the virtual abandonment of any attempt by the Court to restrain exercise of power under the Commerce Clause. Lawrence H. Tribe, *American Constitutional Law* (Mineola, New York: Foundation Press, 1978), p. 450; Arthur S. Miller, *The Supreme Court and American Capitalism* (New York: Free Press, 1967), 107ff.

23. See Louis Lusky, " 'Government by Judiciary:' What Price Legitimacy," 6 *Hastings Constitutional Law Quarterly* 403 (1979) at 405ff.; Alexander M. Bickel, *The Supreme Court and the Idea of Progress* (New York: Harper and Row, 1970).

24. Herbert Wechsler, "Toward Neutral Principles of Constitutional Law," 73 *Harvard Law Review* 1 (1959); Alexander M. Bickel, *The Least Dangerous Branch* (Indianapolis: Bobbs-Merrill, 1962); Archibald Cox, *The Role of the Supreme Court in American Government* (New York: Oxford University Press, 1976), p. 111.

25. See especially Alexander M. Bickel, *The Supreme Court and the Idea of Progress, op. cit.*

26. Frank I. Michelman, "On Protecting the Poor Through the Fourteenth Amendment," 83 *Harvard Law Review* 7 (1969); Laurence H. Tribe, *op. cit.,* pp. 515ff.; 1077ff.

27. John Hart Ely, *Democracy and Distrust—A Theory of Judicial Review* (Cambridge: Harvard University Press, 1980), p. 58.

28. See Nathan Glazer, "Towards an Imperial Judiciary," 41 *Public Interest* 104 (1976).

29. *Wisconsin v. Yoder,* 406 U.S. 205 (1972). Amy Gutman, "Children, Paternalism, and Education," 9 *Philosophy and Public Affairs* 338 (1980).

30. *Moose Lodge v. Iris,* 407 U.S. 163 (1972).

31. *Board of Regents v. Roth,* 408 U.S. 564 (1972).

32. *Goldberg v. Kelly,* 397 U.S. 254 (1970).

33. Ronald Dworkin, *Taking Rights Seriously* (Cambridge: Harvard University Press, 1977), p. 85.

34. My thought here owes much to my colleague, J. Roland Pennock.

35. Among critical and pessimistic views are Ward E. Elliott, *The Rise of Guardian Democracy: The Supreme Court's Role in Voting Rights Disputes* (Cambridge: Harvard University Press, 1974); Lino A. Graglia, *Disaster by Decree: the Supreme Court Decisions on Race and the Schools* (Ithaca: Cornell University Press, 1976); and Donald L. Horowitz, *The Courts and Social Policy* (Washington, D.C.: Brookings Institution, 1977).

36. *Pennhurst State School and Hospital v. Halderman,* 101 S.Ct.1531 (1981); see also Nathan Glazer, "Should Judges Administer Social Services?" 50 *Public Interest* 64 (1978).

37. Whether or not the "wages-fund" doctrine was ever true, there may be a near equivalent in the welfare field. Compare Black dissenting in *Goldberg v. Kelly.*

38. Lon L. Fuller, "The Forms and Limits of Adjudication," 92 *Harvard Law Review* 353 (1978). Jethro K. Lieberman, *The Litigious Society* (New York: Basic Books, 1981), pp. 25–26.

39. For instance, *Roe v. Wade,* 410 U.S. 311 (1973); *Craig v. Boren,* 429 U.S. 190 (1976); *Dayton Board of Education v. Brinkman,* 443 U.S. 526 (1979).

40. 411 U.S. 1 (1973).

41. See Horowitz's discussion of *Hobson v. Hansen* in *The Courts and Social Policy, op. cit.*

42. Ronald Dworkin, "Hard Cases," in *Taking Rights Seriously, op. cit.,* pp. 106–107. Robert F. Nagel, "Review of Laurence H. Tribe, American Constitutional Law," 127 *University of Pennsylvania Law Review* 1174 (1979) at 1178.

43. In *Rodriguez,* for instance, Marshall would seem to be better at political theory and to have the best of the argument, especially in view of the Court's own precedents.

44. Geoffrey C. Hazard, Jr., "The Supreme Court as a Legislature," 64 *Cornell Law Review* 1 (1978) at p. 25.

45. John Hart Ely, *op. cit.,* p. 59; Robert G. McCloskey, "Economic Due Process and the Supreme Court: An Exhumation and Reburial," *Supreme Court Review* (1962), p. 46.

46. Louis Lusky, " 'Government by Judiciary:' What Price Legitimacy," *op. cit.,* p. 412; cf. Ely to the contrary, *op. cit.,* p. 47.

47. To be sure, the Court should sometimes "do good" even in the face of popular sentiment: for instance, school prayer decisions. Unpopularity has its virtues, but not if the principle is weak. Cf. Hans A. Linde, "Judges, Critics, and the Realist Tradition," 82 *Yale Law Journal* 227 (1972).

48. John Hart Ely, *op. cit.,* p. 1.

49. One notes the obvious point that the Constitution, the Bill of Rights, and the Fourteenth Amendment each had a different set of drafters with different intentions.

50. 381 U.S. 479 (1965) at 522.

51. Raoul Berger, *Government by Judiciary—The Transformation of the Fourteenth Amendment* (Cambridge: Harvard University Press, 1977), p. 3.

52. Louis Lusky, " 'Government by Judiciary:' What Price Legitimacy," *op. cit.*, p. 405.

53. Louis Lusky, " 'Government by Judiciary:' What Price Legitimacy," *op. cit.*, p. 405; Raoul Berger, *op. cit.*, Introduction especially.

54. Black dissenting in *Griswold v. Connecticut,* 381 U.S. 479 (1965) at 522.

55. Hans A. Linde, "Judges, Critics, and the Realist Tradition," *op. cit.*, at 233–234.

56. Cf. Powell in concurring opinion in *Frontiero v. Richardson,* 411 U.S. 677 (1973) at 726.

57. Robert H. Bork, "Neutral Principles and Some First Amendment Problems," 47 *Indiana Law Journal* 1 (1971) at p. 33.

58. Thomas C. Gray, "Do We Have an Unwritten Constitution?" 27 *Stanford Law Review* 703 (1975) at p. 708.

59. Laurence H. Tribe, "The Puzzling Persistence of Process-Based Constitutional Theories," 89 *Yale Law Journal* 1063 (1980).

60. Learned Hand, *The Bill of Rights* (Cambridge: Harvard University Press, 1958), p. 14.

61. Though Ely ascribed the approach mainly to Justice Warren. Cf. Ely, *op. cit.* 106ff., 117ff.

62. Especially Lusky, Ely, and Sandalow. Cf. Louis Lusky, *By What Right? Commentary on the Supreme Court's Right to Revise the Constitution* (Charlottesville, Va.: Michie, 1975); John Hart Ely, *op. cit.;* Terrance Sandalow, "Judicial Protection of Minorities," 75 *Michigan Law Review* 1162 (1977).

63. Robert H. Bork, *op. cit.*, p. 2.

64. Terrance Sandalow, *op. cit.*, pp. 1166, 1184.

65. John Hart Ely, *op. cit.*, especially Chs. 4 and 6.

66. Cf. Ely, *op. cit.*, pp. 109–157, *passim.;* Sandalow, *op. cit.*, pp. 1185ff.

67. *Ibid.*, p. 1163.

68. Ely, *op. cit.*, pp. 105, 181.

69. The term "fundamental values approach" is Ely's. *Ibid.*, p. 102.

70. Laurence H. Tribe, "The Puzzling Persistence of Process-Based Constitutional Theories," *op. cit.*, at p. 1075.

71. Ely, *op. cit.*, p. 102.

72. 377 U.S. 533 (1964).

73. 424 U.S. 1 (1976).

74. 427 U.S. 347 (1976).

75. See comment by Lusky, " 'Government by Judiciary:' What Price Legitimacy?" *op. cit.,* esp. 416ff.

76. Ely, *op. cit.,* p. 43.

77. Alexander M. Bickel, *The Least Dangerous Branch, op. cit.*

78. Archibald Cox, *op. cit.,* p. 111; also Henry Wellington, "Common Law Rules and Constitutional Double Standards: Some Notes on Adjudication," 83 *Yale Law Journal* 221 (1973).

79. 410 U.S. 113 (1973); compare Ronald Dworkin, *Taking Rights Seriously, op. cit.,* p. 125.

80. 394 U.S. 618 (1969); compare Frank I. Michelman, "On Protecting the Poor Through the Fourteenth Amendment," 83 *Harvard Law Review* 7 (1969) and "In Pursuit of Constitutional Welfare Rights: One View of Rawls's Theory of Justice," 121 *University of Pennsylvania Law Review* 962 (1973).

81. 438 U.S. 265 (1978); compare Laurence H. Tribe, "Perspectives on *Bakke:* Equal Protection, Procedural Fairness, or Structural Justice?" 92 *Harvard Law Review* 846 (1979); Robert Nagel, "Review of Laurence H. Tribe, *American Constitutional Law," op. cit.*

82. Ronald Dworkin, *Taking Rights Seriously, op. cit.,* p. 106.

83. Ronald Dworkin, "Hard Cases," 88 *Harvard Law Review* 1057 (1975) at 1964.

84. See Robert H. Bork, "Neutral Principles and Some First Amendment Problems," *op. cit.;* also Professor Tribe's discussion, "Policy Science: Analysis or Ideology?," 2 *Philosophy and Public Affairs* 66 (1972).

85. As Dworkin's argument would seem to imply.

86. 339 U.S. 56 (1949) at 68ff.

87. 381 U.S. 479 (1965) at 484ff.

88. 376 U.S. 255 (1964) at 270ff.

89. 411 U.S. 1 (1973) esp. 98ff.

90. Ely, *op. cit.,* p. 44.

91. For instance, *Spano v. New York* 360 U.S. 315 (1959); or *Malloy v. Hogan,* 378 U.S. 1 (1964). *Spano v. New York* dealt with custodial interrogation of a man accused of murder. *Malloy v. Hogan* involved a defendant's refusal to testify to incriminating events. Both cases were important for their attention to developing doctrine in the law and as steps toward the so-called "Miranda revolution" that greatly extended Fourteenth Amendment protections of the accused.

92. Louis D. Brandeis and Samuel D. Warren, "The Right to Privacy," 4 *Harvard Law Review* 193 (1890); Alan F. Westin, *Privacy*

and Freedom (New York: Atheneum, 1967); Lawrence H. Tribe, *op. cit.,* esp. Ch. 15.

93. Robert H. Bork, *op. cit.,* p. 10.

94. Gerald Gunther, "In Search of Evolving Doctrine on a Changing Court: A Model for a Newer Equal Protection," 86 *Harvard Law Review* 1 (1970).

95. *Ibid.,* p. 39.

96. John Hart Ely, *op. cit.,* pp. 129, 144; Terrance Sandalow, *op. cit.,* 1186ff.

97. Some test cases for application of this method are *Goss v. Lopez,* 419 U.S. 565 (1975); and *Goldberg v. Kelly,* 397 U.S. 254 (1970). *Goss v. Lopez* involved school suspensions without a prior hearing. *Goldberg v. Kelly* raised a similar issue of termination of welfare benefits without a prior hearing, though a subsequent full hearing was available. In these cases, entitlements or quasi-rights confront complicated social interests. Hence the appropriateness of a more systematic weighing and balancing.

98. Cf. Guy Miller Struve, "The Less-Restrictive-Alternative Principle and Economic Due Process," 80 *Harvard Law Review* 1143 (1967).

99. The term is Robert Bork's. See his "Neutral Principles and Some First Amendment Problems," *op. cit.,* p. 8.

100. Herbert Wechsler, "Toward Neutral Principles of Constitutional Law," *op. cit.*

101. George C. Christie, "Objectivity in the Law," 78 *Yale Law Journal* 1311 (1969), p. 1329. This same theme is systematically and philosophically developed in Bruce A. Ackerman's *Social Justice in the Liberal State* (New Haven: Yale University Press, 1980).

PART IV

FREEDOM OF SPEECH

10

FREE SPEECH AND THE ARGUMENT FROM DEMOCRACY

FREDERICK SCHAUER

I. THE IMPORTANCE OF
A POLITICAL JUSTIFICATION

Hardly more than a glance at the daily newspapers is necessary to show that freedom of speech is important in appraising contemporary governments. Governments are called "democracies" when they permit freedom of speech and press. States that put down critics are taken to be undemocratic.

This instinctive reaction suggests a close connection between freedom of speech[1] and democracy, and this is reflected in the theoretical literature.[2] Yet all too often the connection is assumed rather than explained, and even the explanations have serious flaws. I want therefore to explore the relation between democratic theory and the principle of free speech. I ask, first, is freedom of speech intrinsic to the *definition* of democracy? Second, if democracy is *not* defined partly in terms of free speech, then to what extent does democracy serve to justify free speech? To answer these questions requires analysis of the concepts of both democracy and freedom of speech. My strategy will be to look primarily at the ways in which democracy can be taken to justify free speech. This will enable us to refine our conception of democracy, and so to decide whether freedom of speech is a necessary condition of democracy.

Concentrating on a particular justification for freedom of speech runs the risk of assuming, erroneously, that free speech is a unitary principle. But it is more likely that "freedom of speech" is a bundle of interrelated principles, related by no more than a family resemblance. These principles may each have their own justification, and the scope and strength of the principles will be determined by those justifications. What counts as freedom of speech, and therefore what counts as an infringement, necessarily depends on the reason or reasons for recognizing the principles, just as the contours of a political or legal *right* to free speech will turn on the particular principle or principles that are taken to justify the right.[3]

Among the justifications offered for recognizing a principle of freedom of speech, I want to attend to a group that I call collectively the "Argument from Democracy." These justifications all presuppose the value of some (rarely clarified) form of democracy, and seek to show how acceptance of democracy entails recognition of freedom of speech as a distinct principle of political philosophy. Without assuming at the outset that we need recognize *any* principle of free speech, I want to scrutinize the "Argument from Democracy."

A close look at this line of argument is essential to understanding the philosophical aspects of freedom of speech. The importance of the "Argument from Democracy" arises from the weaknesses of other justifications of free speech. For example, much theory from Milton to the present has been based on some version of the "Argument from Truth."[4] Often associated with the metaphor of the "marketplace of ideas," here truth is thought most likely to be discovered when all ideas are allowed freely to compete. This claim rests on some rather tenuous psychological and epistemological assumptions. All too often history shows that truth does not inevitably prevail in its battle with error. It may be that a variation on Gresham's Law is the more appropriate metaphor, with bad ideas driving out the good.[5] None of this is limpid, but the assumption that truth has some special power to prevail is questionable, and without this assumption the "Argument from Truth" is dubious.

Freedom of speech has also been defended in a less consequentialist manner, with emphasis on liberty of the speaker to achieve self-expression and self-fulfillment.[6] The trouble with

"Arguments from Personal Liberty," however, is not that they rest on erroneous premises, but that they do not lead to the desired conclusion. They do not justify a principle of freedom of speech. Unlike many claimed personal liberties, such as use of narcotics, homosexuality, gambling, and riding a motorcycle without a helmet, speech is obviously not self-regarding.[7] We speak for the very purpose of informing or influencing others, and frequently for the purpose of moving them to action. Speech can and often does produce good, but it also can and often does produce harm. Frequently speech is protected not because it does no harm, but *despite* the fact that it does so. To maintain that the march of the American Nazi Party in Skokie, virulent criticism of government and its officials, or a particularly caustic book review, for example, cause no harm is quite implausible. These acts, and many others, do harms that would normally be taken as sufficient to call for government intervention, but they are protected nevertheless by a principle of free speech. It is true that in many instances speech is self-regarding, and that even other-regarding speech has its self-regarding aspects. To that extent free speech can be justified as part of a broader personal liberty. But this would justify free speech in only a minor way, because most putative restrictions on speech are based on the other-regarding features of the speech, and it is those restrictions at which a principle of free speech is primarily addressed. A useful principle of free speech cannot therefore be based significantly on the self-regarding nature of the actions, and consequently the standard arguments for liberty or individuality are not available.

Weaknesses in some of the well-known justifications of free speech suggest that we look further to find a foundation for our intuition that protection of speech is an important feature of properly designed political and legal institutions. Part of the attractiveness of the "Argument from Democracy" is derived from the weaknesses of some of the other candidates for theoretical justification.

Moreover, there is an intuitive feeling that public policy is at the core of the concept of free speech, and that deliberation on policy should receive especially strong protection, even beyond that provided by a general principle of free speech. If political deliberation is in fact central in our conception of freedom of speech, then the implication is that political considerations explain this special solicitude. Laws and practices that protect political talk may occupy a crucial position in the ideal state, and the "Argument from Democracy" justifies this.

II. SOME HISTORY

The "Argument from Democracy" is commonly associated with Alexander Meiklejohn,[8] and his thinking will be scrutinized in the next section of this essay. But the "Argument from Democracy" has a rather ancient lineage. Spinoza, for example, in *A Theologico-Political Treatise*, argued that public criticism of laws serves the interests of the state, in part because such criticism increases the likelihood that the laws will reflect the views of the majority, in accord with democratic ideals, which Spinoza took to be "the most natural form of government."[9]

Spinoza was especially concerned with unjust *laws*, but in the eighteenth century related sentiments were expressed in terms of the value of freedom of speech and press in controlling bad *governments*.[10] John Trenchard and Thomas Gordon, writing in the early part of the eighteenth century under the pseudonym "Cato," looked at freedom of speech as a way of preventing "publick Mischief."[11] Similar views were expressed by John Wilkes, and by two anonymous essayists, "Junius" and "Father of Candor."[12] The theme of all of these essays was that without the check of speech and press, governments would much more likely act against the wishes and best interests of the populace. Implicit here is the assumption that popular control promotes just government. For these thinkers democratic assumptions provided the basis for a case for freedom of speech, and they are the first to set forth a version of the "Argument from Democracy."

Kant's reasons for "freedom of the pen" reflect similar themes, although he does not refer to "democracy" as such.[13] But he took political authority to be legitimate only insofar as it represented the general will, and he saw the freedom of the pen as the only way of ensuring that the sovereign would be aware of that general will. But an important and interesting variation is found in Hume's unfortunately neglected essay, "Of the Liberty of the Press."[14] In a pure monarchy, Hume says, there would be no need for liberty of the press, because the monarch would have no cause to distrust the subjects and could work his will without interference of public criticism. And in a pure republic, there would again be no reason to permit liberty of the press, because all decisions would reflect the popular will, and any criticism inconsistent with that will could be suppressed in the name of the people. But in a mixed form of government, where the assumption of popular control is combined with a strong magistrate, liberty of the press is necessary so that the people can exercise "watchful *jealousy* over the magistrates." In cases where the central government exceeded its authority, liberty of the press would permit "conveying the alarm from one end of the kingdom to the other," and so would enable citizens "to curb the ambition of the court." Hume thought liberty of the press increasingly necessary as a government becomes strong. Liberty of the press was not a component of "pure" democracy, but instead desirable because democracies are rarely pure.

In the early part of this century a number of opinions of the United States Supreme Court held that freedom of speech is vital for political responsiveness. Chief Justice Hughes relied on this principle in several opinions.[15] In *Gilbert v. Minnesota*,[16] Brandeis, dissenting, held that democracy was based on the idea of political participation by the citizenry, a participation that could be effective only if the citizens could speak out and attempt to influence both each other and government on matters of public policy.

III. FREE SPEECH AND POPULAR SOVEREIGNTY

Although the "Argument from Democracy" has been hinted at in the past, the first fully worked out theory along these lines is offered by Alexander Meiklejohn.[17] Analysis of Meiklejohn's ideas is therefore a useful way of exploring the implications of the "Argument from Democracy."

Meiklejohn presented his thinking by way of an interpretation of the Constitution, but his ideas are best viewed as political philosophy rather than constitutional theory. Whether his theories can be located in the text or history of a particular document is irrelevant to their philosophical validity. The First Amendment, even interpreted in light of the rest of the Constitution, is indeterminate as to the philosophical rationale for "the freedom of speech."[18]

Moreover, it is equally important to divorce evaluation of the Meiklejohn thesis from his belief that his principle is, within its rather narrowly delineated scope, absolute. In seeking to justify a principle of free speech, the first task is to locate those arguments that will generate a side constraint on the permissibility of otherwise acceptable government action.[19] But side constraints need not be absolute, or for that matter even close to absolute.[20] Implicit in the operational political theory of any society is what we might call a *baseline rule,* establishing the normal criterion for government action. Examples would be a rule allowing any action in the public interest, or allowing government action only when necessary to promote the general welfare, or permitting intervention only to protect persons and property. To the extent that a side constraint establishes a standard of justification higher than the baseline rule, a distinctive principle is in operation. Thus a side constraint that makes it somewhat, or even slightly, more difficult to regulate speech than other objects of government concern still operates as a check on some actions, even if the higher standard applicable to speech is capable of being met.[21] In looking for a justification for a principle of free speech, we are looking for a reason to create a stricter criterion. If we find a reason, we have justified a principle of free speech, even if the principle is far short of absolute. It is possible, therefore, for Meiklejohn's arguments to justify a principle of freedom of speech even if they fail to justify the absoluteness he claimed.

Meiklejohn based his theory of free speech on the concept of self-government. This is hardly a precisely specified concept, but to Meiklejohn it means popular sovereignty in its purest form. He was greatly influenced by the New England town meeting, in which all major decisions are taken by the assembled adult population. Although some more modern forms utilize selectmen as elected representatives, the pure town meeting in a smaller town has no officials in the sense of legislators or executives. There is only a moderator entrusted with organizing the meeting and enforcing rules of order. All adults can propose policies, debate the proposals, and vote.

Meiklejohn sees democratic government as a New England town meeting writ large. Final authority in the modern republic lies with the population at large. And he feels that the open debate and deliberation that precedes decisions of the town meeting are equally necessary for decisions in any self governing society.

According to Meiklejohn, freedom of speech is essential in part because it is the way in which all relevant information is made available to the sovereign electorate which can then, on the basis of that information, decide on policy. Because full information is requisite to intelligent voting, denying access to information was to Meiklejohn as serious damage to self-government as would be denial of the right to vote.

Meiklejohn also saw freedom of speech as a corollary of the truism that if the people are sovereign, then officials are servants and not rulers. Servants must know the wishes of the master, so the people need a way to tell the masters what to do. Thus Meiklejohn thought it quite anomalous that the servants might filter the information available to the master.

The "Argument from Democracy" has an epistemological basis as well. If it is formulated in terms of popular sovereignty, it incorporates the view that political truths are, by definition, those made so by the majority. At times this "survival theory of truth" has been used to justify free speaking on anything. This is commonly associated with Holmes and his dictum that "the best test of truth is the power of the thought to get itself accepted in the competition of the market."[22] His radical skepticism, however, seems counterintuitive. The Earth was no more round in 1491, when that proposition was widely accepted, than it is now, and many current opinions are equally false. The same holds true for many ethical propositions. Nazism was not "right" in Germany in the 1930s, slavery was not "right" in the United States, and it is ludicrous to hold that any prevailing American view on anything is correct merely because there is now virtually unlimited freedom of speech. As a general proposition, to define truth as popular acceptance is so at odds with our moral and epistemological understandings that it can only be an extremely weak defense for a principle of free speech.

Yet we are likely much further from certainty on matters of policy and political theory than we are in other realms of thought. In light of disagreement on almost all political issues, as well as about even the criteria to be used for assessing political ideas, an implicit assumption of democracy is that here majority rule *is* the best test of truth. Similarly, democratic theory assumes that truth is not really the issue, for implicit in any version of majority rule is the majority's right to be wrong. If we assume the validity of the case for democracy, the Holmesian marketplace of ideas follows naturally. And if the people have the right to be wrong, then wrongness cannot serve as the criterion for denying the population access to information that may bear upon their decisions.

IV. THE IMPLICATIONS OF SOVEREIGNTY

Meiklejohn's version of the "Argument from Democracy" is parasitic on his conception of democracy as the supremacy of the electorate. In looking at the implications of popular sovereignty, it is crucial to bear in mind the point made in Part I, that speech is almost always other-regarding, and is frequently the source of the kinds of harm with which governments normally deal. We must be wary of falling into what I call the "ratchet fallacy," by which speech is assumed to go in one direction only, producing good and causing no harm. Speech, even on political matters, can do a lot of damage to important interests. If we understand democracy as popular sovereignty, then the unlimited powers normally associated with sovereignty would permit the people to restrict speech to the same extent that they can regulate other forms of conduct.

The idea of popular sovereignty that supports this version of the "Argument from Democracy" thus argues against a limitation on that sovereignty, and militates against recognition of an independent principle of free speech that restricts popular sovereignty. By accepting popular sovereignty as the premise of the "Argument from Democracy," we are precluded from impinging on majority power. If the "Argument from Democracy" would allow things to be said that the people do not want to hear, then the argument is not so much based on popular will as it is an argument against it.

Although there is nothing internally inconsistent about defining either democracy or popular sovereignty in a way that prevents a democracy from committing suicide by alienating its sovereignty, still to rely totally on the concept of majority rule is somewhat paradoxical, for we would hardly agree that majorities can withdraw the minority's right to vote, or can grant permanent and unlimited power to a tyrant. One reason that such paradoxical conclusions are not compelled is that equal participation by all is much more fundamental to self-government than is majority rule. And equal participation offers a much stronger form of the "Argument from Democracy." If all participate equally, then they must have the information necessary to make participation meaningful. The "Argument from Democracy" in this form supports a liberty to speak openly.[23] Shifting from democracy as majority rule to democracy as equal participation enables us to avoid the paradox of majority rule, and thus helps to explain why freedom of speech is an exception to, rather than a conclusion from, the practice of popular control.

Similarly, freedom of speech can be seen as a conclusion from some of the considerations relating to legal and political obligation. I do not want here to rehearse the entire question of why a minority might have an obligation to obey a particular law enacted by the majority, but one answer is especially germane to the question of freedom of speech. One condition of the morality of the rule of law is that everyone has the right to attempt to influence the majority and thus to participate in the formulation of policy. To the extent that a majority limits the ability of the minority to participate by speaking out, then an important prop for the moral authority of *anything* that the majority does is removed.[24]

It should come as no surprise that the "Argument from Democracy" is seen to move further and further away from its origin, at least as Meiklejohn saw it, in theories of sovereignty. The problem is that the conception of democracy as popular sovereignty is flawed as a general theory of democracy. Karl Popper and others have made penetrating attacks on oversimplified views of popular sovereignty, and we need not recapitulate their arguments here.[25] But in this context, the problem is that overemphasis on electoral sovereignty in the "Argument from Democracy" provides little assistance by itself in explaining why a right to free speech is a right against a majority, and why speech should have a special immunity from principles of majority rule.

These problems are but an instance of a much broader problem of democratic theory. When presented in extreme form, such as the people electing a despot, many of the paradoxes of democracy seem unrealistic. But the important question is the extent to which a democratic government may itself define the procedures of democracy. Whenever a majority legislates with respect to any aspect of the electoral machinery, or with respect to the allocation of operational (as opposed to ultimate) authority between government officials and the electorate itself, or with respect to the openness of government, it is acting in a way that is different from other varieties of legislation. Any action of this type brings into play the very same considerations that generate, in more extreme forms, the paradoxes of popular sovereignty. It is not unreasonable, therefore, to hold that any action by the majority that does or can affect the processes of government must be tested under standards other than an absolute presumption in favor of action taken by the majority.[26] Freedom of speech pertaining to subjects germane to politics, public policy, and the conduct of public officials, as an important part of an effective electoral process, is therefore but an instance of this more general problem. As long as we are reluctant to permit the majority to define or modify the practices of democracy, then we must be similarly reluctant to permit the majority to define the permissible limits of political discourse.

V. THE ARGUMENT FROM DEMOCRACY AND THE ARGUMENT FROM TRUTH

As government structures become increasingly complex, they diverge more and more from Meiklejohn's paradigm of the New England town meeting. This phenomenon points us toward a conception of the "Argument from Democracy" that is closer to Hume's than to Meiklejohn's. When officials begin to appear more like elected rulers than servants, the government superstructure is likely to be more concerned with perpetuation of its own power than with acting in what it takes to be public interest. Many of the motives that lead people to aspire to office lead to desire to stay in office. Liberty to criticize government can be seen as a control on this instinct for survival. Freedom of speech operates as part of a system of checks and balances.[27] This defense is not inconsistent with other formulations of the "Argument from Democracy." But by deemphasizing the role of the electorate as a national debating society, and by emphasizing the function of speech as a force for control of government, we follow Popper's admonition "to replace the question: *Who should rule?* by the new question: *How can we so organize political institutions that bad or incompetent rulers can be prevented from doing too much damage?*"[28]

Earlier I doubted the validity of the "Argument from Truth" as a justification for freedom of speech, noting that its rationalist assumptions are questionable. This does not mean, however, that the "Argument from Truth" is of no value. Although it seems true that open discussion does not necessarily lead to more knowledge or sounder beliefs, that may not be the correct question. Instead we should be asking whether the *institution*[29] of government selection among competing ideas is a more reliable determinant of truth than the institution of selection through an open marketplace of ideas. The question is one of relative unreliability. Looked at in this way, it is plausible to argue that government, with its own lack of perfect rationality compounded by the self-interest of the individual governors, is more likely to commit errors than the marketplace of ideas. We need not then be committed to the tenuous proposition that the marketplace of ideas is a good way of determining truth. But it is perhaps a less bad way, and the least bad of the available evils.

If this is the case, then we should no longer treat the "Argument from Democracy" as wholly distinct from the "Argument from Truth." Meiklejohn saw the two as opposing theories, and ridiculed the "Argument from Truth" as a game for "intellectual aristocrats" such as Holmes whom he saw as unconcerned with issues of self-government.[30] But the arguments are not nearly so separate, and the "Argument from Democracy" is more usefully viewed as an important variation on the "Argument from Truth."

As recast above, the "Argument from Truth" reflects doubts about a particular method of determining truth, *viz.*, government selection among ideas. But as we need protection against government, so do we need protection against the far from perfect wisdom, temper, and prudence of majorities. Majorities may have fewer victims than despots, but they can be wrong as well. If majority rule is seen as an imperfect system, yet still better than unaccountable authority, then similarly majority rule with the check of open criticism may be seen as a further effort to contain the probability and consequences of error. The best formulation of the "Argument from Truth" is as an "Argument from Error," that open discussion is the practice least likely to perpetuate error when measured in terms of a large number of decisions over time. And the best formulation of the "Argument from Democracy" seems to be an application of this "Argument from Error" to decisions of government, including majorities.

This does not mean that the "Argument from Democracy" collapses completely into the "Argument from Truth." For the "Argument from Democracy" reminds us that when we are dealing with public policy, and with the qualifications and acts of our leaders, we are in an area where self-interest is especially strong, and where we are playing for higher stakes.[31] The more power we grant to government, the more damage it can do. Special concern for freedom to discuss public issues and criticize government decisions and officials, stronger than the freedom of speech in a broader and more general sense, is a form of the "Argument from Truth," reinforced by the subjects discussed. There is little certainty in questions of public policy, and the consequences of mistakes are particularly serious. With a greater than normal likelihood of error, and a greater than normal harm when error occurs, the risk of assuming infallibility in governmental decisions is especially large. In this sense the "Argument from Democracy" tells us that political speech is different in kind as well as degree. The next advance in free speech theory may come when we recognize and incorporate into our theorizing the fact that different categories of discourse bring different considerations into play, and may require different forms of legal protection. The "Argument from Democracy," by focusing on the special values of a certain kind of discourse, is the first step in this process.

NOTES

1. For my purposes I draw no distinction between freedom of speech and freedom of the press. Although the special reference to "the Press" in the United States Constitution *may* suggest additional protections for the institutional press, this is tangential to my theme, and I treat freedom of the press as simply a particular form of freedom of speech.

2. Examples of theories of democracy that incorporate principles of freedom of speech include William Nelson, *On Justifying Democracy* (London: Routledge & Kegan Paul, 1980), chap. 6; J. Roland Pennock, *Liberal Democracy: Its Merits and Prospects* (New York: Rinehart, 1950), pp. 72–77, 292–94, 320–33; D.D. Raphael, *Problems of Political Philosophy* (London: Macmillan, 1976), pp. 150, 162.

3. A similar point is implicit in distinctions among the "foundational level," the "level of rights," and the "level of policy." T.M. Scanlon, Jr., "Freedom of Expression and Categories of Expression," *University of Pittsburgh Law Review*, 40 (1979), 519, at p. 535.

4. Among the most prominent statements of the "Argument from Truth" are Walter Bagehot, "The Metaphysical Basis of Toleration," in *Literary Studies*, R.H. Hutton, ed. (London, 1884), 422; John Stuart Mill, *On Liberty*, D. Spitz, ed. (New York: Norton, 1975), chap. 2; John Milton, *Areopagitica*, J.C. Suffolk, ed. (London: University Tutorial Press, 1968). Important critiques include Willmoore Kendall, "The 'Open Society' and Its Fallacies," *American Political Science Review*, 54 (1960), 972; H.J. McCloskey, "Liberty of Expression: Its Grounds and Limits," *Inquiry*, 13 (1970), 219. The "Argument from Truth" views open competition among ideas as the process by which truth, defined independently of that process, emerges. An important variation on the doctrine is the pragmatic/skeptical view of Holmes, who *defined* truth in terms of the process of open discussion. See especially his dissent in *Abrams v. United States*, 250 U.S. 616 (1919), at 630.

5. See *Report of the Committee on Obscenity and Film Censorship*, Bernard Williams, chairman (London: HMSO, 1979, Cmnd 7772), 55.

6. Arguments for the self-expression justification of freedom of

speech are found in Edwin Baker, "Scope of the First Amend-
ment Freedom of Speech," *UCLA Law Review,* 25 (1978), 964;
Ronald Dworkin, "Introduction," in *The Philosophy of Law,* R.M.
Dworkin, ed. (Oxford: Oxford University Press, 1977, 1; Ronald
Dworkin, "Is the Press Losing the First Amendment," *New York
Review of Books* (December 4, 1980), 49; Ronald Dworkin, "Liberalism," in *Public and Private Morality,* Stuart Hampshire, ed. (Cambridge: Cambridge University Press, 1978), 113; Ronald Dworkin,
"The Rights of Myron Farber," *New York Review of Books* (October
26, 1978), with exchange (December 7, 1978); David A.J. Richards, "Free Speech and Obscenity Law: Toward a Moral Theory
of the First Amendment," *University of Pennsylvania Law Review,*
123 (1974), 45. For a more extensive critique, see Frederick
Schauer, "Speech and 'Speech'–Obscenity and 'Obscenity:' An Exercise in the Interpretation of Constitutional Language," *George-
town Law Journal,* 67 (1979), 899.

7. I do not claim that there necessarily is such a thing as a self-
   regarding act, which is itself a rather controversial proposition.
   But if there are self-regarding acts, no matter how defined, speech
   is rather plainly not among them.

8. See especially Alexander Meiklejohn, *Free Speech and Its Relation to
   Self-Government* (New York: Harper & Brothers, 1948). Among
   Meiklejohn's other writings about free speech are "The Balancing
   of Self-Preservation Against Political Freedom," *California Law Re-
   view,* 49 (1961), 4; "The First Amendment is an Absolute," *The
   Supreme Court Review* (1961), 245.

9. Benedict de Spinoza, *A Theologico-Political Treatise,* R.H.M. Elwes,
   trans. (New York: Dover Publications, 1951), chap. XX.

10. For an excellent analysis and survey of the literature, see Vincent
    Blasi, "The Checking Value in First Amendment Theory," *Ameri-
    can Bar Foundation Research Journal* (1977), 521.

11. [John Trenchard & Thomas Gordon], *Cato's Letters: Essays on Lib-
    erty, Civil and Religous, and Other Important Subjects* (London, 1755),
    especially letters 15, 32, 100, and 101.

12. See Blasi, op. cit. note 10, at pp. 530–33.

13. Immanuel Kant, *On The Old Saw: That May Be Right in Theory But
    It Won't Work in Practice,* E.B. Ashton, trans. (Philadelphia: Uni-
    versity of Pennsylvania Press, 1974), pp. 72–73.

14. David Hume, "Of the Liberty of the Press," in *Essays, Moral, Polit-
    ical and Literary* (Edinburgh, 1817), pp. 8–11.

15. *DeJonge v. Oregon,* 299 U.S. 353, 365 (1937); *Stromberg v. Califor-
    nia,* 283 U.S. 359, 369 (1931). In *Near v. Minnesota,* 283 U.S. 697,
    717 (1931), Hughes quoted the Letter to the Inhabitants of Que-
    bec (1775) that freedom of the press is the device "whereby op-

pressive officers are shamed or intimidated, into more honourable and just modes of conducting affairs."

16. *Gilbert v. Minnesota,* 254 U.S. 325, 337 (1920).

17. See above, note 8. For other versions of the argument, see Lillian BeVier, "The First Amendment and Political Speech: An Inquiry into the Substance and Limits of Principle," *Stanford Law Review,* 30 (1978), 299; Robert Bork, "Neutral Principles and Some First Amendment Problems," *Indiana Law Journal,* 47 (1971), 1; Frank Morrow, "Speech, Expression, and the Constitution," *Ethics,* 85 (1975), 235.

18. In this respect perhaps one of the most important words in the First Amendment is "the," which suggests a particular pre-constitutional and theory-based limited realm of freedom of speech. See Frederick Schauer, "Categories and the First Amendment: A Play in Three Acts," *Vanderbilt Law Review,* 34 (1981), 265, esp. pp. 267–82.

19. On side constraints, see Robert Nozick, *Anarchy, State, and Utopia* (New York: Basic Books, 1974), pp. 28–35; Ronald Dworkin, *Taking Rights Seriously* (Cambridge: Harvard University Press, 1977), pp. 190–92. See also Charles Fried, *Right and Wrong* (Cambridge: Harvard University Press, 1978), p. 81. It is commonly assumed that side constraints are deontological restrictions on utilitarian goals, but side constraints may also be derived from consequentialist theories, such as rule-utilitarianism, that take account of long-term consequences. See D.W. Haslett, "The General Theory of Rights," *Social Theory and Practice,* 5 (1980), 427; David Lyons, "Human Rights and the General Welfare," *Philosophy and Public Affairs,* 6 (1977), 113.

20. Nozick and others recognize the possibility of an exception for catastrophes, but my point is that the notion of a side constraint is useful even if it can be overridden in circumstances far short of a catastrophe.

21. See Thomas Scanlon, "A Theory of Freedom of Expression," *Philosophy and Public Affairs,* 1 (1972), 204.

22. *Abrams,* op. cit. note 4, at p. 630.

23. It is important to remember that the "Argument from Democracy" produces a principle of free speech rather limited in scope, although not necessarily in strength. When it is claimed, as Meiklejohn did in his later writings, that the principle generated by the argument encompasses art, literature, and the like, much of the force of the argument is diluted.

24. For an excellent recent study of the moral nature of political obligation, see A. John Simmons, *Moral Principles and Political Obligations* (Princeton: Princeton University Press, 1980).

25. See K.R. Popper, *The Open Society and Its Enemies* (London: Rout-ledge & Kegan Paul, Fifth Edition, 1966), chap. 7. See also J. Ro-land Pennock, *Democratic Political Theory* (Princeton: Princeton University Press, 1979), pp. 376–78.

26. For a theory of judicial review based on this premise, see John Hart Ely, *Democracy and Distrust: A Theory of Judicial Review* (Cam-bridge: Harvard University Press, 1980).

27. For such a structural view of freedom of the press, see William J. Brennan, Jr., "Address," *Rutgers Law Review*, 32 (1979), 173.

28. K.R. Popper, op. cit. note 25, vol. 1, p. 121.

29. See John Rawls, "Two Concepts of Rules," *Philosophical Review*, 64 (1955), 3.

30. Alexander Meiklejohn, *Political Freedom: The Constitutional Powers of the People* (New York: Oxford University Press, 1960), p. 42.

31. Thus we might say that freedom of speech is derived not so much from any special value of speech, above and beyond other useful forms of activity, but from a special distrust of government, and of government regulation of communication. See C. Hyneman, "Free Speech at What Price?" *American Political Science Review*, 57 (1962), 847.

11

IS FREEDOM ACADEMIC?:
THE RELATIVE AUTONOMY
OF UNIVERSITIES
IN A LIBERAL DEMOCRACY

AMY GUTMANN

What freedoms of universities should a democratic state respect? My answer has many parts because there are many freedoms that universities can value and assert against the state. These are not just academic freedoms, although even academic freedom (as I shall argue) is constituted by several freedoms. There are freedoms specific to three analytically separable identities of American universities, to universities as territorial, educational, and membership associations. With regard to each of these identities, I build a case based upon liberal democratic theory for their relative autonomy from the state.

But first I consider a simpler answer that is now frequently given by presidents, trustees and legal counsel of private American universities. It reflects a more absolutist position, that a democratic state should respect the right of every university, or at least of every private university, to make and apply its own policies, whenever those policies affect its academic life. In a recent Supreme Court case, for example, Princeton University defends its right to limit political speech on its campus with the argument that "it is constitutionally wrong for state officials to determine what [Princeton's educational] policy is or what activities are consonant with it."[1] In a more generally directed statement, Dallin Oaks, former president of the American Association of Presidents of Independent Colleges and Universities, calls upon "our nation's teachers—especially in higher education—. . . [to] stoutly defend the academic freedom of their colleges and universities from government regulation of the educational process."[2] He then cites thirteen major pieces of federal legislation since 1963 as violations of the right of private universities to academic freedom.[3]

An absolutist defense of institutional autonomy for private universities is understandably attractive these days given the enormous increase in governmental regulation of private universities since 1960. Those of us who value democratic freedoms have much less to fear from the economic and political power of private universities than we do from that of commercial corporations. Universities have educational and intellectual purposes that demand more insulation from state power than that required for the efficient production of material goods.[4] Moreover, unlike most commercial corporations, universities are genuine intellectual, sometimes also religious and cultural, communities. They are usually in limited measure also self-governing collegial communities that would be destroyed by state control over their academic affairs.

Despite these many attractions, the arguments supporting institutional autonomy for private universities have unacceptable consequences for both universities and democratic society. They have implications for democratic theory, especially for what they can tell us about a view of politics that I call corporate pluralism.

Corporate pluralism is best understood as a libertarian theory of the second best. It results from applying the fundamental libertarian principle that owners have an absolute right to control their property to contemporary American society without challenging the legitimacy of the democratic state itself or the corporate institutions that have survived because of the state's support. Instead, the corporate pluralist view supports the right of the present legal owners of institutions to control them, and thus distinguishes between the right of private institutions to be independent from the state and the right of the democratic state to control the associations that it legally owns.

On this understanding, democracy is a means of exercising a collective right of ownership. The constitutional rights of citizens provide the ground rules for exercising collective ownership over public institutions, but these rights extend only as far as the institutions and territories that are publicly owned.

The basic principles of corporate pluralism are not explicitly stated or consistently followed by those who defend the absolute autonomy of private universities. But the reasons that they offer for their defense, and the defense itself, is more consistent with corporate pluralist principles than with any other consistent set of political principles. And only by constructing a consistent set of political principles from the expressed views of those who defend the absolute autonomy of private universities can we understand and evaluate their position and its broader political implications.

By contrast to corporate pluralism the basic postulate of what I call liberal democracy is that each individual's rights of democratic citizenship—included in which are rights to political equality, freedom of speech, association and religion, and equality of opportunity[5]—must be protected within *all* institutions unless someone else's rights are thereby violated. On this understanding, free speech is not a right against the government only, as the wording of the First Amendment might suggest ("Congress shall make no law . . . abridging . . . freedom of speech"). On liberal democratic grounds, we can criticize the wording of the First Amendment, interpret it more broadly, or argue that most institutions, including universities, are subject to sufficient state action to trigger the potential for free speech protection.

Even a properly revised First Amendment or a finding of state action will not suffice to decide any case in favor of protecting free speech within a private institution. The purposes of that institution must always be taken into account. A liberal democratic standard admits of hard cases whenever citizenship rights, such as the right of free speech or equal educational opportunity, conflict with membership rights within a secondary institution, membership rights that result from citizens' legitimate use of their right of free association.

Later, I shall suggest a standard by which a liberal democratic state can decide when universities have a legitimate claim to resist being constrained by the universal rights of citizenship. In contrast to the absolutist position of corporate pluralism, this is a standard of autonomy relative to the value and purposes of membership within the university and to the importance of citizenship rights when they conflict with those purposes. But first let us examine the more straightforward, absolutist position of corporate pluralism by applying its principled distinction between public and private ownership to the issue of university autonomy.

1. CORPORATE PLURALISM AND THE UNIVERSITY

The trustees of private universities claim complete authority on the corporate view to determine the policies of their universities or to delegate their authority within the university as they see fit. Their authority is limited by two provisos on the rights of private property internal to the logic of corporate pluralism. The first is that private institutions have no right to make policies that injure people, members or nonmembers. The force of this proviso as a limitation upon the rights of private universities clearly will depend upon what constitutes an injury, as distinguished from denial of a benefit. The authority of university trustees to hire whomever they wish or to restrict free speech on their campus would be seriously constrained by an argument that to deny someone employment or a right to speak constitutes a harm, not merely denial of a benefit. Perhaps few corporate pluralists would be willing to move in this direction, but it is worth noting that the most extreme corporate defense of the autonomy of private universities rests upon a narrow interpretation of injury as coercion, and a correspondingly sharp distinction between injuring people and denying them benefits.[6]

The second proviso on the absolute right of ownership is that private owners must not violate legitimate (i.e., noncoerced) contracts or contractual understandings. This requirement is necessary to secure the right of private property in the first place, and it is the basis for a corporate defense of academic freedom within private universities dedicated to liberal education. Faculty within private universities have a right to academic freedom if and only if it is (explicitly or implicitly) included in their contract.

With these two provisos on the right of private ownership, the corporate defense of university autonomy can plausibly claim to safeguard three traditional democratic ideals. It supports pluralism by permitting diversity among institutions of higher education. There will be Catholic, Jewish and Fundamentalist, libertarian, socialist as well as liberal universities as long as some groups of trustees decide to dedicate their universities to these purposes. The political life within universities may also vary. Some may be governed hierarchically by a church, others collegially by the faculty, still others democratically by all their members.

Corporate pluralism also claims to secure the particular rights of faculty, students and staff by permitting the state to enforce the contracts made between the university and these individuals. Those faculty members whose contracts include the right to free inquiry and expression will thereby have a legally enforceable right to academic freedom. Those who contracted into a sectarian university will not be guaranteed academic freedom, but their membership rights are also justified as a product of their free choice. Thus, corporate democracy provides a means of enforcing the academic freedom of faculty without elevating that freedom to a constitutional right that precludes diversity within higher education. Students as well as faculty are free to choose between membership within non-liberal and liberal universities, that freedom being safeguarded by the autonomy of private universities.

Yet the corporate view also leaves room for a public sector of liberal higher education by respecting the collective right of the democratic community to regulate and control the universities it owns. Public universities will be liberal in their educational philosophy and practices so long as the constitutional or legislative authority of the democratic community requires them to be.

Thus, by extending the logic of its first principle, the world of corporate pluralism provides for academic freedom and liberal higher education in both private and public universities while also reserving space for sectarian religious and political education in private universities. This view is thus corporatist

in ascribing a right to autonomy to private institutions, and pluralist in proclaiming the value of diversity among those institutions. At least on first impression, corporate pluralism is a
theory well-suited to defending our present system of diversi-
fied higher education in which Oral Roberts, Notre Dame and
Yeshiva Universities compete with Ohio State, Chicago and Columbia, and thereby provide a choice among educational philosophies and cultural communities to prospective students and
faculty.

But this first impression is misleading because of what it neglects to say about how authority could be used within both
private and public universities. The corporate rights of university ownership, both public and private, could have the effect
of limiting or eliminating the academic and associational freedoms of members of universities, and thereby diminishing the
value of higher education as the primary source of critical
knowledge in a democratic society. The idea that our present
system of higher education is consistent with the corporate view
is also misleading, for it fails to take account of the effects that
the requirements of state chartering and other regulations have
already had upon academic life and what life within universities might have been like without enforcement of some uni-
versalistic standards. My criticism of the corporate pluralist argument, however, depends upon the possibility of finding an
alternative theory of university autonomy that is more consistent with democratic values rather than one that is more defensive of our present system. I now turn to that alternative.

2. LIBERAL DEMOCRACY AND THE UNIVERSITY

A liberal democratic state must respect both the universal
rights of citizens and the particular rights of owners and members of secondary associations. By dedicating their resources to
creating a university, or by choosing to teach or to be educated
within that university, citizens use their universal rights of
property and free association to create rights that may be unique
to membership in a particular university. Membership rights
within sectarian universities depend upon a limited right of private property: the right of individuals or groups to dedicate

their property to particular purposes that would not have been chosen by a democratic majority. This right of dedication constitutes only a small part of the bundle of private property rights supported by corporate pluralists. It does not prevent a liberal state from regulating private universities in a manner consistent with their declared purposes nor does it release the state from a responsibility to determine whether the particular rights claimed by trustees violate more valuable rights of members or citizens. The principles of liberal democracy thus permit a state to constrain the rights of dedication and of university governance to those purposes and policies that are not incompatible with the effective exercise of other basic rights supporting citizenship in a democratic society.

Liberal democracy lays claim to the same values with regard to higher education as does corporate pluralism, but for different reasons and often to different practical effect. Pluralism is supported by the right of trustees to dedicate their universities to diverse educational philosophies. The right of free association includes this limited right of private property and thereby commits a liberal democratic state to accepting the importance of sectarian or nonliberal higher education for those citizens who voluntarily choose it.

A democratic state has the responsibility to uphold academic freedom within all universities unless their explicit purposes are incompatible with academic freedom and are sufficiently valuable to override the presumption in favor of academic freedom in higher education. This presumption is based upon the need within a democratic society for an institutional sanctuary for the process of free intellectual inquiry essential to democratic politics. Limitations upon academic freedom within universities therefore demand sufficient institutional reasons, which in some cases can be found within the established religious or other ideological purposes of a private university. For example, a university with explicitly nonliberal religious purposes may need to restrict the academic freedom of its faculty as a means of furthering its purposes. But these limitations upon academic freedom must be apparent to faculty and students before they agree to become members of such a university.

A liberal democratic state supports liberal higher education directly through its own universities, and also indirectly by se-

curing rights of democratic citizenship within private universities, rights that are more compatible with the practices of liberal than with nonliberal education. The reasons for this bias
in favor of liberal universities is quite simple: a democratic state
has a greater need for liberal universities than for nonliberal
ones. Democratic politics, and the effective exercise of the political rights of citizens, depend upon the free development and
dissemination of ideas to which liberal universities are uniquely
dedicated as social institutions.

3. AN ILLUSTRATIVE CASE:
THE UNIVERSITY AS TERRITORY

Consider a recent case that illustrates quite starkly the difference between the corporate pluralist and liberal democratic
standards of university autonomy. A private university dedicated to liberal education claims the right to restrict political
speech on campus. In 1978 Princeton University had a policy
requiring any outsiders who wished to leaflet on campus to get
an invitation from a member of the University or else to obtain
permission from the Office of the Dean of Student Affairs.
Princeton's Security Department arrested Chris Schmid and
charged him under a New Jersey statute with trespass for
leafletting on campus. Schmid was distributing and selling political literature on the mayoral race in Newark and the politics
of the United States Labor Party, of which he was a member.
He had not been invited by any member of the University and
had failed to get permission from the Dean's office.[7]

For the corporate pluralist, the right claimed by Princeton
University to restrict political speech on its campus is a clearly
justified exercise of the territorial right of a private university,
and the decision of the New Jersey Supreme Court to require
free political speech on Princeton's campus is an unjustified exercise of state power. Princeton's policy on solicitation coerced
no one and they violated no contract in keeping Chris Schmid
off campus. Schmid therefore should be free to leaflet on
Princeton's publicly owned streets, but not on the University's
privately owned campus.[8]

The University's defense in the Schmid case was consistent

with corporate principles in admitting that were Princeton a public university dedicated to the same liberal educational purposes, it would be constitutionally required to permit political speech on its campus.[9] The state would be within its authority to insist that no administrator be free to determine which uninvited speakers could have access to campus. But, Princeton's legal counsel argued, a private university has the right to exclude all political speech on campus or to discriminate among political speakers even when it can provide no educational rationale for so doing. The state simply has no authority: "In the case of a private university, where governmental constraints on educational policy are forbidden by the First Amendment, expressive activities on university property may or may not conflict with its educational purposes."[10]

To the liberal democrat, ownership alone does not determine whether the state has authority to require a university to open its campus to political speech. The right of free speech, especially the right of free political speech, is too fundamental to the democratic process to be subordinated to the claim that "it is our university to govern as we see fit." A democratic state is responsible for protecting the value of private property, particularly its value in furthering freedom of association in higher education, but it also has a legitimate concern in protecting the interests of those citizens who wish to communicate their political views to students who live as well as study on university campuses. Therefore, the state must try, as the New Jersey Supreme Court did in its unanimous opinion in favor of the defendant Schmid, "to achieve the optimal balance between the protections to be accorded private property and those to be given to expressional freedoms exercised upon such property."[11]

4. THE RELATIVE AUTONOMY OF THE UNIVERSITY

On this view of liberal democracy, the protection that a democratic state should accord a private university or any other private institution will depend upon the nature and value of the purposes served by the institution; the value of the right of citizenship at stake; and the extent to which those purposes

conflict with the citizenship right. A balance must be struck between the injury to the right of citizenship resulting from recognizing institutional autonomy and the damage to legitimate
institutional purposes resulting from requiring an institution to
respect that right.

Several rules based upon these considerations can guide us
in deciding particular cases regarding university autonomy. If
no conflict exists between a private university's purposes and a
citizenship right, then the state is justified in requiring the university to recognize that right. If some conflict exists, the state
can require recognition only if (a) the injury to the university's
purposes is small or its purposes are not valued; and (b) the
value of the right at stake for some citizens will be significantly
enhanced by requiring that the university (and similar universities) recognize the right. Under the converse conditions, private universities will be justified in restricting a right of citizenship.

This standard will leave a democratic state with some hard
choices, since the educational and associational purposes of
universities are highly valued in our society, as is the right to
political speech and equality of educational opportunity. But in
the case of *Princeton v. Schmid,* the choice is not difficult. The
University does not claim that any injury to its educational purposes will result from admitting political speech by uninvited
outsiders. (I assume that it would retain the authority to regulate the time, place and manner of speech on its campus in
order to prevent disruption of its educational functions.) The
remaining consideration is injury to freedom of association
within the university: the freedom of students, faculty and administrators collectively to shape the environment in which they
live and work. I have more to say later about the importance
of internal democracy for university autonomy, but suffice it to
say here that Princeton's representative body never voted upon,
nor did it have the authority to institute, the solicitation rule
under which Chris Schmid was arrested.[12]

Princeton's defense of its right to limit political speech on its
campus illustrates in the extreme the difference between corporate pluralist and liberal democratic standards for university
autonomy. Since arresting Schmid, the University changed its
internal policy so as to permit political solicitation on campus

by uninvited outsiders, thus, in the opinion of Justice Handler, "exemply[ing] the approaches open to private educational entities seeking to protect their institutional integrity while at the same time recognizing individual rights of speech and assembly . . ."[13] Despite this fact and that it claims no educational rationale for its original restrictive policy, Princeton insists upon its absolute right as a private university not to have its educational policies regulated by the state, and thus to reinstitute its original policy or a more restrictive one if it sees fit.[14]

The most obvious appeal of the liberal democratic, in contrast to the corporate pluralist, standard of university autonomy is that it does not subordinate rights of citizenship to the right of private property without some institutional rationale for so doing. Liberal residential universities whose purposes are consonant with, or arguably even furthered by, free political speech on campus are legitimately subject to the same free speech requirements as the state requires of its own universities. This standard enables a democratic state to stem the tide that is sweeping away channels of inexpensive and easily accessible political communication. Only those private universities, shopping malls, residential communities, and industrial parks that can plausibly claim a conflict between their institutional purposes (protected by a right of free association) and free political speech on their territory have a prima facie case for special treatment by the state, the strength of their cases varying with the specific nature and degree of the conflict.[15]

This standard, however, is less decisive than the corporate one, leaving room among those who agree upon it for disagreement as to where the balance of social justice lies in any particular case. Take a secluded residential college dedicated to religious indoctrination, which values its campus as a retreat from the corrupt practices and ideas of the surrounding society and therefore uses its standard of truth to determine the political views that can be voiced on campus. To achieve this educational purpose, the college administration screens all campus speakers according to the content of their proposed messages. The college's religious purposes are valued by our society, and its students, who are no longer children, certainly have a right to choose membership in such an educational community. But should this college be permitted to close its campus to local political candidates who wish to distribute campaign literature to its students? This is a harder case for the democratic standard than the Princeton case because this college, unlike Princeton, is not dedicated to liberal education. The conflict between the college's educational purposes and free political speech therefore is greater, while both the membership and the citizenship rights at stake are highly valued by our society.

Given only these facts of a hypothetical case, one might reasonably argue that the right of political communication is more seriously restricted by a closed campus than the right of religious education is by one open to political speech. The college can retain exclusive rights to control the use of its classrooms and extensive rights to limit nonpolitical speech on its campus, even if the state requires it to tolerate political speech. The only inexpensive option available to local political candidates who want to address resident students may be direct solicitation, and local elections are frequently decided by a margin smaller than the number of registered student voters in the community. While this hypothetical case certainly leaves room for disagreement as to where the balance of social justice lies on the democratic standard, few actual colleges treat their campuses as classrooms or monastic enclaves, as this case assumes. The alternative corporate standard of declaring the right of private association trump in all situations resolves the normative tension between rights of membership and citizenship by claiming that it does not, or should not, exit.

5. THE CHOICE BETWEEN ACADEMIC FREEDOMS

How do we choose between these two general theoretical positions regarding university autonomy? Although both theories claim to support the same ideals, we have seen that what it means to achieve pluralism, academic freedom and liberal higher education varies according to the distinct moral foundations laid by each theory. One way of evaluating the two theories is by comparing how well they defend the ideals they profess. Another is to ask which understanding of university autonomy, if implemented, would result in a more acceptable system of higher education for a democratic society. I shall argue that by both criteria the liberal democratic theory is superior to the corporate pluralist one.

Unfortunately, but I think unavoidably, both criteria are somewhat circular. That is, a corporate pluralist defense of private property and free association will probably be more convincing to someone who approves of its results. Similarly, those of us who accept a liberal democratic defense of the relative autonomy of universities are likely to find this system of higher education more compatible with our view of a good society at least in part because that view has been shaped by liberal democratic principles.

But these circles of justification are not as tight as I have just drawn them. All but the most committed corporate pluralists are likely to worry about the effects of corporatism on the academic freedom of scholars if private universities are determined to limit that freedom in the name of their institutional autonomy. And only the most dogmatic democrats will not be concerned about whether the defense of academic freedom as an individual right is adequate to protect universities in the face of governmental regulations that significantly constrain admissions and hiring practices of all universities.

It therefore may be difficult, but not impossible, to determine which view better defends pluralism, academic freedom, and liberal education and which supports a system of higher education better suited to a democratic society.

6. THE MARKETPLACE OF IDEAS

Both views support pluralism by permitting private universities to dedicate themselves to a variety of religious, political and educational purposes. On the corporate view, pluralism is directly justified as the product of exercising the right of ownership, and indirectly defended because the educational purposes pursued by different universities create a marketplace of ideas within a democratic society: "From the variety of such groups, each urging its own viewpoint, society as a whole is enriched."[16] On the democratic view, pluralism is justified insofar as it is a necessary condition for exercising our right of free association, and indirectly as a means by which unorthodox ideas are taken seriously within our society.[17]

Our decision of whether and where to go to college is among the more important and deliberate associational choices we make in our lives. But that a variety of colleges and universities exist is no guarantee that we have much choice. If the tuition, hiring and admissions policies of private universities restrict choice for qualified blacks, women or the poor, then the democratic value of pluralism has not been achieved. Public universities in a corporate society may guarantee some choice for all qualified students, but if private universities discriminate on grounds of race, sex or class, some will have many more educational options than others due to factors totally unrelated to their intellectual capacities or interests. The corporate view is oblivious to this possible critique of "laissez-faire pluralism" because the only corporate right of citizenship at stake in justifying pluralism is that of university trustees, not the potential students or faculty of private universities.

The indirect purpose of pluralism—enriching the marketplace of ideas—is also better understood and defended by the democratic view. The marketplace of ideas is a democratic good only if the political and personal choices of citizens are informed by their exposure to competing ideas and theories. Corporate pluralists are mistaken if they assume that a system of diverse sectarian universities is a sufficient means for such exposure. If every private university shields its students from the burden of being exposed to ideas it deems unworthy of consideration, then the marketplace of ideas will have no privately educated and informed consumers. The idea that "society as a whole is enriched" by every university promoting its own theory of the good life ignores the fact that the idea of intellectual enrichment presumes a thinking subject.

Even the most intellectually sectarian universities may still contribute to political and personal freedom by providing us with knowledge and a set of educational choices that by their very nature cannot be supplied by liberal universities. They enable some of us to understand and others of us to choose among systems of beliefs that require suspension or denial of intellectual doubt. But a system of higher education consisting only of such universities would be an impoverished marketplace from a democratic perspective. Students would not be free to expose themselves to competing theories, nor would they be held responsible for evaluating theories on intellectual grounds. University faculty would be constrained by political and religious authorities rather than by the canons of thought in their disciplines. Consequently, citizens would be exposed only to theories that had not been tested by scholarly standards.

Public universities can supply the missing product of liberal education in the ideological marketplace of a corporate pluralist society. The commitment of corporate pluralism to liberal higher education is dependent upon a clear constitutional or legislative mandate. One might argue over whether we can find a clear requirement that publicly owned American universities respect free speech, academic freedom and nondiscriminatory standards of admission. But even if we can agree upon this interpretation of our constitutional contract, the corporate view provides us with no reasons for adopting such a constitution in the first place. A contract view of the constitution is blind to the idea that democracies need liberal universities because they serve an essential function of protecting citizens from both private and public tyranny over freedom of inquiry, which, in turn, serves as a means for freedom of political and personal choice.

The liberal democratic view not only gives a more plausible defense of liberal universities, it also alerts us to a potential tension within a democratic society if private universities are not required to respect citizenship rights. A system of higher education, tied to corporate pluralist principles, would create two educational cultures: one public and by law intellectually tolerant and supportive of equal citizenship; the other private and legally free to be intellectually intolerant and to discriminate upon any religious or political criteria chosen by university trustees.

Whether these two cultures could peacefully coexist is not a question I am prepared to answer, and in any case it is probably not the most crucial question. A democracy in which only the publicly educated are exposed to secular canons of intellectual inquiry or taught political tolerance is not merely a culturally divided society. It is also a fundamentally inegalitarian one: a society in which all citizens have democratic rights, but only some bear the corresponding responsibilities of democratic citizenship. Corporate pluralism sanctions the division of civil society into two radically different spheres. The publicly educated constitute a civic culture of political and intellectual tolerance in accepting citizenship rights as constraints upon their particular ends, while the privately educated substantiate the need for tolerance of the intolerant in asserting their freedom to pursue their own educational ends without such constraints.

A Marxist critique of this dual educational culture would assume the possibility of uniting particular and universal wills by abolishing those social conditions that create sectarianism. But this solution creates many more problems. By underestimating the importance of our particular identities as members of different associations and cultures, it fails to acknowledge the cost of eliminating, at least from American society, the tensions between rights of membership and citizenship. Instead of taking an abolitionist stance towards nonliberal universities, we need to find a means of spreading the responsibility of political tolerance and respect for universal rights as widely as possible, thereby narrowing the gap between the two cultures.

7. ACADEMIC FREEDOM AND FREEDOM OF THE ACADEMY

If its name is more than a pretext for tax exemption, every college and university in the United States is dedicated to furthering the life of the mind. But universities disagree upon the standards that are to guide that life, and who within them should determine those standards. American universities, public and private, sectarian and liberal, share one, perhaps only one, common point of agreement: that the state should not determine what those standards are.

The claim that universities should be free from governmental control over determining their academic standards can be understood on the corporate view as an assertion of academic freedom for those private institutions dedicated to furthering the life of the mind. But this is a rather recent and peculiar understanding of academic freedom, which has found its way into our constitutional law via a concurring opinion of Justice Frankfurter in the case of *Sweezy v. New Hampshire.* Quoting a statement made in a conference on the "Open University in South Africa," Frankfurter declared " 'four essential freedoms' of a university—to determine for itself on academic grounds who may teach, what may be taught, how it shall be taught, and who may be admitted to study."[18] The corporate interpretation of Frankfurter's statement emphasizes the freedom of every university as an institution to determine its own educational policies and relativizes the meaning of academic standards to those accepted by each university.[19] On this corporate understanding of academic freedom, because private universities are free to determine what constitutes an academic standard, their trustees may suppress what has traditionally been identified as the core of academic freedom: the freedom of scholars to assess existing theories, established institutions and widely held beliefs according to the canons of truth adopted by their academic disciplines, without fear of sanction by anyone if they arrive at unpopular conclusions.

This idea of academic freedom for scholars, as derived from the German concept of *Lehrfreiheit,* is neither a universal right of citizenship nor a contractual right of university employees. It is perhaps best understood as a special right tied to the particular role or office of scholar, similar in form (but different in content) to the particular rights of priests, doctors, lawyers, and journalists. This traditional understanding of academic freedom as inhering in the scholar's office is not derived simply from the basic principles of liberal democracy or corporate pluralism, but it is more compatible with the former than with the latter. The corporate pluralist understanding of the property rights of university trustees gives academic freedom the same status as any other contractual right within the university, reducing the privileges of the scholar's office to those contractually ceded to him by his university.[20] On the liberal democratic understanding, just as universal rights are those freedoms necessary to carrying out the role of a responsible citizen, so particular rights are attached to nonuniversal offices according to what is essential to carrying out those roles. The particular right of individual scholars to academic freedom—to an institutional environment conducive to creating and disseminating ideas—is justified, as is every particular right of office, because democratic society benefits from recognizing such a right.[21]

But is this understanding of academic freedom as an individual right of scholars adequate to discriminate between justified and unjustified governmental constraints upon the autonomy of universities? Executive Order 11246 defining affirmative action guidelines for universities, Title IX forbidding sex discrimination in student athletic programs, and legislation extending the age of mandatory retirement, are not direct assaults upon the academic freedom of faculty, yet they do limit the rights of universities to determine their own educational practices. On its face, liberal democracy's ascription of academic freedom to scholars seems too individualistic even to recognize that this legislation *might* threaten something valuable within the university. When HUAC and state legislative committees pressured universities in the 1950s to dismiss faculty members for their alleged Communist loyalties or for their failure to testify concerning their political beliefs, universities could legitimately assert their autonomy on liberal democratic grounds as a means of protecting the academic freedom of their faculty.[22] But can liberal democracy defend university autonomy when the academic freedom of individual faculty members is not at stake?

The corporate pluralist view of academic freedom as an institutional right provides a simple and direct way of defending university autonomy in the face of recent governmental regulation that does not directly affect the academic freedom of faculty. But it is disturbingly indiscriminate in defending private universities against all governmental regulation of their educational affairs. And it is unjustifiably discriminating in exempting private universities from any legally enforceable responsibility to recognize the rights of citizens, while leaving public universities totally vulnerable to governmental regulation. Nothing in principle, and (arguably) very little in the United States Constitution, prevents the state from requiring loyalty oaths for the faculty of public universities or from requiring public universities to teach (or ban) certain courses on political grounds.[23] At best, public universities may find protection for their autonomy in constitutional rights. But corporate principles offer little aid to someone who wishes to use necessarily general constitutional language to defend public universities against state regulation that is nondiscriminatory but restrictive of intellectual freedom.

So, we are left with one set of principles that provides a correct, but seemingly incomplete, understanding of academic freedom as a scholar's individual right, and another that provides a misleading and incomplete understanding of academic freedom as an institutional right of private universities. Our task is no longer to decide which theory offers a better defense of academic freedom, but to see whether we can extend the logic of liberal democracy to account for our intuition that there is more to academic freedom of universities than the right to defend themselves against attacks upon the academic freedom of their faculty. Can we grant an institutional right without succumbing to the absolutist defense of private universities and the irrelevant distinction of the corporate view between private and public universities?

The part of academic freedom most often neglected by its liberal democratic defenders is control of the educational environment within which scholarship and teaching take place. The historical reason for this neglect is not difficult to discern. Whereas German universities were generally self-governing bodies of scholars who made administrative decisions either collegially or through democratically elected administrators, American universities (with few exceptions) are administered by lay governing boards and administrators chosen by those boards.[24] Therefore, while the scholar's right of academic freedom in the German context could readily be extended to a right collectively to control the academic environment of the university, the academic freedom of faculty in the American context had to be used as a defense *against* the university's legally constituted administrative authority. Recurrent threats by university trustees and administrators to the academic freedom of faculty members made it easy for them to overlook their stake in defending their universities against state regulation of educational policies.[25] Despite this historical neglect, the liberal democratic view leaves room for universities to assert an institutional right to academic freedom, even when the freedom of no particular faculty member is directly threatened by governmental regulation. Constraints upon a university's hiring and admissions standards are likely to affect the future academic standards within disciplines and the environment within which scholarship and teaching take place. Administrative time and money spent complying with state regulations may be time and money not spent on improving an academic department or responding to the concerns of faculty and students. When a governmental regulation threatens to worsen the environment for scholarship and teaching, either by lowering the intellectual quality of faculty and students or by shifting the distribution of valuable resources from academic to nonacademic areas, universities can legitimately assert an institutional right to academic freedom consistent with, indeed derived from, the individual right of scholars.

But this understanding of academic freedom as an institutional right, and its concommitant defense of university autonomy, diverges significantly from the corporate understanding. It can only be properly invoked by universities dedicated to defending the traditional academic freedom of their faculty. It applies with equal force to public and private universities so dedicated. And it is not so broad as to permit any university to defend itself against those governmental regulations that are compatible with, or instrumental to achieving, a university's self-proclaimed educational purposes.

By these criteria, it is not clear that any of the thirteen major pieces of federal legislation now regulating colleges and universities—beginning with the Equal Pay Act of 1963 and ending with the sex discrimination regulations under Title IX of the Educational Amendments of 1972—violates the academic freedom of universities.[26] One can therefore agree with the general claim that "teachers should realize that an institution which lacks freedom from government interference in the management of its educational functions cannot protect its faculty from government interference in theirs" and yet refuse to shout "Academic Freedom!" whenever a university defends itself against governmental regulations of its admissions, hiring or educational programs.[27] These regulations are compatible with the educational purposes of most American universities. In some cases, a conflict arises from the fact that a university is not committed to academic freedom at all, but to certain sectarian religious purposes that are incompatible with the state's commitment to equal opportunity or to free speech. The proper institutional defense against such regulations is not academic freedom, but freedom of association.[28] And in each of these cases, a democratic state must determine with which of the competing rights—of citizenship or of membership—the balance of social justice lies.

8. FREEDOM OF ASSOCIATION

Universities are not only institutes for advanced study; many of them are also communities of scholars, students and administrators, preferably of administrators who share the intellectual and educational concerns of scholars and students.[29] Although they will not be truly voluntary communities as long as a college diploma is necessary for respectable employment in our society, many students and some faculty (to an unfortunately diminishing extent) choose where they want to study or teach. The relative intellectual worth of various institutions is only one factor in their decisions. Universities are also chosen for the kinds of communities they are. In the case of many private universities, trustees first determined the cultural and social standards of their institutions, but in most cases they do not remain the sole force behind perpetuating or redefining those standards. Faculty and students as well as administrators also influence, if not determine, the social and cultural life of their university. They have more of an interest in defining the standards of their community than do nonmembers, except in cases where their university's policies violate the rights of nonmembers.

In many instances where affirmative action regulations are compatible with a university's academic standards, they nevertheless may threaten the value of free association by redirecting administrative attention away from the preferences of university members towards those of governmental agencies and by placing another external limit upon the range of policies available to university members in determining standards of membership in their community. This does not constitute a complete argument against state-imposed affirmative action, but it is an argument that advocates of affirmative action often neglect even to consider. A complete defense (or critique) of affirmative action would have to compare the social gain in equality of educational opportunity or compensatory justice with the limits thereby placed upon freedom of association within university communities. Should the state use universities as instruments for achieving a more just distribution of education, income and office if the price of that achievement is constraining associational freedom within universities? In a society like our own in which past discrimination has created a seriously skewed racial and sexual distribution among university members, the answer in most cases will probably be "yes." But a fully reasoned answer would have to follow a detailed inquiry into what is gained and lost by particular affirmative action regulations within university communities.

If freedom of association provides universities with a prima facie defense against affirmative action regulations imposed by the state, it must also give them authority to institute their own standards of preferential admissions. Other things being equal, free association makes self-imposed affirmative action less problematic than state-imposed standards. But other things are not equal in our society. Under what circumstances may the state legimately overturn a university's self-imposed standards?

The starting point for an analysis along corporate democratic lines is reflected in Judith Thomson's essay on affirmative action: "It is the fact of public support," she argues, "that makes preferential hiring in the universities problematic," since "where a community pays the bills, the community owns the university."[30] But the next step in the corporate argument is not clear. Does collective ownership imply that the public has a right to control the admissions policies of its universities through democratic legislation? Or does it follow that joint ownership gives every equally qualified citizen a right to an equal chance of being admitted or hired by a public university? Thomson assumes the latter for the sake of justifying a limited form of affirmative action within public universities: giving preference to equally qualified women and minorities over men.[31] On either assumption, private universities are free to adopt any admission policies they wish, so long as they do not violate contractual obligations.

One might simply accept the corporate distinction between

public and private universities and then argue that in practice the distinction is moot because no American college or university is wholly private. Even those few that accept no direct government subsidies are publicly supported by tax-free use of land and of income, and tax-deductible contributions.[32] But I want to argue that the very starting point of corporatism—the presumption that the right of ownership distinguishes problematic from nonproblematic cases of self-imposed preferential hiring—is misleading. If a public university's policy of preferring women to equally qualified men violates the right of male citizens to equal educational opportunity, then so does the same policy adopted by a private university with similar educational and associational purposes. Conversely, once one justifies preferential hiring by private universities, public ownership will not be sufficient to render the same policies by similarly dedicated public universities unjust. Both private and public universities should be permitted to exercise discretion in determining their admissions policies among the broad range that are compatible with their purposes. Discretion leaves room for associational as well as academic freedom. Arbitrariness effectively precludes the pursuit of any purposes. It is not private ownership per se that can give private universities still more latitude in determining their admission and hiring standards, but their special right of dedication to nonliberal educational or associational purposes. That right of dedication will sometimes require a democratic state to make a hard choice between its interests in respecting educational pluralism or freedom of association and its responsibility in furthering equality of educational opportunity.

But hard choices arise only when a private university's educational or associational purposes leave no room for admissions and hiring standards consistent with the liberal standard of equal educational opportunity. The state is therefore forced either to violate the educational purposes and limit the associational freedom of a university or to relax its standard of equality.

The *Bakke* case was not a hard one in this sense, nor would it have been an easier one had the Medical School at Davis been privately owned. Justice Powell's concurring opinion in the case, in favor of overturning Davis's preferential hiring standards, did not rely upon the fact of public ownership, but rather upon a more generally applicable standard of equality of educational opportunity. While acknowledging that a university should have "wide discretion in making the sensitive judgments as to who should be admitted," Powell also recognized that "constitutional limitations protecting individual rights may not be disregarded."[33] Were Davis's quota system a reasonable means to achieving its educational goal of diversity, Bakke's right to equal consideration would not have been violated. In his subsequent argument, Powell not only denies Davis's claim that its social admissions program is the *only* effective means of serving its educational interests in diversity, he also denies that it is *an* effective means at all, because it disregards any qualifications other than race or ethnicity: "The diversity that furthers a compelling state interest encompasses a far broader array of qualifications and characteristics of which racial or ethnic origin is but a single though important element. Petitioner's special admissions program, focused solely on ethnic diversity, would hinder rather than further attainment of genuine diversity."[34]

If Powell's empirical claims are correct, the choice facing the Court in the *Bakke* case was between Davis's associational right to determine its own admissions standards and Bakke's right to equal consideration in the distribution of places in medical school. Freedom of association provided Davis with a legitimate, although in this case insufficient, defense of its preferential hiring program, despite the (presumed) fact that it offered no convincing educational rationale for its policy.

Of course, some universities (Davis may be one example) are not self-governing communities in any meaningful sense, but rather autocratically governed institutions even on issues central to the interests and expertise of their faculty. In professedly liberal universities where the faculty are denied power over academic issues most central to their interests and expertise, the role of a liberal democratic state should be to support more freedom of association for faculty rather than to take over the administrative role in order to enforce policies more favorable to the faculty's interests. By preserving a university's right to make its own educational policies, subject only to nonviolation of individual rights, a democratic state increases the possibility of more self-governance in the future. It is easier for faculty members to fight their board of trustees or administration than for them to wrest policy-making authority from their state legislature or the U.S. Supreme Court.

I have concentrated upon the membership interests of faculty, but students too have significant and legitimate interests in influencing university policy, especially in matters concerning their social and political life on campus. The demand of Berkeley students in 1964 for a right of political advocacy on a 26-foot strip of brick walkway at the campus entrance was widely interpreted as a demand for more student and faculty participation in governing the university.[35] Had the students taken the free speech issue to the California courts, they might have won the right of political advocacy on that corner of Bancroft Way and Telegraph Avenue. Instead, by directing their protest internally against the Berkeley administration, they brought about some significant changes in university governance. The administration ceded faculty and students more influence over university policy than they previously had.

Even faculty members who were not totally sympathetic to the aims of the Free Speech Movement became critics of the way Berkeley had been governed. "The constitution of the university—the distribution of powers among its various elements—may well be out of joint," Nathan Glazer conceded.[36] Often, as in the Free Speech Movement, the internal fight to redistribute those powers is costly and the results not entirely satisfactory. But if the alternative is to have courts continually determine university policy, when that policy primarily affects university members, the costs may be worth bearing in the hopes of ultimately creating a genuine university community. In any case, the job of redistributing powers within the university must be internally initiated.

9. IN CONCLUSION

On the liberal democratic view, relative autonomy for liberal universities is justified as the means by which they are most likely to fulfill their educational purposes within a democratic society and also enrich the associational life of their members. Autonomy from state control does not release trustees of lib-

eral private universities from the moral responsibility of furthering the democratic and associational purposes of higher
education. While corporate pluralists can commend liberal educational goals as their personal preferences, nothing in the
theory of corporatism indicates why liberal higher education or
the participation of members within liberal universities are valuable social goods.

On the corporate view, the goods we value as a society are
identified by the goods for which we have contracted, either as
individuals or as a society. Perhaps we already have a social
contract that requires the trustees of all nonsectarian universities to respect the academic freedom of their faculty and the
associational interests of their members. If so, the corporate
pluralist and liberal democratic perspectives will support the
same degree of freedom for universities from the state, only
for different reasons. But this is not likely to be the case in fact,
because our social contract is metaphorical rather than real; in
any case, it does not explicitly grant academic freedom to scholars. Moreover, the real contract between university trustees and
faculty is not usually explicit in its guarantee of academic freedom, thus leaving plenty of room for disputes over implied understandings. These disputes will not easily be settled in favor
of faculty members in a court of law informed by corporate
principles. Therefore, in fact as in theory, those of us who wish
to defend the university against unjustified governmental regulation will have to choose between a corporate pluralist and
liberal democratic defense.

I have argued that the more absolutist defense of the autonomy of private universities is not the more adequate from the
standpoint of democratic values, and that the better defense is
one that recognizes both the interest of democratic citizens in
regulating higher education and that of university members in
governing their own associations. Therefore, freedom of the
academy and within the academy may conflict at times with the
freedoms of nonmembers. My argument in favor of the liberal
and against the corporate defense of university autonomy ultimately rests upon a reluctance to sacrifice either citizenship or
membership rights, and a corresponding willingness to acknowledge that democratic states may face hard choices when

those rights conflict, as I assume they will for a long time to come.[37]

NOTES

1. "Brief of Appellant," *Princeton and State of New Jersey v. Chris Schmid* (July 13, 1981), p. 19. Hereafter cited as *Brief of Princeton.*
2. "A Private University Looks at Government Regulation," *Journal of College and University Law,* Vol. 4, No. 1 (Fall 1976), p. 3.
3. Ibid., pp. 3–4.
4. For evidence of "the limited competence of markets" and for a balanced account of the problems created for a democracy by unregulated private enterprise, see Charles E. Lindblom, *Politics and Markets: The World's Political-Economic Systems* (New York: Basic Books, 1977), pp. 76–116 and 170–213.
5. The meaning of equality of opportunity is notoriously elusive, but my argument depends only upon a fairly minimal notion of nondiscrimination in the distribution of social offices and valuable places. Equality of opportunity is violated if a person is denied admission to college or an academic job on the basis of a characteristic irrelevant to his or her ability successfully to satisfy reasonable requirements of that position. The full meaning of equal opportunity is broader and more controversial than this one. See John Rawls's general discussion in *A Theory of Justice* (Cambridge, Mass.: Harvard University Press, 1971), pp. 65–80. Gutmann, *Liberal Equality* (New York: Cambridge University Press, 1980), pp. 191–197 is directed to the specific problem of equalizing educational opportunity in a liberal democracy.
6. For an informative essay that attempts to make use of this distinction, see Judith Jarvis Thomson, "Preferential Hiring," *Philosophy & Public Affairs,* Vol. 2, No. 4 (Summer 1973), pp. 364–384; see esp. pp. 370–371.
7. These facts are all cited in the opinion of the Supreme Court of New Jersey, *State of New Jersey v. Chris Schmid,* 84 N.J. 535 at 538–542. Also reprinted in "Jurisdictional Statement of Appellant Princeton University" (March 17, 1981), pp. 1a–4a (hereafter cited as *J.S.*).
8. See *J.S.,* pp. 12–15.
9. *Brief of Princeton,* pp. 10–11; and "Reply Brief of Appellant-Princeton University" (October 14, 1981), p.8.
10. *Brief of Princeton,* p.10.
11. *State of New Jersey v. Chris Schmid,* 84 N.J. 535, at 562.

12. The solicitation rule in question was written in 1977 by the Assistant Counsel of the University in consultation with the staff of the Office of the Dean of Student Affairs, and it was added to the University's "Rights, Rules, and Responsibilities" booklet in 1977 without a vote by the Council of the Princeton University Community. While the added paragraph on solicitation was intended to codify the long-standing practice of the University administration, the previously existing legislation (which had been passed by the CPUC) gave no clear answer to the question of whether uninvited outsiders could peacefully leaflet or solicit for political and religious causes on Princeton's campus.

13. *State of New Jersey v. Chris Schmid*, 84 N.J. 535, at 568.

14. "Princeton contends that the judgment as to what is or is not discordant with its philosophy is for Princeton alone to determine." *Brief of Princeton*, p. 6.

    "What Princeton has sought to defend in this case is the freedom of the university to govern its own affairs, including the formulation and reformulation of its own rules of access to the campus." Thomas H. Wright, "N.J. v. Schmid: The University's Case," *The Daily Princetonian*, Tuesday, December 2, 1981, p. 6.

15. For a legal argument to this effect, based upon state constitutional protections of free speech, see "Note: Private Abridgement of Speech and the State Constitutions," *The Yale Law Journal*, Vol. 90, pp. 165–188.

16. "Brief of Appellant Princeton University Opposing Motion to Dismiss or Affirm," *Princeton University and State of New Jersey v. Chris Schmid* (April 30, 1981), p. 4.

17. One might take this argument one step further: the liberal educational ideal itself may be parasitic upon the existence of communities that depend for their survival on nonliberal forms of education. If different ways of life cannot be seriously considered unless they actually exist within a society, and if liberal education (even liberal higher education) conduces to conformity without living examples of radically different ways of life, then liberal democracy may have to foster, not simply to tolerate, sectarian forms of higher and lower education.

18. *Sweezy v. New Hampshire*, 354 U.S. 234, at 263 (1957).

19. E.g. in the *J.S.* of Princeton University, pp. 7 and 8: "The purpose of a private educational institution is research and education—to deal with ideas and concepts from whatever viewpoint, doctrine, cause or perspective it chooses. It may educate its students with the purpose of indoctrination in virtually any set of beliefs it espouses—popular or unpopular, reasonable or unreasonable. . . . [T]he institution's choice is totally protected by the U.S. Constitu-

tion from either perfidious or benign governmental interference, direction or control." With regard to restricting political speech on its campus: "[T]he issue is not simply whether the property owner may or may not be identified with the views expressed on its property by others but whether it must dedicate its property to expressive uses by others which, *in its opinion,* are incompatible with its own educational purposes."

20. Princeton acknowledges its faculty's right to academic freedom in these terms: "Of course, Princeton, like any other person, would be bound by any voluntary contractual limitations on its First Amendment rights. When *amicus* AAUP suggests that Princeton would offer its First Amendment rights as a defense to tenure and other breach of contract claims asserted by the faculty, it grossly misreads Princeton's argument. Here, the state police power is involved." *Reply Brief of Appellant Princeton University* (October 14, 1981), p. 8, note 9.

21. See "1940 Statement of Principles on Academic Freedom and Tenure," in Joughin, ed., op. cit., p. 34; and Machlup, "Some Misconceptions Concerning Academic Freedom," in Joughin, ed., op. cit., pp. 181–182; and Machlup, "In Defense of Academic Tenure," in Joughin, ed., op. cit., pp. 326–328.

22. For an account of these governmental attacks upon academic freedom in the 1950s, see MacIver, *Academic Freedom in Our Time,* pp. 46–55, 158–187.

23. Some states still require loyalty oaths of all public employees, including faculty at state universities. Profession of loyalty to the U.S. Constitution may be a reasonable requirement for government employees whose jobs require implementation of governmental policies, but the responsibility of a scholar is to be led to his political principles by intellectual standards, not by the requirements of his job. Loyalty to the constitution of a liberal democracy requires no more nor less of faculty within public universities. For an account of an oath of loyalty that required more, see David P. Gardner, *The California Oath Controversy* (Berkeley, Calif.: University of California Press, 1967).

24. See Ralph F. Fuchs, "Academic Freedom—Its Basic Philosophy, Function, and History," in Hans W. Baade and Robinson O. Everett, eds., *Academic Freedom: The Scholar's Place in Modern Society* (Dobbs Ferry, N.Y.: Oceana Publications, 1964), pp. 5 and 6; and Hofstadter and Metzger, op. cit., pp. 383–398. The first systematic formulation of this understanding of academic freedom seems to have been Friedrich Paulsen's in *The German Universities and University Study* (1902), trans. F. Thilly and W. W. Elwang (New York: C. Scribner's Sons, 1906), pp. 228–231.

AMY GUTMANN

25. See the AAUP's list of "Censured Administrations, 1930–1967" in Joughin, ed., op. cit., pp. 143–146.
26. This list includes also the Minimum Wage Laws, the Occupational Safety and Health Act of 1970 (OSHA), Title VII of the Civil Rights Act of 1964, and Executive Order 11246, as amended to require affirmative action to correct past discriminations in employment. For the list of thirteen, see Dallin Oaks, "A Private University Looks at Government Regulation," pp. 3–4.
27. Oaks, op. cit., p. 3.
28. This is the position taken by the American Association of University Professors in their "Brief Amicus Curiae," *Princeton University and State of New Jersey v. Chris Schmid*, pp. 4–10.
29. Cf. Clark Kerr, *The Uses of the University* (Cambridge, Mass.: Harvard University Press, 1963) where Kerr's description of the "multiversity" as "a city of infinite variety" leads him to define the role of a university president as a mediator among all the university's constituencies (pp. 21 45). This definition is dangerous if mediation entails sacrificing in response to external pressures the intellectual freedoms and culture unique to universities as social institutions.
30. Judith Jarvis Thomson, "Preferential Hiring," pp. 369, 374.
31. Ibid., pp. 374–384.
32. Ibid., pp. 369, 374.
33. *University of California Regents v. Allan Bakke,* 438 U.S. 265, at 314 (1978).
34. Ibid., at 315.
35. For an extensive account of the Berkeley Free Speech Movement upon which my discussion is based, see Seymour Martin Lipset and Sheldon S. Wolin, eds., *The Berkeley Student Revolt: Facts and Interpretations* (Garden City, N.Y.: Doubleday & Co., 1965).
36. "What Happened at Berkeley," in Lipset and Wolin, eds., op. cit., p. 301.
37. I would like to thank John Chapman, Marshall Cohen, Michael Doyle, Michael McPherson, Walter Murphy, Roland Pennock, Thomas Scanlon, Jr., Dennis Thompson, and Michael Walzer for their helpful comments. I also benefited from discussions of the *Schmid* case with Sanford Levinson and Thomas Wright, Jr.

PART V

RATIONALITY, RESPONSIBILITY, AND INDIVIDUALITY

12

LIBERAL DEMOCRACY AND THE SOCIAL DETERMINATION OF IDEAS

BARRY HOLDEN

I.

My aim is to counter an insidious form of those "anti-democratic" arguments which contend that "liberal democracies" are not in fact the democracies they purport to be. The variety of "anti-democratic" argument with which I am concerned involves or arises from a challenge to a fundamental pre-supposition of liberal-democratic theory—the intellectual autonomy of the electorate. The counter-argument I shall deploy focusses on the way in which the notion of intellectual autonomy can be saved by a proper recognition of the role of true ideas: in other words my aim will be to re-affirm the existence of democracy by stressing the importance of truth as a source of ideas.

The challenge to the intellectual autonomy of the electorate springs primarily from certain aspects of modern socio-philosophic thought, especially from Marxism. The challenge is insufficiently recognised; when recognised, it is inadequately dealt with.

Marxist and neo-Marxist critiques of Western or liberal democracies are faced with—and must, as it were, "explain away"—the brute fact of free elections and mass electorates, i.e. competitive elections based on universal suffrage and the secret ballot. Marxist arguments, then, to the effect that the so-called "liberal democracies" are but sham democracies in which the people do not in fact rule, come up against the difficulty that (apparently) in these systems the people *do* make the basic political decisions through free elections. Marx and Engels had various views about whether, or to what extent, the existence of universal suffrage gives power to the people. However, with the passage of time, and the persistence of what Marxists see as essentially undiminished bourgeois power in the "democracies," only one type of view has become possible: that the establishment and continued existence of universal suffrage and competitive elections has not put the people in control.[1] But how can this be so when, apparently, at elections the people *do* make the ultimate political decisions?

Two main types of argument tend to figure in answers to this question—and often both are used together. In the first emphasis is on the idea that it is economic power that is basic: political institutions are subordinate to economic power. Hence even though (or even if) the people genuinely make basic policy decisions at elections this does not mean that they have power: the capitalists will frustrate the implementation of any decisions that threaten their own interests.[2]

The second category of arguments focusses not so much on the (paucity of) effects of elections as on the elections themselves, and calls into question the significance of the electoral process. The basic contention is that the so-called free elections of liberal democracies do not actually express the views of the people: the electoral "decision" (if such it can be called) is not the verdict of the people. Thus, even if elections were to control subsequent policy, still the "will" of the people would not prevail.

This set of arguments subdivides. First, it is often said (and not just by Marxists) that it is the restricted range of available options that prevents an election from being an expression of the people's views. The people cannot vote for what they want because what they want is not there to vote for. And the Marxist would say that the range of options is restricted to those that comply with the interests of the ruling class. I do not intend to consider this contention, although I think that it is basically mistaken (even if it may have some truth as applied to the short term). The view is surely basically correct that sees the adoption of policies by political parties (including new parties) as stemming, to an important extent, from the need to win votes by satisfying the wishes of the electors. But this "restriction-of-options" line frequently becomes transmogrified into one that is more fundamental, and which is more worrying for the Western liberal democrat. And it is arguments of this latter kind that bring us to the central problem with which I am concerned.

II.

The more fundamental claims of this sort are to the effect that elections do not express the views of the people because, in a crucial sense, the people cannot be said to have views—that the views they express cannot properly be said to be theirs. The key notion is that these views—or, more generally, thoughts or ideas—have been "put into" people's heads. The Marxist notion is, of course, that these ideas serve the interests of the "ruling class." Marx himself said that "the ideas of the ruling class are in every epoch the ruling ideas."[3] This theme was developed by Gramsci and Marcuse; indeed, it became the basic inspiration of so-called "critical theory."[4] In a Marxist perspective, then, the mass of the people, even in "liberal democracies," have been indocrinated with the ideas—the ideology—of the ruling class. In a word, they are victims of "false consciousness." Electoral activity, then, simply reflects back the outlook of the ruling class.

Whether the ideas of the ruling class are deliberately imposed or whether they flow directly from the class structure is not our present concern.[5] The fundamental point is the notion that the ideas expressed by the mass of the people are not, properly speaking, their own—whether or not deliberate action by the ruling class is responsible for this state of affairs.

III.

Marxism may be the most prominent source of the notion that ideas are put into people's heads; it is from a Marxist perspective that its "anti-democratic" use usually arises. However, this notion is not, of course, restricted to Marxist thought: the conception of ideas serving the interests of the ruling class is characteristically Marxist, but the belief that ideas expressed by the people are not their own has two other components that are by no means uniquely Marxist. The first of these is an emphasis on the extent to which ideas exist independently of, rather than being generated by, the people who express them (the reference is primarily—but not exclusively—to concepts rather than to the propositions, beliefs, opinions, etc., constituted from them.) The second component is that concepts, opinions and so on are induced in the minds of the individuals who express them, rather than being spontaneously adopted. The first component would be widely accepted as valid,[6] although it should be kept in mind that the liberal democrat thinks as much in terms of an individual's desires, wants or preferences as in terms of his ideas: and desires, wants and preferences *are* generated by the individuals who express them. We shall return to this point later. The second assertion is more distinctive and has implications that are more clearly and directly anti-democratic, but the point to be made here is that neither contention is restricted to Marxist analyses. Not only are they central to the whole sociology of knowledge but they are also important in conventional positivist political analysis: studies of political socialization *consist* in analyses of the processes by which people are induced to absorb—to "internalize"—the ingredients of their political culture. In other words, the subject of such studies is how ideas, which pre-exist "outside" them, are induced into individuals' minds.

The two contentions add up to the claim that thinking is socially determined. And, as we have just noticed, this is widely accepted. But this means that a fundamental critique of Western liberal democracy is pretty much taken for granted. It is true that when not associated with the Marxist vision of a ruling ideology, its anti-democratic implications are not explicit—nor, indeed, are these implications usually recognised or intended. But let us be clear about it: the anti-democratic implications *are* there. If thinking is socially determined the people's expressed ideas are not their own (this point is further discussed below), but if this is so then the people cannot be said to rule. This is the case whether or not those ideas belong to, or further the interests of, a ruling class.

Wide acceptance of the premise for these implications is a very serious matter. It creates crucial difficulties for the theoretical (and therefore also the practical) defence of Western liberal democracy. Nor is the situation made any better by the fact that those who do not recognize its insidious implications are frequently advocates of liberal democracy (most positivist political scientists support liberal democracy even though their "scientific value relativism" is supposed to rule this out). Worse still, these implications are even suggested in the writings of modern democratic theorists, as shown by the frequent identification of consensus with political socialization: a clear example is Dahl's emphasis on the dependence of consensus on *social training* in the norms of democracy, which implies that people's ideas are nothing *but* the product of social training.[7]

IV.

One possible response to a critique of liberal democracy based on, or implied by, the thesis that the people have ideas put into their minds, is to demur that this does not really matter. The important thing, according to this line of argument, is that the ideas *are expressed* by the people: those ideas *are* the people's simply by virtue of the fact that they express them, and should be respected as such. People have the thoughts they express, however they came to have them. To explain the existence of something is not to explain it away.

This type of argument has some merit, but in the end it will not really do. This is because the concern, here, with the issue of whether the ideas expressed by the people can be said to be their own involves more than simply an interest in the question of the proper criteria of intellectual ownership. The underlying, and crucial, issue is that of intellectual autonomy. Does the mere fact of expression of ideas by a person in itself amount to a manifestation or signification of his intellectual autonomy? The key contention here is that autonomy (if it exists) consists to an important extent in intellectual autonomy—which must involve autonomous thought, i.e. *inner* directed control of ideas. To put the point another way, the important issue is whether people themselves *decide* on the ideas they express: whether those ideas are ones they have themselves deliberately decided to adopt—which cannot be the case if thought is socially determined.

The position, then, is this: democracy is a system in which the people have control, but control presupposes that the people are autonomous; this autonomy entails intellectual autonomy, and intellectual autonomy is precisely what is precluded by insistence that their ideas are determined. Intellectual defense of liberal democracy—demonstration that what are called liberal democracies are really so—thus requires refutation of the doctrine that popular thought is socially determined. It would be impossible here to undertake a full analysis of the issues this raises, but in what follows I will point to some key arguments essential to such a refutation.

V.

Arguments supporting the notion that popular thinking is socially determined can, in the first place, be rejected as incoherent. The key point is that these presume or assert the relativity of thought. Or, to put the point somewhat more circumspectly, such arguments gain much of their force from their implicit—and, in their extreme form, their explicit—assumption that social thought is relative. This contention is incoherent.

The notions, then, that ideas are socially determined and that they are relative—and do not express truths—are closely tied together. If ideas do not express truth they must come from somewhere else, from social forces or whatever. And, conversely, if ideas are "caused" in this way, then it is not because they express truths that they come to mind. If the proposition that ideas are relative is incoherent, then the notion of the social determination of ideas is seriously undermined.

Central to the theory that social thought is relative, then, is the contention that the content of thought (about social reality, at least) arises from, or is provided by, something other than the object (or alleged object) of that thought. The content of the ideas people have about society does not arise from rational contemplation of that society. Their ideas do not consist in apprehensions or representations of the society any more than nightmares caused by indigestion consist in apprehensions or representations of the digestive system. Instead, according to the relativity of thought doctrine, people misapprehend or misrepresent reality because they merely react to the social environment. In short, understandings of social reality do not grasp truths but are outcomes of social processes.

Thought is relative in the sense that its content is relative to the thinker's situation rather than being an objective representation of that which is the purported object of the thinking. (Of course, this contrast does not imply that if thought were nonrelative its content would *necessarily* be true; rather it implies that a crucial determinant of the content of thought could well be—and frequently would be—the nature of the social reality that was the object of reflection, and that, accordingly, the content of the thought might well be true, or, at least, embody a large measure of truth.) Often, this relativity of thought is explicitly focussed on. The concept of the ideology of the "ruling class," for instance, contains an explicit contrast between objective truths and the distortions and falsehoods constituting the awareness of those subjected to the ideology. But in other cases there is little or no recognition that the relativity of thought is implied. Thus, it is seldom recognized or acknowledged that the concept of "political socialization"—at least if not carefully formulated to avoid this—carries the implication that thought is relative. The point is that when exposure to social processes is taken as a necessary and sufficient explanation for people having the ideas that they have, then it is no longer necessary or possible to say that they are held because they are true. No connection—or only an arbitrary connection—remains between the truth and what is in people's minds.

Let us return now to the contention that the doctrine of the social determination of popular thought has a basis that is incoherent.

First of all the very idea of cognitive relativity is incoherent. The idea self-destructs. This point is often made,[8] but just as often ignored. If *all* thought is relative, if ideas never express objective truths, then the idea of the relativity of thought is itself relative, i.e. it does not express an objective truth. Hence, either the relativity-of-thought doctrine is not correct, and it is not the case that all thinking is relative; or it *is* correct—but this means that there is here a true idea, and this shows that not *all* thought is relative.

It can, of course, still be maintained that much thought is relative even though not *all* of it is—and, in particular, that the thought of the masses is. This kind of argument is commonly used or implied by Marxists, for instance, when the contention that Marxist analysis is true is combined with the contention (which plays a key role in the substance of that analysis) that most people's thought is relative. However, to admit that some thinking is not relative is to deny the *intrinsic* relativity of thought. But this is seriously to undermine the most important basis for the claim that the ideas of the masses are socially determined, i.e. that thought is *by nature* socially determined.

To maintain, then, that all thought is relative, is incoherent, but to modify this contention can also be self-defeating, since this is to destroy the usual foundation for alleging relativity in particular instances. This has a concomitantly corrosive effect on particular allegations of social determination.

Besides the general incoherence charge there is, in effect, a particular application of it. Our Marxist "anti-democratic" argument rests on what purports to be an analysis of the objective position of the people and the true character of their ideas. This is to say that the mass of the people express ideas that are contrary to their interests and favorable to the interests of the "ruling class." But this presumes or involves (what are held to be) objectively true accounts of the interests of the "ruling class," and of the interests of the people and the character of the ideas they express. In other words, an analysis (i.e., that which purports to demonstrate the false consciousness of the masses) that presupposes that thought is by nature relative, makes crucial use of arguments that assert (what are held to be) objective truths about society. Moreover, those versions of this polemic that conceive of the "ruling class" as more or less deliberately inducing ideas in the minds of the people, presuppose that it is not just Marxist analysts who have true ideas: i.e. the members of the ruling class themselves must have an objectively true view of social reality in order to know what their interests are and to know how to manipulate the thinking of the masses on behalf of those interests.

VI.

The "incoherence argument" against relativity-of-thought doctrines—and the particular application of this argument to Marxist critiques of Western democracy—shows that it must be admitted that true ideas are possible. This is of central importance as a key part of the incoherence argument itself, but of even greater importance here is an implication the significance of which is not always properly appreciated. To acknowledge the possibility of true ideas is to recognize the possibility of another reason, besides social causation, for the presence of ideas, namely, the truth that those ideas express (i.e., those ideas that *are* true). This is a crucially important reason. This point seems blindingly obvious to me, but, oddly, few people seem explicitly to recognize or accept it. Of course, a statement as bald as this brushes aside complex and controversial issues, some of which are touched on below, but in the end it must surely be admitted that it affirms an inescapable truth that in practice we all accept. It is difficult to deny, for instance, that a sufficient explanation for the existence of, say, the idea that birds build nests is that birds do build nests.[9] (One of the range of issues that is brushed over here concerns the fundamental philosophical issue of whether, or the extent to which, concepts in some sense shape reality—or, at least, shape one's view of it—as distinct from merely reflecting it; indeed, this issue is itself intimately connected with the question of the social determination of ideas. What is being posited or assumed is some version of realism. I do not intend to defend this view, but three points may be briefly made. First, it can be argued that any denial of realism falls victim to what is, in effect, a generalization of the incoherence argument that we have just looked at. Second, although the complexities of epistemological issues relating to social reality are in some ways greater than those relating to physical reality, it is also true that in an important way the former are less complex. Thus because of the "conceptual character" of social reality[10] in an important sense we have a more direct comprehension of social reality than we do of physical reality. Third, *in practice* we all do accept that some ideas are, to at least some extent, valid—that they express truths in the sense of "reflecting" reality—whilst others are untrue, or at least less true.)

Ideas, then, can be produced by something other than social interactions, (variable and capricious) cultural development, requirements of propaganda, furthering or protecting of interests, or whatever. So, also, can people hold them for reasons other than subjection to social or cultural pressures ("socialization") or indoctrination—i.e., they can hold them because they are true. The truth of an idea can account not only for its existence but also for why people adopt it. Despite qualifications to be made in a moment I maintain that, at the very least, the truth of a (true) idea can be, and usually is, a crucial part of the explanation for its existence and for its being held.

This alternative explanation for the existence and holding of ideas (an alternative to explanations in terms of social causation and manipulation) is implied as soon as the existence of any true idea is admitted. The mere acknowledgement of the possibility of this alternative type of explanation corrodes social determinist theses. But this corrosive effect is even more apparent where an "active" role for the "ruling class" is postulated. As we have seen, postulation of this role implies that the "ruling class" has true ideas: but to allow that some members of a polity (the ruling class) have true ideas is to concede that this alternative explanation does have direct application to the members—and not just to the analysts—of that polity. And if, in principle, the thinking of *some* members can be explained in this way, it becomes more difficult to show why, in principle, that of the great majority of members cannot be so explained.

It may be argued—indeed some Marxists, for example, do argue—that the veracity of an idea is a matter quite independent of the issue of whether it is socially determined. The argument is that true ideas are still socially determined. Some men are just lucky enough to have ideas that are true socially implanted in their minds.[11] In other words, truth as such is not a reason for the presence of ideas. Now, it may be that the truth is not the only possible reason for the existence and adoption of a true idea—but it does seem the most likely given the infinite number of possible ideas. It really does seem to be pushing coincidence too far to accept that anyone—let alone significant groups of people—should just happen to have acquired those particular ideas that happen to express the truth! In any case, even if, the truth *might* not be what accounts for an idea that is true, it certainly *can* be. In short, that they are true remains as a possible—and indeed, the most likely—reason for the existence and holding of ideas that are true.

VII.

Let us now summarize, and consider further, the significance of admitting the reality of true ideas; that is to say, its significance for the thesis that the people's ideas are not, in some important sense, their own.

The key points in the analysis so far are (a) that the "easy" argument for the relativity of popular thought—that since all thought is relative the ideas of the masses must be—is refuted; and, (b) that a crucially important additional factor is made available for explaining why the people have in their minds the ideas they do; i.e., the ideas of the people may be true, and if they are this explains why they hold them, and no other explanation is necessary. Thus, even where the ideas of the masses are in line with, or support, the interests of the "ruling class" it need not be the case that those ideas are induced by the "ruling class." It could be that the ideas are true, and their support for the "ruling class" would then be incidental.[12] For instance, it might be that the people in Western capitalist democracies *are* better off under capitalism than under communism.[13] If the ideas are true, at the very least we do not *have* to account for them in some other way.

Notice the reasoning is not that the ideas of the populace in some, or all, Western democracies are in fact true, and that they are not induced by the capitalists. Rather, the argument here is that it is *possible* that those ideas are true. Whether or not popular ideas are true is a large issue in itself. But, by the same token, so is the question of whether those ideas support the interests of the "ruling class." Not only is the nature and significance of the ideas at issue, but so also is the whole notion of a "ruling class," what its interests might be and whether these are incompatible with, or hostile to, those of the community at large, or of other sections of it.

We must now ask what is the further significance of this thesis that popular ideas may be true, and that this can account for their being held. The question that arises is whether the holding of ideas by people because they are true demonstrates that those ideas are their own in any significant sense.

Two issues appear. First, there is the matter of the distinction (the significance of which has so far been glossed over) between explaining the existence of an idea and explaining its presence in someone's mind. The argument so far has been concerned with both sorts of explanation, but its main force applies only to the first type: the truth of an idea may very well be the reason for its existence, but why it should be adopted by someone may well be considered a separate question. That an idea is true may sufficiently explain why a person upon whom it impinges adopts it; what also needs explaining is how a person comes to be in contact with true ideas—how is it that those ideas are available to him.

Truths, complex ones at any rate, are rarely directly apprehended and normally need to be made accessible to individuals by way of pre-formulated ideas. Hence, the possibility of an individual having true beliefs is dependent upon true ideas being available to him in the culture he inhabits. The holding of true ideas, then, is dependent on cultural situation. But does this not mean that what ideas people hold are, after all, determined by their culture? Does this not mean that the usual sociology of knowledge and socialization arguments *are* correct? The answer is complicated, but the crucial point is that it is not the culture *rather than* the truth that is the reason for the ideas being held. Note two considerations. First, a decisive part of an explanation of why true ideas occur and persist in a culture must be that they are true. This can be only dogmatically asserted here, but as before, it does seem obvious that the reason for the persistence of, say, the idea that the world is round is that the world *is* round (or, at least, the persistence of the idea is due to the rational acceptability of the idea of the world being round—see below). Hence the truth of a person's ideas is at least an indirect reason for his holding them. Second, within cultures ideas compete, and individuals have to select. Selection of a true idea can be explained by its truth, so that in such cases the truth of an idea is a direct reason for its acceptance. In these two ways it can still be maintained that a crucial part of the explanation for the holding of true ideas is that they are true. (The significance of the restricted availability of ideas is further discussed below.)

The second, and related, issue that arises in considering whether true ideas expressed by people can properly be said to be their own, concerns what is meant by the term "their own." To say that someone holds an idea *because* it is true—to say that the holding of an idea is "caused" by the truth it reflects or expresses—seems to suggest that person has no choice in the matter. Moreover, as we have already recognized, true ideas are *available to,* rather than being created by, the people who hold them. People normally adopt existing ideas (whether true or not) rather than originating them.

Despite these objections, in a significant sense the true ideas held by someone are his own. If the ideas are true they are rationally acceptable, and the individual holds them because— or very probably because[14]—he rationally accepts them. This is not to say that all rationally accepted ideas are true (this point is taken up below), but that all true ideas are—or very probably are—rationally accepted. A rationally accepted idea is one to which an individual gives his rational acquiescence—one that he freely accepts because rational consideration of the idea, its implications, the relevant evidence and so on convinces him that he should. He takes the idea as his own: it is not perpetrated upon him.

It does appear then that people's true ideas can in a significant sense be said to be their own. This is the key to the refutation of a major argument used against the notion that electorates in the Western liberal democracies are autonomous. To be sure, not all such arguments can be refuted in this way: it is still possible that the ideas (or some of them) of the electors (or some of them) are not true and that they are induced. But there is no general reason, no reason in principle, for saying that this should be so. Indeed, demonstration of electors' lack of intellectual autonomy can now be seen to require detailed and specific demonstration that the ideas they express are false. It is not sufficient, for instance, merely to indicate (even *if* this is the case) that the electorate's views coincide with, or help to advance, the interests of the "ruling class" (even *if* such a thing exists).

VIII.

So far our defense of democracy has been confined to ideas that are true; intellectual autonomy has been tied to the actual veracity of the electorate's ideas. However, this may be too severe. Must it be said that electorates have autonomy only when their ideas are true?

There are three main points here. First, it may be a mistake to limit analysis to the role of ideas and a strict conception of intellectual autonomy, rather than to consider decisions, needs, preferences and so on. This issue will be taken up in the next section. Second, it is not implied by the preceding argument that false ideas are necessarily induced, but merely that there is no underlying reason for saying that they are not: the implication is that quite possibly, but *not necessarily,* it is the case that false ideas are induced. Falsehoods might be generated or adopted for a variety of reasons, only some of which would imply that ideas are induced or "put into" people's minds. Indeed, untrue ideas of one type arguably have as close a connection with intellectual autonomy as do those which are true. This brings us to the third point.

This third point arises from the notion of rational acceptance. I said just now that true ideas expressed by a person can be regarded as his own because they are ideas that he can be said rationally to accept. But rational acceptance need not involve only the truth. It may be that true ideas provide the "paradigm case" for rational acceptability and acceptance, and that such acceptance is most clearly evident in the case of ideas that are true. But there are others that can be said to be rationally acceptable and rationally accepted, those for which it can be said that there are "good grounds"—good grounds for accepting the ideas, even though they are not true. Truth and the criterion of "good grounds" are clearly connected, but there may be good grounds for accepting an idea which in fact is not true when there are good reasons for thinking that it is. One might even call such ideas "valid," despite their being untrue.

Complex issues beyond the scope of this essay are raised here, but one point to notice is that the notion of "good grounds" copes with a difficulty arising from restrictions on the "availability" of true ideas—the difficulty of avoiding the implication that only those individuals lucky enough to have true ideas available to them can have ideas that are rationally accepted.[15] Thus persons who—through the nature of the culture they inhabit or the absence of necessary conditions for arriving at the truth (and the two can be very much interconnected)—do not have true ideas available, can nonetheless hold ideas for which there are good grounds and which are therefore rationally acceptable and so rationally accepted.[16] At one time there were, for instance, good grounds for believing that the sun went round the earth.

It might be held that there is an obvious and important difficulty connected with this criterion that deprives it of any explanatory power, since what are to be counted as good grounds is an inherently controversial issue. With little agreement on what are "good grounds" there would seem to be no way of distinguishing ideas that are held on "good grounds" from those that are not. However, rather than constituting a difficulty this reinforces traditional arguments for democracy. Since there is no certain test of what should count as good grounds, the people themselves should, in effect, be the judge of this. (This is in some ways similar to the widely accepted "relativist justification" of democracy,[17] which is essentially that since there is no certain criterion of what is right, decisions about what ought to be done can only be left to all the citizens.) This is not to say that there can be no objective analysis of whether there are good grounds for the people's beliefs,[18] nor is it to say that the people's own assessment can never be wrong. Rather, it is to say that in the last analysis, when a decision has to be made on whether to *treat* ideas as well grounded, that decision should, in effect, be made democratically. (Of course, this parallels the traditional pro-democratic contention that substantive political decisions should in the last analysis be made by the people.) In other words, it should be assumed that the people's expressed ideas *are* their own. From this it follows, given the traditional case for democracy,[19] that these ideas should prevail. The argument for the people in effect making "procedural" decisions about the grounds for popular ideas rehabilitates, and reflects, the case for the people making substantive decisions giving effect to the content of those ideas.

It may, of course, happen that the people's ideas are not well-grounded and that they are in fact socially determined (not that "invalid" ideas are *necessarily* socially determined). Here their expressed views will not, properly speaking, be their own. In this case the forms of democracy will exist but not its substance. But it only *may* be so; the argument is that the best response to uncertainty here is to treat ideas as being well-grounded where the people themselves so regard them. (The contrast is not so much with people actually regarding their ideas as being ill-grounded—an unlikely state of affairs—as with an unthinking acceptance and a lack of reflection by people on the grounds for their ideas.) Any alternative stance, and this is the crucially important point, is likely to lead to the people's expressed views being dismissed and ignored on the grounds that those views are not their own—even when they are.

To develop the point another way, it is better, far better, to treat a specious democracy as if it were an actual one, than to treat an actual, as if it were only an apparent, democracy. The forms of liberal democracy—in particular free elections—ought to be preserved even if and when they do not actually provide democracy, since they are a vital protection against tyranny. (It is true that one of the typical contentions of our "anti-democratic" arguments is that hidden control over the minds of people is also tyranny. However, even if the kind of "control" over minds referred to can be properly so called, it is surely a far less pernicious form of tyranny, if such it can be called, than that denounced by liberal democrats: the latter may well involve incarceration and torture whereas the former involves only "deprivations" of which the "victims" are not even properly aware.) Even a specious democracy should be preserved since it is a system that is not only more tolerable than, but is also a protection against, out-and-out tyranny.

Finally, before we leave rational acceptability and the criterion of "good grounds," note that some potential difficulties relating to true ideas are also covered by our analysis. At first glance the concept of true ideas seems free of the difficulties connected with ideas that are not true but are merely well-grounded—since the criterion of truth is objective in a way that the criterion of good grounds is not. However, the notion of truth, and establishing what is and is not true, raises so many difficulties that in practice the application of this criterion raises the same problems about lack of agreement as does the "good grounds" criterion. But to the extent that these issues are resolvable in the latter case, so are they also in the former.

In fact, it is only because these same issues do arise that the truth criterion does not pose fundamental difficulties of its own. If the truth, or otherwise, of an idea was a matter to be straightforwardly settled with certainty and finality, claims to have true ideas would be open to definitive test, and possible refutation. And, of course, down the ages the case against democracy has been that the ordinary people are less able to judge what is true than are experts.

This kind of definitive validation would render defence against the social-determination-of-ideas arguments very precarious. The case would remain that if people held ideas that were true then this would show that their thinking was not socially determined. But it is a big "if," and those who sought to demonstrate social determination of ideas could plausibly claim the ability to show conclusively that people's ideas were untrue. However, because in practice the question of establishing whether ideas are true is as controversial as establishing whether the grounds for ideas are good, this kind of certainty and finality, and the associated claims of expert knowledge, do not arise.

IX.

I now take up two considerations that have so far been barely mentioned. These might seem to call into question the whole point of our analysis since they challenge the assumption that ideas are the key to intellectual autonomy. Or, to speak more directly, what counts is not "intellectual autonomy" so much as "autonomy of the will."

The first concerns the use of the word "idea." So far this

concept has been used to cover such diverse aspects of thought as beliefs, attitudes and value judgements. But it might well be said that (a) there is a crucial difference between beliefs on the one hand and attitudes and value judgements on the other;(b) implicitly—if not always explicitly and intentionally—it is only beliefs that have so far been referred to by the use of the word "ideas;" (c) the key conception in the notion of popular power—and therefore of democracy—is that the people make political decisions; and (d) making political decisions is essentially a matter of which values or attitudes are to prevail, and hence it is in those of the people doing so that popular decision-making consists.[20] Now, since it is said that value judgements and attitudes are essentially expressions of preference and have no cognitive status, the question of the truth of, or the grounds for, what the people think does not arise; hence the issue of whether the people's thought is really their own does not turn on this question.

However, this line of argument cannot be accepted, for three interconnected reasons. First, even if value judgements and attitudes are essentially expressions of preference they are not the only, nor even perhaps the most important, constituents of political decision making. People necessarily make value judgements about, and have attitudes towards, something. Since here the relevant something is social and political reality, people's beliefs about it necessarily play a part in shaping their judgements and attitudes. Secondly, the claim that value judgements are nothing but expressions of preference is mistaken. Rather, they are *judgements* about reality that, though they relate to preferences, are indeed judgements about the nature of that reality and, as such, contain or involve as essential elements beliefs that are true or false. Thirdly, attitudes also have cognitive dimensions. But in any case, in politics attitudes are not separate from value judgements so much as one of the factors that enter into or affect them. For these reasons, it can still be maintained that the relevant aspects of the people's thought have truth value, and that the question of how true or well-grounded their thought is remains central to the issue of whether that thought is really their own. And despite—or, rather, because of—its cognitive implications it was proper to give "idea" a central role in the exposition.

This brings us to the second of the challenges to the notion of intellectual autonomy as I have used it. Even when ideas are widely, and properly, conceived as including an amalgam of beliefs, attitudes and valuations, the question remains as to whether *decisions* are to be understood in terms of ideas. Again the point of our presentation is called into question. Since it is decision-making by the people that is salient, if decisions are not understood in terms of ideas it is pointless to worry about the nature and role of electors' ideas.

So far, I have treated "the ideas expressed by the electorate" and "the decisions made by the electorate" as more or less interchangeable. Voting has been taken as registration of ideas. However, this is an oversimplification, since holding or expressing ideas and making a decision are—though interrelated—importantly different. An idea is something distinct from the individual by whom it is held, hence the difficulties that can arise with the notion that the idea is his own. But a decision ineluctably belongs to the individual—it is something *done by* him. Choosing intimately involves the ideas held by a person, but the decision itself is an operation with or upon these ideas. It is something that is performed by the individual and that performance makes it. Moreover, a decision is based on desires or preferences as well as ideas. It is taken for granted that desires or preferences unambiguously belong to individuals in a way that ideas do not. A decision is not the same thing as the expression of a desire. Indeed, one *decides whether* to express a desire, i.e., whether to act so as to signify or satisfy that desire. Such decisions will be taken in the light of one's perception of the world, in the light of one's ideas. Hence a decision is not simply a direct manifestation of subjectivity to the extent, and in the same way, that a desire is. Nonetheless, the fact that a decision can express a desire does give the *content* of decisions a subjective dimension. A decision, then, can be subjective in content as well as in form; hence a decision can in a double sense intrinsically "belong to" the individual who makes it.

To an important extent, then, what is expressed by individuals by way of decisions necessarily "belongs to" those individuals. Since an election in a Western democracy is conceived as a *decision* by the electorate, it might seem that such an election is quite clearly and straightforwardly something done by the

electors. That is to say, it might appear that the whole issue of
the nature and role of the ideas expressed by the electorate is
shown to be irrelevant before it is off the ground.

However, this is to oversimplify. To begin with, although decisions *may* only be based on—or express—desires, this need
not be so. A decision can equally be based on—or reflect or be
the outcome of—ideas. Most decisions combine both aspects.
One might simply decide to satisfy one's hunger by having
something to eat, or decide to go to a restaurant that one *believed* to have certain characteristics.

More fundamentally, it oversimplifies to maintain or assume
a necessarily clear distinction between ideas and desires or
preferences in the first place. The objects of desire are often
given by ideas. This has two important and interrelated implications. First, it means that desires (or at least the operations of
desires) are not always entirely subjective. They are strongly
affected by ideas, which are in an important sense external to
the individual. (It was precisely this externality of ideas that
gave rise to the analysis in the first place.) Second, to the extent
that an individual's ideas are not his own, then the desires affected by these ideas can in a real sense be seen, to a degree,
as externally directed and distorted.

In short, even if voting were to be understood in terms of
desires, there would remain a sense in which electoral decisions
might be distorted, and fail to be authentic actions by the people.

This point can be pushed further and connected with the
conception of "false needs." Desires and preferences may be
regarded as the maifestations of needs. Needs generate, and
reveal themselves through, desires and preferences. Now, needs,
like desires, are often taken as purely subjective, "internally
fixed," attributes of individuals. However, it has been argued—
most forcefully by Herbert Marcuse—that needs can also be
created by society. Moreover, such needs may be at odds with
the individuals' true nature. They may indeed be false needs;
it is these that "distorted" desires reflect. For Marcuse, of course,
the "false needs" and "social determination of ideas" arguments
are intermeshed: false needs are created by (and in turn help
to sustain) ideas flowing from the ideology and culture of the
"ruling class." People lack autonomy because neither their ideas

nor their needs are their own. It is not, of course, the idea of autonomous people that Marcuse is attacking—indeed the contrast between false and true needs presupposes the possibility of autonomous individuals. Rather, he disputes that Western electorates are composed of such people, or indeed, that such people comprise the masses anywhere in the present world.

More generally, the connection between the "true needs" and the "true ideas" lines of argument points to the parallel between two dichotomies. On the one hand, individual autonomy is connected with true ideas and opposed to the absence of individual autonomy and the social determination of ideas. On the other hand, individual autonomy is linked with true human nature and opposed to lack of autonomy deriving from social determination of character. In both cases the antithesis is between individuals conceived on the one hand as without autonomy because they are but creatures of their particular social environment, and on the other hand as autonomous because truths—those about human nature and those reflected in valid ideas—provide a universal basis, independent of that environment, for their character, thought, and action.

The question of the intellectual autonomy of the electorate is thus enmeshed in perennial and fundamental issues of social and political philosophy concerning the relation between individuals and society.[21] Perhaps this analysis could be seen as one way of approaching these issues. The main aims, however, have been not only to attempt to deal with the autonomy question, but to draw proper attention to its nature, and, indeed, to its existence.

NOTES

1. See, for example, Ralph Miliband, *The State in Capitalist Society* (London: Quartet Books, 1973), pp. 161–3.
2. *Ibid.*, pp. 80, 88–106, Chapter 6.
3. Or, more accurately, Marx and Engels said it: K. Marx and F. Engels, *The German Ideology*, (London: Lawrence and Wishart, 1965) p. 64.
4. A lucid exposition, relevant to this point, is William Leiss, "Critical Theory and its Future," *Political Theory*, 2 (August 1974), pp. 330–349.

5. See, for example, R. Miliband, "Poulantzas and the Capitalist State," *New Left Review*, 82 (November–December 1973), pp. 83–92, and N. Poulantzas, "The Capitalist State: A Reply to Miliband and La-clau," *New Left Review*, 95 (January–February 1976), pp. 63–83. Also, David Easton, "The Political System Besieged by the State," *Political Theory*, 9 (August 1981), pp. 303–325.

6. Of course, some concepts are, to an important extent, created by particular individuals, but this is very much the exception. More-over, propositions, beliefs, etc., even though in one sense quite often (at least partially) generated by particular individuals, are (arguably) heavily, perhaps even decisively, shaped by the concepts used in their formulation.

7. Robert Dahl, *A Preface to Democratic Theory*, (Chicago: Phoenix Books, 1963) pp. 76–7.

8. One of the best known statements of this is by Robert Merton. In the context of a discussion of Mannheim's conception of ideology, he refers to ". . . radical relativism with its familiar vicious circle in which the very propositions asserting such relativism are *ipso facto* invalid." Merton, *Social Theory and Social Structure*, (Glencoe: The Free Press, 1957), p. 503.

9. To be more precise, three separate but interrelated points are being made here. First, that some concepts "reflect" reality and exist be-cause they do so. Secondly, the existence of true propositions—which make use of such concepts—is due to their *being* true. Thirdly, that people accept such concepts and propositions be-cause of their truth (this is further discussed in the main text).

10. The position with regard to *social* reality is in one way complicated by the fact that, to an important extent, this reality is itself consti-tuted by ideas—or, as is often said, by concepts or "meanings." However, it is people's ideas *about* the constitutive concepts—their ideas about social reality—that are, among others, those that di-rectly concern us here. That is to say, we are not here directly concerned with the question of the truth of the concepts consti-tuting the reality—whether they can be said to be, and if so whether they are, true or false—but merely the question of the truth of people's ideas about the constitutive concepts, ideas concerning what these concepts are and what their significance is. To an im-portant extent social reality can be more directly grasped than physical reality precisely because (or insofar as) it is a direct com-prehension of concepts that is involved, rather than an "interpre-tation" of sense data.

A position is here taken on a central methodological and epis-temological issue in sociology. However, few would deny that to *some* extent social phenomena have a meaningful character. For an outline of what is meant by asserting that social reality is constituted by meanings, and for a discussion of the issues involved, see W. Outhwaite, *Understanding Social Life* (London: Allen and Unwin, 1975). From the point of view of political analysis, see J.D. Moon, "The Logic of Political Inquiry," in F. Greenstein and N. Polsby, eds., *Handbook of Political Science* (Reading, Mass.: Addison-Wesley, 1975), Vol. 1, pp. 131–228.

11. A key factor is the "availability" of true ideas.

12. Conversely, to attempt to explain ideas in terms of their advantage to the "ruling class" is thereby to cast doubt on their validity. Consider the example used in the text: the idea that we are better off under capitalism than communism.

13. The issue of the cognitive status of value judgements is touched on later.

14. People (especially children) may often *initially* be "induced" to adopt even true ideas. But the most likely, even if not the only possible, reason for a true idea continuing to be held is that it is rationally accepted.

15. Exceptional individuals (but only exceptional individuals) will on occasion create their own ideas and have insights that transcend the limitations of their culture.

16. This argument is to be distinguished from the argument that rationality is itself culture-dependent. For a lucid discussion of the relevant issues see Steven Lukes, "Some Problems about Rationality," *European Journal of Sociology*, 8 (1967), pp. 247–264, reprinted in Steven Lukes, *Essays in Social Theory*, (London: Macmillan, 1977), pp. 121–137. The latter argument asserts that the criteria of rationality vary with different cultures. The argument used here posits a universal standard of rationality but asserts that judged by the *same* criteria what it is rational to believe varies to some extent with the cultural context.

17. See, for example, Barry Holden, *The Nature of Democracy* (New York: Barnes & Noble, 1974), p. 213; Thomas Landon Thorson, *The Logic of Democracy* (New York: Holt, Rinehart and Winston, 1962); Edward A. Purcell, Jr., *The Crisis of Democratic Theory* (Lexington, Kentucky: The University Press of Kentucky, 1973). There is also a very important difference between the relativist justification of democracy and the case for democracy that I am advancing. The latter avoids the incoherence of the former. In the relativist justification a definite moral judgement, one in favor of democracy, is based on the contention that moral judgements, as normally understood, cannot be made. In the argument I am advancing, however, the moral judgement is independently based and does not rest on a denial of its own possibility.

18. Indeed, the task of a political analyst may well include an assessment of the degree to which popular beliefs are well-grounded.

19. I am not concerned directly with the issue of whether political decisions ought to be made by the people, but with the issue of whether what purport to be political decisions made by the people are such. Nonetheless, there is a connection, since establishing the authenticity of the people's expressed ideas involves commenting on their validity. (I do not argue, however, that all "authentically popular" ideas are valid, but merely that all popularly expressed ideas that are valid are, most probably, *authentically* popular.)

20. Brevity requires that we leave aside the matter of how it can be said, given the normal diversity of opinions, what the values and attitudes of "the people" are.

21. John Rawls's *A Theory of Justice* (London and New York: Oxford University Press, 1972) is significant here as a systematic attempt to base justification of liberal democracy on a conception of individuals stripped of specific, socially determined characteristics.

13

TOWARD A LIBERAL CONCEPTION OF LEGISLATION*

KENNETH I. WINSTON

Liberal theorists in the United States have expended considerable energy in worrying about the undemocratic character of judicial review. In most instances, this concern has generated theoretical efforts to restrict the functions of the judicial office or to narrow the range of its competence. At one extreme is an almost complete deference to the legislative power, with the judiciary confined to the task of fixing the outer boundaries of reasonable legislative action beyond which it impinges on constitutionally protected rights.[1] Other theorists have sought to minimize what is accepted as inevitable judicial overruling of some preferences of popularly elected legislatures by placing formal constraints on the way judicial power is exercised (e.g., invalidation of legislation is acceptable only when based on neutral principles) or by limiting the substantive focus of judicial concern (e.g., to values connected to the enlargement of democratic participation).[2] From time to time, however, liberal theorists have adopted a less defensive posture, arguing that judicial protection of constitutional rights against legislative majorities is itself democratic in character, since it relies on a shared background morality that expresses the deeper and more abiding commitments of all citizens.[3]

Whatever the merits of these views, the democratic (or undemocratic) character of judicial review is clearly a subject of

313

lively debate. It seems to me, however, that there is much less worrying, indeed much too little worrying, about the liberal, or rather non-liberal, character of legislative policy-making. Yet the one concern is the reciprocal of the other. This neglect is especially curious since traditional liberal theorists made it a central aim of their work to devise institutional strategies for limiting the exercise of legislative power. Only by rendering that power impersonal, they thought, could democratic government be made consistent with liberal ideals, particularly protection of individual rights.[4] To be sure, remnants of traditional liberal strategies are still evident in contemporary, progressive liberal theory. The work of John Rawls offers good illustrations. For example, as Rawls has his contractors move from the original position to the legislative stage, he partially lifts the veil of ignorance behind which decision-making is conducted so that legislators are aware of the full range of economic and social facts characterizing their society. The representative legislator, however, assesses proposed laws without knowing any particular facts about himself.[5] The restriction is designed to ensure that personal interests or biases do not skew the choice of legislative proposals, but Rawls says nothing as to how this partial veil might actually be instituted and the requisite disinterestedness made operative.

Again, in a discussion of the rule of law, Rawls, following a suggestion of Lon Fuller, defines a legal system in terms of the ideals toward which it aims (and which any existing system would embody only imperfectly).[6] In this way he captures the liberal insight that the definition of law has moral implications for the relation between lawmaker and citizen. A legal system, in Rawls's terms, is a coercive order of public rules addressed to rational persons for the purpose of providing a framework for social cooperation and a basis for legitimate expectations regarding one another's conduct. This purpose cannot be fulfilled without official adherence to various principles—what Fuller called *the internal morality of law*—that we associate with the idea of the rule of law. One of these principles, applicable to legislators, is that "statutes be general both in statement and intent and not be used as a way of harming particular individuals who may be expressly named."[7] Although Rawls invokes this principle only in the context of the application of criminal sanctions (*nulla crimen sine lege*), it is precisely this requirement of generality that classical liberals most insisted on as an essential formal property of all legislation whatever, a property that would guarantee the impersonality needed for protection of individual rights. Why the scope of the requirement has been reduced from all to only criminal legislation is a point that Rawls does not raise.

Curiously, the most famous and most systematic use of the traditional liberal strategy is made by Rousseau, whose credentials are a matter of some controversy. In a letter to Mirabeau, Rousseau declared that the great problem of politics is finding a form of government that places laws above men. This could be done, he thought, "taking men such as they are, and [fashioning] laws such as they may be made."[8] Specifically, laws must meet the requirement of generality. They must be general in their *origin* (i.e., approved by every citizen), general in their *content* (i.e., aiming at the common good), and general in their *form* (i.e., referring to classes of acts and persons, not named individuals or particular acts). Of these three kinds of generality, the third—generality of form—is decisive for the other two. The argument runs roughly as follows. Since laws containing class terms do not specify to whom they apply, they apply equally to all citizens. As a consequence, only laws containing class terms will be approved by all citizens. That yields generality of consent. Similarly, since the laws apply equally to all, any law injurious to one person or group will be injurious to everyone. Hence, no one has an interest in an injurious law; everyone can be expected to aim at the common good.

This argument is fallacious, of course, relying principally on equivocations in "applying equally to all." (I shall review some variations on the argument in section 2 below.) Though the requirement of generality is still a shibboleth of some liberal thinkers, many now agree that generality, in the words of Edwin Patterson, is an "ethically neutral characteristic of law."[9] This neutrality is quite compatible, obviously, with its performing important social functions. Holmes once remarked, for example, that the generality of statutes makes them easier to remember.[10] And H.L.A. Hart stresses the practical benefits of generality in observing that "no society could support the number of officials necessary to secure that every member of the society was officially and separately informed of every act which he was required to do."[11] But, while Patterson's declaration seems to express the commonly accepted view, the current neglect of conceptions of legislation suggests that progressive liberals may be unaware of what was lost by the demise of generality as a morally significant feature of law. This sense is confirmed by the fact that they do not seek to fashion an alternative conception of legislation which would play the role in progressive liberalism that generality played in classical theory.

This essay is an attempt to come to terms with the present neglect by reviewing why the requirement of generality fails to perform the function desired by classical liberals. I shall not engage in an exegesis of traditional liberal texts, as helpful as such an exercise might be, but instead shall trace successive refinements of the idea of generality that yield alternative formulations of the requirement. Probing the reasons for the unsatisfactoriness of these formulations will lead to an examination of the underlying concerns of classical liberals that explain their attachment to generality. I then clarify why I think these concerns cannot serve progressive liberals as touchstones for a conception of legislation.[12]

1. THE GENERALITY OF LAW

Richard Wollheim observes that legal theorists who insist on generality as a defining property of law are nonetheless uncertain "whether the required generality is of actions involved (Austin) or of persons affected (Blackstone) or of both (Rousseau)."[13] This uncertainty is well founded, for no satisfactory way of formulating a logical criterion for determining when a law is general in the appropriate (formal) sense has been discovered. In this section, I shall review the technical details that establish why this is so. This analysis will set the stage for identifying the rationale of the requirement of generality.

Let's begin with a law that is obviously *specific* in its form: for example, legislation granting a divorce between two named parties. In saying that the law is obviously specific, I mean only that, whatever criterion one finally accepts for distinguishing generality and specificity, this law would have to be classed as specific. It serves as a touchstone of an acceptable criterion. Yet, as John Salmond has pointed out, the act implies permission to every unmarried person to marry one of the divorced parties without committing bigamy.[14] Thus what is specific in one way is general in another. The specificity is that of *language* (the law refers to a single act of named individuals rather than multiple acts of indefinite members of a class); the generality is that of *effect* (it alters the legal options of a large group of persons). The respects in which the law is specific or general are therefore distinct. However, the question arises why these respects are not of equal importance. Why should the law be taken as a paradigmatic instance of specificity? Are there theoretical grounds for favoring a criterion of language over a criterion of effect? The technical answer to these questions is that generality of effect is not a satisfactory criterion because it is not a formal property of the law. It is rather the consequence of a contingent relation between the law and the world. If the world had been different—if, to take extreme cases, there were no other unmarried persons or the divorced parties had taken unalterable vows of celibacy—then the effect of the law would have been substantially different, without any change having occurred in the act of the legislature. Since the point of the requirement of generality is to constrain legislative conduct in a certain way, generality of effect will not do.

However, generality of language involves a difficulty that is in a way the converse of that raised by the divorce act. A law that is admittedly general in its terms may nonetheless be specific in its effect, and liberal theorists want to exclude that result as well. For example, a law that uses general language may apply only to events that have already taken place. Such a law, in effect, refers to specific persons. Since the past is fixed and the number of events finite, an enumeration of named individuals and their acts would provide a complete and exhaustive substitute for the general language in the law. Thus a logical corollary of the requirement of generality, when properly construed, is prohibition of retroactive statutes.[15] Theorists make the point by observing that the terms of a statute are general in the appropriate sense only if they stand for *logically open classes*. In Lucas's words: "If legislation is to be properly so called, it must be about the legal consequences of the *future* actions of people. For only these constitute a genuinely open class."[16]

The requirement of logically open classes, however, also fails to exclude all undesired forms of specificity. A common example is legislation phrased in such a way as to circumscribe its effects to the advantage (or disadvantage) of a particular city or county within a state's jurisdiction, while nominally conforming to a constitutional prohibition against specific or local laws.[17] The terms of such statutes describe logically open classes. Yet they constitute what Rawls calls *rigged definite descriptions,* that is, the general predicates contained in the statutes function, despite their generality, as if they constituted proper names (of the cities or counties in question).[18] The problem for courts in reviewing legislation of this sort has been, in Cardozo's words, that of determining where classification finds an end and designation a beginning.[19] Unfortunately, the task of distinguishing classification and designation in this context is no more possible, in principle, than that of finding a formal way of identifying "genuinely open" classes. Whether any particular set of predicates actually yields the objectionable specificity of reference is, again, a matter of contingent fact. Hence there is logically no formal way of precluding it. Cardozo confronted this problem when interpreting the New York constitution after it had been amended so as to add generality of effect to generality of terms as a condition of permissible state laws relating to cities. Cardozo allowed that it would be futile to try to say precisely what would count as meeting this condition, but he proposed the following: "If the class in its formation is so unnatural and wayward that only by the rarest coincidence can the range of its extension include more than one locality, and at best but two or three, the act so hedged and circumscribed is local in effect."[20] He then proposed that, if the waywardness of the law was obvious on its face, he would regard it as also local *in its terms.* Thus, in a remarkable tour de force, Cardozo made the generality of language in a statute depend on contingent facts about the world.[21]

In the pursuit of a formal criterion of generality, it is more helpful to examine what is perhaps the most famous example of a statute describing a logically open class that is nonetheless specific in its reference. It is the German customs tariff of 1902, which provided for a special rate of duty for "brown or dappled cows reared at a level of at least 300 metres above the sea and passing at least one month in every summer at a height of at least 800 metres."[22] That this statute, which was designed to avoid a most-favored-nations obligation, is regarded by classical liberals as problematic for the requirement of generality is itself revealing. For in many contexts the implicit reference to Swiss and Austrian cows would be understood as a reference to one class of cows among other classes (and thus would be unobjectionably general) and not, as it is understood here, a reference to particular countries (and thus unallowably specific). What is critical to the characterization of this statute as specific is neither the language nor the effect of the statute but the *intent* of the legislators in writing it in such a way as to discriminate among the members of a known group, to the detriment (or benefit) of some of them. For this purpose, it is a matter of indifference whether the legislators accomplish their aim explicitly through language or implicitly through effect, just as it is a matter of indifference whether the members singled out for special treatment are individuals or classes. What is fatal is that the legislators have deliberately designed their instrument for an identifiable target.

Bentham underscored this point, that the generality or specificity of both language and effect is strictly irrelevant, when he held that "there is not so much as a single article [in the English common law] which can with propriety receive the appellation of *a* law."[23] The reason is that common law opinions, no matter how sweeping the formulation of rules, are always addressed to identifiable individuals and hence are specific, whereas law must be general, that is, applicable to individuals not then assignable. Friedrich Hayek has insisted on the same point in proposing that, for a legislative act to count as a law, its effect on identifiable individuals must be unforeseeable at the time of promulgation.[24] In essence, Hayek suggests that legislators must stand behind a veil of ignorance that screens out not only particular knowledge of themselves (as possible beneficiaries of legislation) but also particular knowledge of other citizens. Only then will a legislative act have the requisite *generality of intent,* even if it happens in fact to apply to a single person. With this proposal, of course, we arrive at the opposite pole from our starting point, generality of effect. Since legislators must not know whose interests are at stake in any item of legislation, one direct consequence of this formulation of the generality criterion is the abolition of lobbying or at least any efforts by known individuals or groups to influence the content of laws. Indeed all sources of information about the relation of legislation to specific persons would have to be excluded from the legislator's purview. Only knowledge of general social facts could be allowed: the level of economic development, types of institutional arrangements, pervasive beliefs and practices, the extent of social and economic differentiation, and so on. Implicit in this knowledge may lurk the pattern of interests existing in the society, but favoring particular interests by legislation is not ruled out, as long as the legislators do not know which individuals possess the interests in question. Thus I presume that a law adjusting the capacity to grant mortgage loans so as to favor commercial banks over savings cooperatives would be acceptable under this criterion of generality, providing legislators are not aware that David Rockefeller runs a commercial bank.

This last refinement of the generality requirement hardly represents a significant advance over preceding formulations, yet it has the virtue of revealing a fundamental concern of classical liberals in their pursuit of a satisfactory conception of legislation. In brief, they believed (or still believe) that generality as a formal property of law would ensure a kind of impersonality in legislative decision-making. I propose now to leave behind the technical problems involved in formulating a criterion of generality and look more closely at its supposed connection with the idea of impersonality.[25]

2. THE IMPERSONALITY OF LAW

Roscoe Pound observed that almost all legislation assigning rights or duties to specific parties (such as grants of divorce, bills of attainder or of pains and penalties, awards of new trials, adjudications of claims against the state) came to an end in the United States by the middle of the nineteenth century.[26] The demise of what he calls *legislative justice* was fortunate, Pound suggests, because it exhibits all the bad features of governance without rules: (1) it is unequal, uncertain, and capricious; (2) it is influenced by personal solicitation, lobbying, and even corruption; (3) it always proves highly susceptible to the influence of passion and prejudice; (4) it is subject to a preponderance of purely partisan or political motives as grounds of decision; and (5) it is distorted by the participation in argument and decision of many who have not heard (or, one might add, have not attempted to understand and assess) all the relevant evidence.

This is a curious list of vices, all variations on the theme that legislative decision-making of this sort is neither principled nor disinterested. More curious still is the implied contrast with legislative acts containing only general rules, as though the latter were not subject to these enumerated defects. Of course, in this historical review, Pound is concerned mainly to mark the limits of legislative justice, as compared to judicial justice, in the treatment of individuals. Judicial justice is not subject to the failings of legislative justice because judges are trained to be responsive to legal reason rather than interest or external pressure. They are experienced in the systematic exposition and logical development of legal principles and are watched carefully by a learned public that has available to it the judges' elaborate justifications of their decisions.[27] The only advantage in the legislative administration of justice to be set against its defects, Pound says, is that it is more responsive to the popular will. But whatever one may think of this contrast, the claim implicit in Pound's description is that, when the legislatures of the nation ceased to issue specific directives to named parties and instead promulgated only general rules, the moral character of lawmaking was significantly transformed. Like classical liberals, Pound seemed to believe that the requirement of generality cleaned up the legislative act.

I want to explore some of the reasons why liberals thought this would be so. I think the crux of the matter is expressed by Lucas when he observes that, while generality is not a guarantee against wicked laws, it is nonetheless a safeguard "in that legislators will not enact laws to other men's detriment if the laws must work to their own detriment also."[28] This is what I shall call the "Rousseauian effect" of generality, since it was Rousseau, as I have pointed out, who thought that generality of form would distribute all legislatively enacted burdens equally and thus give each citizen, whether legislator or not,· an interest in legislation that did not impose an untoward burden on anyone. The Rousseauian effect appears to be a direct consequence of the fact that enacted laws are impersonal; they apply as well to one person as to another or, in other words, citizens are subject to mutual regulation by shared rules. It is clear that, for Rousseau, mutual regulation of conduct by shared rules was conceived as substituting a moral equality among citizens for the physical inequality ordained by nature. Not all classical liberals were similarly committed to finding institutional forms for counteracting the differential distribution of natural assets, but I think it is fair to say that the limited moral equality granted to citizens by the sharing of rules animated liberal conceptions of legislation.

It strikes me as something of a puzzle, however, why so much weight is placed on shared rules, that is, rules that apply as well to one person as to another.[29] Games are typically regarded as paradigmatic cases where it is "only fair" that the same rules apply equally to each participant, and the derivative ideas of "fair play" and "sportsmanship" have done much to shape Anglo-American attitudes toward public institutions. Yet it is rather obvious that game rules are not designed to make every individual an equal competitor regardless of native or acquired ability. To the contrary, game rules systematically advantage some players over others, on the basis of, say, height (basketball), quickness of reflex (fencing), memory (blackjack), and so on. This partiality may be acceptable in any particular instance if the point of the game is to winnow out those possessing the favored abilities. But since almost all games can be equally well constituted by rules that distribute advantages along different dimensions, there is no neutral way of choosing among possible sets of rules. Consequently the fairness of applying the same rules to different persons presupposes that the persons affected are characterized by a rough equality with regard to relevant abilities, or at least that strength in one respect will compensate for weakness in another. The analogous assumption regarding competition for coveted social and economic opportunities is the Hobbesian thesis that "when all is reckoned together, the difference between man and man is not so considerable." [30]

This assumption reveals itself in liberal writings in many ways, perhaps the most obvious being the frequent appeal to game analogies to support accounts of the obligation to obey enacted laws. A more subtle use of the assumption is evident in what I take to be the main argument for shared rules, an argument that rests the impersonality of general rules on the supposed equivalence of the individuals to whom they apply. The argument begins with a principle that could be considered an *ad hominem* version of Kant's categorical imperative: a person cannot act toward others in accordance with a given rule without rendering legitimate similar acts by others in accordance with the same rule in relation to that person. If this principle is correct, it follows that, when citizens act in accordance with a shared set of rules, they each, by their acts toward others, authorize the similar acts of others toward themselves whenever their roles are reversed. Thus they have no basis for complaint if some unwanted burden befalls them as a consequence of others following the rules, since their own acts validate the rules in question. In order for this reciprocal legitimation to operate, of course, it is necessary for each citizen to validate each rule; that is, it must be more than a speculative possibility that the roles of citizens will in fact be reversed. There must be sufficient fluidity in the relations among citizens that roles are indeed actually and constantly being reversed, so that the duties owed by one citizen to a second today will be owed by the second to the first tomorrow. Such fluidity, in turn, makes sense only on the assumption that the abilities of citizens are sufficiently alike that any individual could occupy any social or economic role. "The self and the [other] become, so to speak, fungible entities." [31]

That the assumption of the fungibility of persons would render the idea of the Rousseauian effect plausible I do not doubt, but why that assumption should be considered plausible is a point that eludes me. It is certainly not a basis for even the most progressive idea of equality of opportunity, the one area (if any) where it might be thought to have some application. To the contrary, it is a presupposition of a system of equal opportunity that not every person, even eventually, achieves every position or obtains every good.[32] It does not even require that people have roughly equal chances of obtaining the positions and goods they desire. The opportunities a person has to pursue a particular vocation are not independent of its social utility or of the person's capacity to perform it. So, in a society characterized by elaborate stratification and a complex division of labor, the mental and physical virtues of individuals are not interchangeable. Far from being encouraged to expect the beneficent results of the Rousseauian effect, we are forced to see the aptness of both legislators and ordinary citizens asking the question posed by Rousseau himself in a different context: "[W]here is the precise reason for me, being myself, to act as if I were another, especially when I am morally certain of never finding myself in the same situation?"[33] This question is apt even though rules are shared. The sharing of rules is quite compatible with a division of citizens into numerous and widely disparate groups, entailing equally disparate rights and duties. Creditors may be treated differently from debtors, optometrists differently from opticians, men differently from women. Even fundamental rights may apply to individuals in different ways. For example, every citizen may enjoy the protection of property, but what this means to a wage-earner, whose automobile is bought on credit, is quite different from what it means to a corporate executive, who owns a large share of the company's stock. Rules containing class terms (logically open classes, let us say) are shared insofar as they leave open the possibility, however remote it may be in particular cases, of individuals moving from one class to another and thus altering their opportunities or their liabilities. The rules are also shared in the minimal sense that the legal claim of any one class of persons must be consistent with the claims of other, related classes. But neither sense is sufficient to justify the claim that citizens engage in mutual validation of the rules through their actions, and hence to establish the proposition that shared rules are impersonal in a morally significant way.

I think, rather, that the moral equality among citizens to be achieved by mutual regulation in accordance with general rules can be of significance only if a strategy is devised to restrict possible discriminations in the rules, such that some classifications are permitted and some are not. But I am fairly certain this cannot be done in terms of a formal feature of law. Hayek recognizes this point and suggests that the requirement of generality could be supplemented by the test of consent: when a law is limited in scope to a defined class, both those inside and those outside the class (or at least a majority of them) must acknowledge the legitimacy of the discrimination.[34] This test, however, makes the requirement of generality superfluous. For if a law that is *specific* in form obtains the consent of those named and those not named in the law, what force has the objection that the law is not general? The same superfluity obtains if we understand the consent to be not the actual consent of the two groups but a kind of hypothetical consent. Let us say, for example, that a person's view of the discrimination should not depend on his being inside or outside of the class. Since laws containing class terms provide benefits or burdens to those inside, but not those outside, the class, we could expect the required indifference of individuals only if they did not know whether they personally were members of the class in question. Thus we would need to place them, once again, behind a veil of ignorance, where they would approve or disapprove permissible classifications without knowing whether they stood to gain or lose thereby. In order to give their approval, the individuals behind the veil would need to be guided by some general principles (principles of justice, perhaps, or an idea of the common good) that would provide grounds for permitting some classifications and not others. However, once we can assess possible laws in terms of broad principles of justice, the requirement that laws be general is unnecessary. Indeed, if laws can be said to accord with accepted principles, it does not even matter if the legislators know to whom they apply, including themselves.

We must conclude, then, that the supposed connection between generality and the impersonality of law is tenuous at best. Furthermore, the requirement of impersonality, that laws apply as well to one person as another, leaves somewhat vague exactly what classical liberals seek to gain by making this feature a criterion of all law. I propose to make one more attempt, therefore. at ferreting out the value underlying generality, using as a clue the fear expressed by Lucas (and indeed by Rousseau and every classical liberal) that legislators will enact laws to other people's detriment.

3. LAW AND AUTONOMY

Classical liberalism characteristically regards legislating with suspicion. It is suspect because it offers opportunities, on the largest possible scale, for some individuals to impose their will on others. The hope embodied in the Rousseauian effect is that it would virtually eliminate the ominous temptation that the office of lawmaker provides. While that hope is futile, it reveals that the classical liberal ideal is a form of political association that maximizes opportunity for individual self-determination or autonomy. Of course, the presumption in favor of self-determination can be overcome, sometimes quite easily, for example, when an individual's conduct is harmful to others or when the interests at stake for an individual are trivial in comparison to some public good. In some activities, however, the presumption is so strong that it is marked by identification of specific *liberties* that can be violated only in the most extreme circumstances. Typically, the identified liberties relate to matters of religious conviction, economic exchange, or political participation. Whatever the list, fundamental liberties are said to constitute a basic set of rights attaching to individuals independently of the decrees of legislative (or judicial) bodies. Indeed in the traditional view the principal aim of government is just to secure these rights.[35]

The implications of this way of thinking for a conception of legislation were hinted at by Kant and spelled out by later liberal theorists.[36] To act in accordance with one's own will means to pursue only such ends (goals, projects) as one sets for oneself. The sole constraint imposed by a common social life is that each individual's freedom to choose his own ends must be compatible with the like freedom of other individuals to choose *their* ends. It follows that the task of legislators who respect citizens' autonomy is to promulgate only such laws as allow individual self-determination to occur. Their aim will be to facilitate private choice; hence they will not use the coercive power at their disposal to compel citizens to adopt any specific ends of action.[37] In this sense, legislation is characterized, at least negatively, by its content: it does not express or reflect any preferences of the legislator (or of anyone else, for that matter) regarding what is good or worthwhile. Legislation properly (i.e., liberally) conceived permits citizens to act according to their own desires—to pursue their own good in their own way, in John Stuart Mill's phrase—which they do through forms of voluntary association. In accord with this conception, contract would be the principal modality of social ordering, at least if it were broadly construed to include the law of property and negotiable instruments, the law of corporations, and so on. Legislation regulating commercial transactions would not embody any stipulations as to what the terms of a fair or reasonable deal might be, and a judge with the task of enforcing a contract would not seek to determine if the contractors benefited, or benefited equally, from their agreement. The judge would be concerned solely with the form of the relation, that is, whether the parties freely engaged in the transaction according to a law applying to both.[38] Criminal laws and the law of torts would play a critical role in defining boundaries—marking the area of permissible freedom—within which private pursuits take place. In sum, legislative enactments and judicial rules would establish baselines for self-directed actions by citizens, securing those minimal conditions necessary for continuing voluntary interaction.[39]

It is important to observe that in this formulation of the classical liberal conception it is a material, not a formal, property of law that restricts the reach of legislative regulation. Laws must acknowledge the autonomy of citizens by not imposing any specific ends of action. In this respect, the formulation fails to meet the original goal of basing the reconciliation of democratic decision-making with liberal ideals on a formal property of law. On the other hand, the formulation does give a definite (even if negative) sense to the idea of generality, and it bears a sufficient resemblance to a logical property of law, even though material, to make conceivable its embodiment in the legislative process without resorting to any artificial devices, such as a veil of ignorance. With some justification, therefore, one might conclude that the original aim has been achieved. At any rate,

I shall not cavil at this conclusion. Having arrived at one of the most persistent strains in classical liberal thinking about legislation (preservation of individual autonomy), I want now to shift gears and explore the advance from classical to progressive liberalism. I shall argue that this development has so transformed the valuation of autonomy in liberal thought that, whether or not it once served as the principal support of a liberal conception of legislation, it can no longer do so. Consequently an alternative framework must be erected for assessing models of the legislative process. In clarifying this claim I shall briefly sketch the central concerns of progressive liberals.

The shift in liberal attitudes regarding autonomy had much to do with a series of transformations that began in the nineteenth century, including:

> the demise of a classical market economy (and indeed of the conditions that made it possible), which undermined liberal confidence in the public good to be achieved by an economy built on private property and contract;

> profound demographic and technological changes magnifying the interdependence of people (manifest principally in elaborate occupational differentiation and pervasive institutional dependency), rendering self-contained action increasingly improbable;

> the remarkable growth of affluence, which fostered the conviction that poverty is a social, not a natural, phenomenon (or, at any rate, that the regime of property and contract could not meet the needs of the dispossessed).

I shall not attempt any sustained account of the effects of these transformations, a task in any case better left to others.[40] For my purposes it will be sufficient to note two conceptual shifts in liberal thinking that explain the decreased preoccupation with personal autonomy.

The first shift coincides with a change in the nature of the perceived threats to human liberty. Most illuminating in this regard is Mill's account in the opening pages of *On Liberty*, where he observes that, in olden times, the struggle between liberty and authority was based on the premise that rulers were necessarily antagonistic to (the majority of) the people whom they ruled. When democratic control was sufficiently advanced, however, rulers became servants, not opponents, of the people, and the struggle for liberty became a contest of nonconforming minorities against a potential tyranny of the majority.[41] Although Mill offers this brief history as though it represented a development taking place over many centuries, it is probably a sounder reading to see it as Mill's attempt to distinguish the pressing concerns of his day from those of the previous generation of liberals, including Bentham and his father.[42] In any event, the threat posed by democratic majorities is not, as liberals from Locke to Kant might have thought, to rights of property and autonomous control over economic instrumentalities, but to rights of personality, specifically the right to be an individual. Thus when Mill proceeds, in the remainder of the essay, to discuss "the appropriate region of human liberty" he concentrates on the liberty "of framing the plan of our life to suit our own character" without interference from others.[43] The emphasis on autonomy remains central, to be sure, but is now largely confined to decisions about how to live, to matters of belief and feeling and taste—in a word, to the realm that we imperfectly capture under the rubric of privacy. The range of conduct "affected with a public interest," on the other hand, has burgeoned, and the final responsibility that liberals were formerly willing to accord individuals, especially in their economic affairs, has been replaced by public accountability.

The second shift involved in the move from classical to progressive liberalism derives from the realization that social conditions can as easily attenuate and distort the development of individuality as support and promote it. Let me explain the importance of this. It is a fundamental tenet of both forms of liberalism that the good of individuals is distributive (i.e., a property of each separately), not collective. For this reason basic rights attach to individuals simply in virtue of their humanity and carry weight even against the desires of a majority. But liberalism does not promote a particular conception of what the good of individuals consists in (though progressive liberals, as I will indicate in the next section, have a theory of basic goods). What liberals offer is instead a conception of how the good is to be achieved—differently for different individuals. Specifically, individuals flourish by engaging in activities for which they have both aptitude and ambition, and this flourishing is enhanced when it is the result of the individual's own choice. It follows that a basic right of individuals will be that of acting in accord with a personal conception of their own good, as long as they do not infringe on the similar right of others. As Mill succinctly says: "To give any fair play to the nature of each, it is essential that different persons should be allowed to lead different lives."[44] Where progressive liberals move away from classical liberals is in stressing that development and execution of a plan of life require not only liberty (the absence of external interference) but also opportunity and control over resources.[45] This has many consequences, both practical and theoretical. One practical consequence is that progressive liberals are less suspicious of legislative regulation; ensuring opportunity for individual development, especially equal opportunity, requires a very active, even meddling government. This shift in attitude is also reflected at the theoretical level by an extension of the list of basic rights, an extension that introduces an affirmative role for the legislature and further confines the range of personal autonomy.

4. BASIC GOODS AND "THE RIGHT OF FREE INDUSTRY"

To give expression to this development, I borrow Martin Golding's distinction between two kinds of rights that may be said to belong to individuals: option rights and welfare rights.[46] Option rights define spheres of freedom within which individuals may act as they choose (i.e., autonomously). Individuals have final responsibility for their choices, and others have a duty not to interfere with the exercise of choice or to foreclose available options. A typical list of option rights would include liberties of religious belief, speech, voluntary association, and private property. Welfare rights, on the other hand, are entitlements to some benefit that others have a duty to provide. Examples include the rights to an education, to decent housing, and to adequate health care.

Now the claim I want to make is that classical liberals are

principally concerned to protect and defend option rights for individuals, while progressive liberals have expanded their concern to include welfare rights. This is not to say that progressive liberals neglect option rights; to the contrary, welfare rights enlarge the opportunities for individuals to take advantage of their option rights and distribute such opportunities more equally among all citizens. Thus, while recognition of welfare rights is often regarded as reflecting a commitment to material equality, strictly it is a commitment to equalizing the worth of liberty. Welfare rights generally provide for individuals who are the victims of ill-fortune the minimum conditions necessary for realizing the independence prized by traditional liberals; that is, the ability to form for themselves and act on the basis of personal conceptions of how they ought to live. Yet, if this claim is correct, it would seem at first glance irrational for classical liberals to oppose recognition of welfare rights, since they appear to complement and enhance the exercise of option rights. The fact of the matter, however, is that the two sets of rights sometimes conflict, and it is by giving priority to welfare rights when conflict occurs that progressive liberals further reduce the acceptable range of autonomous choice.

I cannot hope to substantiate this claim fully in this essay, but discussion of a single illustration will at least convey my meaning. Part of the classical liberal understanding is that, in forming a plan of life to suit one's character, each citizen has the right not only to be free from physical restraint but also the right

> to be free in the enjoyment of all his faculties; to be free to use them in all lawful ways; to live and work where he will; to earn his livelihood by any lawful calling; to pursue any livelihood or avocation, and for that purpose to enter into all contracts which may be proper, necessary and essential to his carrying out to a successful conclusion the purposes above mentioned.[47]

In one of the classic formulations of this view, Herbert Spencer describes *the right of free industry* as "the right of each man to carry on his occupation, whatever it may be, after whatever manner he prefers or thinks best, so long as he does not trespass against his neighbors."[48] To be sure, various restrictions on occupational choice have been imposed at times by liberals on the basis of sex or race or age, but eliminating these restrictions is only a way of broadening the class of people to whom "the right of free industry" is available. Similarly, the right to engage in any lawful calling does not necessarily preclude state regulation in the form of licensing, provided the criteria to be met for obtaining a license are appropriate to the profession and can be reasonably satisfied—even if by difficult study and application.[49] The justification for licensing lies in the state's power to protect its citizens from fraud (in this respect analogous to the regulation of all contractual relations) and to protect them from their own ignorance and incapacity (a form of paternalism that has long been mixed with liberal principles). Within these limits, individuals should be free, in the classical view, to contract their services on any and only those terms they choose to accept.

This right of occupational choice was put to the test, and upheld, in a remarkable Indiana case at the turn of the century. A man became dangerously ill and sent for the family physician. The messenger informed the doctor of the man's illness, tendered him his fee for his services, and stated (truly) that no other physician was available in time to be of any use. The doctor's services were not required in fact by anyone else, and he could have gone to the sick man if he had been willing. However, he refused, and the man died. His heirs sued the doctor for wrongfully causing the man's death by refusing to enter into a contract of employment, but the court affirmed the doctor's freedom to contract or not as he wished. "In obtaining the State's license (permission) to practice medicine, the State does not require, and the licensee does not engage, that he will practice at all or on other terms than he may choose to accept."[50]

Now there are many ways of appraising this decision. One response does not depend, or depends only marginally, on the fact that the doctor was the family physician. That relation could be taken to indicate existence of a prior obligation, founded on a long-standing commitment, and would form the basis of a suit in tort rather than contract (which would have a much better chance of succeeding). Even if the doctor were a stranger, however, and the other circumstances of the case remained the same, one might feel that the doctor failed to fulfill an obligation for which he could be held liable. It is tempting to account for this feeling by calling upon the idea of Good Samaritanism. After all, the obligation to aid people in distress, especially when one is in the best position to act and the risk or cost to oneself would be minimal, is a clear moral requirement. Yet the principle of Good Samaritanism assimilates the situation to a broad category of cases and does not reach what is special in these circumstances. (The historical reluctance of legislators and judges in the United States to use the law to enforce benevolence would also pose a problem.) I think, rather, that the deeper intuition that leads to a contrary conclusion focuses on two reciprocal features of the case: first, that the claim put forth by the dying man was for the sake of a basic good (namely, life or health) and, second, that the person against whom the claim was made was a professional whose job is to promote the basic good in question. This intuition, at any rate, appears to underlie progressive liberalism's recognition of a basic right to medical care and its willingness to impose duties on doctors to secure that right to all citizens.[51] There is, of course, an element of paradox here; for the provision of health care (or education or housing) to all citizens is justified as a prerequisite for each person's being able to execute a self-chosen conception of how to live, which would ordinarily include a choice of vocation. Yet this goal can be accomplished only by regulating some choices. The resolution of this paradox within progressive principles seems to me doubtful. What is clear is only that progressive liberals believe an equitable distribution of some basic goods cannot be secured through a regime of autonomous ordering, and they consider legislative recognition of appropriate welfare rights (with correlative duties imposed on others) warranted. (Obviously this does not preclude a balancing of option rights and welfare rights in situations where the interest in liberty is too important to sacrifice.)

How rigorous legislative regulation would have to be depends on the list of basic goods. I want to close this section by quickly reviewing four sets of basic goods that would be of con-

cern to designers of a just society. I shall not attempt to elaborate the legislation that would be needed to realize these goods,
but it is evident that it would be extensive.

1. The first set consists of *primary goods,* which are the general means necessary to carrying out any plan of life. These
include basic liberties, educational and vocational opportunity,
the rights and powers connected to a democratic structure of
government, financial security, and a sense of one's own worth.[52]
These are goods that rational persons want, whatever else they
want. Stated with sufficient abstractness, of course, classical liberals would not necessarily quarrel about the importance of the
goods mentioned, but disagreement over priorities would
emerge as details were filled in and conflicts between goods
arose. Thus, for a society to provide individuals with genuine
equality of opportunity the undeserved inequalities of natural
endowment and birth (i.e., social class) must somehow be com-
pensated for, which means that the society may have to enact
preferential legislation that would devote greater resources to
these less favored individuals.[53]

2. The second set of goods consists of what Rawls calls *natural goods,* which also provide means necessary for carrying out
a life-plan. The principal examples are health and vigor. Rawls
separates these goods from the first group, I think, because
their realization rests in part on factors beyond the control of
individuals or social institutions. So these goods will figure in
the design of a just society only to the extent their possession is
influenced, or can be influenced, by social factors.[54] One of
these, as I indicated in my discussion of *Hurley,* is the practice
of medicine. Here again the extent of legislative control will
depend on details. Norman Daniels has suggested that the basic
good of health encompasses the following needs: (1) adequate
nutrition and shelter; (2) sanitary, safe, unpolluted living and
working conditions; (3) exercise, rest, and other features of a
healthy way of life; (4) preventive, curative, and rehabilitative
personal medical services; and (5) non-medical support services.[55]

3. The legislative task becomes still more complex if we add
to the designers' concerns other goods that have a central place
in each person's life, without being primary or natural. First

there are *human goods,* which include "personal affection and friendship, meaningful work and social cooperation, the pursuit of knowledge and the fashioning and contemplation of beautiful objects."[56] Human goods would be favored by the designers because of their intrinsic importance: the pursuit of such goods tends to enhance the good of all (distributively). Exactly what forms of legislative intervention would be appropriate for the promotion of these goods is difficult to say, but it seems clear that a legislature would be justified in giving priority in the allocation of resources to some occupations over others, such as those connected to basic research and artistic endeavors.

4. Finally, when the designers regard what it would be rational for them to want, they should focus on a fourth set of goods, namely those broadly based traits of character that it would be desirable for fellow citizens to possess regardless of their social roles. These *excellences* include essential moral virtues and various natural assets, such as intelligence, imagination, wit, strength, and endurance.[57] Excellences are more than requirements of justice, they are conditions of human flourishing generally and as such would be considered good from everyone's point of view. To the extent that they are also influenced by social factors, life-plans that promote them would be legitimately favored by legislation. Or so at least the designers could conclude. They would still leave a large area for individuality of taste and feeling and belief (the area of personal autonomy), but the conditions of cooperative life, they would think, require extensive accountability to one another.

5. TOWARD LEGISLATIVE REFORM

I have argued that the classical liberal conception of legislation as general rules is incoherent, and that the ideal of personal autonomy that motivated it has been displaced in liberal thought by a theory of basic goods. I would like to be able to conclude these reflections on the interplay of form and substance by elaborating a conception of the legislative process consonant with progressive goals, but I have not yet seen my way clear to such a conception. The history of liberal thought does not provide much guidance on this matter. Whatever structural reforms have on occasion been proposed are now largely, and perhaps deservedly, forgotten.[58]

Even to suggest the possibility of reform, however, stands in sharp contrast to the current despair among progressive theorists regarding the legislative process. Instead of thinking about structural changes, they have fallen into an exaggerated reliance on courts as protectors of liberal values in the face of illiberal legislative majorities. As a consequence, they implicitly advance a conception of legislation that effectively relieves legislators of the duty recognized in classical liberalism of acting as guardians of citizens' rights. The task of protecting rights is seen to be part of neither the function nor the responsibility of legislators; if such bills happen to be enacted (e.g., the various Civil Rights Acts of the 1960s) that is fortunate but entirely fortuitous. Thus they end up placing on judges the enormous burden of keeping their liberal heads while all about them are losing theirs. Such a division of responsibility is neither desirable nor possible.

NOTES

*Parts of this essay were sketched in my paper "Dworkin's Liberalism," presented to the New England Political Science Association in April, 1979. A research fellowship from the National Endowment for the Humanities provided time to develop the ideas further. For a critical reading of earlier drafts, I am indebted to Mary Jo Bane, J. Roland Pennock, Philip Selznick, and Alan Soble.

1. See, e.g., Justice Frankfurter's dissent in *West Virginia State Board of Education v. Barnette,* 319 U.S. 624, 646 (1943). The classic statement of this position is James Bradley Thayer, "The Origin and Scope of the American Doctrine of Constitutional Law," *Harvard Law Review,* 7 (October 1893), 131–156.

2. See Herbert Wechsler, "Toward Neutral Principles of Constitutional Law," *Harvard Law Review,* 73 (November 1959), 1–35, and John Hart Ely, *Democracy and Distrust: A Theory of Judicial Review* (Cambridge: Harvard Univ. Press, 1980).

3. See James Coolidge Carter, *Law: Its Origin, Growth and Function* (New York: G.P. Putnam's Sons, 1907), and Ronald Dworkin, *Taking Rights Seriously* (Cambridge: Harvard Univ. Press, 1977).

4. For classic formulations, see John Locke, *Two Treatises of Govern-*

ment, ed. Peter Laslett (Cambridge, Eng.: Cambridge Univ. Press, 1963), secs. 87 and 131; David Hume, *Political Essays,* ed. Charles Hendel (Indianapolis: Library of Liberal Arts, 1953), esp. ch. V, "Of the Origin of Government," and ch. XIV, "Of the Rise and Progress of the Arts and Sciences;" Immanuel Kant, *The Metaphysical Elements of Justice,* ed. John Ladd (Indianapolis: Library of Liberal Arts, 1965), pp. 33–45. For contemporary versions of classical liberalism, see F.A. Hayek, *The Constitution of Liberty* (Chicago: Univ. of Chicago Press, 1960), and J.R. Lucas, *The Principles of Politics* (London: Oxford at the Clarendon Press, 1966).

5. John Rawls, *A Theory of Justice* (Cambridge: Harvard Univ. Press, 1971), p. 198.

6. Ibid., sec. 38.

7. Ibid., p. 238. See Lon L. Fuller, *The Morality of Law,* rev. ed. (New Haven: Yale Univ. Press, 1969), pp. 46–49, and *The Principles of Social Order: Selected Essays of Lon L. Fuller,* ed. Winston (Durham: Duke Univ. Press, 1981), pp. 33–40.

8. Jean-Jacques Rousseau, *The Social Contract,* ed. Charles Frankel (New York: Hafner, 1947), p. 5.

9. Edwin Patterson, *Jurisprudence: Men and Ideas of the Law* (Brooklyn: Foundation Press, 1953), p. 98.

10. O.W. Holmes, Jr., "The Path of the Law," *Harvard Law Review,* 10 (March 1897), 458.

11. H.L.A. Hart, *The Concept of Law* (London: Oxford at the Clarendon Press, 1961), p. 21. However, note Hart's claim that "there is, in the very nature of law consisting of general rules, something which prevents us from treating it as if morally it is utterly neutral, without any necessary contact with moral principles." Hart, "Positivism and the Separation of Law and Morals," *Harvard Law Review,* 71 (February 1958), 624. The claim of a necessary connection between justice and general rules also underlies Theodore Lowi's attack on interest-group liberalism in *The End of Liberalism* (New York: W.W. Norton, 1969), pp. 290–291. I have demonstrated elsewhere that this claim rests on the conflation of a principle of justice (that like cases ought to be treated alike) with a principle of judicial conservatism. Winston, "On Treating Like Cases Alike," *California Law Review,* 62 (January 1974), 1–39.

12. Although the distinction between two forms of liberalism is common, no one seems to have devised completely satisfactory terminology for referring to them. The former is alternately called *traditional, atomistic,* or *individualistic* liberalism; the latter is *modern, collectivistic,* or *welfare* liberalism. My own preference is for *classical* and *progressive* liberalism. Whatever the terms, it is important to note that the historically older form has many contemporary

adherents and that the newer form has deep roots in the nine-teenth century. See John Dewey, *Liberalism and Social Action* (New York: Capricorn, 1963).

13. Richard Wollheim, "The Nature of Law," *Political Studies*, 2 (1954), 131.

14. John W. Salmond, *Jurisprudence*, ed. Granville Williams (London: Sweet & Maxwell, 1957), 11th ed., p. 40. In the case of *Vanzant v. Waddel*, Judge Peck says of the legislative grant of incorporation to a bank: since "all manner of persons might have some transaction with or demand against [the bank], it follows that the act was made for all persons, and is therefore a general law." 2 Yerg. (Tenn.) 260, 267 (1829).

15. See Franz Neumann, *The Democratic and the Authoritarian State*, ed. Herbert Marcuse (New York: Free Press, 1957), p. 36.

16. Lucas, op. cit., pp. 134–135.

17. For examples that both do and do not meet this condition, see Patterson, op. cit., pp. 114–116.

18. Rawls, op. cit., p. 131.

19. *In the Matter of the Mayor*, 246 N.Y. 72, 76 (1927), referring to *Matter of Henneberger*, 155 N.Y. 420 (1898).

20. Ibid., at 78.

21. The opposite tack of allowing that general terms may have sin-gularity of reference is adopted by Quine. Thus the expression "natural satellite of Earth" refers in fact to a single object but is counted as a general term. This is explained by saying that the singularity of reference is not purported in the term. W.V.O. Quine, *Methods of Logic*, 3d ed. (New York: Holt, Rinehart and Winston, 1972), sec. 39.

22. Gottfried von Haberler, *The Theory of International Trade*, trans. A. Stonier and F. Benham (New York: Macmillan, 1936), p. 339, quoted by Hayek, op. cit., p. 489n, and by Lucas, op. cit., p. 116.

23. Jeremy Bentham, *Of Laws in General*, ed. H.L.A. Hart (London: Athlone Press, 1970), p. 153. See also pp. 76–92.

24. Hayek, op. cit., pp. 149–153. In arguing for a narrow construc-tion of the crime of treason, Chief Justice Marshall observes that "the framers of our constitution . . . must have conceived it more safe, that punishment, in such cases, should be ordained by gen-eral laws, formed upon deliberation, under the influence of no resentments, and without knowing on whom they were to operate. . . ." However, the contrast Marshall is drawing is between pro-visions of the constitution (which satisfy the above conditions) and acts of Congress (which inflict punishment "under the influence of those passions which the occasion seldom fails to excite"). *Ex Parte Bollman*, 4 Cranch 74, 126 (1807).

25. I should note that I do not address myself in this paper to a defect of general rules that results from vagueness of language. This problem has been of concern to liberals in connection with legislative delegations of authority to administrative agencies, empowering officials to exercise unguided discretion in areas of economic regulation. However, Lowi has pointed out that the difficulties generated by vagueness can be met by legislative elaboration of guidelines and by early and frequent administrative rule-making. See Lowi, op. cit., ch. 10.

26. Roscoe Pound, "Justice According to Law," reprinted in *Essays on Jurisprudence from the Columbia Law Review* (New York: Columbia Univ. Press, 1963), pp. 241–245.

27. Ibid., pp. 261–266.

28. Lucas, op. cit., p. 115.

29. See Winston, "On Treating Like Cases Alike," op. cit., pp. 14–15. Ely finds a version of what I call the Rousseauian effect invoked by Chief Justice Marshall in *McCullock v. Maryland,* 4 Wheat. 316, 436 (1819). Ely seems to think the Rousseauian effect is achieved by what he calls *virtual representation.* Generality might be the condition of law by means of which virtual representation is realized, but Ely's discussion is too opaque to tell for certain. See Ely, op. cit., pp. 85–86.

30. Thomas Hobbes, *Leviathan,* ed. C.B. Macpherson (Baltimore: Penguin, 1968), p. 183.

31. Giorgio Del Vecchio, *Justice: An Historical and Philosophical Essay,* ed. A.H. Campbell (New York: Philosophical Library, 1953), p. 84. The argument of this paragraph is most explicit in Fuller, *The Morality of Law,* op. cit., p. 23. Hayek says that "complete equality before the law" means that no attribute belonging to some persons (but not others) would alter their position under the law. *The Political Ideal of the Rule of Law* (Cairo: National Bank of Egypt, 1955), p. 36. For the idea of mutual validation of rules, see Peter C. Williams, "Losing Claims of Rights," *Journal of Value Inquiry,* 12 (Autumn 1978), 178–196.

32. See John Plamenatz, "Equality of Opportunity," in *Aspects of Human Equality,* eds. L. Bryson et al. (New York: Conference on Science, Philosophy and Religion, 1956), pp. 79–107.

33. Jean-Jacques Rousseau, *Emile,* ed. Allan Bloom (New York: Basic Books, 1979), p. 235n, quoted in French by Del Vecchio, op. cit., p. 96.

34. Hayek, op. cit., p. 154.

35. In the words of William Blackstone: "the principal aim of society is to protect individuals in the enjoyment of those absolute rights, which were vested in them by immutable laws of nature. . . ."

Commentaries on the Laws of England (Chicago: Univ. of Chicago Press, 1979), vol. I, p. 120. (This edition is a facsimile of the first edition of 1765–1769.)

36. I do not wish to be understood here as engaging in textual exegesis. I am merely utilizing certain suggestive passages in *The Metaphysical Elements of Justice*.

37. It is perhaps worth noting that this point follows as a simple consequence of Kant's *metaphysical thesis* that it is impossible for one individual to compel another to adopt an end. The choice of an end is necessarily an act of inner determination of the mind, a matter of internal legislation. See Mary Gregor, *Laws of Freedom* (New York: Barnes and Noble, 1963), pp. 64–66. Subsequent theorists were committed only to the weaker *normative thesis* that legislation should not posit or embody any specific ends of action. See Hayek, op. cit., pp. 152–153.

38. Kant, op. cit., p. 34.

39. See Fuller, op. cit., pp. 162, 207, 210, 229. Fuller found support for this view in an elegant little essay by Stuart Hampshire that identifies "unrestricted liberalism" as a form of radicalism. "For a radical the right of each man to choose for himself his own manner of life, as long as he does not disregard the equal right of others to do the same, is *the sole criterion of political decision.*" Hampshire, "In Defence of Radicalism," *Encounter*, 5 (August 1955), 38 (emphasis added). It should be noted that a weaker conception of autonomy would require only that citizens be treated in conformity with principles to which all could consent in a hypothetical situation of rational choice. This weaker conception would not necessarily yield legislative deference to private ends. Cf. David A.J. Richards, "Human Rights and Moral Ideals: An Essay on the Moral Theory of Liberalism," *Social Theory and Practice*, 5 (1980), 461–488.

40. On the critical decades at the end of the nineteenth century, see especially Michael Freeden, *The New Liberalism* (Oxford: Clarendon Press, 1978), and Thomas Haskell, *The Emergence of Professional Social Science* (Urbana: Univ. of Illinois Press, 1977), chs. I and II.

41. John Stuart Mill, *On Liberty*, ed. Elizabeth Rapaport (Indianapolis: Hackett, 1978), pp. 1–5. See Winston, "Forms of Tyranny," *Working Papers for a New Society*, 5 (1977), 90–95.

42. Robert D. Cumming, *Human Nature and History: A Study of the Development of Liberal Political Thought* (Chicago: Univ. of Chicago Press, 1969), vol. I, p. 30.

43. The quoted phrases are from Mill, op. cit., pp. 11–12.

44. Ibid., p. 61. See also Ronald Dworkin, "Liberalism," in *Public and*

Private Morality, ed. Hampshire (Cambridge: Cambridge University Press, 1978), pp. 113–143.

45. As John Dewey says, liberals must be as much interested in the construction of favorable institutions as in the removal of abuses and oppression. "The Future of Liberalism" in *Problems of Men* (New York: Philosophical Library, 1946), p. 136.
46. Martin P. Golding, "Toward A Theory of Human Rights," *The Monist,* 52 (October 1968), 521–549. See also D.D. Raphael, "Human Rights," *Aristotelian Society Proceedings Supp.,* 39 (1965), p. 211.
47. This is Justice Peckham's explication of "liberty" in the 14th Amendment, *Allgeyer v. Louisiana,* 165 U.S. 578, 589 (1897).
48. Herbert Spencer, *The Principles of Ethics* (Indianapolis: Liberty Classics, 1978), vol. II, p. 149.
49. *Dent v. West Virginia,* 129 U.S. 114 (1889).
50. *Hurley v. Eddingfield,* 156 U.S. 416 (1901).
51. Most of the substantive due process cases in the forty-year period between 1897 and 1937 dealt specifically with the issue of whether and under what conditions individuals are subject to legislative control in the pursuit of a business, trade, occupation, or profession. When the court finally ceased invalidating such legislation on the basis of freedom of contract or rights of private property, it moved from the classical to the progressive liberal position. The physician's sacrifice of liberty entailed by my rejection of the result in *Hurley* "is merely the imposition of a burden already faced by much of the working population." Norman Daniels, "Health Care and Distributive Justice," *Philosophy and Public Affairs,* 10 (Spring 1981), 176. For a recent polemical treatment of substantive due process, see Bernard Siegan, *Economic Liberties and the Constitution* (Chicago: University of Chicago Press, 1980).
52. Rawls, op. cit., pp. 92–95; David A.J. Richards, *A Theory of Reasons for Action* (London: Oxford at the Clarendon Press, 1971), p. 120.
53. For applications of this principle in educational settings, see Mary Jo Bane and Kenneth I. Winston, "Equity in Higher Education," a report to the National Institute of Education (March 1980), pp. 136–147, 167–175.
54. Rawls, op. cit., p. 93.
55. Daniels, op. cit., p. 158.
56. Rawls, op. cit., p. 425. Compare the discussion of basic goods by John Finnis, *Natural Law and Natural Rights* (Oxford: Clarendon Press, 1980), pp. 85–90.
57. Rawls, ibid., p. 435.
58. A notable exception, I think, is John Stuart Mill's suggestion for improving the quality of democratic lawmaking by separating the task of *formulating* laws, which he would assign to a special Legis-

lative Commission, and the task of *enacting* laws, which is the proper work of the representative assembly. Mill's design would not guarantee any substantive results and, for that reason, is not a model for progressive theorists. Nonetheless, his willingness to take reform seriously is instructive. See Mill, *Considerations on Representative Government,* ed. Currin Shields (New York: Library of Liberal Arts, 1958), pp. 68–84.

14

EFFICIENCY, RESPONSIBILITY, AND DEMOCRATIC POLITICS

WILLIAM C. MITCHELL

In politics, more than anywhere else, we have no possibility
of distinguishing between being and appearance.
—Hannah Arendt, *On Revolution*

Today, nearly all social phenomena have become politicized,
and almost all social difficulties are assumed to have only political solutions. The politicizing of life can be seen in every basic
relation: between parents and children, between husband and
wife, employers and unions, businessmen and consumers, professors and students, between races, between men and women.
All this stands in sharp contrast to an earlier period when individuals perceived their difficulties as essentially private and
to be dealt with privately through private institutions of family,
church, and the market. Today, the initiative is collective and
the solution bureaucratic.

Collectivizing society inevitably leads to aggrandizement of
the state and enshrinement of power. Politicians and bureaucrats become more significant in our lives than businessmen,
and public institutions supplant the private. Coercion and compulsory philanthropy replace voluntary agreements and persuasion. Individuals increasingly must seek permission to "do
their own thing." As a result, the individual has become more
dependent on the state, a dependence that leads necessarily to

personal frustration, impotence, anger, and irresponsibility. The discrepancy between reality and millennium promised by the intellectual "left" only makes these realities more difficult to explain and accept. Conflict, passion, hatred, revolution are now made respectable by social theorists while the ideals of eighteenth- and nineteenth-century liberalism are derided as an amusing ideology of the not-so-wonderful past when men were enslaved by the industrial revolution.

My theme is this: As society becomes more collectivized, responsible individual participation and governmental rationality are seriously weakened. A diminished sense of responsibility leads, in turn, to greater conflict and injustice in the distribution of wealth and income than might otherwise be obtained through market and other private choices. More generally, public policy is characterized by extraordinary perversities from which come hopelessness and anger. Since one is not in command of one's fate in a collectivized society, blind adjustment, i.e., irrational conduct, is not only permitted but exalted. I cannot believe that much good will result from these developments.

RESPONSIBLE PARTICIPATION IN MARKETS AND POLITICS

The many and varied roles we play in a modern democracy help to shape our perceptions, beliefs, and values. Because the activities of a modern market economy and democracy are decentralized, specialized, and intricate, we cannot expect that all social effects or consequences of actions taken by individuals will be considered. Both ignorance and disincentives combine to produce ill-considered or "irresponsible" choices and policies. We must assume, too, that people find it difficult to assign "responsibility" correctly. We do not know to whom credit is due for our good fortune nor whom to blame when things go wrong.

My argument is simple: Utility-maximizing individuals find fewer incentives for responsible behavior in the polity than in the market. Indeed, collective choice, whether direct or representative, is unusually productive of both irresponsible conduct and irrational policies. Collective choice generates frustration, alienation, and impotence in individuals and extraordinary collective inefficiencies and inequities. To politicize life is to invite individuals to ignore the consequences of their choices. Since voting is acting for others one might assume that each would consider social consequences, or so romantic democrats would have us believe. I maintain that we act most responsibly when we act on our own behalf within well-defined property rights and liability rules. That leads me to a definition of "responsibility."

Responsibility is defined in a slightly unfamiliar way as rational choice. Rational choice, in turn, is defined as decisions that take full accounting of relevant consequences, i.e., the costs and benefits of alternatives. An efficient or responsible choice is, therefore, one in which all possible gains are exhausted; it is no longer possible to make anyone better-off without someone else being less well-off. Few individuals and no great societies attain perfect efficiency in the employment of resources. Rather, efficiency is concerned with moves in the right direction, i.e., putting resources into more highly valued uses. When resources are misallocated less-valued uses dominate choices. Foregone productive contributions are greater than the value of the existing or actual contribution of resources. The source of misallocation may be attributed chiefly to ignorance—to the allocation of resources at prices that do not reflect true costs and future preferences, income and prices. Accordingly, opportunities are presented to the better-informed or lucky to profit by these misallocations. An individual who discovers these unexploited opportunities redirects the flow of resources and thereby makes himself and others better-off. This is responsible market behavior.

Unfortunately, the responsible entrepreneur may earn greater profits by not considering all costs. These unaccounted costs are known variously as externalities, spillover or neighborhood effects, and social costs. In many activities social costs considerably exceed private costs, as in air and water pollution, congestion, deforestation and employment damaging to the health or development of the employee. Too many of these unintended bads will be produced by private markets. Hence, resources are misallocated. Although people act rationally in ignoring these costs, they are real and will be paid by someone.

Moralizing about these matters is not likely to solve anything as long as each continues to see a huge gap between the high cost to him of "responsible" behavior and the low cost of "irresponsible" behavior—especially when he thinks that his own sacrifice will make no noticeable difference to the community, and will not induce others to follow his lead. Every private act has social consequences; the more completely these consequences are taken into account, the more satisfactory will be the resulting allocation of resources. Since the spillovers of private choices become larger in advanced society, we should attend to more effective ways of assigning responsibility to people for their actions.

So-called irresponsible action resulting in externalities is actually not an imperfection or failure of the market so much as it is a political failure. More efficient allocations of resources can be achieved by assigning responsibility through voluntary exchange on the basis of property rights that are more fully specified. What is needed is not more restriction on property rights but rather their extension into those areas that are presently treated as communal property. Nothing invites irresponsible conduct so much as resources "owned" by everyone. We should devise institutions that internalize relevant costs and benefits. Internalization forces people to consider consequences because they are brought home to them. Accordingly, individuals become more responsible.

The market system obviously fails to internalize all externalities. Still, it does manage to handle an extraordinary number of externalities. In particular, the market induces people to do good by enabling them to capture a share of the benefits for themselves. Surely most writers believe in copyrights! Every new or improved commodity is made because people expect to exchange their own work for something they want. While the market does internalize many costs and benefits it may fail to calculate long-term or intergenerational allocations. Whether a political process could do a better job is debatable. Just as future consumers are unable to register their demands so, too, the unborn voter has no voice.

Whereas the market encourages production of the right goods it may not always call forth the right amounts. Political activity (or politics), however, may do neither; worse, it stimulates un-productive transfer activity. Rational thought in politics is de-voted not to the discovery of new ideas, new products, new resources, new and more efficient means of production but to new means of exploitation. One cannot readily redistribute wealth and income in the economy without doing good for oth-ers; since making oneself better-off through political means or-dinarily requires less than unanimous consent, doing good at the expense of others is facilitated. Such behavior is irrespon-sible.

POLITICAL SETTINGS

The unique and rather disturbing aspects of politics gain sig-nificance when contrasted with the economics of a market economy. The economy generates resource allocation through a host of individual transactions. These transactions take place on the basis of private property and freedom of contract. There are rules for deciding who owns each piece of property. Each person has substantial control over the use of his property. Property can change hands only by free exchange or by free gift. A person's wealth increases rapidly if he gets large gifts, if he produces, if others are willing to offer high prices for what he owns, and if he saves wisely. Because of free contract, no one is forced to accept a position that he thinks inferior to that his original property secures. If anyone can produce something that is more valuable than the resources used up, then he can gain from its production. If he can find other people who trade things that he regards as more valuable than what he gives up, then he can gain from exchange. Under certain well-known conditions, freedom of exchange leads to an optimal allocation of resources. The role of prices in this entire process is of ex-traordinary importance, for prices constitute the essential in-formation sellers and buyers need in making their respective decisions.

Collective choice, on the other hand, is based on some speci-fied, minimal agreement, and choices are binding on all. Coer-cion is, therefore, a hallmark of the political system. In the market men generally act directly for themselves, but most public decisions are made by representatives or fiduciaries rather than by individual voters. Still, every representative and voter is a potential dictator in that each attempts to choose for all others as well as for oneself. Benevolent would-be dictators though we may be, we attempt to impose our values, views, policies and preferences on all others if only because laws must be of general application. A market choice, on the other hand, is not an attempt to persuade or impose that choice on other consumers.

In addition to being coercive, polities can exist only if their governments possess monopoly powers. Governments do not tolerate competitors. Accordingly, citizens cannot switch to competing bureaucracies whenever they become dissatisfied with a service. "Voting with one's feet" has, therefore, distinct and readily apparent limitations as an effective control over politicians and bureaucrats, whereas in the market it (or "exit") is common practice.

Although governments are monopolies, they engage in peculiar economic decision-making. They are not permitted to seek profits. Instead, the government normally finances its activities by payments from taxpayers unrelated to specific goods or services. When government distributes services and goods, it does so at zero prices or less-than-cost prices. The beneficiaries pay unequal "prices" for the same services. Markets, on the other hand, charge a uniform price to all regardless of personal and economic characteristics. The very existence of prices enables not only precise but systematic comparison of values and costs. In the world of politics most services go unpriced.

That governments engage in these odd forms of fiscal behavior has enormous consequences not only for the overall allocation of resources, distribution of welfare and burdens, but also for the daily life of citizens, politicians, and bureaucrats. Economists and public choice theorists are exploring choices in terms of their efficiency and equity. Political scientists have examined some of this behavior but have, for the most part, chosen to emphasize non-monetary interrelations of personality and politics. While many of these investigations are valuable, most appear to have been conducted without knowledge of the political setting. Without an understanding of the distinctive properties of the political process and government one lacks at least part of the explanation of irresponsible conduct.

In order to analyze the actual processes by which irresponsibility is generated in politics and minimized in markets we must examine on the one hand the immediate situations and incentives of politicians, voters, bureaucrats and buyers and sellers, on the other.

My analysis assumes that all behavior is self-interested. Insofar as this assumption is valid it follows that abolishing self-interest is fruitless; it also follows that abolition of private property in the instruments of production, for example, brings no fundamental change in human nature. Any set of political and economic institutions, including socialism, creates characteristic patterns of incentives and costs. The abolition of property or the administering of public property does not remove private control over and private use of resources. Someone, somehow, administers the resources, determining the opportunities for their employment and thus tempts public decision makers to make use of public resources at the expense of the general public.

VOTERS AND VOTING: IGNORANCE, ILLUSION AND CONFUSION

While voting rights or "assets" are typically distributed to adults universally, equally, and free of charge, they cannot be used without incurring some cost. The costs may have an enormous range, but they are rarely in accord with the benefits that might be sought by voting. Just as the vote is given all, regardless of knowledge, effort and achievement, so that same vote cannot be bought and sold. I point to these fundamental properties of the vote because none of them is conducive to responsible choice. Because voting rights are free and universal, there is little incentive to develop expertise, to specialize, and to economize in their exercise. Voters can rationally remain ignorant. In a market equivalent ignorance would impose severe penalties.

Normally, prospective voters face a highly biased and discouraging situation. They not only confront powerful constraints but have only the slightest influence over outcomes. They have influence without having real choices. More exactly, their choices can be exercised only at prearranged times. These opportunities would be analogous to a market in which consumers were asked to supply themselves with goods for a four-year stretch without rights to return. And, unlike the consumer faced with a plethora of marginal choices, the voter faces binary, i.e., either/or, and future-oriented or uncertain options. One cannot have a little more or a little less of a candidate nor even a little more or less public expenditures and revenues. In two-party systems the choice generally presented is one involving homogeneous promises, or between "Tweedledee" and "Tweedledum." Were genuine choices offered no expression of intensity would be permitted and while tie-in purchases are rare in the market, they are characteristic of politics. Furthermore, the voter is confined to a single constituency; he is unable to vote for favorite politicians in districts other than his own.

The voter is free of a "reality test" in the sense that (a) he has little incentive to be informed, and (b) he need not consider the fiscal consistency of his choices. Voters rarely face price tags and explicit contracts on policies. If they did, they could not enforce compliance from politicians; no court will uphold campaign promises. Voters can only choose "process" characteristics and hope for the best.[1] Typically, consumers buy "results" rather than promises and leave the process to those who specialize in producing the goods and services. While any purchase is made under some uncertainty, the uncertainty confronting the voter is far greater.

A reduced sense of reality and disconnection of benefits and costs accounts not only for irresponsibility but also for apathy. The paradox of participation, i.e., the lessened value of one's vote as the electorate grows, is felt by the lowliest of voters. No such paradox exists in the market. In any event, the ordinary citizen is likely to view himself in an uncontrollable system. So he expends less effort on political issues than he spends on almost any economic choice. As usual, Schumpeter was right when he wrote:

> It will help to clarify the point if we ask ourselves why so much more intelligence and clearheadedness show up at a bridge table than in, say, political discussion among non-politicians. At the bridge table, we have a definite task; we have rules that discipline us; success and failure are clearly

defined; and we are prevented from behaving irresponsibly because every mistake we make will not only immediately tell us but also be immediately allocated to us. These conditions, by their failure to be fulfilled for political behavior of the ordinary citizen, show why it is that in politics he lacks the alertness and judgment he may display in his profession.[2]

Consider now the citizen-voter as citizen-consumer in a "government store." The store is, of course, operated by politicians and bureaucrats, all of whom are expected to serve in "the public interest." The government store is, then, a sort of cooperative. But it is a peculiar one in that it is destined to frustrate its members. Most of our public goods and an increasing volume of private goods are being offered in these "stores." These goods have no price tags but differential prices (taxes) are imposed, having little to do with the evaluations of the citizen-consumer. Not only are prices absent but consumers are required to finance unwanted goods or goods in unwanted quantities. Unlike the market, consumption is not subject to consumer discretion.

Consumer advocates have found private markets wanting in protections for the consumer; so they support government regulation. Suppose now that we ask for consumer protection in the political market. Surely protection is needed when government administers more than a third of the GNP. Unlike government, and unless they have monopoly power, private firms can neither require consumers to purchase goods nor charge differential prices. Furthermore, firms operate under laws of contract and tort, whereas the public producers can be sued only with their own consent. Many public services are of such a nature that consumer appraisal of them is all but impossible. Many political decisions are confounded by the presence of goods that have not been bought and sold and are therefore unpriced. People cannot decide whether these goods are worth having in what amounts by comparing price to cost. Nor can they choose among goods on the basis of comparative prices.

In effect, the producer does the judging, as is clearly the case when professors grade their students. Like professors, governments decide what to produce, in what quantities, and to whom it will go. Neither faces an independently generated demand curve. In fact, the demand for many public services is decided by the politicians and bureaucrats rather than by the ultimate consumers. Needless to say, demand curves are shifted to the right either by political fiat or advertising. While private advertisers must appeal to a vast number of individuals to change demand, governmental agencies need appeal only to small numbers of congressmen, suppliers of resources, and beneficiaries of specific services. Of course, the money for advertising comes not from sales but from unknown taxpayers who know not the uses being made of their untagged dollars.

William Buckley, in an obvious play on a famous passage from Galbraith's *The Affluent Society,* suggests that our "social imbalance" has a political explanation:

> A modern Justine could in New York City, wake up in the morning in a room she shares with her unemployed husband and two children, crowd into a subway in which she is hardly able to breathe, disembark at Grand Central and take a crosstown bus which takes twenty minutes to go the ten blocks to her textile loft, work a full day and receive her paycheck from which a sizeable deduction is withdrawn in taxes and union fees, return via the same ordeal, prepare supper for her family and tune up the radio to full blast to shield the children from the gamey denunciations her next-door neighbor is hurling at her husband, walk a few blocks past hideous buildings to the neighborhood park to breathe a little fresh air, and fall into a coughing fit as the sulphur dioxide excites her latent asthma, go home, and on the way lose her handbag to a purse-snatcher, sit down to oversee her son's homework only to trip over the fact that he doesn't really know the alphabet even though he had his fourteenth birthday yesterday, which he spent in company of a well-known pusher. She hauls off and smacks him, but he dodges and she bangs her head against the table. The ambulance is slow in coming and at the hospital there is no doctor in attendance. An intern finally materializes and sticks her with a shot of morphine, and she dozes off to sleep. And dreams of John Lindsay.[3]

That politics might have something to do with unemployment, union monopoly, education, transit, and medical services seems reasonable.

While citizens may be victimized by governments, they are continuously encouraged to get something for nothing. While the same motive prevails in the economy, price tags veto the wish. Not so in the polity; one can get something for nothing because government, with its coercive powers, can award benefits to some while it charges others. As the LSE joke about the democratic process goes: "Give me your vote, and I'll give you somebody else's money!" So universally accepted is this practice that redistribution is now widely viewed as a major function of government. So powerful is the conviction that eminent economists—Lester Thurow,[4] Harold M. Hochman[5] and James D. Rodgers[6]—treat redistribution as a pure public good. That suggests a close look at those who spend some people's money on others.

POLITICIANS: VOTE GATHERING AND IRRESPONSIBILITY

We can understand the politician's contribution to irresponsibility once we appreciate his incentives, disincentives, and resources. My analysis proceeds in much the same manner as the analysis of voters and voting. The results are similar in that behavior is peculiar but hardly irrational given the rules of the game.

Those who occupy decision-making posts gain them by a competitive struggle for votes from utility-maximizing but mostly uninformed, part-time voters. The quest for votes encourages the politician to take short-run perspectives and buy support. He opts for programs that will be highly visible to specific groups, each of whom he expects or hopes will contribute to his coalition of minorities at election time. He rewards those whose support is most contingent rather than those of whom he is sure: money must be spent in the "right" places at the "right times." And, it must be spent in the "right" ways! For example, politicians prefer programs that confer benefits through regulation or tax reductions rather than outright transfers. Accordingly, the politician is able to advance the welfare of some without arousing and annoying others. Legislative review is also avoided. Welfare payments "in-kind" are preferred to income grants, but this practice may reflect taxpayer rather than beneficiary interests. In any event, he can spend money in ways denied the private businessman and the consumer. They must decide within a known budget constraint; they confront opportunity costs in a most direct manner. This is not so for most politicians, who decide both spending and tax policies without the constraint of a fixed fund. Log-rolling is a typical consequence; if one interest group is gaining an "unfair" advantage, the response of legislators is not to end the "injustice," but to seek similar advantages for their own constituents. While log-rolling makes compelling political sense it has slight economic justification. Still, it is a basic political process.

Spending programs must ultimately be financed by someone, some way, for as the cliché now has it, "there ain't no such thing as a free lunch." Unless constrained by Constitutional rule or an alert and informed electorate, politicians may ignore the Friedman dictum. But even these "controls" offer no guarantee of responsible action, because the redistributive preferences of voters outweigh their concern for collective efficiencies. Voters and politicians alike can simultaneously advocate massive spending, lower taxes, and balanced budgets without going broke.

Tax policies are the obverse of spending decisions, i.e., the politician attempts to diffuse taxes over as many people as possible. Taxes may be made less visible and onerous by shifting them to non-voters, making payment less noticeable, and changes in bases and rates as gradual as possible. As in spending politicians are concerned with the impact of taxing on marginal voters and votes, not with the efficiency of markets. Most legislators are uninterested in the economist's criterion of fiscal neutrality; if market intervention or inefficient regulation will garner more votes they will be done in spite of known inefficiencies.

Regardless of ideology, politicians encourage citizens to use the political system. Once the polity has significant control over the economy citizens must resort to political activity if they are to protect or advance personal welfare. Their activity necessarily creates work, status, and power for the politicians. So they will select policies that make voters still more dependent on the state: a politician will, for example, advise people to seek state aid rather than take an independent private course of action. In the aftermath of the Mount St. Helens eruption, Northwest politicians, regardless of party, attempted to outdo one another in well-publicized efforts to obtain federal disaster monies, rather than advising local residents to leave the area. Politicians are most reluctant to tell obsolescent industries and occupations to heed the market signals. Instead, they protect the dying with tariffs, import quotas, subsidies, favorable tax legislation—all those schemes known as the "new protectionism." State support for local interests demonstrates care, a compassion that cannot be demonstrated with efficient policies. The latter will always appear as cold and impersonal long-run solutions. Again, we conclude that the politician is simply uninterested in efficiency; his attitude is dictated not by the equi-marginal calculus ($MB = MC$), but by the truly important political consideration of *whose* gains and *whose* losses. The ever-present prospect of receiving great benefits at little or no extra personal cost brings forth a persistent demand for redistribution.

The invisible hand of self-interest has produced remarkable results in the marketplace, but the same practice applied to political intervention in the economy may work in reverse. The universal pursuit of protection and redistribution—import quotas, fuel allocations, legalized monopolies, tax privileges, etc.—may so encumber the system as to generate a gigantic prisoners' dilemma in which everyone ends up worse-off. This may be one of the great tragedies of modern democracies: The better a political system performs in representing the narrow interests of its citizens, the worse it may be at managing its economy. If each citizen's collective interests are overwhelmed by the promise and necessity of seeking more immediate gains from redistribution, then all will share a smaller GNP. The fundamental problem for the politician stems from his having to satisfy ever-increasing demands for larger shares from a possibly less productive economy and more reluctant taxpayers. His dilemma is eased somewhat by the ignorance of consequences that is so characteristic of politics: The people who are helped by any particular policy are often those who have not struggled for it, while those who are injured include many who know not the source of their difficulties.

Aside from a necessary and important interest in the fiscal

behavior of elective officials, we must take note of certain other facts and incentives. Politicians have become full-time professionals, earning considerable salaries, commanding many valuable perquisites of office, but having little influence on bureaucrats and the programs they administer. In the political division of labor, politicians must pay for most of the decision costs of policy-making and governing. They do not take on the external costs of their policies. Hence they want to reduce decision costs but show little desire to reduce externalities levied at the rest of us. That the politician treats the federal budget as a "common pool resource" should occasion no surprise.[7] When private and public costs diverge, as they do in politics, one may expect fiscal irresponsibility.

Those who seek elective office are seldom those who would find an entrepreneurial career attractive. Once one grasps the differences between government and business, the reasons are apparent. Political life is much more exciting, ego-rewarding, and visible than private business. If few can name very many public officials, fewer still can name any of the top 500 businessmen.

In business appearance and reality cannot long be separated; in the crudest sense, this means there is a "bottom line" to discipline executives. Profits, or the lack thereof, can be disguised only in the very short run. In government there is no stock market, and that is why a politician or an entire administration can play at image-making. The very criteria of political success are controversial. Having returned to private life after a stint in government, many businessmen have noted that appearance is much more important than reality, a distinction that would not even occur in the business world. In politics power depends on what others think you have in the way of influence. Frequently people appear to have influence when they have none or little; occasionally, politicians seem not to have influence when in fact they are quite powerful. Would-be politicians soon learn that diligent cultivation of appearances is of the utmost importance.

Aspiring politicians also learn that while the appearance of consistency may or may not be the hobgoblin of small minds, it is important for a political career. Businessmen are expected and entitled to change their minds about future action as conditions change. Responsible decision-making demands adaptability. In politics those who vacillate are accused of inconsistency by other politicians, the Russians, and the press, as was Jimmy Carter. In consequence, much political language is double-talk. Politicians go to great lengths to avoid appearing to have changed their principles, priorities, and assessments. The media exploit these linguistic gymnastics, because mistakes and inconsistencies are newsworthy. Businessmen are not subjected to this kind of scrutiny; money does the talking.

Politicians interested in imagery learn, too, the importance of posing as the person who not only devised a policy but convinced others to go along. Who gets to announce policies and when are matters of the highest strategic import. Inclusion in decision-making is of primary significance to politicians; to be excluded is costly not only to his constituents but for his reputation. That is why Congressmen insist on having pictures taken with the President and, more importantly, of having the President appear to be listening or congratulating.

If appearances and reality are so inconsistent and power so critical, we should expect that those who go into politics either are or soon become vain, shallow, and unprincipled. All too often, politics seems tantamount to expedience. Everyone is obliged to say what we cannot possibly believe, promise the impossible, force practitioners to reckon with fools, flatter people who repel us, deprecate those we esteem, and all this for the sake of power whose possession will prove disappointing. Milton Friedman, in a recent *Newsweek* column, observed that

> Most members of Congress are honest, decent people whom you and I would be proud to have as personal friends and whom we would trust implicitly to tell us the truth and to honor their obligations. Yet, as "public servants," they consistently behave very differently, making assertions that they know to be untrue, making promises that they know will not be kept. Voting for legislation that they know to be undesirable.[8]

Politicians speak often but say as little of consequences as possible. Historians inform us that Lincoln was a partial exception for he did not make a single campaign speech in 1860 and

refused to answer any questions about his intentions. He said
he would stand on his "record." Ironically, politicians must dress
up their virtue of compromising in the language of "principle,"
the greatest of political vices. In the phrase, "Words that Succeed and Policies that Fail," Murray Edelman conveys much of
what I have attempted to characterize as compassion without
responsibility.[9]

Aside from the fact that politicians are forced to conceal, shift
positions, smooth feelings, evade, and the like, their task is extraordinarily difficult. They are expected to rush in where the
market fears to tread, providing services such as defense and
clean air that the market ignores. But the dictates of economic
efficiency are of little appeal and guidance in the public sector.
The criterion of efficiency simply dictates that the best policy is
that which yields the largest net benefits; questions of who is to
get how much of the benefits and who is to pay how much of
the costs are not addressed. Economists may know how to
choose between two housing projects but not know how to advise a politician on which one to support, because they cannot
advise on who should have better housing. The politician has
no such out from choice. When equity is not relevant, as in the
provision of public goods, the politician faces an equally difficult task—deciding how much or the optimal supplies of both
public goods and bads. Public choice theory is fairly certain that
no institutional arrangements can provide a definitive answer
to this question. Some citizens will always prefer more than is
offered; others with differing tastes will always prefer less,
whatever the amount supplied. But once the decision is made
to supply a particular quantity of a public good, the same
amount is available to all. As a result, and unlike the market,
individuals cannot adjust their consumption. If all individuals
must "consume" the same amount, many are going to be frustrated. Politicians must live with this fact.

BUREAUCRATIC APPEARANCES AND REALITY

We continue our inquiry into the divergence of appearance
and reality by examining bureaucracy and its incumbents the
bureaucrats. Again, we discover a gulf leading to irresponsible

conduct as well as a number of other well-known bureaucratic maladies, including even severe personality disorders. Once more the analysis is not meant to condemn intelligent, well-educated, hard-working servants of the public; in fact, most bureaucrats display all of these virtues. Ironically, dedicated and efficient effort may violate the norm of Paretian optimality and, of course, infringe upon individual freedom. In the words of Stephan Michelson, we are dealing with the "working bureaucrat and the nonworking bureaucracy." [10]

Bureaucrats work within the powerful constraints of a formal, hierarchical organization whose mission is defined by legislative fiat and whose task is to supply the public with not-for-profit services. The bureau finances its activities not by the sale of services but from a periodic budgetary commitment provided by the legislative branch. These funds are based on the government's right to print money, collect taxes, issue tax-free bonds, and even conscript and expropriate. Needless to say, private firms are denied these unique financial instruments. Public organizations so financed are not likely to go out of business, since they can shape the demand for their own services by collusion with private suppliers, beneficiaries, and, of course, interested politicians. Once an agency is in the budget, it is borne along year after year without close legislative oversight and certainly without the daily scrutiny of a marketplace.

These external differences tend to be more significant than the internal differences between a private firm and a public agency. However, one important internal difference pertains to the working conditions of employees; private competitive firms place much greater reliance on financial rewards and employment sanctions. Higher-level employees may obtain a substantial proportion of their income in the form of contingent claims, i.e., bonuses and stock options, and their employment is far less secure. In addition, government agencies account for their finances in a radically different way from that of profit-making firms. Accounts in private enterprises include both a balance sheet and an accrual-based income statement. Hardly any government agency prepares a balance sheet, and no decisions are made on "bottom-line" considerations, i.e., on the basis of net worth. Cash flow statements are used by agencies because capital expenditures are budgeted at time of purchase and never again. Private firms are quite flexible in their capital decisions since they shift capital expenditures on the basis of expected returns. Public agencies, on the other hand, are relatively inflexible since sales are not important. Instead, entrenched beneficiaries are able to maintain services even when public demand has shifted to other services. One might, therefore, claim that new agencies tend to be capital-deficient, while established agencies are capital-rich.

These curious economics of bureaucracies are not in the least peculiar to politics, a point made with considerable imagination by Gordon Tullock[11] and Anthony Downs[12] and with rigor by William A. Niskanen, Jr.[13] Public bureaucracies, operated by some 14 million employees, many strongly unionized, and several million more part-time employees, are now an electoral group that cannot be ignored.[14] Of greater significance, however, is the role played by bureaucrats in managing the economy, in supplying public goods, and redistributing income. Bureaucracies can and typically do ignore the marginal cost/benefit nexus in deciding their levels of operation; in short, they expand their services as far beyond that point as the size of the consumer surplus will permit. Excessive production then constitutes exploitation of those who finance the excess capacities and levels of operation. We should be careful to note that this form of exploitation is frequently done in the guise of "doing good," and meeting "social" or "merit" needs. Bureaucracies provide services and goods but not always in accord with citizen preferences; some people get more than they want and obviously are willing to finance. Even if production is excessive, the intended beneficiaries may complain because of insufficient personal allocations, excessive red tape, inopportune investigations, impersonality, and arbitrary decisions.

Bureaucracies and the political processes that decide their financing are notoriously inadequate in accurately and speedily reflecting societal preferences. A bureaucracy is, nevertheless, able to reflect its own preferences for larger budgets and have those preferences enacted. The important point here is that bureaucrats will want higher levels of public output, not because their preferences are necessarily different but because they face a different constraint; in this case, the relative prices of public and private goods confronting bureaucrats are different from those confronting the citizenry. For the same level of utility, bureaucrats will prefer a mix that contains more public goods and fewer private goods. As producer roles are more significant for the average citizen-voter, so too is the producer role more important to a government worker than is his other role as a citizen-voter. The stakes are larger and the chances greater that one can affect one's fate as a producer than as a consumer and citizen.

While private producers are constrained by the market to keep costs down, such incentives are largely nonexistent or weak in the public sector. In fact, the dominant incentives work in exactly the opposite direction. A bureaucrat gains status, income, and power by supervising more subordinates and not by what he produces in the way of valuable services to the public. It is in the interest of higher-level bureaucrats to overstaff their agencies and to increase the flow of paper or even the complexity of the organization. Making work for the agency has a payoff for every member, at the expense of citizens. The drive is to use as much as possible to achieve any given output. Legislators need to know that these costs are highly visible so that the agency has a persuasive rationale for a still larger budget. As was noted above, a bureaucracy can shift its demand curve in order to justify greater appropriations, but the same result can also be attained by increasing the alleged costs or by charging below-cost prices. When prices are reduced and/or below-cost prices adopted, demand for the service will increase.

Bureaucracies are meddlesome, inefficient, and therefore irresponsible. The extent of their costly behavior varies from one agency to another, from one time to another, from one nation to another, but it is always limited somewhat by prevailing institutions and the contrary interests of citizens. Unfortunately, the costs of organizing these opposing interests are far higher than might ideally be the case and certainly higher than the costs of efficient rent-seeking by the bureaucracies themselves.

NEGATIVE-SUM GAMES, HARM AND FAILURE

One acts positively to further one's welfare. That social costs or externalities may follow is incidental—a consequence that is unintentional and often unknown at the moment of decision. If the externalities are negative, complaints are certain and political action demanded; if operations are beneficial, few speak out. While one acts politically to advance personal welfare, this is mostly achieved not by seeking mutually desired exchanges but through negative and even destructive actions taken with the express purpose of harming others. Voters, bureaucrats, and politicians act against other members of the polity. Policies are deliberately enacted that restrict the alternatives available to others. Indeed the state is the enemy of Paretian choice. And, worse, Fromm's "escape from freedom" has become a fear of freedom for other people. As M. Bruce Johnson aptly observes:

> More and more products and activities that were voluntarily chosen by private decision are becoming involuntarily imposed, restricted, or eliminated by state mandate. Yet, it does not follow that because we are all one people, we all want the same diets, automobiles, medical services, pension benefits, and environmental amenities—or that we all are willing to bear the same costs to obtain a given benefit.[15]

George Stigler is unfortunately correct in asserting that Uncle Sam is really "Uncle Same" in his bureaucratic treatment of citizens, except, of course, at tax and subsidy times.[16]

Because the imposition of harm is so characteristic of political action, we should expect that as society is politicized, zero-sum and, increasingly, negative-sum games will replace the positive-sum games of the market. Potential benefactors turn to the state as the lowest-cost way of protecting themselves and intentionally or not imposing their own values on others. Evidently, politicians and bureaucrats are willing to supply the demand for security; evidently, many intellectuals and others are willing to justify their claims.

Since imposition of harm is so characteristic of political action, we should probably expect that politics will attract those who wish to see others controlled or harmed. In the worst circumstances sadists will go into politics, and in less horrendous situations well-meaning ideologists wanting to save mankind will crusade for ill-conceived reforms.

Those concerned about the failures of markets and market economies have a legitimate concern. We should worry also about the modern democratic polity and its impact on individualism and responsible conduct. Since the polity is treated by many as a substitute rather than a complement to the market, analysis of political, as opposed to economic, failure becomes imperative.

Failure is indigenous to politics. The polity, unlike the economy, is characterized by costly and infrequent trading, expensive information, high organizational and entry costs, many externalities. The consequences of any decision are therefore less fully thrust upon the political than the market participant. To offset this tendency of reduced cost-bearing, special constraints are imposed on officials and public employees. But such constraints, adopted in the interest of responsibility, are a poor substitute for the internalization of consequences. They contribute mightily to inflexibility. More importantly, the failure or inability of politics to internalize costs and benefits induces the kind of irresponsible behavior described as inefficient by public choice theorists and irrational by some political psychologists. As society becomes increasingly politicized, we may expect more of both public inefficiency and private irresponsibility.

Individuals are rarely ennobled by political action; instead, they are enticed to become less informed, less fair-minded, and less responsible. The waste of scarce resources is a tragic yet inevitable consequence of political choice.

POLITICAL DYNAMICS AND POLITICAL PARTICIPATION

Readers may find my analysis and its implications disturbing if not downright perverse, outlandish, or even churlish. Nowhere might these reactions be more quick and strong than on the important issue of political participation in a democracy. For the obvious conclusion is that "participatory" democracy is bound further to weaken our sense of responsibility, already woefully weak.

Nevertheless, given the assumption of utility maximization and the unique properties of public choice, participation is eminently rational. To be sure, the motivation assumed here may not possess the ethical qualities many political philosophers seem to prefer and, indeed, may even believe prevail. Still, my analysis should be understood as favoring individual and organizational political effort. We are in the grip of a new political dynamic.

Regardless of the reasons for the growth of the "State," the facts are that taxation consumes a major portion of current income; that government is the single largest purchaser of goods and services; that regulation of individuals, businesses, etc., is pervasive and costly (an estimated $2 billion in administrative costs and $100 billion per year in compliance costs);[17] that changing rules, expenditures, taxes and regulations alter property rights which, in turn, affect the income and wealth of every single citizen; and finally, that federal transfer payments totalled more than $300 billion in 1980.[18] *In a world like ours "participation" in politics and administration becomes mandatory.* We are driven to it. A mundane happening illustrates our predicament. After the Carter Administration forced recreational boat owners to purchase and install expensive anti-pollution devices and then proposed that weekend boating during energy shortages be banned, the membership of the Boat Owners Association soon increased from 50,000 to its current level of more than 80,000.[19] Democratic politics becomes both more aggressive and more defensive. The advocates of participatory democracy will get their way for reasons they will not like and try to ignore.

There is more to the dynamic of our situation than these facts suggest. In attempting to improve their lot, people do not merely adjust to economic contingency. They alter the rules and policies to their own advantage. The effort they will expend to alter rules and policies depends on the relationship between costs and expected gains. This is the rational principle that explains the political dynamic of collectivistic liberalism.

What appears to have happened over the past century is nothing less than a dramatic shift in the cost-benefit schedules of political action. While the state has always provided basic services and redistributed income and wealth, we observe rapid intensification during the twentieth century. As this has occurred, the returns from using the political process have increased at a far greater rate than the also mounting costs. Almost any economic decision can now be challenged in the political arena and with a reasonable expectation of success. To be sure, as more citizens have entered politics and as their pressure has become more continuous and professionalized, the costs have increased. But the ratio has widened, and that is the crucial calculation. The question is no longer one of participation, if it ever was, but of the shape of effective action. (The dynamic of participation is set forth in simple diagrammatic form in Appendix A.) The question of effectiveness is not considered. It is exhaustively dealt with by David Truman in his classic *The Governmental Process* and in countless texts on political parties and interest groups.

The conclusion is that the liberal democratic welfare state has generated a distinctive form of politics. People try to obtain income and wealth at the expense of others and attempt to protect themselves against government. Economic man has put on political clothes. While a definitive estimate of outcomes is probably impossible, there does seem to be considerable agreement among analysts of redistributive politics and economics that (1) income and wealth are redistributed both vertically and horizontally; (2) that almost every citizen is both beneficiary and donor; (3) that significant transfers take place among members of the same income bracket; (4) that lower-income groups have made significant gains during the past forty years; (5) that total transfers have not altered the basic market distribution by very much; and finally, (6) that inequality prevails.[20]

All this is very costly, i.e., the opportunity costs are enormous since the energy expended is not productive. The person busy in the halls of government advancing his own prosperity is obviously not working for others. These opportunity costs are probably unmeasurable. Anyway, the overall distribution remains unequal and, as noted throughout this essay, many programs are perverse. Contrary to liberal intention and expectation, many of the rich become richer and some of the poor, poorer. After all the frenetic action and transfers, most people still occupy the same relative positions. Rational individual and group action will increase transaction costs, produce a smaller social product, and in the end leave most worse off. This is the disastrous dynamic of our democracy. But not to seek subsidies when others may be expected to, and not to demand tax privileges when others do, makes no sense. Everyone is caught up in a tragedy of the budgetary "commons." These "games" are neither ennobling nor socially optimal.

In the words of Robert A. Dahl, ". . . the making of governmental decisions is not a majestic march of great majorities united upon certain matters of policy. It is the steady appeasement of relatively small groups."[21] We face the dilemma of individual and collective rationality, that general ruin can be the outcome of rational action.[22]

Political "participation" is self-interested and rational, yet in the long term highly irrational. This finding goes against conventional radical wisdom. Political participation is usually held to be an intrinsic good and productive of good consequences. A healthy democracy is one in which citizens participate in public-spirited ways, more or less continuously, enjoy the comradeship of cooperative action and, of course, resolve social problems. The polity is really a commune writ large. Others consider democracy an arena for class conflicts, yet one in which fighting stops short of violence. Both views make political participation the most significant and noble of human actions. Our present politics is not what Hannah Arendt had in mind.

Curiously, economic behavior is generally considered mundane, selfish, uninteresting and even "unproductive." Neither saints nor heroes appear in the marketplace! This being the case, no one worries about economic life except that it is seen as demeaning, inhuman, and a realm of domination. Markets are zero-sum games. They exhibit fraud, coercion, monopoly, and capitalistic pathologies. Political action is treated as selfless, communal, exhilarating, and productive. If so, some thinkers have some difficulty in explaining why so rewarding an activity is so unattractive to so many Americans. The answer is found, not in the opportunity costs of politics, but in the institutional and policy constraints imposed by "establishments," "power elites" and "corporate pluralism."

But surely this attitude is mistaken. Political "participation" is far more intense than our pollsters and radicals think. Indeed, one cannot be apolitical; even the simple act of "not voting" or declaring that one "doesn't know" are political acts because they have consequences for the resolution of political and economic issues. Likewise, to obey or disobey a law, to pay or cheat on one's taxes, to receive or not receive a subsidy, to sing or not sing the national anthem, to watch a TV newscast, to love or hate one's country are political statements. Americans are a highly politicized people and becoming more so, as are the British. Given the importance of government they have no choice.

"Participatory" politics is not well informed. Why does a highly politicized people remain ignorant of political strategy and public policies? Again, the competitive dynamic provides the answer. We have marketized, not humanized, politics.

Politics is highly uncertain. Reduction of uncertainty is costly and not often worth anyone's while. In these discouraging conditions few are apt to become expert in political matters. Instead, the individual will become an ideologue or depend upon hired experts to represent him. In consequence, the distribution of political information is highly skewed. (A diagrammatical presentation of these conclusions is found in Appendix B.)

Throughout this essay I have maintained that the polity remains an inferior mechanism to the market when it comes to the allocation of scarce resources between myriad and conflicting individual preferences. All markets, of course, work imperfectly compared to the ideals of the textbooks. Still, the realities of imperfect markets—externalities, consumer ignorance, advertising, monopoly, oligopoly, non-optimal provisions of public goods—are overwhelmed by the universality and magnitude of public failure. While this failure is intractable democracy remains superior to other forms of politics because individual liberty and preferences are honored as ideals, and institutions of collective choice at least make some effort to discern and act upon them. Finally, I, for one, have not despaired of the possibilities of institutional reform. Certain recently proposed constitutional amendments pertaining to the fiscal and monetary powers of government provide more suitable settings for enacting efficient policies. Moreover, recent imaginative work on "demand revelation" reveals means of coping with the free-rider problem, as well as offering further testimony to the inventiveness of the human mind.[23] While collective choice stands in the sharpest contrast to the market, marginal improvements are possible. But of all improvements the most effective is a steady diminution of the scope of government.

APPENDIX A

In order to maximize gains from redistributive government, the politically active must find that amount of "participation" at which the difference between total expected gains and expected costs is maximized. As shown in Figure 1, maximizing activity must satisfy the condition that, at that level, the slopes of the total gain curve and the total cost curve are equal. At lower levels of action than 0Q, total gains could be greater if the individual or organization increased its effort. Similarly, at all higher levels than the maximum, costs will exceed gains and at some level total cost will exceed total return. On the other hand, total costs typically exceed gains at the beginning of redistributive efforts, as indeed they do for almost all human endeavors. The rational participant then is not one who maxi-

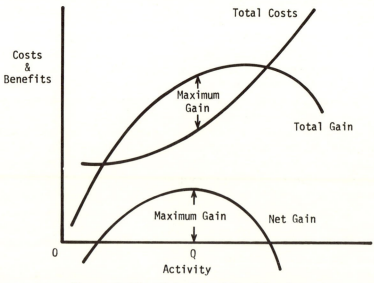

Figure 1. The Calculus of Participation

mizes gains while minimizing costs, for that is logically impossible; instead the rational participant must know by how much an additional act raises both costs and gains. Maximization requires finding the point where marginal cost equals marginal gain; that is found where total gain exceeds total cost by the largest amount. Accordingly, most citizens could engage in vastly more political action, but to do so would ignore the dictates of rationality. Even if some social scientists do not understand the fundamental importance of opportunity costs, ordinary citizens act as though they do.

APPENDIX B

Appendix A sets forth the calculus of participation without reference to the equally important question of optimal levels of information. "Participation" may be intelligent or ignorant. The question is how informed should one be. The answer will shed light on how well informed citizens are and how their information compares with consumers' knowledge.

In deciding how informed to become, the individual considers both the anticipated cost of acquiring and interpreting information and anticipated cost of remaining ignorant. These two types of costs are set forth in Figure 2, with the former cost (C_1) depicted as an increasing function of the amount of information, while the second cost (C_2) is shown as a decreasing function of the amount of information sought. In short, more information costs more and more information decreases the probability of reaching incorrect decisions. It should also be observed that the slope of C_1 is increasing, i.e., the marginal cost of information increases. On the other hand, the slope of C_2 suggests that the initial acquisition of information reduces the chances of making mistakes much more than do successive units. By vertical addition of the two costs, one finds the total costs (c_3); by locating the low point of the total cost curve the individual determines the optimal degree of knowledge for whatever activity is contemplated.

The above analysis is completely general and in no way depicts the specific situations of a citizen and consumer. Figure 3 provides such a comparison, enabling us to understand why a citizen typically chooses to engage in uninformed political activity and highly informed (by contrast) economic action.

C_1 and C_2 are drawn to depict the situation of a consumer and resemble similar curves shown in Figure 2. One might think of these as costs of purchasing an automobile or house. A second set of the same costs is included to portray the situation of a voter considering whether to vote and for whom in a Presidential election. These cost schedules are shown in dotted lines. The cost of political information is assumed to be higher per unit than economic costs because economic information is both more readily available and in more meaningful terms to individuals. One does not require a Ph.D in economics or engineering to buy a good automobile. A sensible choice of a President may not require either degree, but surely acquisition of knowledge about various economic alternatives is more demanding than buying a car. On the other hand, the cost of

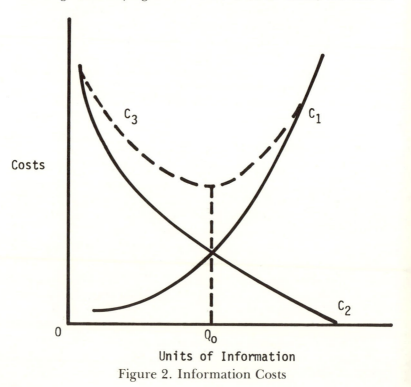

Units of Information
Figure 2. Information Costs

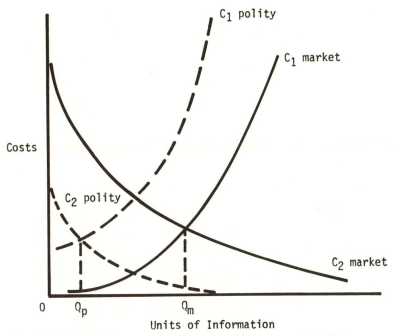

Figure 3. Information Costs: In Markets and Polities

economic and political ignorance is hardly as enraging as buying a "lemon." The total costs of choosing the "wrong" President may be enormous, but they are diffused through the entire population and would probably have been incurred regardless of how any given individual voted. If these assumptions are correct, a person will choose to be better informed in markets than in politics. Whereas the optimal quantity of market information is Q_m, the optimal quantity of political information is Q_p. Thus it is contended that individuals choose to remain more ignorant regarding the bases for political choices than they do with regard to market choice.

NOTES

1. Thomas Sowell, *Knowledge and Decisions* (New York: Basic Books, 1980), pp. 140–141.
2. Joseph A. Schumpeter, *Capitalism, Socialism and Democracy, third edition* (New York: Harper and Row, 1975), p. 261.

3. William F. Buckley, Jr., *The Unmaking of a Mayor* (New York: Viking Press, 1966), pp. 30–31, as quoted in Richard E. Wagner, "Advertising and the Public Economy: Some Preliminary Ruminations," in David G. Tuerch (ed.), *The Political Economy of Advertising* (Washington, D.C.: American Enterprise Institute, 1978), p. 98.

4. Lester C. Thurow, "The Income Distribution as a Pure Public Good," *Quarterly Journal of Economics,* 85 (May 1971), pp. 327–336.

5. Harold M. Hochman, "Individual Preferences and Distributional Adjustment," *American Economic Review,* LXII (May 1972), pp. 353–360.

6. Harold M. Hochman and James D. Rodgers, "Pareto Optimal Redistribution," *American Economic Review,* LIX (September 1969), pp. 542–557.

7. John Baden and Rodney D. Fort, "Natural Resources and Bureaucratic Predators," *Policy Review* (Winter 1980), pp. 69–81.

8. Milton Friedman, "Balanced on Paper," *Newsweek* (June 23, 1980), p. 68.

9. Murray Edelman, *Political Language: Words that Succeed and Policies that Fail* (New York: Academic Press, 1977).

10. Stephan Michelson, "The Working Bureaucrat and the Non-Working Bureaucracy," in Carol H. Weiss and Allen H. Barton (eds.), *Making Bureaucracies Work* (Los Angeles: Sage Publications, 1980), pp. 175–200.

11. Gordon Tullock, *The Politics of Bureaucracy* (Washington, D.C.: Public Affairs Press, 1965).

12. Anthony Downs, *Inside Bureaucracy* (Boston: Little, Brown & Co., 1967).

13. William A. Niskanen, Jr., *Bureaucracy and Representative Government* (Chicago: Aldine-Atherton, 1971), p. 137.

14. Winston C. Bush and Arthur T. Denzau, "The Voting Behavior of Bureaucrats and Public Sector Growth," in Thomas E. Borcherding (ed.), *Budgets and Bureaucrats* (Durham, N.C.: Duke University Press, 1977).

15. M. Bruce Johnson, "The Economics and America's Third Century," in Robert I. Rooney and M. Bruce Johnson, *The Economics of America's Third Century: A Discussion* (Los Angeles: The International Institute for Economic Research, 1978), p. 23.

16. George J. Stigler, "The Government of the Economy," *A Dialogue on the Proper Economic Role of the State* (Selected Papers No. 7, Graduate School of Business, University of Chicago, 1963).

17. Roy Ash, *The Political World, Government Regulation, and Spending* (Los Angeles: International Institute for Economic Research, 1979), p. 5.

18. Edgar K. Browning and Jacqueline M. Browning, *Public Finance and the Price System* (New York: Macmillan Publishing Co., 1980), p. 194.
19. Brooks Jackson, "Reagan Plan to Tax Yachts and Boats Has Owners Angry," *Wall Street Journal* (May 8, 1981), p. 29.
20. See, for example, Edgar K. Browning, *Redistribution and the Welfare System* (Washington, D.C.: American Enterprise Institute, 1975); James N. Morgan et al., *Income and Welfare in the United States* (New York: McGraw-Hill Book Company, 1972); and especially, Morton Paglin, "The Measurement and Trend of Inequality: A Basic Revision," *The American Economic Review*, 65 (September 1975), pp. 598–609.
21. Robert A. Dahl, *A Preface to Democratic Theory* (Chicago: University of Chicago Press, 1956), p. 146.
22. The relationship between rational individual choice and collective irrationality is imaginatively explored in Jon Elster, *Ulysses and the Sirens* (Cambridge: Cambridge University Press, 1979); J. Roland Pennock, *Democratic Political Theory* (Princeton: Princeton University Press, 1979); and E.L. Jones, *The European Miracle* (Cambridge: Cambridge University Press, 1981).
23. Edward Clarke, *Demand Revelation and the Provision of Public Goods* (Cambridge: Ballinger Publishing Co., 1980).

15

INDIVIDUALISM AND THE MARKET SOCIETY[1]

ROBERT E. LANE

> The ancient conception in which man always appears (in however narrowly national, religious, or political a definition) as the aim of production, seems very much more exalted than the modern world in which production is the aim of man and wealth the aim of production.
>
> —Karl Marx

Of all the varied elements of liberalism, individualism probably evokes the greatest ambivalence among liberals. *Individualism* is the perception of the individual distinguished from his social group, the definition of the individual in terms of qualities that are distinctively his own as contrasted to group qualities, and the evaluation of the individual separate from the evaluaton of his group. These perceptions, definitions, and evaluations are attributed both to the individuals themselves and to the culture; that is, they are socially endorsed and widely shared.

An *individualistic society* is one where individualism prevails and where control over behavior and thought is vested in the individual relatively more than in custom, tradition, and consensus (as is the case in primitive and traditional societies), and relatively more than in authority (as in command economies and authoritarian societies). Usage gives the term "individual-

ism" many additional meanings,[2] some of which pertain to societies and some to individuals; we shall find it useful to treat
many of these as the properties of the individual necessary to
enable an individualistic society to function adequately, that is,
to energize and coordinate the tasks which such societies usually set for themselves. I shall call the set of individual properties necessary for that purpose "functional individualism." Beyond that a further definition follows from an evaluation of the
individual that is not only separate from the evaluation of the
group, but which, in accord with much humanistic thought,
gives priority to the individual over the group and its codes and
practices. I shall call that set of individual properties "developmental individualism," for it represents a conviction that the
"ultimate value" lies in the development of the individual to his
full powers, and a repudiation of the view "that the individual
did not exist for his own sake, but for the sake of the whole
society."[3] Functional individualism, on the other hand, carries
with it no such implication, for the properties are conceived to
be necessary precisely because they are functional to any society
where neither tradition nor authority serves as an adequate
guide to behavior. As the term implies, in the functional version man is a means; in developmental individualism, man is
an end.

We will tread gingerly around the question of the origins of
the individualistic society, whether these be in religion (Weber),
the modes of production (Marx), the division of labor (Durkheim), technology (Mumford, Landes), philosophy (Arendt),
epistemology (Comte), evolutionary processes (Spencer), and
focus on a somewhat different question. That question is: why,
given the relative emphasis on the individual (in place of tradition and authority) as a principal energizing and coordinating social instrument, do individuals assume a certain character? Among the variety of forces shaping character, our concern
is with only one, the market economy. After offering a brief
sketch of the individual in a tradition-oriented society, we turn
to the characterological requirements of an individualistic society, the individual properties that are necessary for the operation of such a society. Does it require, as alleged, "one-dimensional man," "cheerful robots," machine-like calculators,
organization men, emotionless performers, role identities, ego-

ists, atoms but not individuals? Or, in spite of the market's in-difference to personality and individuality, is the logic of the system such that it develops relatively individuated, autono-mous, emotionally mature persons who accept responsibility for their fates and think for themselves? We then turn to some evidence on the still-changing character of modern man, and conclude with an exploration of how the market might have produced these results.

THE INDIVIDUAL IN COMMUNITY

In the beginning was community. Man is a social animal; non-human primates live in groups commonly varying from ten to fifty; prolonged human immaturity requires prolonged mother-child relations and their defense; the human isolate is sick and lacking in many properties we regard as human; attachment or bonding is instinctive.[4] Where the community is dominant, as among primitive societies or isolated traditional villages, the in-dividual sees himself and others chiefly as parts of the group; individuals derive their properties from their group relations. There are perceptual as well as motivational reasons for this definition of self and others only in the group context. Percep-tually, no categories or schema aid in defining the individual self. Hobhouse, reflecting the anthropology of his time but also anticipating later cross-cultural research, suggests that in prim-itive societies "the familiar categories of human experience are not fully distinguished . . . distinct individuals melt away into one another and preserve no clear-cut identity."[5] Inevitably, language is likely to reflect this priority of the community over the individual. The developed and often intricate language for kinship in primitive societies seems to contrast with a relatively impoverished language for states of mind. In advanced socie-ties, in those situations where it is assume that everyone shares a common background, people employ a "restricted linguistic code," failing to elaborate on the properties of persons men-tioned because of the assumption that they are personally known to others.[6] Behaviorally, when small children spend all their time together, they are less likely than those who spend only briefer periods together, to assert themselves over their possessions.[7] Motivationally, in a total community incentives to separate the self from the group or to examine the properties of the self are unlikely. A separate identity is not valued; distinctiveness beyond the permitted variation in value orientations is neither functional nor approved: indeed, it is unthinkable. Furthermore, "self-focused attention" is painful, even under modern conditions where it is sometimes socially encouraged.[8]

The perceptual problem has structural explanations. As Durkheim argues, primitive and traditional societies, with little division of labor, create similar or "segmental" personalities, more or less alike because of exposure to like formative experiences. Even the differentiated roles required in these societies are often such that almost any member of the appropriate age and sex can fill any of them.[9] Perception thrives on contrast; without contrast, differences among individuals are minimized.

Education and exposure to alternative cultures create individual differences,[10] but thse are rare in traditional, as well as primitive societies. Writing in 1885, F.C. Montague argues that the apparent differentiation of persons in medieval society was deceptive:

> Beneath the varied and gorgeous pageant of the Middle Age an acute observer might have detected a widespread monotony. Peasant, burgher, and knight differed much more in garb and bearing than in their inner life. Perhaps not one of the three could read; perhaps not one of the three had travelled, save on a pilgrimage to some popular shrine; their minds were imprisoned within the narrow limits of their generation and of their neighborhood. . . . Modern civilization is so vast as to furnish an infinite variety of pursuits. Every one of these, if earnestly pursued, will develop a distinct habit of thought and feeling . . . not less strongly marked because they all wear broadcloth and converse[d] in the dialect of good society.[11]

Not long ago, the "man in the gray flannel suit," like his broadcloth-wearing nineteenth-century British cousin, was taken as the prototype of the stereotyped, deindividuated American. Montague is telling us that the Middle Age character types were embedded in their cultures and roles; that freedom from such roles and conventions lies in diversity of occupation and varied inner life improved by education.

While the history of social philosophy is by no means the same as the history of social experience, the late "discovery" of the individual offers a clue to the timing of the emergence of the self from the matrix of society. Even the individualistic Greeks interpreted the individual in terms of such properties of society as the division of labor; men's acts and fates were as much determined by the gods as by men's own wills; *The Republic*, for example, offers little scope for individuality. Von Mises suggests that the "Copernican revolution in social science" was the shift in the seventeenth century from a focus on society and the state to the individual;[12] Burckhardt traces individualism from the Renaissance, and, as Lukes points out, others have placed its origins in the Reformation, the decline of aristocracy, the church, traditional religion, or the industrial revolution, the rise of capitalism, and democracy.[13] By common consent, however, the age of Enlightenment is a major turning point.

The social contracts of the seventeenth and eighteenth centuries offer a mixed contribution to the concept of individualism. On the one hand, they seem to have had the historical and analytical sequence wrong. Men do not consciously come together to achieve peace and prosperity, for, as we said, there always was community. Rather, out of the matrix of community gradually emerged concepts of the distinct, differentiated, separately valued individual. On the other hand, the social contract was important in the development of concepts of distinct and valued individuals, for it reversed the causal order: by coming together to create society, individuals were converted from objects to subjects, from that which is acted upon to that which initiates action. Through successive reformulations, the idea of a social contract served to break the grip of the customary order, for it implied that people can create their own institutions, and it led to concepts of popular sovereignty thrusting responsibility back upon individuals. But this is functional individualism, not yet developmental individualism.

One other feature of intellectual history bears on the altered view of the individual over more recent history. In tracing the change in the content and definition of liberalism over the last two hundred years, Girvetz identifies the original classical version with an "atomistic" view of man in society, a mode of perception that, he said, was consonant with a general reductionism, the tendency to see parts as unchanged by participation in the functioning of the whole.[14] The change from "classical liberalism" to "contemporary liberalism" was prompted by recognition of the more complex interrelations between parts and wholes, assisted, one might add, by the shift from a mechanical to an organic metaphor. The parts of a machine are separable; they have independent identities; they may be recombined in a variety of different ways. An individualism reflecting the mechanical metaphor might, indeed, be reductionist, atomistic. On the other hand, "A thing is called organic when it is made up of parts which are quite distinct from one another, but which are destroyed or vitally altered when they are removed from the whole."[15] An individualism based on an organic metaphor must comprehend the relations of the individual to the society of which he is a part. Market economics failed to change its metaphoric base when philosophic liberalism changed. The divisibility of the factors of production is an essential feature of the market's marginal analysis. Consumers are assumed not to have interdependent utilities. As the other components of liberalism changed to an organic metaphor (man *in* society), market economics retained the idea of the individual as a replaceable unit in a productive machine.

PERSONALITY REQUIREMENTS OF AN INDIVIDUALISTIC SOCIETY

By means of the slow accretion of collective experience, traditional communitarian societies develop routines for coordinating and accomplishing communal tasks. Authoritarian societies employ hierarchy and command for these purposes. But individualistic societies require of the individual that he assume some of the functions achieved through tradition and command. In order to perform these functions he must have certain cognitive, motivational, emotional, and behavioral properties. What are these personality requirements of an individualistic society?

In the first place, relatively bereft of other sources of guidance, the individual must learn to think for himself. In the atmosphere of the Enlightenment, Kant gave this capacity of man the highest priority. "Enlightenment," he says, "is man's emergence from his self-imposed nonage. Nonage is the inability to use one's understanding without another's guidance."[16] Like the contemporary humanistic psychologist, Abraham Maslow, he urges us to "Dare to know." Kant ascribes the causes of overly prolonged immaturity to man's laziness, cowardice and learned preference for servitude, qualities which could be modified by the relinquishment of controls by authority. Freedom was the answer. But later experience with freedom of speech and conscience reveals more deep-seated constraints.

Thinking for oneself requires more than motivation and release from constraints; it requires cognitive complexity. Summarizing a vast literature, we may say that cognitive complexity comprises (1) a variety of schemata categories, concepts, models, dimensions held in solution in the mind so that they are available for use in defining and analyzing situations as they present themselves; (2) some internal "rules" for grouping, or "chunking," perceptions to aid in classifying observations and giving them properties, along with the capacities to form intellectual hierarchies and to move flexibly from the concrete to the abstract and back again; therefore (3) a capacity to resist the tendency to think in terms of simple analogies, to avoid the "sweeping concretization" that follows from the use of single schemata without comparisons or consideration of alternatives;[17] (4) the strength to see "good" features in a person or an event which one dislikes and "bad" features in the preferred, that is, the strength to avoid the halo effect[18] or simple good-bad dichotomies, and to endure the pain of ambivalence or what psychologists call a "cognitive imbalance;"[19] (5) openness of mind such that one assimilates new features to old mental structures, sees new uses for familiar objects, employs information to explore the world rather than defend against it, the avoidance, that is, of dogmatism and ridigity;[20] and (6) in Piagetian terms, the capacity for formal operations involving reciprocity and logic—a condition for the moral reasoning that was for Kant the main purpose of thinking for oneself.[21]

These are formidable requirements; few people are fully endowed with these capacities, and fewer still employ them, especially in moral reasoning.[22] But whatever degree of this kind of cognitive complexity a people may possess, they will be discouraged from exercising these capacities by pressure to conform to tradition or public opinion and by demands for unqualified obedience to authority.

Because the individualistic society thrusts decisions upon the individual that require him to attend to his longer-term objectives, to discover for himself what *he* wants to do, it requires a limited form of self-awareness, but hardly a full understanding of his inner conflicts or full potentialities. It is only a beginning. Two basic cognitive styles differentiate those who perceive themselves as separate from the group and those who do not.[23] The articulated or "field independent" style sees the parts of any perceptual whole, and seeing the parts can give them properties, recombine them, use them flexibly. The global or "field dependent" style sees only the gestalt. These two forms of perception or cognition have been tested cross-culturally by such instruments as an "embedded figures test" (where, significantly, the individual is asked to see *faces* in a confused pattern design), a "rod and frame test" where the subject is asked to tell whether an element within the framework or the framework itself is tilted, and a tilted chair test where the subject is himself placed at an angle and asked whether the object to be perceived is either at the same or a different angle.

What is important for our analysis is that the person with a field independent, articulated style can differentiate himself as a separate part of the environment. Witkin, the author of these studies and inventor of the tests, reports one of his findings as follows:

> Persons with articulated (field independent) cognitive styles give evidence of a developed sense of separate identity—that is, they have an awareness of needs, feelings, attributes which they recognize as their own and which they identify as distinct from others. Sense of separate identity implies experience of the self as structured; internal frames of reference have formed and are available as guides for definition of the self. The less developed sense of separate identity of persons with global cognitive styles manifests it-

self in reliance on external sources for definition of their attitudes, judgments, sentiments, and views of themselves.[24]

Thus, in general, any society that requires rationalistic analysis, the breakdown of wholes into parts and the recombination of these parts into new configurations, to the extent that it develops the general field-independent cognitive style also contributes to the sense of separate identity.

The cognitive capacity to achieve a separate identity does not guarantee a "successful identity," for the very elements that require it may at the same time confuse the individual as to his "real self;" too many choices are thrust upon him, his rationality may not help him to discover his central values around which an identity must be built. Further, we know from other experimental work that "objective self-awareness" is actively discouraged by a sense of personal deficiencies, for attention to the self is then painful. An individualistic society is likely to be competitive and often invidious, thus making for painful comparisons between self and others; it is also likely to encourage ambition, creating painful comparisons between aspirations and achievements. On the other hand, this same body of laboratory research finds that "deindividuation . . . a circumstance where individual identity is swallowed up by the environment" (a circumstance encouraged by traditional and communist societies) discourages the individual from facing contradictions between his opinions or norms and his behavior; he is not required to face internal discrepancies.[25] Thus a moderate but not total attention to the self produces a more consistent and reliable personality. The need for individual decisions also encourages the individual to sum up his values and wants, and develop capacities for self-differentiation. It makes individuation and uniqueness a value,[26] encourages field independence, and takes the individual part way toward self-awareness and an identity that he can call his own.

An individualistic society that encourages an individual to consider his own wants and needs might be said to motivate him to forget others, to think only of himself. The motives of the disembedded individual have long been suspect, for they are freighted with connotations of egoism. In condensed form, this egoism may be said to take the form of selfishness and narcissism. Encouraged to see himself as independent from the community, the individual, it is argued, will pursue his self-interest at the cost of others and the community, or will love only himself, giving himself over to pride and envy, to inflated self-concern. Yet others, taking the same theme—a theme which Fromm calls "man for himself"—believe that this self-concern will lead to individual development and growth, to searching for a higher moral code, to self-respect rather than self-love.[27] Some Enlightenment theorists, along with John Stuart Mill and contemporary "romantics," like John Dewey and Abraham Maslow, believe that an underlying "growth instinct," once released, will make for a better version of man, a version not only compatible with but a condition for a humane society. Evidence supports both views,[28] testimony to the variety of motives available to the individual. Once a person is free to develop his personality as he wishes, once the self is made culturally important, individuals in different contexts will give that important self a variety of attractive or unattractive configurations.

Thus, it would seem that individualism is achieved only at the expense of violation of man's natural endowment; man in "the state of nature," that is, man ruled by the human biogram, is more at home embedded in community than he is when disengaged from that community. Under these circumstances, it is quite possible to say with Sabine (and many others) that the rise of doctrines of individualism was dependent on "its agreement with the interests of the class that mainly produced it,"[29] for it appears that there is nothing especially congenial to human nature about individualism. But a motive, quite possibly instinctive,[30] supports a limited form of individualism. It is the motive to control one's own environment. "Man's primary motivational propensity," says the American psychologist Richard DeCharms, reviewing the findings of much research, "is to be effective in producing changes in his environment."[31] That this control can be achieved through combination with others means that it is equally available to market and to socialist economies, but it does imply that to satisfy that motive the individual must see himself as a causal agent. He cannot satisfy it by serving merely as an instrument of authority or the collectivity. To satisfy the motive, three things are necessary: (1) the motive must be aroused or released by a culture that legitimizes it; (2) the individual must believe that he is, in fact, the agent of his own powers, the origin of his own acts and not the pawn of fate; and (3) he must perceive that his acts make a difference, that "outcomes" are contingent on what he does. Like most motives, it is therefore associated with appropriate cognitions.

Here, perhaps more than anywhere else, we have a personality characteristic upon which the individualistic society may rely. If a person is not motivated by fear of authority or stimulus-response mechanisms, or desire to conform to tradition, if, that is, society requires some initiative from him in controlling his own destiny, he must be motivated to do so and must believe that his efforts will not be in vain.

Individualism has been criticized for unleashing the passions, mostly evil: lust, envy, sacrifice, hate—the deadly sins. The supporters of *gemeinschaft* confounded community bonds with the bonds of love, and therefore believed that with the relaxation of these community bonds, love itself would disappear and hostility, restrained only by prudence, would take its place.[32] Relief from this idea came from two sources: the precursors of the market ideology advanced the belief that the passions could be harnessed by self-interest, which was a motive under cognitive control, although hardly controlled by love.[33] And Freud, for different purposes, made men conscious of the power of love, generalized as libido and then extended to encompass all human attachments. (But Freud was uncertain at the end, whether the libido, or Eros, would triumph over men's aggressive instincts.) In fact, our biological endowment includes dispositions prompting both aggression and love and even altruism and sympathy.[34] The culture generally and the economy specifically can shape and use these dispositions in a variety of ways. In an individualistic society the absence of social restraints on aggression requires internal controls without which individuals indulge in impulsive and destructive acts.[35] But with internal controls, removal of social restraints often leads to what psychologists call "pro-social behavior," for the reason that when the individual perceives *himself* (and not others) to be responsible for and effective in altering "outcomes," that is, in removing the duress or pain of another, he is more likely to take the necessary action.[36] Similarly, the libido, or more plausibly the "attachment motive" (they are not the same thing),[37] requires cognitive control or it risks dependency. It is a condition of a successful individualistic society, therefore, that the individual possess these internal controls. They are not given by nature but rather taught and learned in economic as well as in family and social life.

The need for some degree of cognitive control over the emotions implies that the emotions may not be "ego alien," that is, they are not so frightening to the individual that he dare not acknowledge or even examine them. More than that it implies that he does not lose the energizing force of his emotions, treating himself as a "thing," impersonally and coldly. Much of the criticism of modern man lies precisely here: His cognitive apparatus has been overdeveloped to the point where his emotional life is starved.[38] From the clinic evidence emerges that this failure of emotionally charged commitment, may, indeed, constitute one of the casualities of modern society,[39] but no evidence from epidemiological or survey studies support a general indictment of the individualistic society on these grounds.[40] The emotions, like the motivations, are the energizing forces of the individual; to the degree that the individualistic society relies upon the individual's initiative and energy, he must not only have them under cognitive control, he must recognize them and employ them. Impulsiveness, the inability to defer gratification, is disruptive for the individualistic society, but so is emotion-lessness, apathy and listlessness. The risk, and perhaps the reality, is that the emotions will be enlisted to serve some narrow special purpose, perhaps productivity or success, functional, no doubt, for the economy, but constricting for the individual.

Thinking for himself with all the cognitive powers that implies, motivated to do something with this independent self and above all to use it to control his environment, endowed with an emotional life under cognitive control, the individual is now in a position to take up the responsibilities assigned to him by the individualistic society. He is able, that is, to assume responsibility for his own fate. Philip Slater regarded this as the heart of individualism: it is, he said, "the belief that everyone should pursue autonomously his own destiny."[41] Preceding him, Condorcet hoped that the time would come when men "would approach a condition in which everyone will have the knowledge necessary to conduct himself in the ordinary affairs of life, according to the light of his own reason . . . [and] become able to find the means of providing for his own needs. . . ."[42] As a state of mind, this is called "self-reliance;" as a theory of society it is (mistakenly, I think) associated with "laissez-faire."

Not only is the individual responsible for his own fate, he is also responsible for his own acts. The second kind of responsibility arises most acutely in the problem of obedience to authority. The American psychologist Stanley Milgram suggests that through evolutionary processes nature has endowed us with two alternative devices for controlling our behavior: (1) self-censoring devices that prevent members of a group from transgressing against each other, and (2) devices favoring obedience to authority, which permit cohesion and group action. Both favor group survival. In his experiments, where ordinary people were willing to give potentially lethal shocks to others solely because they were asked to do so by someone clothed in scientific authority, most abdicated from control of their self-censoring sense of responsibility for their own acts and accepted control of authority as sufficient justification. Milgram calls this "malignant obedience" and argues that it is the facile granting of legitimacy to authority that permitted these individuals to escape from a sense of responsibility for their own acts.[43]

We are here on the border between developmental individuality, which embodies the sense of responsibility for one's own acts guided by principled moral reasoning, and functional individualism, which allows this responsibility to be shared more easily by authority. We are speaking of conscience, but the individualistic societies with which we are familiar manage to function "well enough" with conventional consciences, guided principally by group norms and concepts of law and order. Individualistic societies of that kind do require self-censoring consciences, for they require a comparatively uncoerced law and order, but they are satisfied by this more limited form of conscience or moral reasoning. It is their greatest weakness. A society whose members are valued only for their services will attend only to those moral norms that facilitate the performance of those services, perhaps honesty in trade and respect for property (or for the chivalric code, or the icons of the church, or whatever). But the fully developed conscience, assuming, as it must, a broad responsibility for a person's acts, is more inclusive and more autonomous. Failing sufficiently rigorous consciences, societies enforce responsibility for individual acts by means of authority and law. In contrast, responsibility for one's own fate is enforced by the economy, for lack of success in tending to one's fate is more often punished by economic than by legal sanctions.

Finally, erosion of the coordinating and motivating forces of both tradition and authority compels individuals to devise their own patterns of interpersonal relations. Contract theories have characterized such a "state of nature" alternatively as a jungle and as a feast of harmony. As Hobbes pointed out, the jungle model would return society to authority rather quickly; some degree of trust, then, is necessary. To get along with each other in the absence of controls, people must trust each other and devise ways whereby their competitiveness does not interfere with their long-term purposes. The machinery for this is not a social contract assigning the police or legislative power to a sovereign or legislator, but rather the socialization of the child in a nurturing family under conditions of relative abundance and reinforcement of trusting behavior by appropriate rewards throughout one's life. Scarcity leads to mistrust because one may not survive, for example, "waiting your turn;" the goods will give out before your turn comes around. For this and other reasons, even functional individualism is a late historical arrival; it had to await relative affluence. Mistrust is common in traditional societies and may be a product of authoritarian communist societies as well.[44] In those primitive societies where maternal care is not nurturing, illness is attributed to personalized malevolent spirits and to witchcraft, and trust disappears.[45] To learn trust is said to be a child's first lesson.[46]

Trust is the foundation for good human relations, but it may be impersonal, lacking in all the qualities that foster genuine friendship, mutual disclosure, warmth, the enjoyment of others. It represents the absence of social pathology, but not the presence of health.

Abraham Maslow sought to define the essential characteristic of the person who had satisfied his needs for safety, physiological supplies, a sense of belongingness and esteem, and is then in a position to develop his full potential. "Independence of

environmental stimuli," said Maslow, "is the defining characteristic of full individuality, of true freedom, of the whole evolutionary process."[47] His statement may serve as a summary of
the ideal, but, of course, not the realized condition, of the
properties that we have said are functional in an individualistic
society.

Functional individualism takes a step in that direction, for
the individualistic society that it serves requires men to think
for themselves, but neither broadly nor deeply; it requires people to be self-aware in the sense that they know their own wants
but not necessarily their own needs and values, from whence
come a reliable identity; it requires men to seek to serve themselves either egoistically or developmentally. That kind of a
society releases and legitimizes men's desires to control their
own environments, that is, to resist external control, for better
or worse; it requires them to master and use their own emotions, but may direct them into narrow channels; it encourages
them to take responsibility for their own fates, but it is deficient
in encouraging a similar sense of responsibility for their own
acts, that is, a concern for one's effects on the welfare of others;
it requires that men trust each other, but not that they love
each other. The logic of the individualistic society is clear, but
systemic logics often miscarry.

THE RISE OF INDIVIDUALISM

The emergence and rise of the *concept* of individualism has
been analyzed by Jacob Burckhardt, Guido de Ruggiero, Élie
Halévy, Steven Lukes and others. Whether in fact the personality properties I have identified have increased has often been
questioned. Earlier works by such authors as Galton, Le Bon,
Giddings, MacDougal and Ortega found contemporary man
marked by "gregarious and slavish instincts," crowd psychology, "the herd instinct," and other properties denying, among
other things, that individuals had come to think for themselves.
As I said at the beginning, a vast contempory literature on organization man, one-dimensional man, "cheerful robots," conformity, other-directedness, and mass man in mass society seems
to document the failure of the individual to develop as indi-

cated, or more likely to have declined in precisely those properties I argued were functional to the individualistic society. According to these authors, the individual has been atomized, not individualized: his links to the community have been broken, but he has not been individuated, does not think for himself, is not self-aware, is not motivated and able to assume responsibility for his own acts or fate, is alienated from his emotional life, and mistrusts others. Together these views of the individualistic society constitute an alternative social model with alternative individual requirements.

Many of these authors, from Tönnies (1887) to Fromm (1955), attribute these deficiencies to the market economy and offer plausible arguments for their cases. The market is impersonal, caring little for the individual. It destroys the old bonds of community without creating in the individual the properties that would permit him to get along well in individualistic society. For its own purposes of production and consumption a market economy creates caricatures of man, exaggerating efficiency considerations and fostering the grosser appetites. By giving to the laws of the economy the status of natural law, it creates a mood of fatality, the very opposite of fate control, and destroys incentives to think of alternatives. Its rationalism erodes emotionality, making not individuals but machine-men.

But at least since the time when systematic evidence began to be collected the evidence on both personality properties and direction of personality change goes against many of these indictments. This is an anomaly. How can a market for which individuals are units of production and consumption and for which personalities are external to a firm's accounting system foster the properties of individuals which, we said, are functional requisites of an individualistic society? Before seeking an explanation, let me present some of the evidence that the kind of personality properties described characterize some important fraction of contemporary populations in individualistic societies.

Without burdening the reader with a mass of details, much of which may be found summarized elsewhere,[48] let me cite some illustrative evidence on the critical issues defined above. Of course people conform to group opinion, but less than has been thought and less than they used to do. Comparing the responses of matched samples in Detroit for 1953 or 1956 and 1971, Duncan and associates found that young parents in the later period were more eager to have their children "think for themselves" than to "do what is right" in certain religious/moral issues. On the basis of this and other findings these authors report "if there was a trend toward other-directedness prior to 1953, it has since been reversed."[49] Tracking a British sample from adolescence to age thirty-three, Himmelweit and Bond (1974) reported, "conforming, being like others, became even less of an important goal," a change which these authors believe was due to "changes in the general climate of opinion."[50] In a recent American study of the influence of peers (cohorts) and family on such core values as "humanism vs. materialism" and "collectivism vs. individualism," Bengsten found weak transmissions by the family and great variability among peer cohorts. He concludes (p. 369) "it is well to avoid the fallacy of an 'over-socialized' perspective on the development of values. Global orientations may be more reflective of the individual's unique personal biography. . . ."[51] Similarly, studies by Jennings and Niemi find only weak family transmission of opinions and such moods as "cynicism;"[52] Butler and Stokes suggest a relaxation of the influence of social class on voting decisions in England;[53] Andrew Greeley finds American ethnic groups retaining their residential cohesion but losing their power to serve as opinion reference groups.[54] The power of these "primordial groups" to decide for the individual or to serve as the reference point for his decisions has declined. As Morris Rosenberg has shown, even black children and adolescents simply disidentify with their group when it serves their purposes.[55] Group reference is increasingly chosen, not given.

Self-awareness, if not identity, comes in part from absence of fear of examining the self. This fear was a feature of the authoritarian personality, a personality configuration that is reported by Nevitt Sanford to have declined in the United States.[56] More specifically, psychoanalysts report that their patients decreasingly suffer from lack of self-knowledge; rather they suffer from lack of commitment to chosen values.[57] That form of cognition that was identified as making identity and consciousness of self possible, field independence, has been found to be higher among wage laborers than among subsistence farmers.[58]

It is not a triumph for mental health, but there does seem to be evidence, however fragile, that modern populations increasingly have a consciousness of self, as might be expected in an individualistic society.

The evidence on egoism or selfishness, as contrasted to altruism or pro-social behavior, is less clear. In developing countries, industrialized workers have more compassion for women and children than traditional villagers;[59] moral reasoning is more sophisticated among American school children than school children of three developing countries,[60] but these scraps of evidence can only suggest caution in accepting allegations about the egoism of individualism; they cannot decide the issue.

On the related matters of the desire to control one's own environment and the belief that this is possible, that is, the desire to control one's own fate: in the United States members of the middle working class believe that they and others can be self-reliant in this sense, but blacks tend not to believe this, and college-educated tend to believe it of themselves but to excuse others for their failures.[61] The American population overwhelmingly believes in the *value* of self-reliance and even the people on welfare tend to support this value even though they cannot live by it.[62]

But personal responsibility for one's own acts when ordered to do something that may conflict with one's own conscience is another matter. When Lieutenant Calley slaughtered women, old men, and children in a Vietnamese village in the belief that he had been ordered to do so, a majority of Americans endorsed his act and said they would have done likewise under similar circumstances.[63] This is an excessively narrow slice of the issue, but crime statistics, accounts of child abuse, battered wives, and vandalism in the United States suggest that large segments of the population either define conscience-violating acts loosely, or have poor control over their emotions; most likely both. Here, it seems, the relaxation of social controls to vest responsibility in the individual was, in the United States, premature. But other individualistic societies such as Sweden, the Netherlands, and Switzerland, have fared better.

Finally, on the issue of interpersonal trust, the extraordinary, relatively unfluctuating high scores on a "faith in people" measure administered to successive samples of the American public for almost twenty years suggests that at least one individualistic society has managed to preserve that trust.[64] That this trust survived racial riots, defeat in war, revelations of unparalleled corruption, and crime waves, and persisted when faith in American institutions declined markedly, is a striking testament to the power of an individualistic society to foster, or at least not discourage, this crucial attitude.

This sampling of evidence, which includes a cluster of analytically distinct dispositions, should not be misread as intended proof of victory of the theory of functional individualism over opposing models. The logic of the individualistic society is not coercive; its history is short; the required standards of performance were placed at a level that guaranteed, according to the theory, satisfactory conditions for survival but not more. A vast field for developmental individualism remains, where the individual, and not the society, is the ultimate value. But given these bits of evidence, let us examine how it might be that the market has taken the individuated personality this far.

THE SELECTIVE CONTRIBUTION OF THE MARKET TO FUNCTIONAL INDIVIDUALISM

In the first place, the economy affects *the structure of society,* in some instances as a prime mover, in many others as an accelerator of the changes that technology creates. As Marx and Engels (1848) observed: "the bourgeoisie cannot exist without constantly revolutionizing the instruments of production, and thereby the relations of production, and with them the whole relations of society. . . ." That this is not merely the work of technology is suggested by the fact that it takes about twice as long in Soviet as in American society for an innovation to proceed from conception to industrial practice.[65] The market's destructive, recombinant, changing quality requires an often painful adaptation by many people, an adaption that causes them to develop and employ certain of their cognitive capacities to the full. They are forced to think for themselves, and, like other painful, life-changing forces short of trauma, they are forced to consider their own life goals, to increase their "objective self-awareness."

Similarly, the proliferation of occupations through the very division of labor that Marx and others have found so unattractive can, if it is not confined to "detail work" but rather to something approaching diversity of careers, require a variety of choices. It has been suggested that the identity crises alleged to occur in modern society have their genesis not in primary socialization, which creates a single world of reality, but in secondary socialization for occupational life, at which time the individual suddenly discovers that there are plural realities, plural worlds.[66] But an "identity crisis," however painful, is a crisis in self-definition, requiring self-awareness, as well as a requirement for thinking for oneself. Unlike command economies where the state offers substantial guidance, a market economy delegates the choices to individuals. At this point, the middle-class youth may take what Erikson has called a psychosocial moratorium, a period of relaxed social constraints, in order to summon his faculties and scrutinize his values for the hard choices with which he is confronted.[67] The very indifference of the market towards the individual requires him to pay special attention to himself, to choose and to think for himself.

Firms in a market economy locate where resources, transportational networks, markets, and labor costs combine to offer the greatest profitability. Guided by these criteria, firms are mobile. This also means that individuals become geographically mobile, leaving their friends, communities, and sometimes their families. These movements (and willingness to move is part of what is called "human capital") break up homogenous ethnic groups, call for making new friendships, buying and selling homes, adjustment to new schools for children; in short, they place demands upon people that are often stressful but also challenging. In general, the person who moves is more successful than the person who does not, attributable in part to the convention-destroying experience of moving.[68] Equally important, compared to mobile urban persons, the rural person who stays and develops a special loyalty to the place in which he lives tends to be "less informed, more prejudiced, less favorable to civil liberties, less tolerant of deviances, more ethnocentric and isolationist . . . less trusting of people.[69]

More generally, both experimental and observational evidence supports the view that environmental complexity produces personality as well as cognitive complexity. Durkheim was among the first to make this point, as mentioned above, and later investigation has revealed some of the mechanisms that produce these complexities. In the experimental evidence, it has been found that the more complex the problems with which an individual is confronted, the more complex does his cognition become, that is, the more differèntiated the schemata he must bring to bear on the problem and the more complex the integrating procedures employed in synthesizing them.[70] Similarly, surveys reveal that in modernizing societies, the transitional individuals, as contrasted to traditionals, perceive the possibility of becoming something other than what they are; they have what has been called "psychological mobility."[71] Observing this phenomenon, Frederick Frey suggests progression from dependence on charismatic leadership to mobilize the society to an information-dependent society, where the individual knows enough efficiently to choose for himself.[72] While this may be as true of societies taking the socialist road to development as it is of the marketizing societies, the emphasis on freely available information and self-choice in the latter impose both a burden and a challenge on the individual. But both experimental and cross-cultural work has found a curvilinear process whereby as choices and environmental complexity increase, a limit is reached which then induces more simplistic thinking and possibly a renewed demand for authoritative direction.

In interpreting the market's effect on the decrease in conformity and rise in "thinking for oneself," both cognitive and social factors are relevant. Cognitively, attribution of causal influence to the self as contrasted to believing that the causes of events lie in some group or society or the nature of things, increases resistance to conformity. Individuals in group situations are less likely to believe that they are causal agents.[73] Hence the market's degrouping of individuals helps us to understand nonconformity. Consensus trends to alter the meaning of a question, for dissensus opens up opportunities for individuals to interpret social questions for themselves. Socially, people who serve as models of independence tend to license disagreement within a group, even if the model is not present; even the imagined behavior of such a model is, therefore, helpful.[74] A combination of fears of group rejection, the possibility of group surveillance in a continuing relationship, and anxiety stemming from previous group rejection all play a role in determining degrees of conformity. The market's contribution to the sometimes painful discontinuity of groups thus makes for nonconformity. Groups having only one dissenter from a group opinion license independence, or at least offer a possibility for conforming to the opinions of a minority leader.[75] And the market tends to throw people together who have heterogeneous backgrounds. Thus cognitive complexity, causal attribution to the self, and heterogeneity contribute to conformity; these, in turn, are partly the products of the differentiated, changing social structure generated by a market economy.

Second, in addition to the structural approach emphasizing the market's contribution in environmental complexity we may take as a theme the *rationalism of the market*. Weber was careful to limit his emphasis on the rationality of market systems to cognitive processes, excluding any suggestion that markets led to "substantive rationality," the more perfect means to achieve the true goals of society.[76] Like others, he contrasted this emphasis on rationality to an impulsive or "affectual orientation," that is, under the strictures of the market the individual was compelled to submit his emotions to cognitive control. Among these controls is the requisite deferral of gratification, the postponement of some pleasure or indulgence now for larger pleasure or more important gratification later. It has been found that this particular form of deferred gratification is most difficult to develop in societies entering a money economy for the first time.[77]

But this rationality of the market is more than simply ends-means rationality, for it constantly presses businessmen and others to imagine situations contrary to fact, something psychologists call "divergent thinking." Prior to the self-regulating market, business as usual could assume the same kind of ritualistic observance of established procedures as those generally characteristic of traditional societies. Indeed, these rituals were protected by the state against competition. But with the rise of market society, as Schumpeter points out, the businessman had to become an entrepreneur.[78] "The ability to free oneself from the common tradition," says Weber, "a sort of liberal enlightenment, seems likely to be the most suitable basis for such a businessman's success."[79] Since it was future-oriented, the new rationality of the market necessarily had to deal with potentiality and possibility as well as certainty and fact. Here we have the elements of cognitive complexity in an elaborated form, for the financial consequences that follow a decision depend upon imagination and knowledge, estimation and precision. The same is true for each person who takes himself as his own enterprise and invests in himself and projects his own future.

Much has been said about the constraining quality of rationalism,[80] but in passing we may note that it is also liberating. As Weber (again) said, we feel most free when we behave rationally, and least free when we behave irrationally, in the grip of some emotion.

We mentioned earlier that a cognitive style called "field independence" tended to help the individual achieve a separate identity. Given what was stated about the utility in a market society of freeing oneself from the common tradition, it is important to note that cross-sectional research locates tendencies toward field independence in societies that are least conformist or ritualistic and require the most initiative. Compared to agricultural societies, for example, persons in fishing and hunting societies, whose means of livelihood demand greater initiative, are more field independent. Further, field independence is found to be relatively low in societies where obedience to authority is emphasized. Indeed, in such societies the field independent person has a notably poorer relation to the authorities. Yet the socialists may take heart, for in solidary communities where the individual is brought up to think for himself, to be an individual, as in the case of the kibbutzim, the members of that society too are field independent.[81] But at least in contrast to economies coordinated either by tradition or by authority, the market society is very likely to encourage the field independent or articulated style of cognition and perception.

A third approach to the solution of our anomaly is through the *usages of money,* an essential ingredient of the market economy that some have said reduces individuality, eradicating all qualitative differences and substituting mere quantitative ones, deindividuating the world. This is atomism, not individualism. The economists' argument that money and price permit all values to be compared, even those not priced (since time and effort spent in their pursuit represents opportunity costs or the loss of the money that might otherwise be earned), is employed by critics of the market to reveal the mechanism eliminating the distinctiveness of values, their homogenization in money terms. And with the elimination of distinctive values follows the elimination of distinctive personalities. "Money is the universal, self-constituting value of all things," said Marx. It has therefore robbed the whole world, both the human world and nature, of its own peculiar value.[82] For the market, the value of money lies in its facilitation of exchange. Picking up this theme, Fromm says that in a market economy, "People are also experienced as the embodiment of a quantitative exchange value."[83] Thus while money may serve to detach the individual from the group, these critics claim that it fails to give him the properties that we said were functional for an individualized society.

Some comments on the American's alleged love of money help to illuminate this aspect of the problem. Although he was writing about a primarily agrarian society, Tocqueville observed, "I know of no country . . . where the love of money has taken a stronger hold on the affections of man. . . ."[84] But later, and with more understanding, Santayana reports that it is not money itself, or what it will buy, that is so attractive to Americans, but rather its symbolic value, for it serves as "the symbol and measure . . . for success."[85] And still later Gorer says that for the Americans money is not important in itself, but, like marks in school, it shows one's relative position in the world, helping people to relate to each other: "until you know the income bracket of a stranger, and he knows yours, your mutual relationship is unsatisfactory and incomplete."[86] While these later observations seem to divorce the love of money from the love of commodities, relaxing the allegation of greed and materialism, they retain the one-dimensional evaluation of the person.

Of course the question at issue is not the American character but the effect of a market society, any market society, on individuality. That according to survey evidence the modern American identifies money with happiness far less than does the Frenchman[87] is less relevant than (as mentioned above) that the urbanized worker in traditional societies identifies happiness with, in this case, possessions, far less than the traditional villager. Nor is it important that in a comparative study of youth values requiring a ranking of the values of "love," "money," and "job," the Americans ranked money lower than the youth of any other country. But comparing three less comercialized countries (Brazil, India, the Philippines) with three advanced, commercial countries (France, Germany, and the United States), it may be significant that the average value attached to money was almost identical in the two groups.[88] What Tocqueville observed in agrarian America may or may not have been accurate; if it were, the commercialization of America has been associated with a decline in the value of money, even as a standard by which to judge the self and others. Other dimensions of evaluation thus may have been restored, and along with them some contribution towards individuation.

People who believe they control their own fates respond more to rewards than punishments;[89] in reverse, rewards (but not punishments) contingent on behavior encourage the belief that one is in command of the environment.[90] The money economy offers rewards contingent on behavior, as contrasted to the coercive features of serfdom, the non-contingent rewards of some traditional societies, and the collective rewards of some command economies. There are many casualties in the market's money economy and there is strong evidence that chance and luck and privilege are as important as effort and skill.[91] But the belief in one's ability to control what happens to oneself remains strong, as we have seen. The money or contingency-reward system may be considered a contribution to this belief.

More theoretically, it has been argued that, in contrast to possessions, money liberates the individual from constraint.[92] If *gemeinschaft* is associated with land and other physical possessions, *gesellschaft*, by which Tönnies meant capitalism, is associated with wealth in the form of money. But possessions are inextricably linked with the personalities of those who made or exchanged them; they are personalized, and they require care and attention, while money, being impersonal, frees the individual from these cares and interpersonal links. He is therefore free to use the money as he chooses, to spend it where and how he wishes, or to save it for future uses. In a curious paradox, the very impersonality of money frees the individual to express his idiosyncratic personality however he may wish. Even in the

labor market this freedom from interpersonal ties and obligations has an expression. When Painville moved from a subsistence economy to a market economy, the farmers in the village
gladly gave up their practices of work-swapping in favor of
money wages. The sense of reciprocal obligation, with all its
ambiguities, was confining; money wage payments released them
from these ambiguous and constraining obligations.[93]

If freedom is, as both Kant and Humboldt argued, the condition for thinking for oneself and for developing one's personality, it may be that, as in the above example, it is the freedom from obligation to others rather than from the commands
of the state that is most important. In marriage freedom to
choose one's own spouse was associated with the rise of the
market curiously, the release from bride price and from consideration of the economic value of the spouse made for "romantic," that is, personalized, choices.[94] In reverse, availability
of alternative sources of income for women both increased their
economic value to men (dual-income households are much better off), and liberated both women and men from the "empty
shell" marriages that otherwise they were destined to endure.
That this has been done with great costs to children and to
what has been called "unemployed wives," that is, wives without
husbands, is a different issue, for individuation does not mean
happiness (perhaps the reverse). But by release from mutual
obligation, a money economy and allied practices grant individuals the freedom to express their individuality with fewer constraints. The money economy is, of course, not the sole source
of these freedoms, but it has contributed to their development.

Compare the working of the price system in a command
economy and in a market economy. Where there are shortages,
if price does not increase with scarcity, whoever commands a
good in short supply commands a bit of leverage against other
goods in short supply. A form of bartering develops. The admissions officer of a selective school barters admission to that
school for the specialized services of a dentist; the proprietor
of a store keeps spare parts under the counter for exchange
against the plumber's services that he urgently needs. But these
exchanges depend upon maintaining the goodwill or grace of
the exchange partners; they represent a form of mutual obligation, free of money because money is useless without access

to the rare good or service. A successful money economy, therefore, liberates individuals from these forms of mutual dependence. This is not to argue that socialism is necessarily associated with scarcity, but rather that scarcity creates mutual dependence as well as deprivation in a command economy, and only deprivation in a market economy. But deprivation, of course, is equally an enemy of freedom and individuality wherever it occurs.

The market economy permits, although it does not stipulate, individualized payments to individuals. Collective goods, elements of a "social wage," and incomes shared with kin do not have this individualized property. While much may be said for collective goods and a social wage, they cannot be said to contribute to the functional individualism we have in mind. But, of course, functional individualism does not take the value of the individual as its criterion; that comes with developmental individualism. In a population of fully mature individuals perhaps social wages would be sufficient.

MARKET SOCIETY AND INCOMPLETE INDIVIDUALITY

In summary, then, the market serves first to destroy the community in which the individual was once embedded, and then to facilitate the development of some of the properties that an individualistic society needs. The social structure that the market creates is subject to constant change, requiring individual decisions that encourage and teach cognitive complexity; these decisions force upon the individual a sometimes painful self-awareness. The market's division of labor both differentiates individuals and exaggerates requirements for complex decisions. The market mechanisms for matching workers with jobs tend to erode ethnic and religious self-sufficient enclaves, making for fragmented heterogeneity where survival requires the perception of the person behind the primordial label. In general, environmental complexity fosters psychological mobility, personality differentiation, and complex thought.

The emphasis on rationality in the market causes emotionality to be subordinated to cognitive control; it encourages divergent, imaginative thinking as well as strict ends-means rationality. Through substituting individual choice for conformity to tradition or obedience to authority, the market encourages a cognitive field independence that permits the individual to achieve a separate identity for himself and to see others as distinctive parts of the communal whole.

The money economy of the market does not reduce individuals to numbers or give them a single monetary dimension; rather, it gives them the means, or illusion, of controlling their own fates by making changes in their personal environments appear to be contingent on their own acts, a perception favored by the use of rewards rather than punishments. By liberating the individual from wealth in land or possessions the money economy facilitates a freer expression of idiosyncracy, and by liberating him from the bounds of interpersonal obligation in work and marriage and other domains of life, the money economy similarly reduces his dependence on other people. Under conditions of scarcity, the price mechanism eliminates the barter of command economies with their dependency relationships, although not the deprivations incident to scarcity.

In all these ways, the impersonal, indifferent market helps the individual to think for himself, to be aware of himself as a distinct person, to assume responsibility for his own fate and sometimes his own acts, to evaluate, if not always to value, himself, and to be independent of environmental stimuli. But while it encourages functional individualism it hinders developmental individualism; it limits further growth. But that is another story.

NOTES

1. I would like to thank the Politics Society, University College, Cardiff, and the member of Professor Jack Pole's American history seminar, Oxford University, for helpful comments on early drafts of this paper. The paper was presented at the Annual Meeting of the American Political Science Association, Washington, D.C., August 1980.
2. See Steven Lukes, *Individualism* (Oxford: Basil Blackwell, 1973).
3. Ibid., pp. 47, 51. See also Silvan Tomkins, "Left and Right: A

402   ROBERT E. LANE

Basic Dimension of Ideology and Personality," in Robert W. White, ed., *The Study of Lives* (New York: Atherton, 1963).

4. John Bowlby, *Attachment and Loss: Volume I, Attachment* (New York: Basic Books, 1969), p. 211; Edward Wilson, *Sociobiology, the New Synthesis* (Cambridge, Mass.: Harvard University Press, 1975).

5. L.T. Hobhouse, *Morals in Evolution* (London: Chapman Hall, 1951), 3rd edition, p. 618.

6. Basil Bernstein, *Class, Codes and Control* (London: Routledge & Kegan Paul, 1968).

7. M. Lakin, M.G. Lakin and P.R. Constanzo, "Group Process in Early Childhood: A Dimension of Human Development," unpublished paper cited in Lita Furby, "The Origins and Early Development of Possessive Behavior," paper presented at the Meeting of the International Society of Political Psychology, Washington, D.C., 1979, p. 13.

8. Robert A. Wicklund, "Objective Self-Awareness," in Leonard Berkowitz, ed., *Advances in Experimental Social Psychology*, vol. 8 (New York: Academic Press, 1975).

9. Ralph Linton, *The Cultural Background of Personality* (London: Routledge & Kegan Paul, 1947).

10. Nevitt Sanford, Jr., *The American College* (New York: Wiley & Sons, 1962).

11. F.C. Montague, *The Limits of Individual Liberty* (London: Rivingtons, 1885), pp. 133–134.

12. Ludwig von Mises, *Epistemological Problems of Economics*, tr. G. Riesman (Princeton, N.J.: Van Nostrand, 1960), p. 154.

13. S. Lukes, *Individualism*, p. 14.

14. Harry K. Girvetz, *The Evolution of Liberalism* (New York: Collier Books, 1963), p. 41.

15. L.T. Hobhouse, *Liberalism* (London: Oxford University Press, 1911), p. 126.

16. Immanuel Kant, "What is Enlightenment?" reprinted in Peter Gay, ed., *The Enlightenment* (New York: Simon & Schuster, 1973), p. 384.

17. Robert P. Abelson, "Script Processing in Attitude Formation and Decision-Making," in J.S. Carroll and J.W. Payne, eds., *Cognition and Social Behavior* (Hillsdale, N.J.: Lawrence Erlbaum, 1976).

18. James Bieri and others, *Clinical and Social Judgment* (New York: Norton, 1966).

19. F. Heider, *The Psychology of Interpersonal Relations* (New York: Wiley & Sons, 1958).

20. Milton Rokeach, *The Open and Closed Mind* (New York: Basic Books, 1960).

21. Lawrence Kohlberg, "Development of Moral Character and Ide-

ology," in Martin L. and Lois W. Hoffman, eds., *Review of Child Development Research,* Vol. 1 (New York: Russell Sage, 1964).

22. Lawrence Kohlberg and R. Kramer, "Continuities and Discontinuities in Childhood and Adult Moral Development," *Human Development,* 12 (1969), 93–120.

23. Herman A. Witkin and others, *Psychological Differentiation* (New York: Wiley & Sons, 1962).

24. Herman A. Witkin, "Psychological Differentiation and Forms of Pathology," *Journal of Abnormal Psychology,* 70 (1965), 317–36; reprinted in Peter B. Warr, ed., *Thought and Personality* (Harmondsworth, England: Penguin, 1970), pp. 201–202.

25. R.A. Wicklund, "Objective Self-Awareness," pp. 263–264.

26. On the value individuals attach to their distinctiveness, see H.L. Fromkin, "Effects of Experimentally Aroused Feelings of Undistinctiveness upon Valuation of Scarce and Novel Experiences," *Journal of Personality and Social Psychology,* 16 (1970), 521–529.

27. Erich Fromm, *Man for Himself* (New York: Rinehart, 1947).

28. Compare P.G. Zimbardo, "The Human Choice: Individuation, Reason, and Order versus Deindividuation, Impulse, and Chaos," in *Nebraska Symposium on Motivation* (Lincoln, Neb.: University of Nebraska Press, 1969) and Carl R. Rogers and others, *Client-Centered Therapy* (Boston: Houghton-Mifflin, 1951).

29. George H. Sabine, *History of Political Theory,* 3rd edition (New York: Holt, Rinehart & Winston, 1963), 531.

30. Robert W. White, "Motivation Reconsidered: The Concept of Competence," *Psychological Review,* 66 (no. 5) (1959), 297–333.

31. Richard DeCharms, *Personal Causation: The Internal Affective Determinants of Behavior* (New York: Academic Press, 1968), p. 269.

32. Ferdinand Tönnies, *Community and Society,* tr. C.P. Loomis (New York: Harper Torchbook, 1963) [1887].

33. Albert O. Hirschman, *The Passions and the Interests: Political Arguments for Capitalism Before its Triumph* (Princeton: Princeton University Press, 1977).

34. E. Wilson, *Sociobiology,* p. 551; I. Devore, ed., *Primate Behavior: Field Studies of Monkeys and Apes* (New York: Holt, Rinehart & Winston, 1965).

35. P.G. Zimbardo, "The Human Choice."

36. Shalom Schwartz, "The Justice of Need and the Activation of Humanitarian Norms," *Journal of Social Issues,* 31, no. 3 (1975), 111–136.

37. J. Bowlby, *Attachment,* p. 230.

38. Jules Henry, *Culture Against Man* (New York: Vintage Press, 1965), p. 12.

39. Frederick A. Weiss, "Self-Alienation: Dynamics and Therapy," reprinted from the *American Journal of Psychoanalysis* in Eric and Mary Josephson, eds., *Man Alone* (New York: Dell, 1962).

40. See, for example, Gerald Gurin, Joseph Veroff, and Sheila Feld, *Americans View Their Mental Health* (New York: Basic Books, 1960).

41. Philip E. Slater, *The Pursuit of Loneliness: American Culture at the Breaking Point* (Boston: Beacon Press, 1970), p. 29.

42. Antoine-Nicolas de Condorcet, *Sketch for a Historical Picture of the Progress of the Human Mind,* reprinted in Peter Gay, ed., *The Enlightenment* (New York: Simon & Schuster, 1973), p. 805.

43. Stanley Milgram, *Obedience to Authority* (New York: Harper & Row, 1974).

44. Oscar Lewis, *La Vida: A Puerto Rican Family in the Culture of Poverty—San Juan and New York* (New York: Random House, 1966); Irving A. Hallowell, "Fear and Anxiety as Cultural and Individual Variables in a Primitive Society," in his *Culture and Experience* (New York: Schocken, 1967); Edward C. Banfield, *The Moral Basis of a Backward Society* (Glencoe, Ill.: Free Press, 1958); J.K. Campbell, "The Honour of the Greeks," *Times Literary Supplement,* November 14, 1975, p. 1355. On communist societies: Ezra Vogel, "From Friendship to Comradeship," *China Quarterly,* 21 (1965), 46–60.

45. John W.M. Whiting and Irvin L. Child, *Child Training and Personality: A Cross-Cultural Study* (New Haven: Yale University Press, 1953).

46. Erik H. Erikson, "The Problem of Ego Identity," *Journal of the American Psychoanalytic Association,* 4 (1956), 58–121.

47. Abraham Maslow, *Toward a Psychology of Being,* 2nd edition (Princeton: Van Nostrand, 1969), p. 36.

48. Robert E. Lane, "Interpersonal Relations and Leadership in a 'Cold Society,'" *Comparative Politics,* 10 (July 1978), 443–59; "Autonomy, Felicity, Futility: The Effects of the Market Economy on Political Personality," *Journal of Politics,* 40 (February 1978), 2–24; *The Dialectics of Freedom in a Market Society* (Urbana, Ill.: University of Illinois Press, 1979), reprinted as "Personal Freedom in a Market Society," *Society,* 18 (March/April 1981), 63–76.

49. Otis D. Duncan, Howard Schuman, and Beverly Duncan, *Social Change in a Metropolitan Community* (New York: Russell Sage, 1973), pp. 30–31.

50. Hilda T. Himmelweit and Roderick Bond, *Social and Political Attitudes: Voting Stability and Change.* Report to the Social Science Research Council (London: mimeographed, May 1974).

51. Vern L. Bengsten, "Generation and Family Effects in Value Socialization," *American Sociological Review,* 40 (June 1975), p. 369.

52. M. Kent Jennings and Richard G. Niemi, "The Transmission of

Political Values from Parent to Child," *American Political Science Review,* LXII (March 1968), 169–184. But see contrary evidence in Russell J. Dalton, "Reassessing Parental Socialization: Indicator Unreliability versus Generational Transfer," *American Political Science Review,* 74 (June 1980), 421–431.

53. David Butler and Donald E. Stokes, *Political Change in Britain,* 2nd edition (London: Macmillan, 1974), p. 116.

54. Andrew M. Greeley, *Ethnicity, Denomination and Inequality* (Beverly Hills, Calif.: Sage, 1976).

55. Morris Rosenberg, "Group Rejection and Self-Rejection," in Roberta G. Simmons, ed., *Research in Community and Mental Health,* Vol. 1 (Greenwich, Conn.: JAI Press, 1979).

56. Nevitt Sanford, "Authoritarian Personality in Contemporary Perspective," in Jeanne N. Knutson, ed., *Handbook of Political Psychology* (San Francisco: Jossey-Bass, 1973), pp. 164–165.

57. Allen Wheelis, *The Quest for Identity* (New York: Norton, 1958): Weiss, "Self-Alienation: Dynamics and Therapy."

58. J.W. Berry, *Human Ecology and Cognitive Style* (New York: Wiley/Sage, 1976).

59. Alex Inkeles and David Smith, *Becoming Modern* (Cambridge, Mass.: Harvard University Press, 1974).

60. Lawrence Kohlberg and R. Kramer, "Continuities and Discontinuities in Childhood and Adult Moral Development."

61. Gerald Gurin and Patricia Gurin, "Personal Efficacy and the Ideology of Individual Responsibility," in Burckhardt Strumpel, ed., *Economic Means for Human Needs* (Ann Arbor, Mich.: Institute for Social Research, 1976).

62. Paul M. Sniderman and Richard A. Brody, "Coping: The Ethic of Self-Reliance," *American Journal of Political Science,* XXI (August 1977), 501–521.

63. Herbert C. Kelman and Lee Hamilton Lawrence, "Assignment of Responsibility in the Case of Lt. Calley: Preliminary Report on a National Survey," *Journal of Social Issues,* 28, no. 1 (1972), 177–212.

64. Warren E. Miller, Arthur H. Miller and Edward J. Schneider, *American National Election Studies Data Sourcebook,* 1952–1978 (Cambridge, Mass.: Harvard University Press, 1980), p. 293.

65. Zbignew K. Brzezinski, *Between Two Ages: America's Role in the Technetronic Era* (New York: Viking Press, 1970), p. 29.

66. Peter L. Berger and Thomas Luckman, *The Social Construction of Reality* (Garden City, N.Y.: Doubleday/Anchor, 1967).

67. Erik Erikson, "The Problem of Ego Identity."

68. Peter Blau and Otis D. Duncan, *The American Occupational Structure* (New York: Wiley & Sons, 1967).

69. Clyde Z. Nunn, Harry J. Crockett, Jr., and J. Allen Williams, Jr., *Tolerance for Nonconformity* (San Francisco: Jossey-Bass, 1978), p. 98.
70. Harold M. Schroder and Peter Suedfeld, *Personality Theory and Information Processing* (New York: Ronald Press, 1971).
71. Daniel Lerner, *The Passing of Traditional Society* (New York: Free Press, 1958).
72. Frederick W. Frey, "Communication and Development," in Ithiel deSola Pool and Wilbur Schramm, eds., *Handbook of Communication* (Chicago: Rand McNally, 1973).
73. Vernon L. Allen, "Social Support for Nonconformity," in Leonard Berkowitz, ed., *Advances in Experimental Social Psychology,* vol. 8 (New York: Academic Press, 1975), pp. 20–21.
74. Ibid., p. 24.
75. S.E. Asch, "Studies of Independence and Conformity: A Minority of One Against a Unanimous Majority," *Psychological Monographs* 70 no. 9 (1956); whole no. 416.
76. Max Weber, *The Theory of Social and Economic Organization,* ed. & tr. Talcott Parsons (New York: Oxford University Press, 1947), pp. 185–186.
77. Leonard Doob, *Becoming More Civilized* (New Haven: Yale University Press, 1960), p. 223.
78. Joseph Schumpeter, *The Theory of Economic Development,* tr. R. Opie (Cambridge, Mass.: Harvard University Press, 1936).
79. Max Weber, *The Protestant Ethic and the Spirit of Capitalism,* tr. T. Parsons (New York: Scribner's, 1958), p. 71.
80. Jacques Ellul, *The Technological Society,* tr. J. Wilkinson (London: Jonathan Cape, 1965); Lewis Mumford, *The Transformation of Man* (New York: Harper Torchbook, 1972); Theodore Roszak, *The Making of a Counterculture* (Garden City, N.Y.: Doubleday, 1969).
81. Harry C. Triandis, "Cultural Training, Cognitive Complexity and Interpersonal Attitudes," in Richard W. Brislin and others, eds., *Cultural Perspectives on Learning* (New York: Halsted/Wiley, 1975), pp. 61–62.
82. Karl Marx, *Economic and Philosophical Manuscripts,* in Erich Fromm, ed., *Marx's Concept of Man* (New York: Ungar, 1961), p. 121.
83. Erich Fromm, *The Sane Society* (New York: Rinehart, 1955), p. 116.
84. Alexis de Tocqueville, *Democracy in America* (New York: Vintage, 1961), p. 53.
85. George Santayana, *Character and Opinion in the United States* (Garden City, N.Y.: Doubleday/Anchor, 1956), p. 116.
86. Geoffrey Gorer, *The American People* (New York: Norton, 1948), p. 180.

87. Hadley Cantril with Mildred Strunk, *Public Opinion, 1935–1946.* (Princeton: Princeton University Press, 1951), p. 281.
88. *Gallup Opinion Index,* Report No. 100, Princeton, N.J. October 1973.
89. D.S. Holmes and T.H. Jackson, "Influence of Locus of Control on Interpersonal Attraction and Affective Rewards," *Journal of Personality and Social Psychology,* 31 (1975), 132–136.
90. Martin E.P. Seligman, *Helplessness* (San Francisco: Freeman, 1975).
91. Christopher Jencks and others, *Who Gets Ahead? The Determinants of Economic Success in America* (New York: Basic Books, 1979).
92. Georg Simmel, *The Philosophy of Money,* tr. T. Bottomore and D. Frisby (London: Routledge & Kegan Paul, 1978).
93. Art Gallaher, Jr., *Plainville Fifteen Years Later* (New York: Columbia University Press, 1961).
94. Paul C. Rosenblatt, "Cross-Cultural Perspectives on Attraction," in Ted L. Huston, ed., *Foundations of Interpersonal Attraction* (New York: Academic Press, 1974).

EPILOGUE: SOME PERPLEXITIES FURTHER CONSIDERED

J. ROLAND PENNOCK

In these concluding remarks I wish to consider a few selected issues, some but not all of which have been discussed in the preceding pages. First, I shall make some comments on the matter of boundaries, both external and internal. This discussion will be followed by a consideration of certain aspects of constitutionalism, especially as they are involved in the contention that the justification of democracy requires sharp departures from the principles now relied upon for that purpose. From here it is but a short step to look at the close linkage between liberalism and democracy, which leads in turn to certain aspects of "deductive" theory, especially Levine's charge of incoherence, based upon preference theory and, more particularly, upon the Sen-Arrow conditions for the aggregation of preferences. Finally, I survey the extent to which the volume as a whole supports the positions taken here regarding coherence.

I.

Whelan's discussion of the problem of establishing and justifying the boundaries of a state finds that democratic theorists have provided no solution to it. Having carefully analyzed the

408

difficulties attending various principles that might be advanced and showing that none of them is satisfactory, he leaves us with the possibility that a given people, residing in a specified territory, must be the *starting point* for democratic theory. Democratic theory provides no way for legitimating a newly formed political entity; it is applied to that entity.

The search for a democratic *procedure* to start and legitimate the democratic process would seem to be foredoomed to failure, as the pursuit of an ever-receding goal. If, however, as I have contended elsewhere, a procedural definition of democracy must always presuppose a standard, an ideal, by which its procedures and accomplishments may be judged—a democratic ideal, or an ideal definition of democracy—the problem becomes more manageable.[1] The ideal is difficult to state succinctly but it relates to a form of government that, given certain requisites, provides a greater probability than does any alternative form for "avoiding tyranny and, further, of maximizing the ends of liberty (including the conditions of personal development) and equality. . . ."[2] If this is accepted as the democratic ideal, then presumably it could be better accomplished with certain groupings of people, territorially delimited, than with others. Obviously this vague principle leaves much to be desired: how should it be determined whether a given grouping is optimal, or whether it even "satisfices"? In the absence of clear tests for these conditions and of general assent of those most directly concerned, force, or the dictum of some powerful polity or group of polities, normally settles the matter. At that point, democratic procedures may be established, although how that should be done involves a great deal of arbitrariness, as did the decision of the United States Constitutional Convention that the constitution it had drafted should become valid on ratification by nine of the thirteen states.

Sooner or later another sticky problem is likely to arise. A constitution, let us assume, has been established. Probably it provides a method for its own amendment, but it is not likely to grant the right of some part to secede from the whole. Yet why should the original agreement continue to bind if the relevant conditions have radically changed; or, for that matter, if the sentiments of some geographically defined portion of the people have altered significantly? I do not intend to pursue this question here. If we must resort to extra-procedural principles to establish the legitimacy of the original agreement, how can we argue that that arrangement was a once-and-for-all, irreversible act? Strong arguments could be made in terms of the general welfare, or of the difficulty of proving that the well-being of the seceders would be improved, or by reference to reasonable expectations on the part of the rest of the united state, or on the grounds that the prohibition removed a divisive temptation to act in a way that would be contrary to the long-run interests even of the seceders, and so on, but would they necessarily be conclusive in all cases? Can it reasonably be contended that the procedural argument (that the rest of the members of the state did not agree) should be definitive?

II.

Dahl raises another question about boundaries, or at least about domain. Recognizing that any sizable state must decentralize many of its decision-making processes, we must face the question whether it can do so, democratically, in a way that gives final authority over certain matters to its subunits.[3] In short, can a federal state be democratic? We might seek an easy answer to this conundrum by saying that the subunits were originally sovereign states, and that they presumably had the power to join with others to form a unitary state, and that if they had this power surely they had the lesser power to yield up certain limited powers to a union, all the while retaining their own original democratic character.[4] The European Community is a case in point. Presumably, using their existing democratic procedures, these states could unite, creating a single democratic state. Can it be then that they cannot do something less, as they have done, without losing their democraticness? But to say that this is something "less" begs the question. If a federal system is by its very nature undemocratic, this fact is not altered by the circumstance that its constituent units were democracies before its formation, nor by the further fact that they *could* have formed a unitary democratic state instead of this hybrid.

We must examine the combined problem of agenda and majority rule. Braybrooke, it seems to me, has succeeded in showing that Dahl dismisses the problem of agendas too easily—that his solution is incomplete, not covering all cases. Consider a possible alternative to Dahl's solution. Begin with a reasonable distribution of power between the central government and what, in American fashion, I shall call the "states." By "a reasonable distribution" I mean one that reserves to the states only those powers the exercise of which will affect chiefly the state that exercises them, having at most a mild effect on others. Another qualification is important: the powers granted (or reserved) to the states must be within their system-capacity to exercise effectively. Once more we are dealing with matters of degree, and of contingency, which can seldom if ever be stated with precision. Granted these conditions it can, I believe, be proved that a federal system in any large and complex society entails less frustration of voter preferences than does a unitary state. Although the formal proof, which I have set forth elsewhere,[5] occupies too much space to merit repetition, the principle is quite simple. It is that having two votes, one for local and one for national matters, enables voters to express their preferences with greater particularity than if one vote had to suffice for all. With two votes they can express certain preferences without negating certain others, where that would be impossible in a unitary state. To be sure, this is an advantage of any system of local government or "home rule." In a federal system, however, the local ("state") units are *guaranteed* against having their wishes overruled by the central government.[6] Accordingly, federalism established in accordance with the conditions set forth above, not only is compatible with democracy, it augments it; Dahl's question "Is one option [unitary or federal] in some reasonable sense *more* democratic?" should be answered in the affirmative. Such federalism also increases the opportunities for political participation and cooperative activity, with whatever self-developmental advantages these may have.[7]

III.

I turn now to certain other aspects of constitutionalism as they relate to democratic theory. First, I shall do so making use of normative concepts and dealing with what is generally called "liberal democracy." In my terminology, I shall be dealing with the democratic ideal and applying it to democratic constitutions. My position can perhaps best be explained, in dialectical fashion, by considering a line of argument that appears to be at odds with my concept of the democratic ideal and with my use of that concept. James S. Fishkin contends that "nontyranny" is a necessary, but not sufficient, condition for "acceptable conditions for social choice," *and* that only by striking out in a radically new direction could democratic theory go beyond this necessary but insufficient principle.[8] Having incorporated the probability of avoiding tyranny in my concept of the democratic ideal, I have no desire to dispute the first half of Fishkin's dual proposition. I do, however, disagree with the second part of this argument, the need for completely new principles, for the following reason. The principle of nontyranny appears to be more simple than it is. The negative conceals a positive. A government policy, Fishkin says, is tyrannous if it unnecessarily imposes severe deprivations "on anyone." By a severe deprivation he means the decisive defeat of a person's life plan.[9] Why "on anyone?" Surely it must be because the government of a democracy must give people equal consideration. *All alike* must be protected against severe deprivation. And why are "life plans" (he also mentions "commitments") so important? It must be because that aspect of liberty we refer to as "autonomy" is likewise of crucial importance. In short, we are back to the democratic fundament, the democratic ideal. The fundament, as I would put it, is the recognition of the dignity of each person, of his or her entitlement to respect, including the right to make his or her own decisions on an equal basis with that of all other persons.[10]

Of course Fishkin does not mean to deny these things.[11] My purpose in making these remarks is simply to point out that, by implication, he is in fact supporting what I call the concept of ideal democracy and its use as a final test for any apparently more precise definition, whether that be in terms of procedures, absolute rights, structural principles, or whatever. In doing so, perhaps unwittingly, he is accepting and relying upon principles that are central to democratic theory; they are by no means "new departures" and they involve no "redirection" in the kinds of principles that are receiving serious attention.[12]

Insofar as these principles admit of differences of opinion as to their precise meaning, as they surely do, and insofar as, by certain interpretations of them, they may conflict with each other, they do involve judgment. Often the judgments in question are about empirical—but very difficult—questions, such as "What would be the consequences of Policy X?" But for some at least (those who do not accept Rawls's "lexical priorities" or their equivalent) they may involve compromises, trade-offs. Call these "ad hoc" if you will; they are no more avoidable for society than they are for each of us when we find our values mutually conflicting.[13] Moreover, the compromises involved in these choices generally fall far short of anything that can be described as "severe deprivations;" nor do they indicate, either for the individual or for society, anything that could be called incoherence. If I say that I prize self-preservation above all else and then go off and climb Mt. Everest, it might properly be said that my declarations and my behavior were incoherent. But if I value both safety and the thrill of adventure and, after careful consideration and preparation decide to make the climb, a charge of incoherence would be misplaced.

If I am right in drawing out the positive implications of Fishkin's negative ("nontyranny") and finding that it amounts to the democratic ideal, or at least relies upon the same values, it follows that his principle, thus elaborated, is not simply a necessary condition for democracy; it is also a sufficient condition. That is to say, any form of government the procedures and structures of which are calculated to operate (and do in fact operate) in such a way as to give reasonable assurance that the ideal will be approached in important degree is properly called a democracy.[14]

An important conclusion deriving from these comments, one that embraces much if not all of what we call "constitutionalism," including especially those checks on governmental power commonly cast in terms of rights against the government, is that these rights and related devices are derivatives of the democratic ideal. They may be thought of as distinctive of what is generally called "liberal" democracy; but my own view is that all democracy worthy of the name is "liberal democracy." This is not to say that a democracy whose constitution did not embody such rights would not be a (liberal) democracy, but it is to say that if it did not govern in accordance with such restraints (whether they be legal, moral, or simply traditional) would be neither liberal nor, properly, democratic.

Incidentally, some of these restraints will be procedural and some substantive. In the United States that highly personal moral right, privacy, for instance, is protected by both kinds of constitutional rights, as is instanced by the ban on unreasonable searches and seizures in the Fourth Amendment (procedural) and by the invalidation of laws interfering with a woman's right (during a certain period) to have an abortion performed (substantive). The First Amendment, perhaps the most important of all from the point of view of democracy even narrowly defined, is clearly substantive.

IV.

The view I have been advancing about the identity, or at the very least the close linkage, of democracy and liberal democracy does not go unchallenged. Nor is the objection confined to those who wish to defend the claim of "people's republics" or "people's democracies" (which are clearly not "liberal") to be democracies. For instance, Andrew Levine has written as follows: "Roughly the liberal holds that there are certain aspects of a person's life, including certain of his actions, that are private and against which others can never rightfully interfere. The democratic judgment holds that what society does should be a function of each individual's preference for what society does, determined according to some decision procedure (such as the method of majority rule)."[15] Using Amartya Sen's proof of the impossibility of a Paretian liberal, he argues that it is impossible to build a liberal democratic theory, barring "the unlikely strategy of delineating the scope of liberal self-determination and democratic choice, respectively, so that the two can never in principle conflict."[16]

Before considering the merits of this argument, let me place it in a wider context than that of whether liberal democracy is a contradiction in terms. We are here at the juncture of justificatory (or, as it is commonly called, "normative") theory and "positive" or (more specifically) "deductive" theory. How are the two to be related to each other? First, what are they? The traditional form of political theory is normative, or at least contains an important normative component. Until the post-World War II period it was the dominant, almost the sole form of theorizing about politics. Since then, in an effort to find a firmer, less subjective, foundation, positive theory has proliferated. For moral philosophy, more specifically for value judgments, positive theorists have substituted the god of rationality, in the limited sense used by economists.[17] With occasional exceptions that seem more like slips, the rational man from whom their deductions are made is the economic man. This "man," is pursuing his or her self-interest. In part, this method is employed because it is assumed that in the political arena, by and large, this is the way humans behave. Without that assumption the theory would be of little value. Beyond this, another assumption is made, for a different reason: the assumption that interpersonal comparisons are impossible. Since it is obvious that such comparisons are not possible in any precise or verifiable way, measurements, calculations, proofs must depend upon getting rid of this element. From this it follows as well that it is preferences that count as interests in the calculation of self-interest, for they can be counted and (within limits) behaviorally determined; counted—not weighed—for the differences in intensity cannot be measured (except as each individual weighs his or her own desires against each other).

While the deductive theorist claims he makes no value judgments and thus avoids the realm of the justificatory, his concern for the aggregation of preferences is one that provides material for utilitarian evaluation. This is the linkage between positive-deductive and justificatory theory.

Continuing the consideration of deductive theory, I shall specify some of its implications. Before doing so, however, two anticipatory comments are in order. The first is that this kind of reasoning has contributed greatly to precision in political theorizing and to the generation of hypotheses for empirical research. The other is that the assumptions, especially that of the impossibility of interpersonal comparisons, are highly artificial. In real life we make such comparisons all the time; no one believes that they are so wide of the mark as to invalidate the whole process. Nor, to make the point, do we need to go so far as me on the bank and Singer's drowning boy in the pond. If I own a valuable antique that I and my two children agree should be kept in the family, should I leave it to the one who has expressed her love of antiques by collecting them or to the one who has spent an equal sum of money (or a sum of equal marginal value to her) on modern artifacts? When one comes to the realm of social, especially political, choice, the comparison is often more difficult. But when Rawls holds that benefits should go to the least advantaged first, he is making an interpersonal comparison (or at least someone must do so if the principle is to be implemented); I suspect that it is one that most of us would strongly agree with *if all other things* (which might include such other things as merit, however judged, and the effect on the future welfare of society) *were equal.* Enough for now. It should be apparent that the denial of interpersonal comparisons ought to be taken as intended, as a heuristic device, or as part of a model that deliberately oversimplifies but is believed to be sufficiently close to reality to be useful.[18]

Now let us consider the argument that has been advanced for the incoherence of democratic theory at the procedural level. It is preferences that are to be counted. They are not assumed to be equal, but it is assumed that they cannot be weighed against one another, for their intensity cannot be measured. It follows that the only way to aggregate the preferences of the individuals in a society, or, rather, the only way to compare social states, is to resort to the test of Pareto optimality. If in one state of society someone is better off and no one is worse off (in terms of the satisfaction of their expressed preferences) than in another, then the former is to be preferred—it is "Pareto superior." But according to Arrow's well-known theorem, this standard of judgment is not compatible with the pairwise comparisons entailed by the democratic process.[19]

Building on Sen's proof regarding liberalism, Levine argues that the liberal and the democratic elements of liberal democracy are mutually incompatible. While I believe some of Levine's arguments are mistaken, it is unnecessary to contest them here, for I agree that the liberal belief that certain aspects of a person's life are private and should not be interfered with is inconsistent with democracy *if* that word be defined, as Levine in effect does, in terms of a society in which the realm of democratic choice is unlimited. The latter is what Arrow calls the requirement of Unrestricted Domain, requisite to a Paretian social-choice rule. Sen states it as follows: "Every logical set of individual orderings is included in the domain of a social choice rule."[20] Liberalism, both in its defense of strong rights and in its weaker preference for granting a great deal of elbow-room for freedom of individual choice, is in conflict with even a weak version of Pareto optimality.

Levine's proof depends upon two elements, both of which are vulnerable: the use of preference as the sole guide for democratic choice and the condition of Unrestricted Domain. I shall deal first with the matter of preferences. They are not the same as interests. (I may prefer ice cream to fruit for dessert but it may be contrary to my interest because it is bad for my health.) Although it is well to bear this fact in mind, in itself it does not take us far. If we were to define democracy simply in terms of satisfaction of individual interests, we would have prepared the way for benevolent despotism. Even if we were to say that democracy is the form of government most likely to satisfy individual interests, we would be on dangerous ground. Let us focus on preference. Feeling the dubiousness of this test as the sole guide to policy, some speak of "ideal preferences."[21] An ideal preference would presumably include at least the following elements: it would be based upon all the relevant information; it would be the product of rational decision as opposed to manipulation; to this end it would follow a period of deliberation and the dialectic of discussion with persons having different points of view; and, as all of this implies, it would not be a merely momentary preference.[22]

What do these considerations imply for democratic theory, for institutions well adapted to achieving maximum approximation of the democratic ideal? Obviously they are sharply opposed to anything like the idea, sometimes suggested, of having a console in every home, through which the citizen can vote on the issues normally decided by a representative assembly. As for participatory democracy in other forms, one can make only certain general remarks. The most important of these is that, whether we consider the goal of individual development or whether we emphasize the effectuation of preferences of the kind discussed above, the kind that presumptively most nearly coincide with real interests, participation must be of the type that entails substantial involvement of the participants. In any sizable polity, this restriction places severe limitations on the number of people who can participate in ways that substitute for representatives.

In short, not only must modern democracy rely for most of its decisions upon representative government, but also the representatives must be guided by more than the actual and immediate preferences of the electorate. Representatives must have discretion to use their own judgment, informed by all available means, supplemented by more effective organizations of groups now seldom heard from. They must judge intensities of preferences, or at least of interests, and they must make judgments about consequences of which the electorate is not in a position to judge. All of this must be subject to the ultimate yea or nay of the electorate, for it is they who must be the final judges of how their representatives have performed. Better, to be sure, that these judgments should be made after the effects of legislative action have become manifest. This is a counsel of perfection, but many may draw the conclusion, which the writer shares, that two years is not long enough to meet this desideratum.

In this connection another point is worth mentioning. Ronald Rogowski concludes that "with the exception of only a few probably unworkable alternatives, fair representation—let alone equally weighted or equally powerful representation—requires PR."[23] Within his framework of analysis, he may be right. The considerations I have been advancing, however, seem to me to call for a broader framework. One must bear in mind that a representative legislature must legislate as well as represent. Anything that furthers the fragmentation of the political process makes governing more difficult and less effective; it seems clear that PR tends to have this consequence. If it tends, as it almost surely does, to weaken our already weak political parties, that is also a result that may be regrettable from the broader point of view. One more point: if voters are to put themselves in their fellow citizens' shoes, as Harsanyi's "ethical preferences" would demand (not to mention Rousseau's prescription for expression of the General Will), they must be subjected to some institutional pressure to do so. Candidates and party platforms that strive to unite a number of special interests, groups that are selected on the basis of group interest, cannot fail to have some influence in this direction. We may well decry how little it seems to be, but this is hardly a reason for running in the opposite direction, as opting for PR almost certainly would be. Nor should these remarks be taken as simply an attack on PR. Rather they are meant to suggest that fair and equal representation, important as it is, should not be allowed to obscure significant objectives that may be hindered by devices aimed at its achievement. We face here another democratic tension—not in this case between ultimate objectives but between means aimed at their realization.

The last several paragraphs have been inspired by Levine's contention that liberal democracy is incoherent, based upon the assumption that democratic choices must be made in accordance with the Arrow-Sen requirements for the aggregation of preferences. Without disputing the logic of these requirements, I have been arguing that the concept of "preference" is ambiguous, that expressed preferences, without further stipulation, are not appropriate determinants for public policy, and that the stipulations requisite for an appropriate determinant would move us far away from the simple rule of the majority (of preferences) on which the logic is based. In short, I have no quarrel with the Arrow-Sen conditions for the aggregation of preferences; rather I am contending that the simple aggregation of preferences is not the appropriate objective of democratic procedures.

V.

I now wish to attack the matter from another point of view, one that deals more directly with Levine's concern about the clash between liberal individualism and democratic choice. This also has to do with the requirement of Unrestricted Domain. If the latter is allowed to stand together with the simple preference theory of democracy, incoherence in the form of direct

inconsistency is inevitable. The same would be true if the preference theory were modified in the direction I have been suggesting. The whole structure of constitutionalism comprises restrictions on domain in the broad sense; much of it, especially
constitutionally protected rights, amounts to a literal restriction
of domain. As Levine says, "Liberalism requires that an individual be decisive over at least some alternatives in contention;
namely those that are private."[24]

Before discussing Unrestricted Domain in detail, however, I
must notice Levine's contention that the liberal position violates
Arrow's condition of Nondictatorship. He declares that "to say
that an individual's choices are ever automatically the society's
choice is to violate the condition of Nondictatorship."[25] Surely
this is a mistake. For a person to be able to control the government's actions with respect to him or her in certain particulars
does not accord with the common understanding of dictatorship. To borrow an example from Sen, if I can paint my bed-
room blue, overriding society's preference, that does not make
me a dictator. It does, however, mean that the state's domain is
limited. It is therefore in the context of Unrestricted Domain
that I shall discuss claims of this kind.

As Braybrooke has remarked, domain is necessarily restricted from the very beginning by the selection of the political
unit and the fixing of its boundaries. Voting cannot take place
until it has been determined who are to be the voters. Thus the
artificiality of the conditions, including that of Unrestricted Domain, is evident from the start.

Furthermore, as has also been noted, the preference theory
of democracy is only a heuristic device. It is useful within limits,
but it must not be made a talisman. It is a theory regarding
democratic procedures, all of which are adopted for a purpose,
specifically for the pursuit of the democratic ideal. The latter
must always be the loadstone for the construction of appropriate arrangements. Indeed both liberalism and democracy, to
separate the concepts momentarily, aim at the same objective,
the well-being of the individual members of a society (including
those as yet unborn) and therefore of the society of which they
are parts.

Ideally, the voting processes of a government serve two broad
purposes: they are a means for aggregating preferences and

giving them effect; and they contribute to focusing the attention of individuals upon their interests vis-à-vis government and upon the interests and needs of their society as a whole. The first of these goals inevitably entails risks. If preferences, as well as interests, did not sometimes conflict they would not need to be aggregated. Since they do conflict, the losers may suffer, and they may suffer unjustly. They may suffer in ways that are not compatible with the dignity and value of the individual; and this suffering may not be necessary for the protection of other persons.

In saying this much I have both laid the foundation for insistence on certain rights against the government, whether they be the elements of fair trial, freedom of expression, privacy, or whatever, and at the same time implied the truth that just where the boundaries of any government's domain ought to be is not susceptible to precise determination. Some rights have objectives in addition to that of respecting individual respect and autonomy. Without freedom of expression and association, for instance, the suffrage would be (as in many parts of the world it is) a hollow sham. Also, at least in most cases, possible effects on others and on the institutions of society must be taken into account. Rights of the accused extended too far may endanger the rights of others. And most societies hold that, at least in the event of violent attack upon them, individuals may be legally required to risk their own lives for the protection of the integrity of the state.

This is not the place to treat of the proper liberal democratic rights (restrictions on domain) in detail. I have simply been trying to sketch out the governing principles and to indicate, by reference to the concept of the democratic ideal, the basis of their legitimacy. Since elements of the ideal, especially liberty and equality, are in tension with each other, the definition of what ought to be protected, as rights, cannot be precise. I have no quarrel with Sen's statement that "the ultimate guarantee for individual liberty may rest not on rules for social choice but on developing individual values that respect each other's personal choices."[26] But until such values prevail the protection of democracy's ideal and even of its procedures must depend upon the enforcement of such rights as those just mentioned.

An additional point in this connection is worth mentioning. Whereas Sen's statement just quoted represents an ideal not likely to be fully attained, Levine's argument that in a liberal democracy "cultivation of individual differences is a social goal" and that accordingly individual value systems in these polities are "radically independent of each other," calls for qualification, as does his contention that "there is every reason to suppose that idiosyncratic standards for evaluating alternatives will supersede any tendency for the universal adoption of common standards."[27] Both of Levine's propositions seem to be to run quite counter to the evidence. In the United States argument over the latest developments respecting rights, whether legislatively or judicially legalized, easily obscures legal advances that are no longer contested, that now represent a consensus. Thus the controversy over whether the right to counsel includes the obligation of police to give "Miranda warnings" should not conceal the fact that the right to counsel itself is no longer questioned, although it was not fully acknowledged as a general right, against state as well as federal government, until the second half of this century. Also, the very idea of social security legislation was highly controversial when it was first enacted, but today, amid all the wrangling about how it should be amended, no serious consideration is given to its repeal. Many other examples could be offered.

VI.

My discussion of domain, of why it can be restricted despite Arrow's contrary condition, and why it must be restricted in order to comply with the liberal element of democracy, might be concluded at this point. But it seems pertinent to add a few words about liberalism's high valuation of liberal democracy that, at least in part, go beyond what has already been said; and also to indicate the relation of this appraisal to classical liberal and democratic thought. The reason for democracy's respect for privacy, ill-defined though that concept is, flows directly and indirectly from democracy's fundamental concern for individual self-respect. In the interest of privacy, democratic theorists have regularly distinguished the private man from the public man. Athenian democracy is often held up (and upheld) as an exemplar of regard for public man; yet Pericles, in his famous apotheosis of that ideal, declared, according to Thucydides, that "the freedom which we enjoy in our government extends also to our ordinary life. There, far from exercising a jealous surveillance over each other, we do not feel called upon to be angry with our neighbor for doing what he likes, or even to indulge in those injurious looks which cannot fail to be offensive, although they inflict no positive penalty."[28]

Man is not an ant. He has his private as well as his public side. The private person must be distinguished from the public person. Individuals must have power in both capacities. How to discriminate between the powers that should be exercised individually and those that should be exercised collectively is one of the perennial problems of governments and constitution makers. Mill's differentiation between self-regarding and other-regarding acts (as it has been generally understood) is nowadays referred to more frequently to assert its limitations than to point to its necessity. But the latter remains. It was recognized by Rousseau, an individualist only in the most extended sense, as well as by Mill. Because Rousseau's insistence upon the importance of this dividing line is often overlooked, it is worth quoting at length. He wrote as follows:

> Besides the public person we have to consider the private person comprising [the body politic], whose life and liberty are naturally dependent upon it. We are bound then to distinguish clearly between the respective rights of the citizens and the Sovereign, and between the duties the former have as subjects, and the natural rights they enjoy as men.
> Each man alienates, I admit, by the social compact, only such part of his powers, goods and liberty as it is important for the community to control; but it must also be granted that the Sovereign is sole judge of what is important.[29]

Emphasis is commonly placed on the final clause, but it by no means negates what precedes it, for, as Rousseau goes on to argue, the sovereign is the General Will, which can never even wish to do anything contrary to the law of reason and the law of nature. Thus one of democracy's greatest champions is insistent upon restriction of the public domain in behalf of the private person, even as is John Stuart Mill.

Rousseau did not even attempt to define the restricted area, except by reference to the law of reason and the law of nature, and the attempt to define it by distinguishing between self-regarding and other-regarding acts is recognized as being at best a rule of thumb, few if any acts being solely self-regarding.[30]

These limitations on governmental activity are based upon what the authors believed essential to the individual for his or her own sake. It is true that liberalism, at least in its classic form, favored even greater restrictions. Hobbes, an individualist but by no means a democrat, expressed part of the theory underlying this position when he declared that "a plain husbandman is more prudent in affairs of his own house, than a privy counsellor in the affairs of another man."[31] More generally, the theory was that of laissez-faire. It is distinguished from the theories of Rousseau and Mill by the fact that its restrictions on economic activities of the state were not designed for the benefit of individuals directly but rather for society's welfare, that is to say for the welfare of individuals collectively, independently of the *direct* effect of governmental actions on the individuals whose conduct it might regulate.

To what extent this theory is sound is still open to question, especially in its application to policy in a democracy. In his contribution to this volume William Mitchell argues vigorously in its support, in modified form. The optimum role for government vis-à-vis the economy is an interesting and important question; but it is not one on which liberal democrats per se need take a stand. Perhaps the statement just made is too strong. Making economic decisions, like making political decisions, no doubt contributes to personal development, but it does so without any pressure toward enlarging the personal outlook in a social direction. It is also true that the throttling effect of overblown bureaucracies is clearly anti-liberal as well as anti-democratic. Liberalism is sensitive to these and other considerations. This bent is part of the general tension between liberty and equality in the democratic ideal itself.

Robert Lane is concerned with the effect of the market system on the individual, particularly on what he calls "functional individualism," as contrasted with "developmental individualism." Far from finding incoherence here, he concludes that the market contributes to the development of individual self-reliance, self-awareness, and responsibility.

VII.

Finally, the volume as a whole supports the general conclusion that, despite what some say, liberal democratic thought is not incoherent in any but a very weak sense of that term. Tensions, yes; contradictions or lack of consistency, no. The chapters on representation argue, in quite different ways, that democracy's fundamental ideal calls for some alterations in present practices (Darwall) or theories of apportionment (Beitz). Both argue that procedures—present procedures, at least—are inadequate to ensure fulfillment of the democratic ideal. Whelan has shown that democracy, like everything else, has a starting point, and that its own theory is bounded by that point, which it cannot itself account for. The chapters on federalism reveal problems, but hardly incoherence. Nor does it appear that the discussions of judicial review are in this respect any different. They do not seem to support the conclusion, sometimes heard, that judicial review is itself antidemocratic, although Railton's position comes close to doing so. Having just referred to Lane and Mitchell, I need say nothing more about them. Holden's chapter is especially in point here, for he deals with an argument that, if sound, would undermine the claim of liberal democratic theory to be fundamentally rational. While he does not pretend to have disproved that contention, his argument at least disposed of its most commonly heard supports.

Possibly Winston's chapter must be noted as an exception to the point I have been arguing, for he flatly concludes that at least one part of democratic thought is incoherent, although the matter in question hardly seems to be central, or even essential, to democratic theory. He also declares that the very foundation of democratic theory, the ideal of personal autonomy, has been abandoned. These statements, however, seem to me to outrun his argument. Liberals, it is true, have set great store by the rule of law; but primarily they have been contrast-

ing it with governance that is arbitrary and capricious, claiming, most reasonably, its superiority to the latter, rather than
holding that the generality of rules itself assures justice. Even
for Rousseau, formal generality of laws was only one of numerous conditions for increasing the likelihood that the Will of All
would approximate the General Will. As for personal autonomy, Winston admits that liberals still defend and attach great
importance to it, while showing, rightly enough, that in the
modern state it has in many respects been necessarily curtailed.
He appears, however, to glosss over the fact that many, perhaps
most, of these curtailments of certain aspects of autonomy either
enlarged other aspects of it or amplified the autonomy of other
people, distributing it more equally.

NOTES

1. J. Roland Pennock, *Democratic Political Theory* (Princeton: Princeton University Press, 1979), pp. 3–6.
2. Ibid. and p. 368.
3. I say "final" authority to avoid the issue of whether the requirement of approval of amendments to the constitution by more than
   a simple majority is "democratic."
4. Whether, having done so, they could individually take back part
   or all of what they had given up, raises the secession question
   referred to above.
5. See J. Roland Pennock, "Federal and Unitary Government—Dis-
   harmony and Frustration," *Behavioral Science* 4 (1959), 147–57.
6. Of course, the relevant conditions may change in such a way that
   the distribution of powers no longer complies with them. The system should therefore provide for alteration of the distribution, by
   constitutional amendment, judicial interpretation, or such devices
   as conditional grants by the central government to the states. These
   may lag, or be abused; but at worst they are not likely to make the
   states (and their citizens) worse off than they would have been
   under a unitary government, although they may be exercised in
   such a way as to minimize the advantages of federalism.
7. As far as concerns the American form of federalism, a more serious problem, for it, or for democratic theory as the case may be,
   is raised by the equal representation of the states in the Senate.
   On the face of it, at least, this provision conflicts with the democratic equality of persons. One can imagine certain lines of de-

fense that might be advanced, and I shall mention two or three without attempting to evaluate them. The most obvious and probably the most acceptable line would be that the provision strengthens the states and thereby advances liberty. This proposition in turn might be supported as follows: by checking the power of the federal government where it conflicted with state interests (as interpreted by the senators), it might be contended, it at once tends to protect the democratic values of federalism discussed in the text above and by the same token minimizes the tendency of the federal bureaucracy to accumulate powers that defy democratic control. A second, closely related, argument would be that, by protecting state governments, federalism provides a power base for those who, at any given time, are the "outs" at the federal level, thus helping to maintain electoral competition. In some measure, it is true, these values would tend to be protected even if the states were not equally represented in the Senate, but arguably the equality provision makes senators think more in terms of state interests than would otherwise be the case.

8. James S. Fiskin, *Tyranny and Legitimacy: A Critique of Political Theories* (Baltimore: Johns Hopkins University Press, 1979), pp. 121 and 122.
9. Ibid., pp. 42–43.
10. Children, up to a certain age, must share this right with their parents or guardians and persons lacking minimal mental capacity also call for somewhat different treatment.
11. In addition to the passage cited, note his statement at another point that a policy is tyrannous if it would "destroy a person's essential interests" when such a policy "could have been avoided for everyone." Ibid., p. 122.
12. Ibid. It is possible that Fishkin would not apply the equality principle to all unnecessary deprivations but only to "serious" ones and that similarly he would not extend the liberty principle as far as I would, but, whether or not he would qualify them, he appears to be relying upon the same fundamental principles of liberty and equality for defining "nontyranny" as are generally relied upon by justificatory democratic theorists. He does not suggest, for instance, that the quality of a person's life, or life plan, should be taken into account. All alike should be protected.

In private correspondence (letter of March 10, 1982), Fishkin states that what he means by "nontyranny" is much more restricted than what I have inferred from it. With due respect, however, it appears to me that my inferences follow logically from his elaboration of the word in terms of deprivations "on anyone" and defeat of "life plans." Perhaps the point is that he is seeking a definition of democracy that is more precise than my definition of ideal democracy.

13. I recognize that the individual's choice for himself, unlike that for society, does not involve an interpersonal comparison. I deal with this matter of interpersonal comparisons below.

14. The wording here is deliberately loose. Among the governments that we (properly) denominate as democratic, some will come closer to realizing the ideal than others, and we will say that some are more democratic than others, while still calling them all democracies.

15. Andrew Levine, "A Conceptual Problem for Liberal Democracy," *Journal of Philosophy* 75 (1978), 302–08, at 302–03.

16. Ibid., p. 303. Sen's article "The Impossibility of a Paretian Liberal" appears in the *Journal of Political Economy* 78 (1970), 152–57.

17. It is something of a measure of their success that the outstanding work in moral-political philosophy of this century to date, that of John Rawls, embraces this method at least in part.

18. For further argument in support of the possibility, subject to wide margins of error, of interpersonal comparisons of utility, see John C. Harsanyi, "Cardinal Welfare, Individualistic Ethics, and Interpersonal Comparisons of Utility," *Journal of Political Economy,* 63 (1955), 309–21.

19. Sen, in "The Impossibility of a Paretian Liberal," uses an even much weaker definition of Pareto optimality, holding only that if *every* individual prefers any alternative x to another alternative y, then society must prefer x to y. P. 153.

20. Ibid. I should also make it explicit that I do not quarrel with the belief Levine attributes to liberalism.

21. Sen distinguishes between a person's "actual preferences" and "what he thinks he would accept as a basis of public policy given the preferences of others and given his values on collective choice procedures." *Collective Choice and Social Welfare,* p. 66. For our purposes that does not alter the situation, since normally a person does not know the preferences of others when he or she votes; therefore it is actual preferences that must be counted in arriving at the social decision. Harsanyi distinguishes a person's "ethical preferences" from his "subjective preferences." "Cardinal Welfare," p. 315. The latter are the preferences a person would have if he thought he had an "equal chance" of being in anyone's position. This Kantian ideal might be a useful ethical standard but it is of dubious value as a guide for constructing democratic procedures.

22. Using the term "ideal interest" and spelling it out in a way not incompatible with what is said above, Ronald Rogowski concludes

that "people's votes, therefore, do not seem to be an adequate standard for judgments about representation; and liberal theory appears to open to endless argument every claim of representation." "Representation in Political Theory and in Law," *Ethics* 91 (1981), 395–430, at 404.

23. Ibid.

24. Levine, "A Conceptual Problem," at p. 304. In the American system it is true that the constitutional restraints are subject to alteration. Whether allowing them to be altered only by our system of extraordinary majorities would be democratic by Levine's standards is not a question I need answer, for it is clear that if they were altered so as to infringe upon fundamental rights that action would be incompatible with liberalism, however it was accomplished.

25. Ibid.

26. "The Impossibility of a Paretian Liberal," pp. 155–56.

27. Levine, p. 309.

28. Thucydides, *History of the Peloponnesian War,* trans. Crawley (New York: Dutton, 1910), p. 122.

29. *The Social Contract,* trans. G.D.H. Cole, Bk. II, chap. iv.

30. The distinction, for which the authority of Mill is commonly cited, probably does not capture Mill's meaning, despite his words at some points. C.L. Ten, *Mill on Liberty* (Oxford: Clarendon Press, 1980), chap. 2 and pp. 45–51.

31. *Leviathan,* Oakeshott edition (Oxford: Blackwell, 1946), p. 45 (Part I, chap. 8).

A QUARTER-CENTURY OF *NOMOS* (INDEX)

Ockham, Susan Moller, XXIII, 230–56 ("Liberty and Welfare: Some Issues in Human Rights Theory")

Oppenheim, Felix E., IV, 274–88 ("Freedom an Empirical Interpretation"); XVII, 280–85 ("Rationality and Egalitarianism")

Parker, Richard B., XX, 269–95 ("The Jurisprudential Uses of John Rawls")

Parsons, Talcott, I, 197–221 ("Authority, Legitimation, and Political Action"); II, 152–79 ("The Principle Structures of Community: A Sociological View")

Participation, political, XVI

Paternalism, IV, 162–75 (Spahr); XV, 174–88 (Bayles), 189–210 (Regan)

Peczenick, Aleksander, XXI, 176–89 ("Cumulation and Compromise of Reasons in the Law")

Pennock, J. Roland, III, 3–27 ("The Problem of Responsibility"); V, 177–82 ("The One and the Many: A Note on the Concept" [of the public interest]); VII, 98–106, ("Reason in Legislative Decisions"); X, 3–27 ("Political Representation: An Overview"); XIV, 1–15 ("Coercion: An Overview"); XXII, 171–86 ("Thoughts on the Right to Private Property"); XXIII, 1–28 ("Rights, Natural Rights, and Human Rights—A General View"); XXV, 408–29 ("Some Perplexities of Democratic Theory Further Considered"); on constitutionalism,

XX, 377–85 ("Epilogue"); on voluntary associations, XI, 285–91 ("Epilogue")

Pettee, George, VIII, 10–33 ("Revolution—Typology and Process")

Pincoffs, Edmund L., XVIII, 172–81 ("Due Process, Fraternity, and a Kantian Injunction")

Pitkin, Hanna, X, 38–42 ("Commentary: The Paradox of Representation")

Plamenatz, John, IX, 79–98 ("Diversity of Rights and Kinds of Equality")

Plato, III, 71 ff. (Leys)

Pluralism, XI, 87–291; XVI, 39–55 (Bachrach); corporate, see Berger

Polin, Raymond, VI, 262–83 ("Justice in Locke's Philosophy")

Political obligation, XII; XIV, 213–42 (Wertheimer)

Primitive societies, see Hoebel

Privacy, VII, 145–59 (Mavrinac); XI, 35–40 (Kariel); XIII

Property, XXII

Public interest, V

Punishment, III, Part Two

Rackman, Emanuel, IX, 154–76 ("Judaism and Equality")

Railton, Peter, XXV, 153–80 ("Judicial Review, Elites, and Liberal Democracy")

Rao, P.S.S. Rama, XII, 440–55 ("Gandhi's Synthesis of Indian Spirituality and Western Politics")

Raphael, D. D., IX, 277–87 ("Equality, Democracy, and International Law")

Rapoport, David C., VIII, 53–74

INDEX